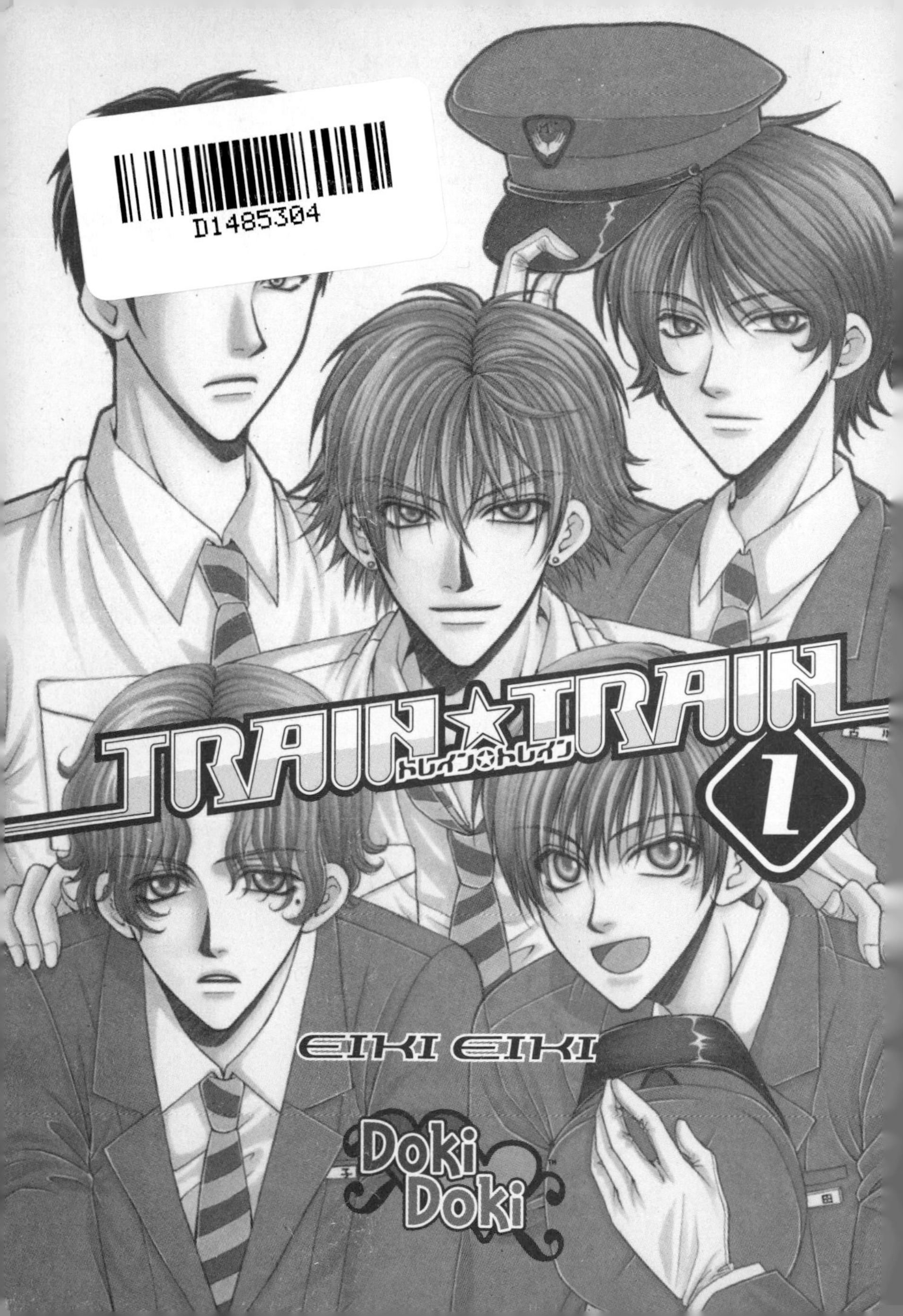
TRAIN☆TRAIN
トレイン☆トレイン
1
EIKI EIKI
Doki Doki

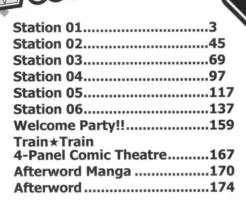

# TRAIN★TRAIN 1

| | |
|---|---|
| Translation | Ken Wakita |
| Editing | Daryl Kuxhouse |
| Lettering | Tawnie Wilson |
| Graphic Design | Matt Akuginow / Daryl Kuxhouse |
| VP Production | Fred Lui |
| Publisher | Hikaru Sasahara |

English Edition Published by
**DIGITAL MANGA PUBLISHING**
A division of DIGITAL MANGA, Inc.
1487 W 178th Street, Suite 300
Gardena, CA 90248

www.dmpbooks.com

First Edition: April 2009
ISBN-10: 1-56970-096-6
ISBN-13: 978-1-56970-096-9

1 3 5 7 9 10 8 6 4 2

Printed in Canada

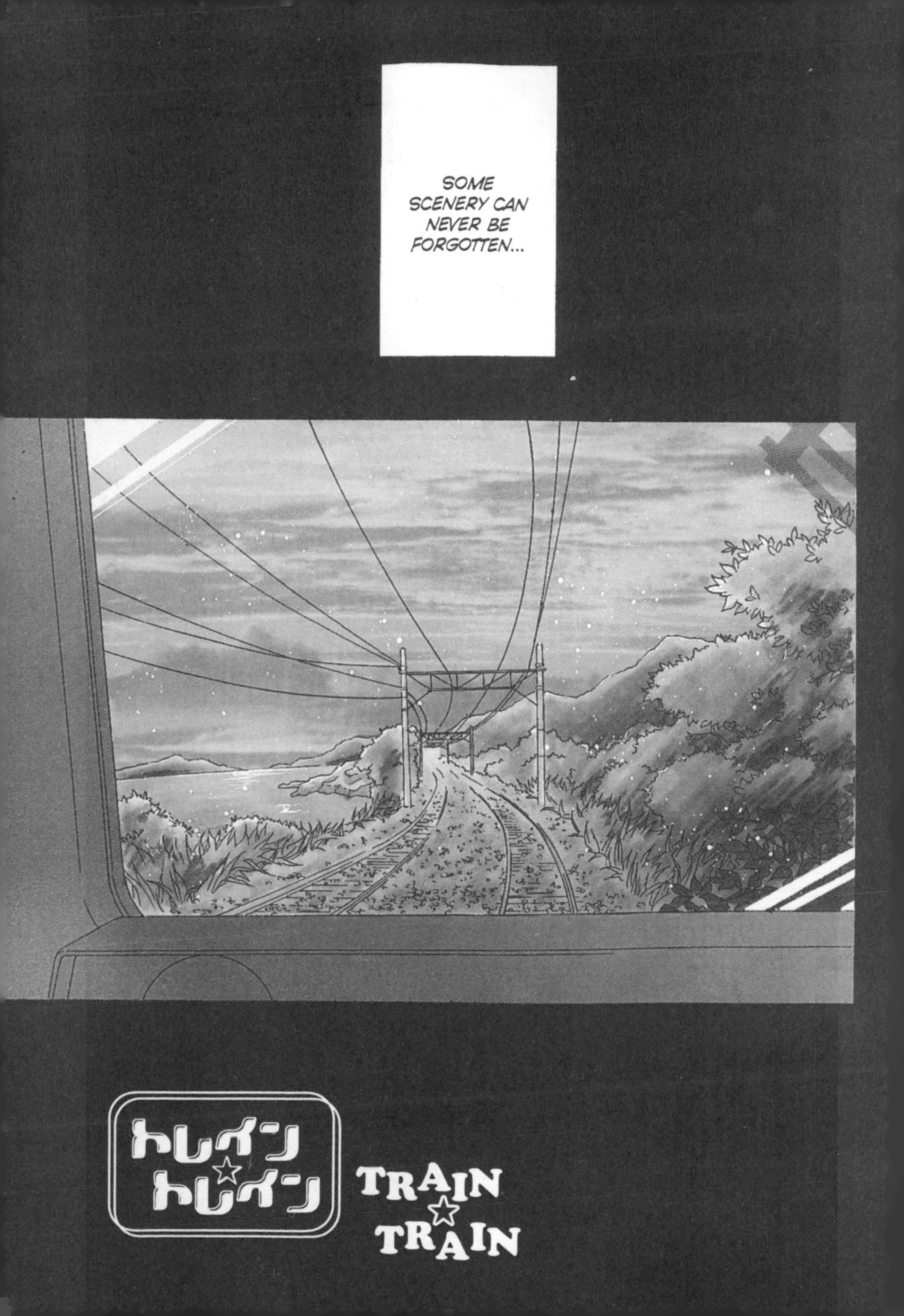
SOME SCENERY CAN NEVER BE FORGOTTEN...
トレイン☆トレイン
TRAIN☆TRAIN

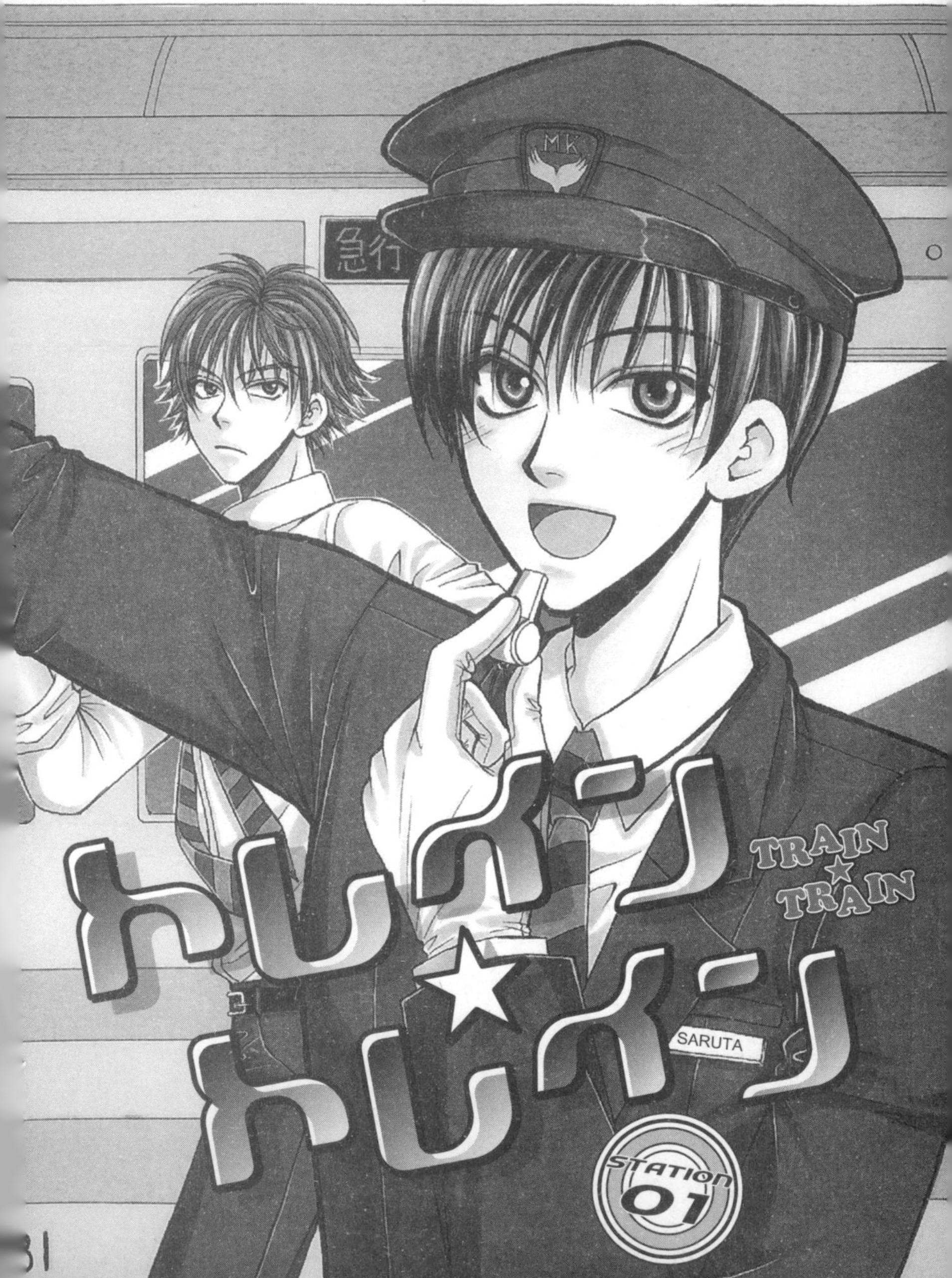
急行
MK
トレイン★トレイン
TRAIN★TRAIN
SARUTA
STATION 01

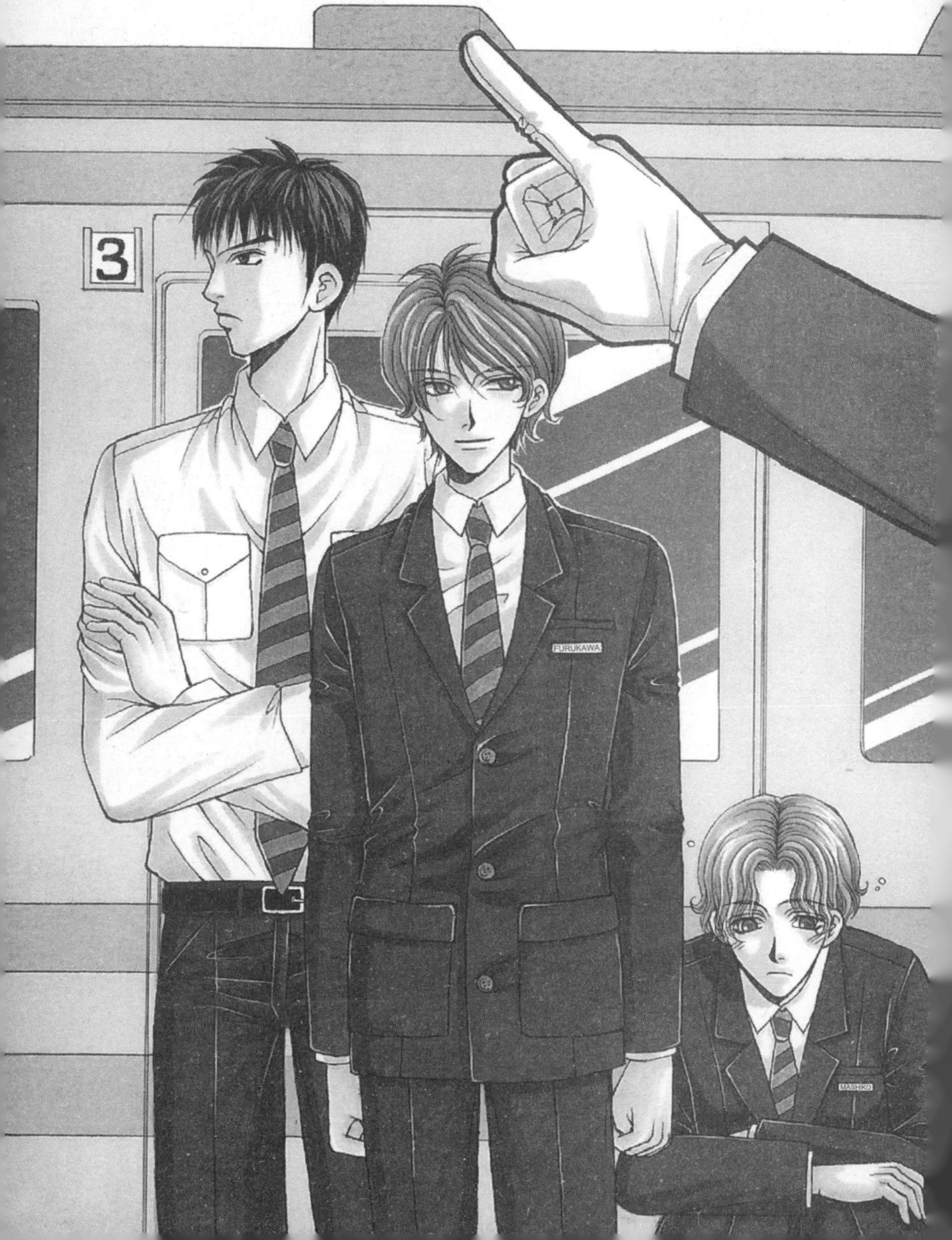
3
FURUKAWA
MASHIKO

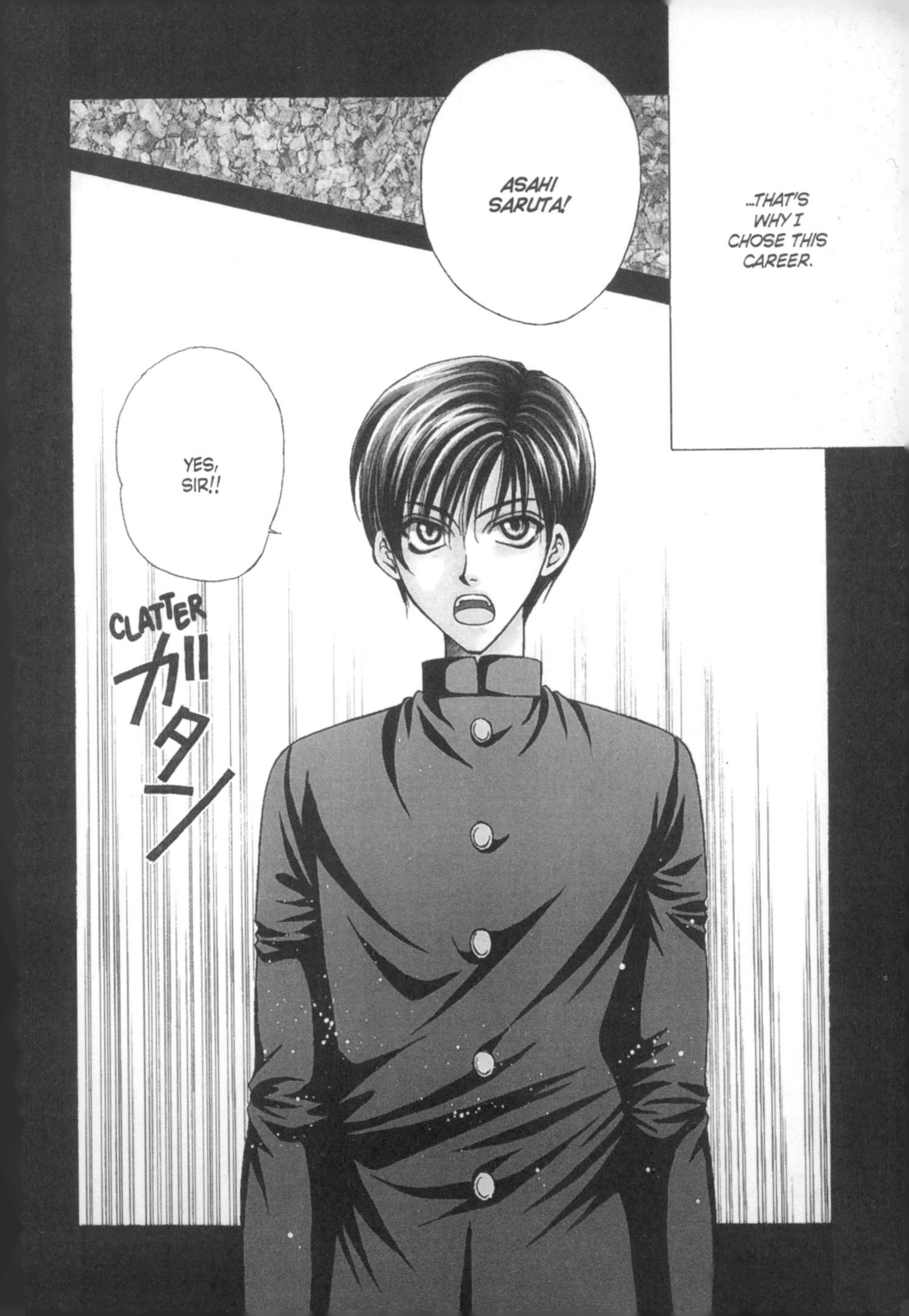
...THAT'S WHY I CHOSE THIS CAREER.
ASAHI SARUTA!
YES, SIR!!
CLATTER
カタン

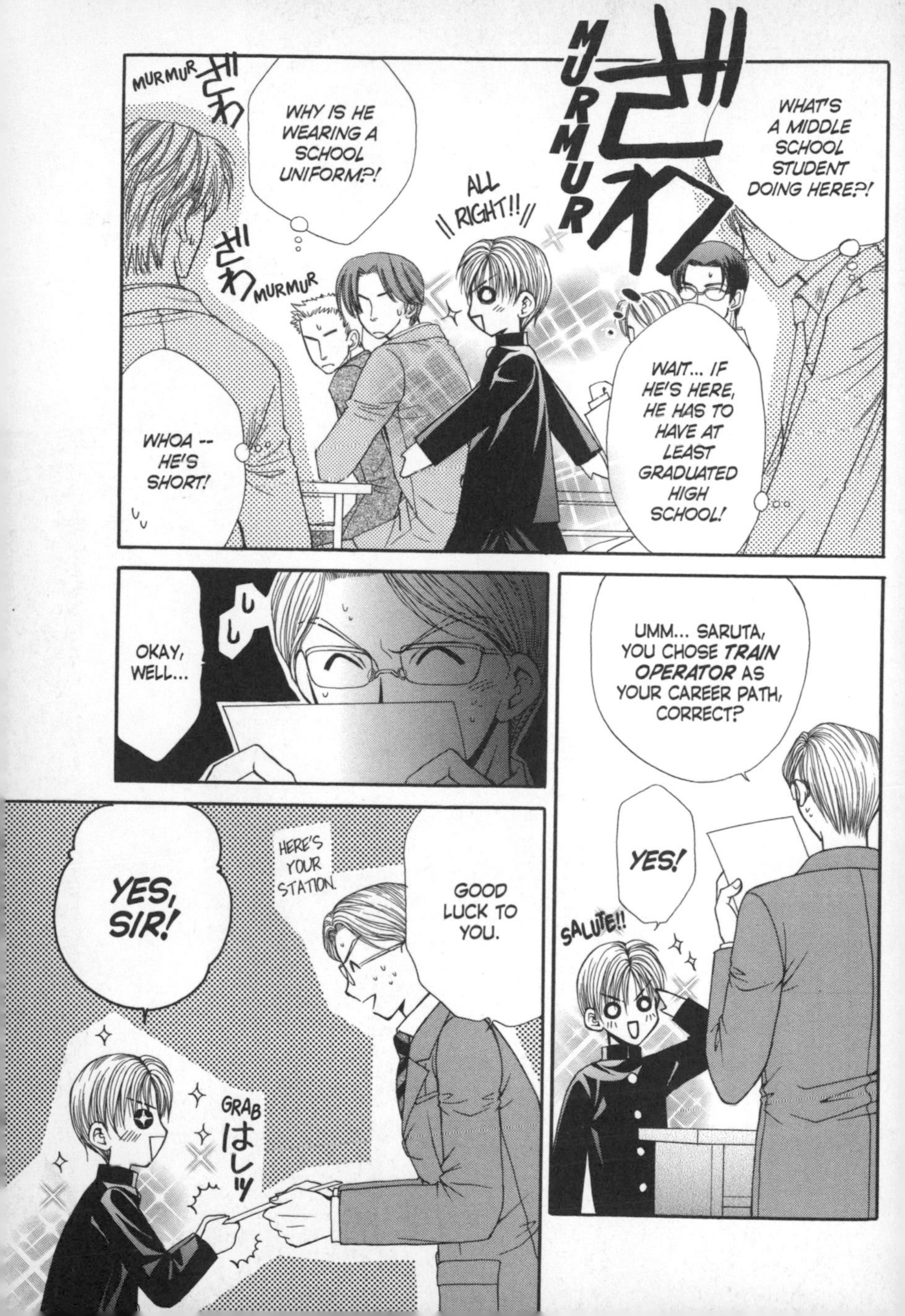
ざわ
MURMUR
WHAT'S A MIDDLE SCHOOL STUDENT DOING HERE?!
ALL RIGHT!!
WHY IS HE WEARING A SCHOOL UNIFORM?!
ざわ MURMUR
WAIT... IF HE'S HERE, HE HAS TO HAVE AT LEAST GRADUATED HIGH SCHOOL!
ざわ MURMUR
WHOA -- HE'S SHORT!
UMM... SARUTA, YOU CHOSE *TRAIN OPERATOR* AS YOUR CAREER PATH, CORRECT?
YES!
SALUTE!!
OKAY, WELL...
GOOD LUCK TO YOU.
HERE'S YOUR STATION.
YES, SIR!
GRAB はしッ

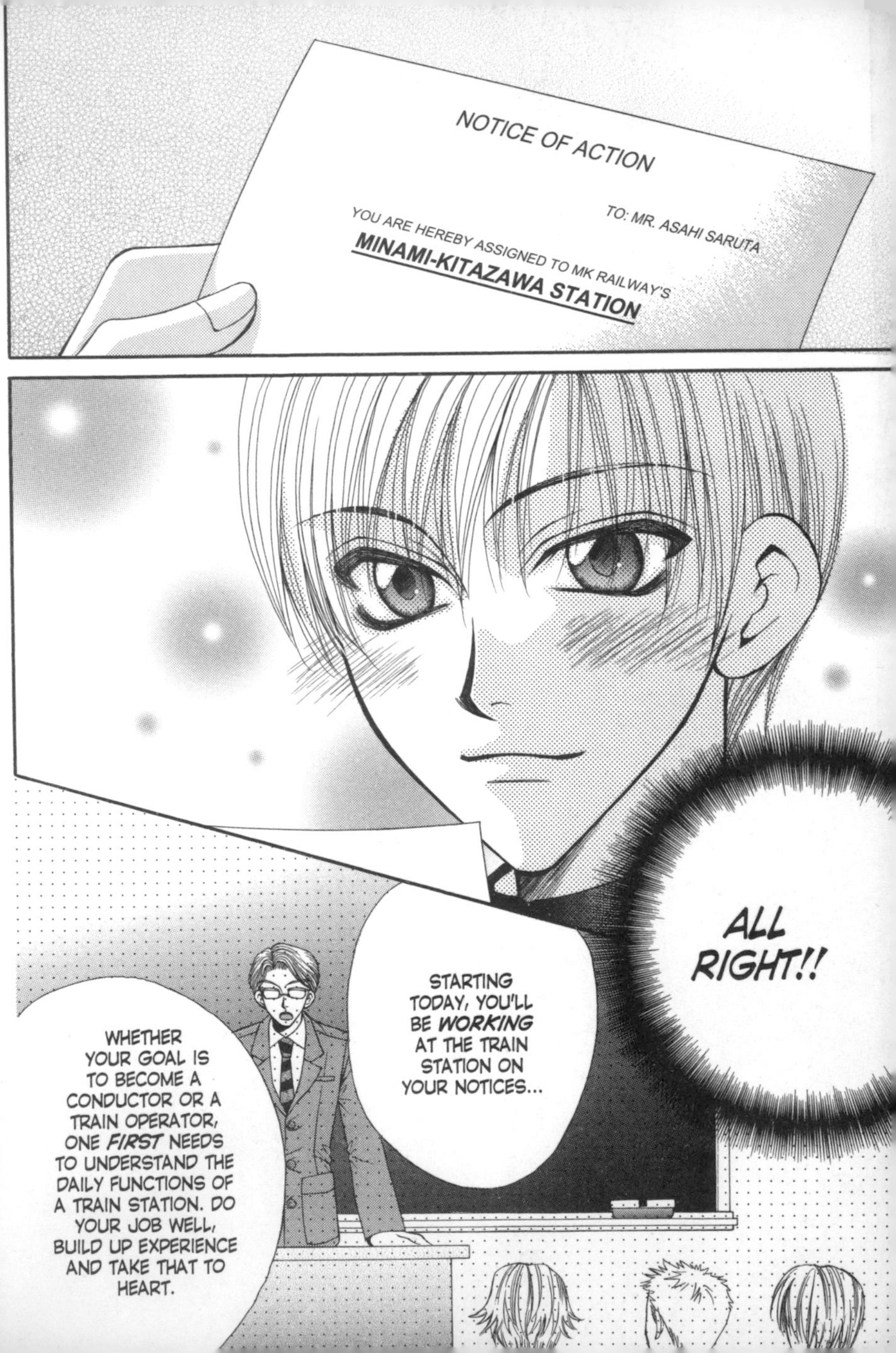
NOTICE OF ACTION
TO: MR. ASAHI SARUTA
YOU ARE HEREBY ASSIGNED TO MK RAILWAY'S
MINAMI-KITAZAWA STATION
ALL RIGHT!!
STARTING TODAY, YOU'LL BE WORKING AT THE TRAIN STATION ON YOUR NOTICES...
WHETHER YOUR GOAL IS TO BECOME A CONDUCTOR OR A TRAIN OPERATOR, ONE FIRST NEEDS TO UNDERSTAND THE DAILY FUNCTIONS OF A TRAIN STATION. DO YOUR JOB WELL, BUILD UP EXPERIENCE AND TAKE THAT TO HEART.

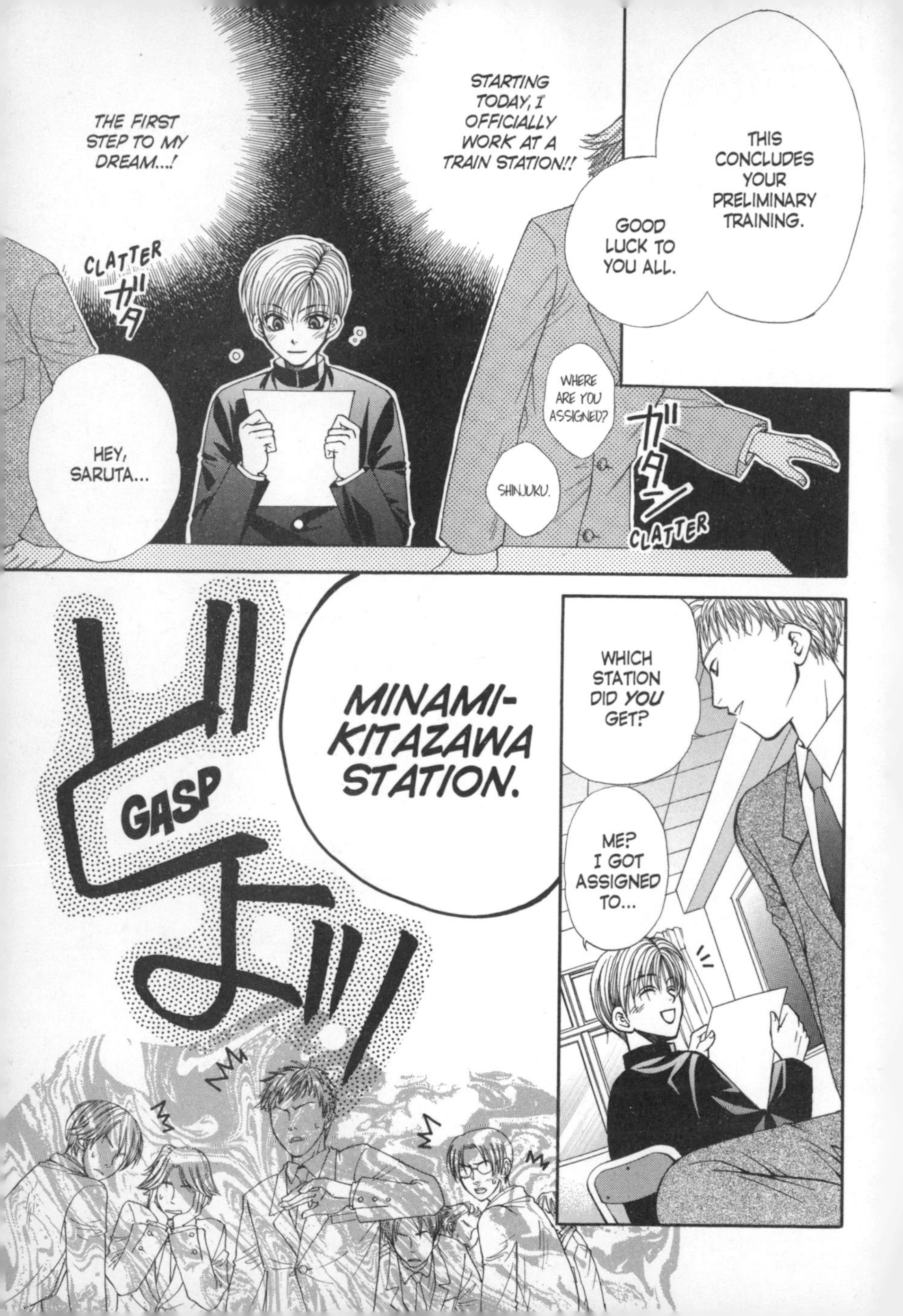
THIS CONCLUDES YOUR PRELIMINARY TRAINING.
GOOD LUCK TO YOU ALL.
STARTING TODAY, I OFFICIALLY WORK AT A TRAIN STATION!!
THE FIRST STEP TO MY DREAM...!
ガタン
CLATTER
WHERE ARE YOU ASSIGNED?
SHINJUKU.
CLATTER
ガタ
HEY, SARUTA...
WHICH STATION DID YOU GET?
ME? I GOT ASSIGNED TO...
MINAMI-KITAZAWA STATION.
GASP

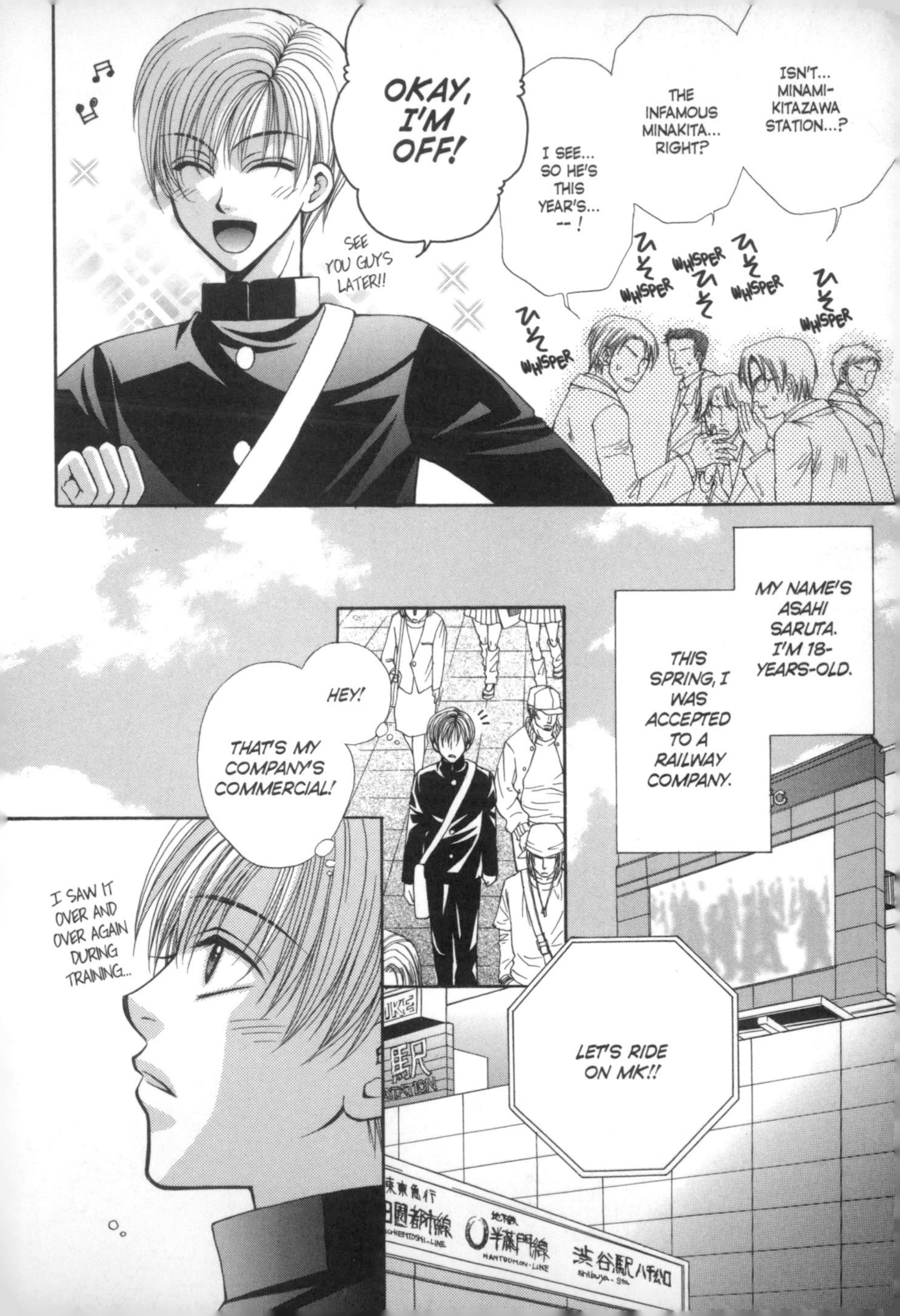
ISN'T... MINAMI-KITAZAWA STATION...?
THE INFAMOUS MINAKITA... RIGHT?
I SEE... SO HE'S THIS YEAR'S... --!
WHISPER WHISPER WHISPER WHISPER WHISPER
OKAY, I'M OFF!
SEE YOU GUYS LATER!!
MY NAME'S ASAHI SARUTA. I'M 18-YEARS-OLD.
THIS SPRING, I WAS ACCEPTED TO A RAILWAY COMPANY.
HEY!
THAT'S MY COMPANY'S COMMERCIAL!
LET'S RIDE ON MK!!
I SAW IT OVER AND OVER AGAIN DURING TRAINING...

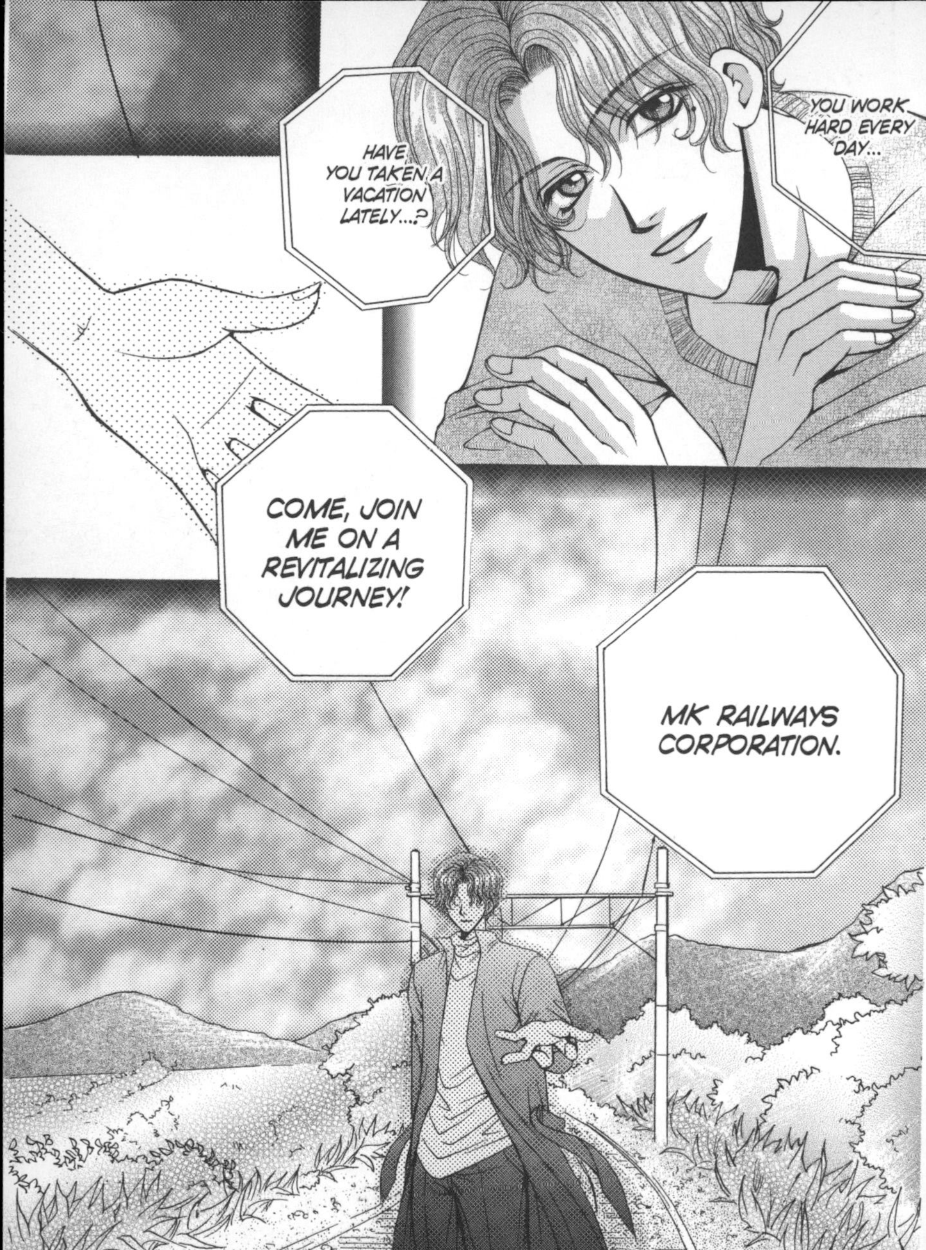
YOU WORK HARD EVERY DAY...
HAVE YOU TAKEN A VACATION LATELY...?
COME, JOIN ME ON A REVITALIZING JOURNEY!
MK RAILWAYS CORPORATION.

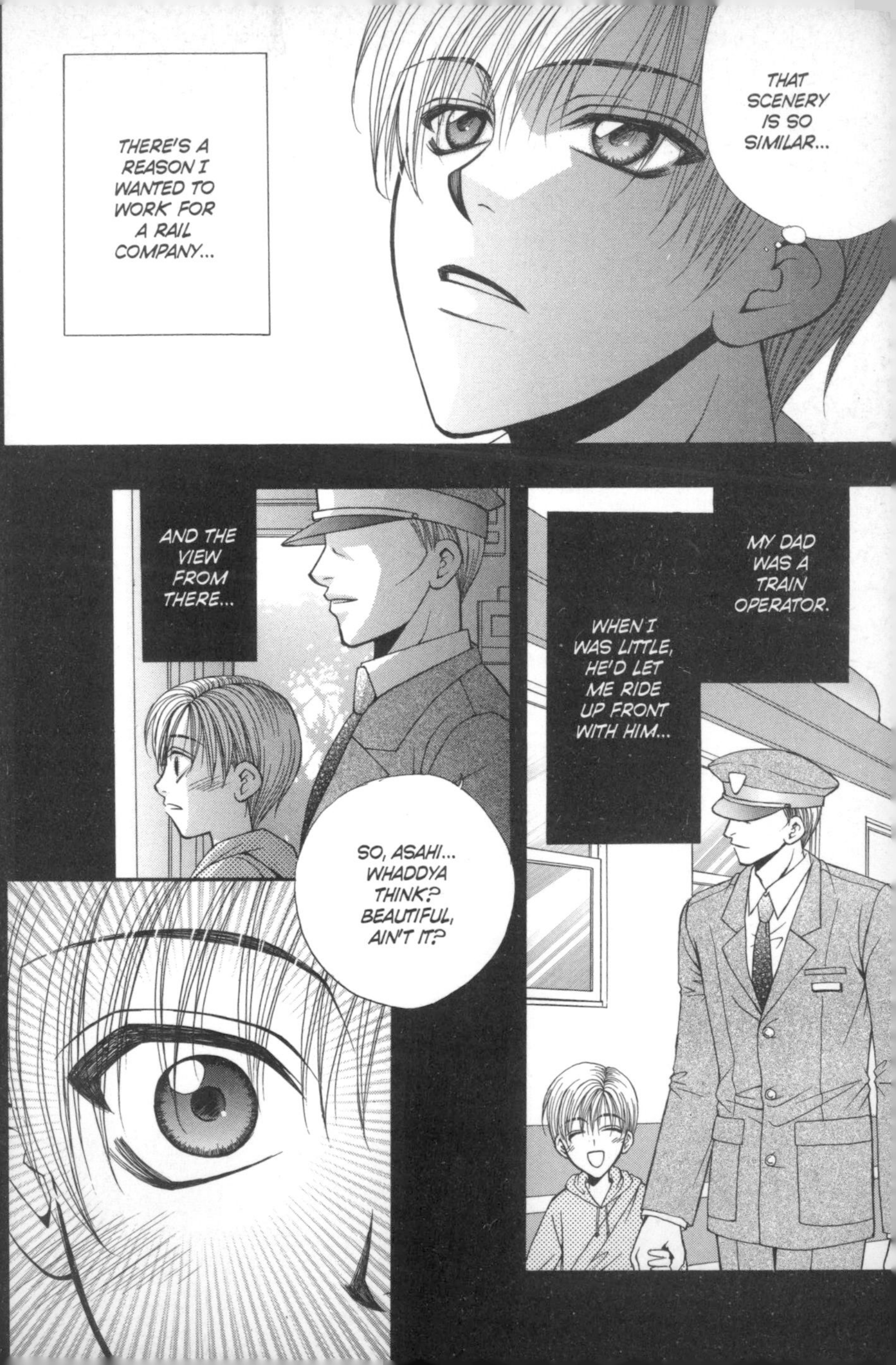
THAT SCENERY IS SO SIMILAR...
THERE'S A REASON I WANTED TO WORK FOR A RAIL COMPANY...
MY DAD WAS A TRAIN OPERATOR.
WHEN I WAS LITTLE, HE'D LET ME RIDE UP FRONT WITH HIM...
AND THE VIEW FROM THERE...
SO, ASAHI... WHADDYA THINK? BEAUTIFUL, AIN'T IT?

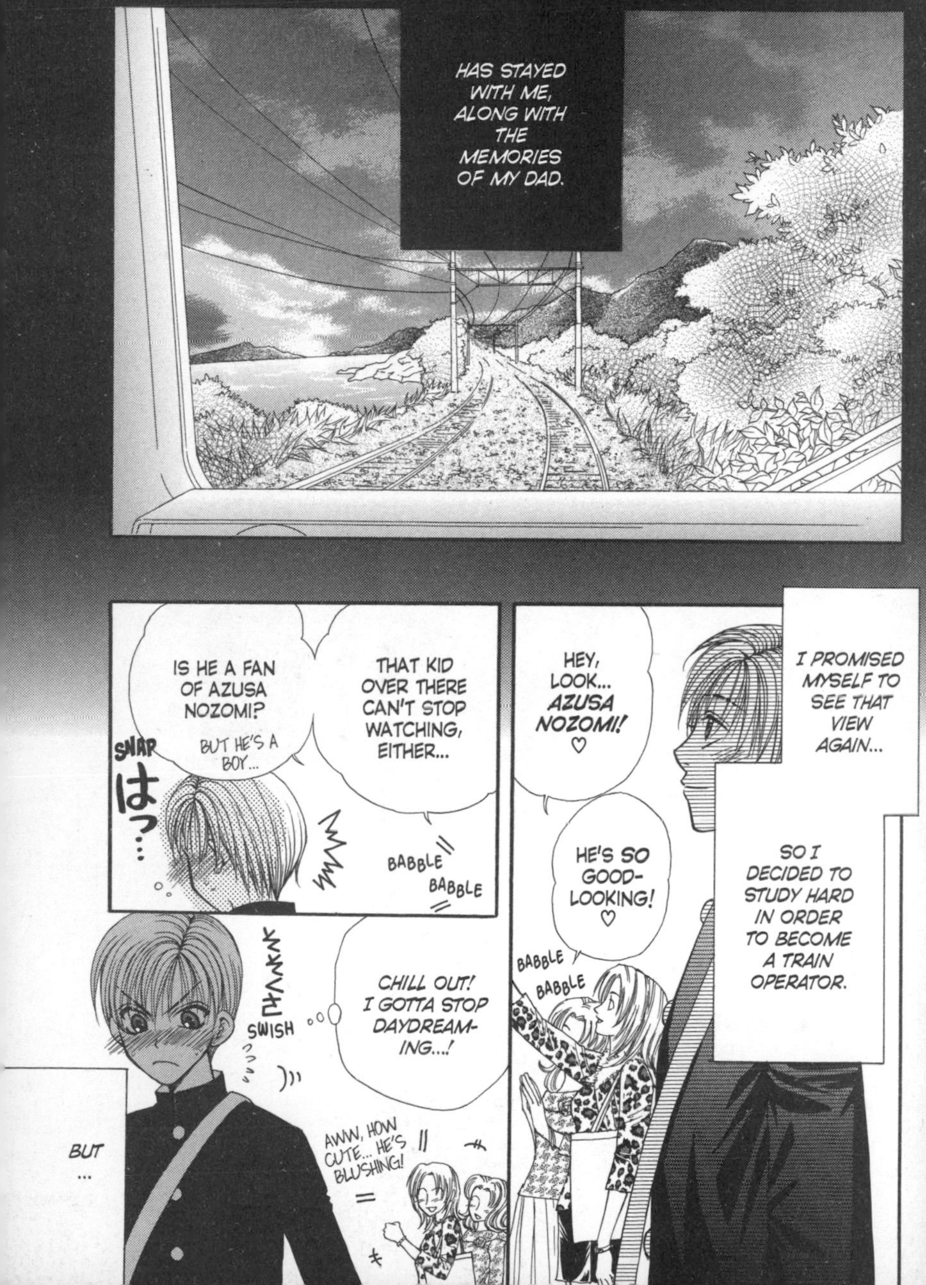
HAS STAYED WITH ME, ALONG WITH THE MEMORIES OF MY DAD.
I PROMISED MYSELF TO SEE THAT VIEW AGAIN...
SO I DECIDED TO STUDY HARD IN ORDER TO BECOME A TRAIN OPERATOR.
HEY, LOOK... AZUSA NOZOMI! ♡
HE'S SO GOOD-LOOKING! ♡
BABBLE BABBLE
THAT KID OVER THERE CAN'T STOP WATCHING, EITHER...
IS HE A FAN OF AZUSA NOZOMI?
BUT HE'S A BOY...
SNAP
はっ...
BABBLE BABBLE
CHILL OUT! I GOTTA STOP DAYDREAMING...!
SWISH
AWW, HOW CUTE... HE'S BLUSHING!
BUT ...

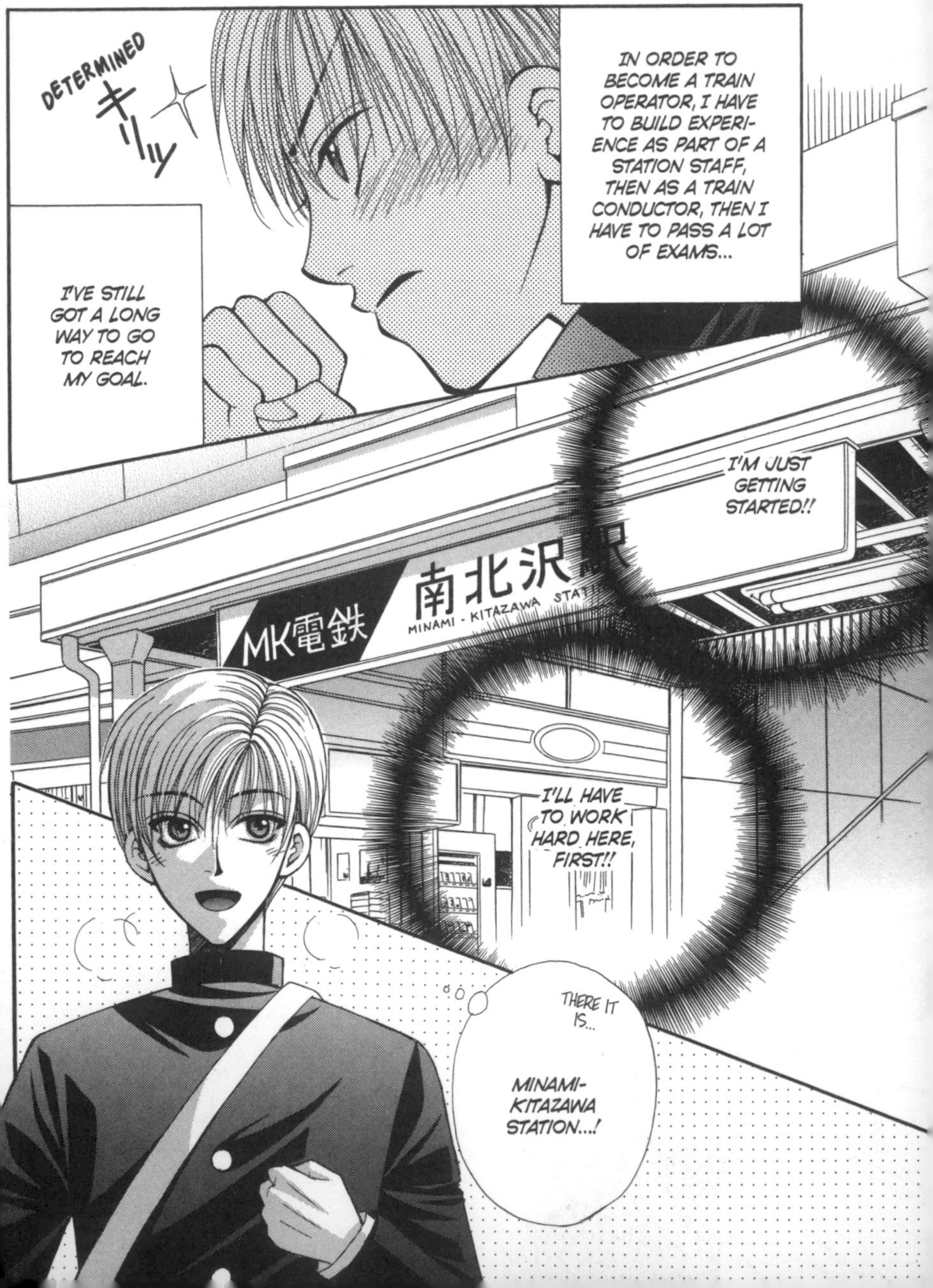
IN ORDER TO BECOME A TRAIN OPERATOR, I HAVE TO BUILD EXPERIENCE AS PART OF A STATION STAFF, THEN AS A TRAIN CONDUCTOR, THEN I HAVE TO PASS A LOT OF EXAMS...
DETERMINED
キリッ
I'VE STILL GOT A LONG WAY TO GO TO REACH MY GOAL.
I'M JUST GETTING STARTED!!
南北沢
MK電鉄
I'LL HAVE TO WORK HARD HERE, FIRST!!
THERE IT IS...
MINAMI-KITAZAWA STATION...!

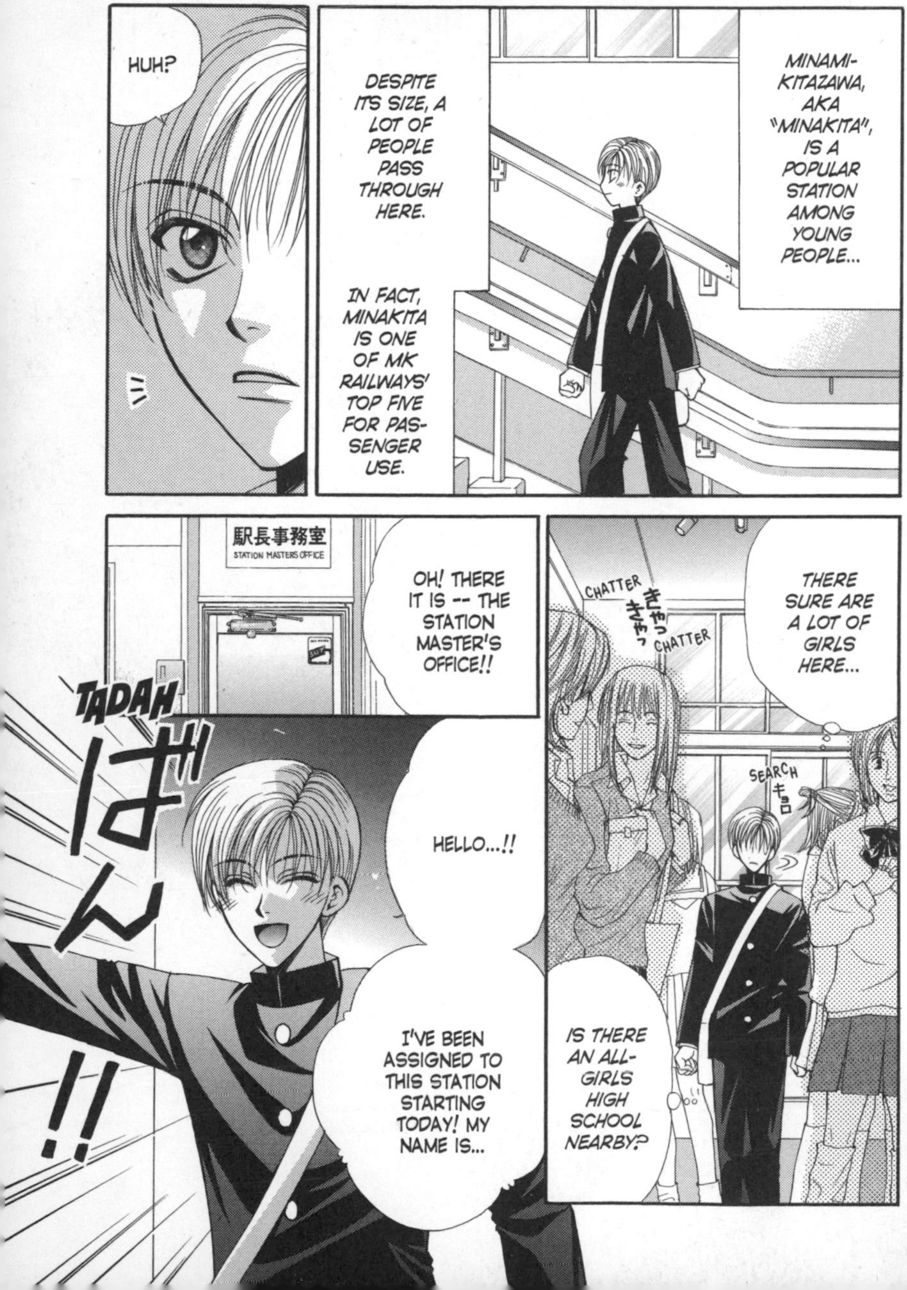
MINAMI-KITAZAWA, AKA "MINAKITA", IS A POPULAR STATION AMONG YOUNG PEOPLE...
DESPITE ITS SIZE, A LOT OF PEOPLE PASS THROUGH HERE.
IN FACT, MINAKITA IS ONE OF MK RAILWAYS' TOP FIVE FOR PAS-SENGER USE.
HUH?
THERE SURE ARE A LOT OF GIRLS HERE...
CHATTER きゃっ
きゃっ CHATTER
SEARCH キョロ
IS THERE AN ALL-GIRLS HIGH SCHOOL NEARBY?
駅長事務室
STATION MASTERS OFFICE
OH! THERE IT IS -- THE STATION MASTER'S OFFICE!!
TADAH
ばん!!
HELLO...!!
I'VE BEEN ASSIGNED TO THIS STATION STARTING TODAY! MY NAME IS...

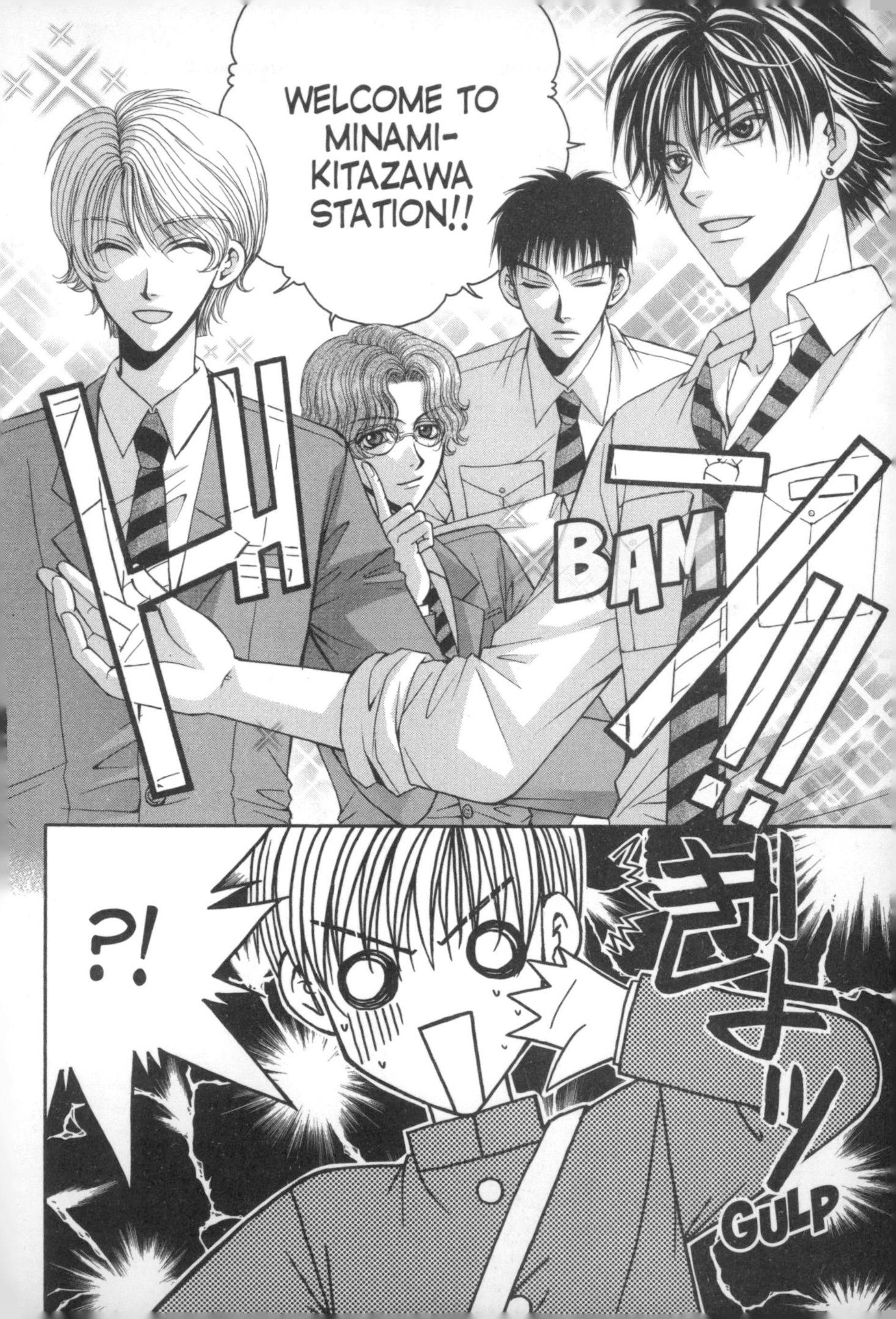
WELCOME TO MINAMI-KITAZAWA STATION!!
BAM
GULP
?!

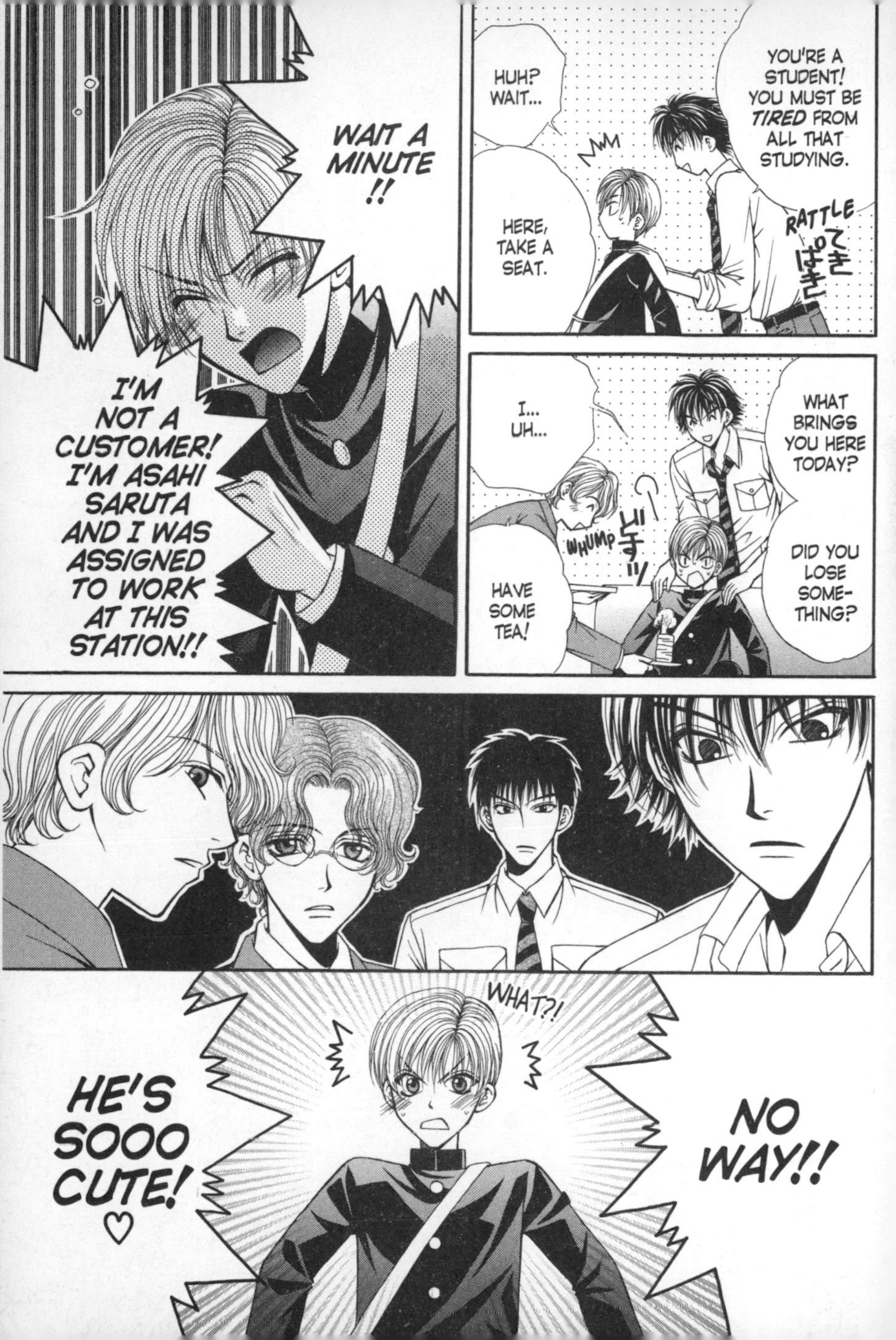
YOU'RE A STUDENT! YOU MUST BE TIRED FROM ALL THAT STUDYING.
HUH? WAIT...
RATTLE てきぱき
HERE, TAKE A SEAT.
WHAT BRINGS YOU HERE TODAY?
DID YOU LOSE SOMETHING?
I... UH...
WHUMP どすッ
HAVE SOME TEA!
WAIT A MINUTE!!
I'M NOT A CUSTOMER! I'M ASAHI SARUTA AND I WAS ASSIGNED TO WORK AT THIS STATION!!
WHAT?!
NO WAY!!
HE'S SOOO CUTE! ♡

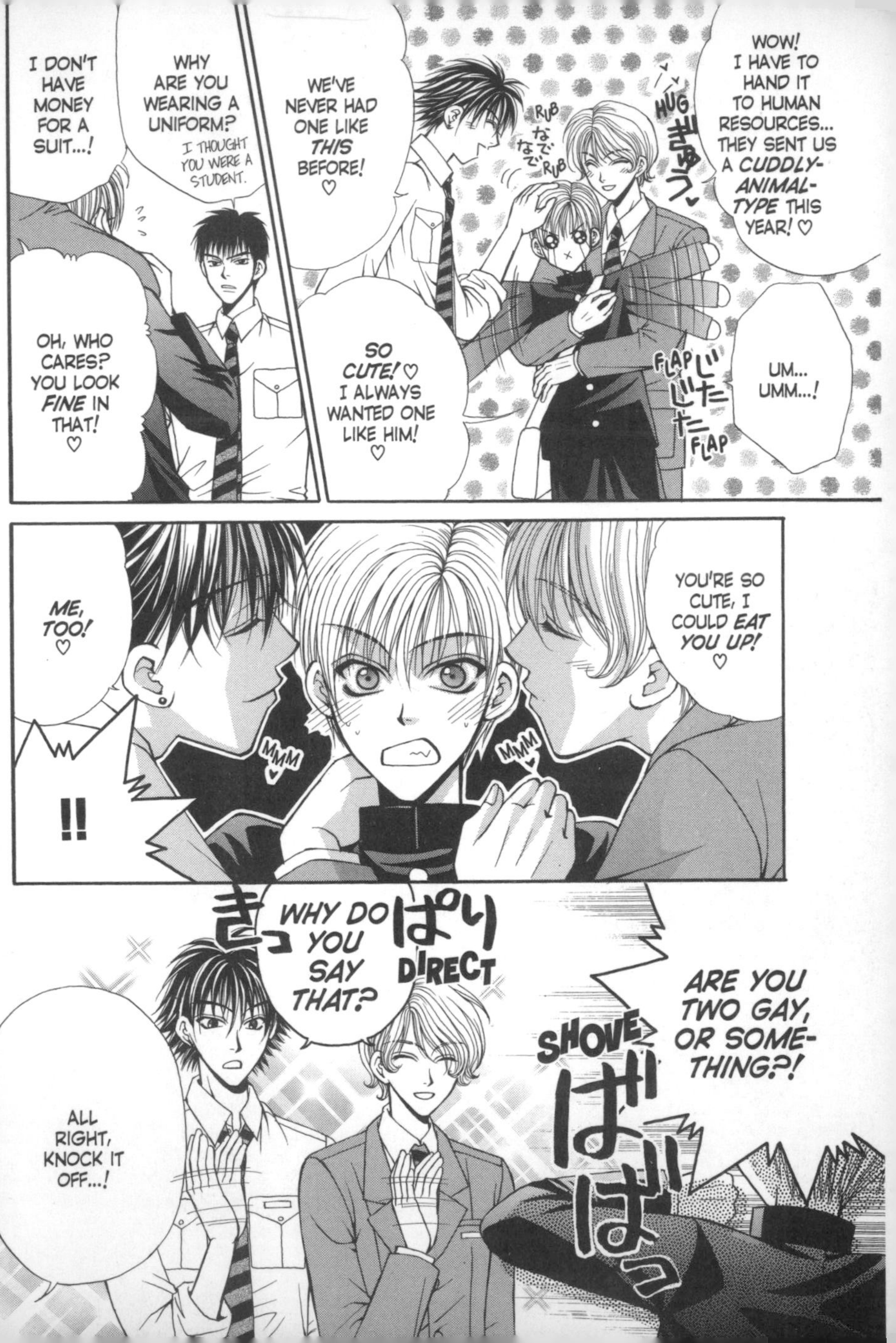
WOW! I HAVE TO HAND IT TO HUMAN RESOURCES... THEY SENT US A *CUDDLY-ANIMAL-TYPE* THIS YEAR! ♡
HUG ぎゅう
RUB なでなで RUB
UM... UMM...!
FLAP じたじた FLAP
WE'VE NEVER HAD ONE LIKE *THIS* BEFORE! ♡
SO *CUTE!* ♡ I ALWAYS WANTED ONE LIKE HIM! ♡
WHY ARE YOU WEARING A UNIFORM?
I THOUGHT YOU WERE A STUDENT.
I DON'T HAVE MONEY FOR A SUIT...!
OH, WHO CARES? YOU LOOK *FINE* IN THAT! ♡
YOU'RE SO CUTE, I COULD *EAT YOU UP!* ♡
MMM ♡
MMM ♡
*ME, TOO!* ♡
!!
*ARE YOU TWO GAY, OR SOME-THING?!*
SHOVE ばばっ
きっぱり DIRECT
WHY DO YOU SAY THAT?
ALL RIGHT, KNOCK IT OFF...!

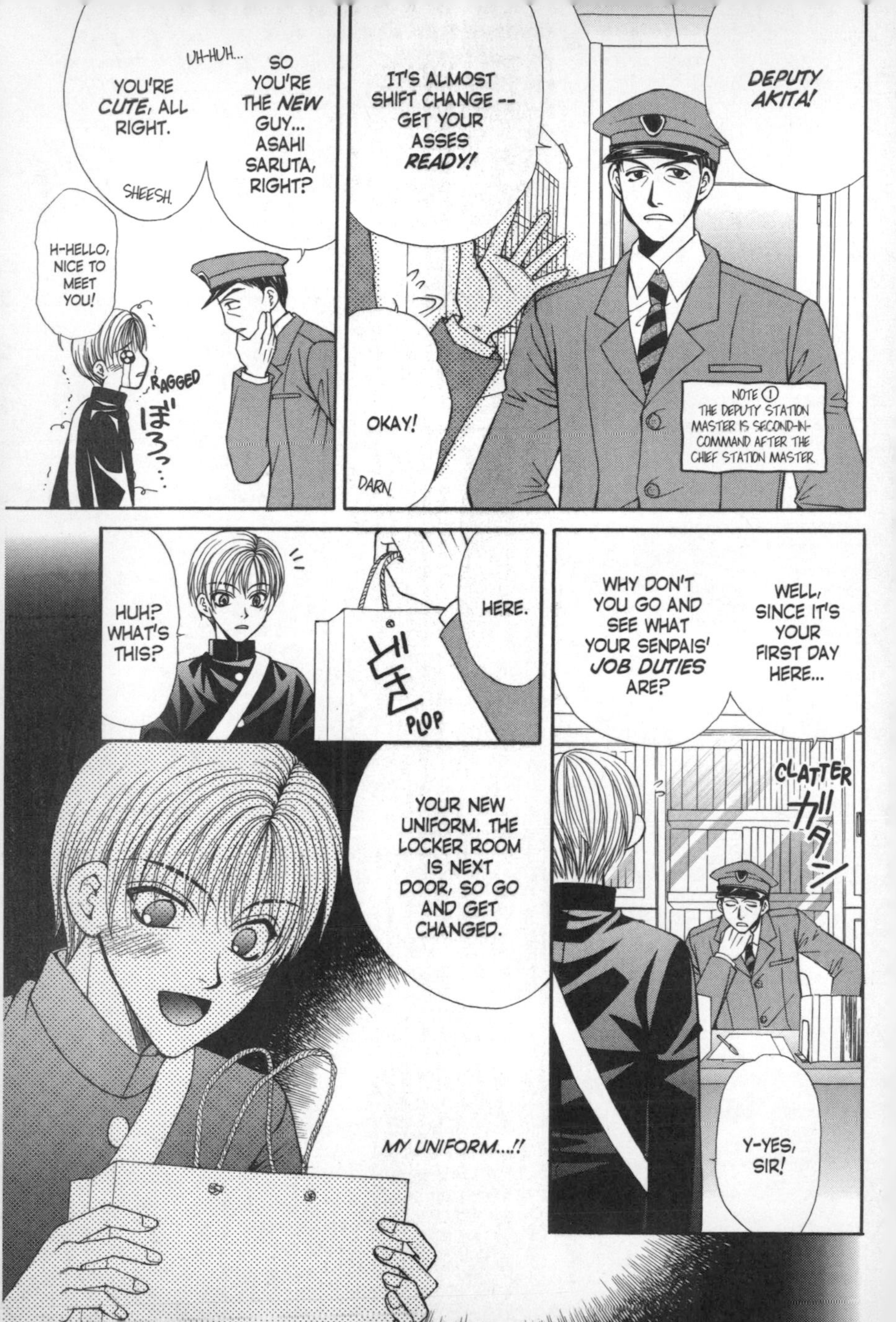
DEPUTY AKITA!
IT'S ALMOST SHIFT CHANGE -- GET YOUR ASSES READY!
OKAY!
DARN.
NOTE ① THE DEPUTY STATION MASTER IS SECOND-IN-COMMAND AFTER THE CHIEF STATION MASTER.
SO YOU'RE THE NEW GUY... ASAHI SARUTA, RIGHT?
UH-HUH...
YOU'RE CUTE, ALL RIGHT.
SHEESH.
H-HELLO, NICE TO MEET YOU!
RAGGED
ぼろっ…
WELL, SINCE IT'S YOUR FIRST DAY HERE...
WHY DON'T YOU GO AND SEE WHAT YOUR SENPAIS' JOB DUTIES ARE?
CLATTER
ガタン
Y-YES, SIR!
HERE.
HUH? WHAT'S THIS?
どさ
PLOP
YOUR NEW UNIFORM. THE LOCKER ROOM IS NEXT DOOR, SO GO AND GET CHANGED.
MY UNIFORM...!!

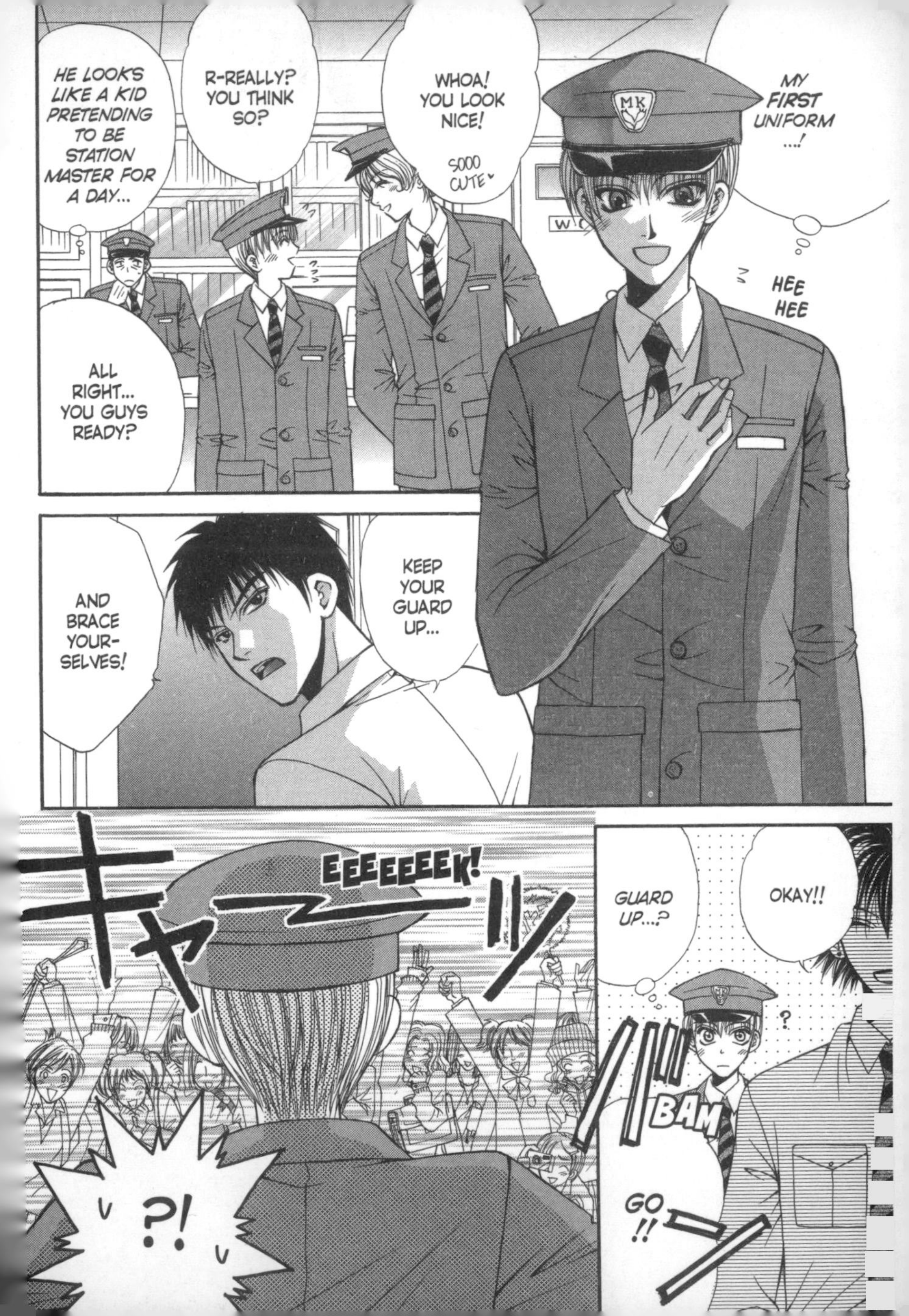
MY FIRST UNIFORM ...!
HEE HEE
WHOA! YOU LOOK NICE!
SOOO CUTE
R-REALLY? YOU THINK SO?
HE LOOKS LIKE A KID PRETENDING TO BE STATION MASTER FOR A DAY...
ALL RIGHT... YOU GUYS READY?
KEEP YOUR GUARD UP...
AND BRACE YOUR-SELVES!
OKAY!!
GUARD UP...?
?
BAM
GO !!
EEEEEEEK!
キャー
?!

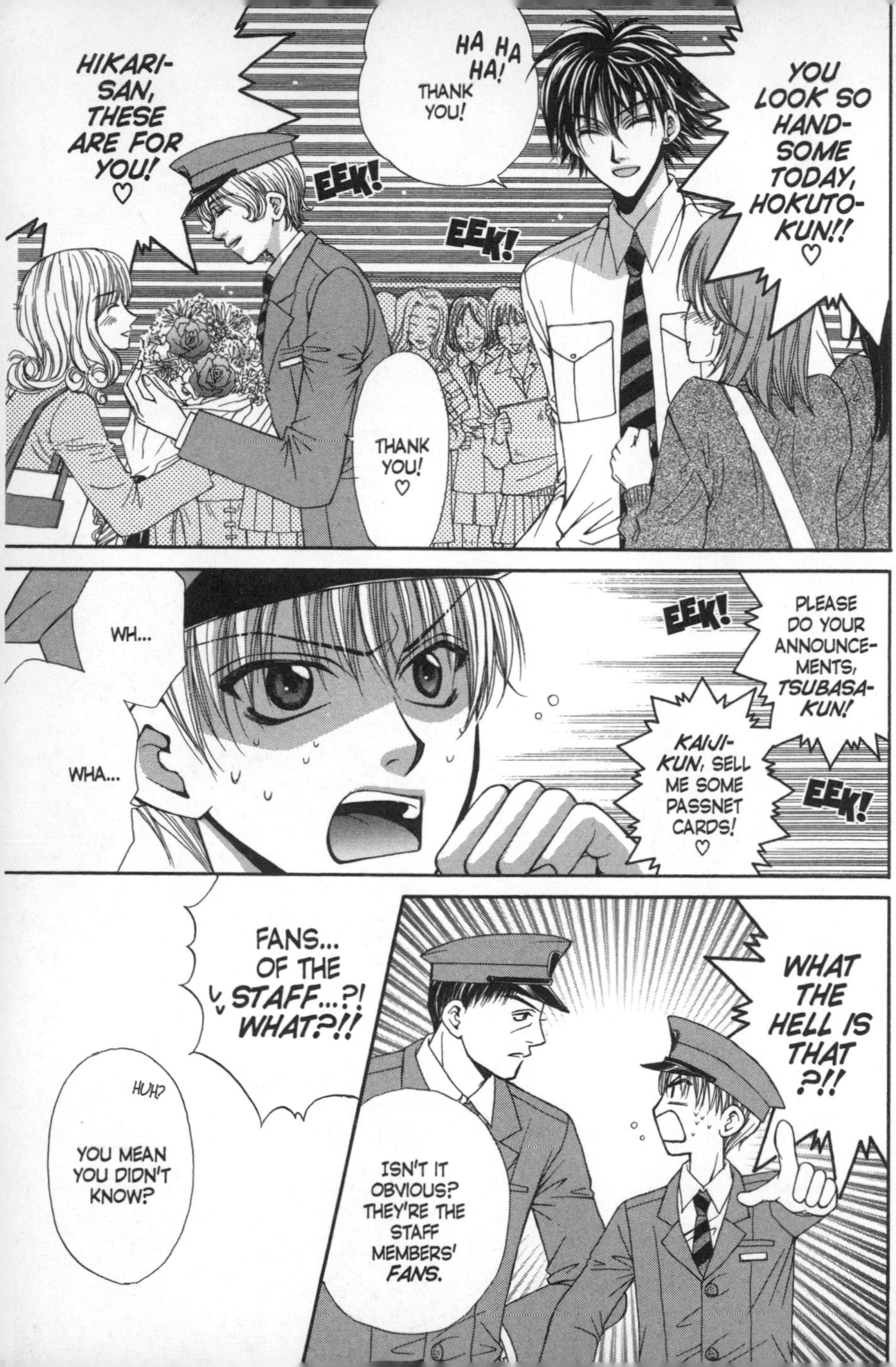
YOU LOOK SO HANDSOME TODAY, HOKUTO-KUN!! ♡
HA HA HA! THANK YOU!
EEK!
EEK!
HIKARI-SAN, THESE ARE FOR YOU! ♡
THANK YOU! ♡
PLEASE DO YOUR ANNOUNCEMENTS, TSUBASA-KUN!
EEK!
EEK!
KAIJI-KUN, SELL ME SOME PASSNET CARDS! ♡
WH...
WHA...
WHAT THE HELL IS THAT?!!
FANS... OF THE STAFF...?! WHAT?!!
ISN'T IT OBVIOUS? THEY'RE THE STAFF MEMBERS' FANS.
HUH?
YOU MEAN YOU DIDN'T KNOW?

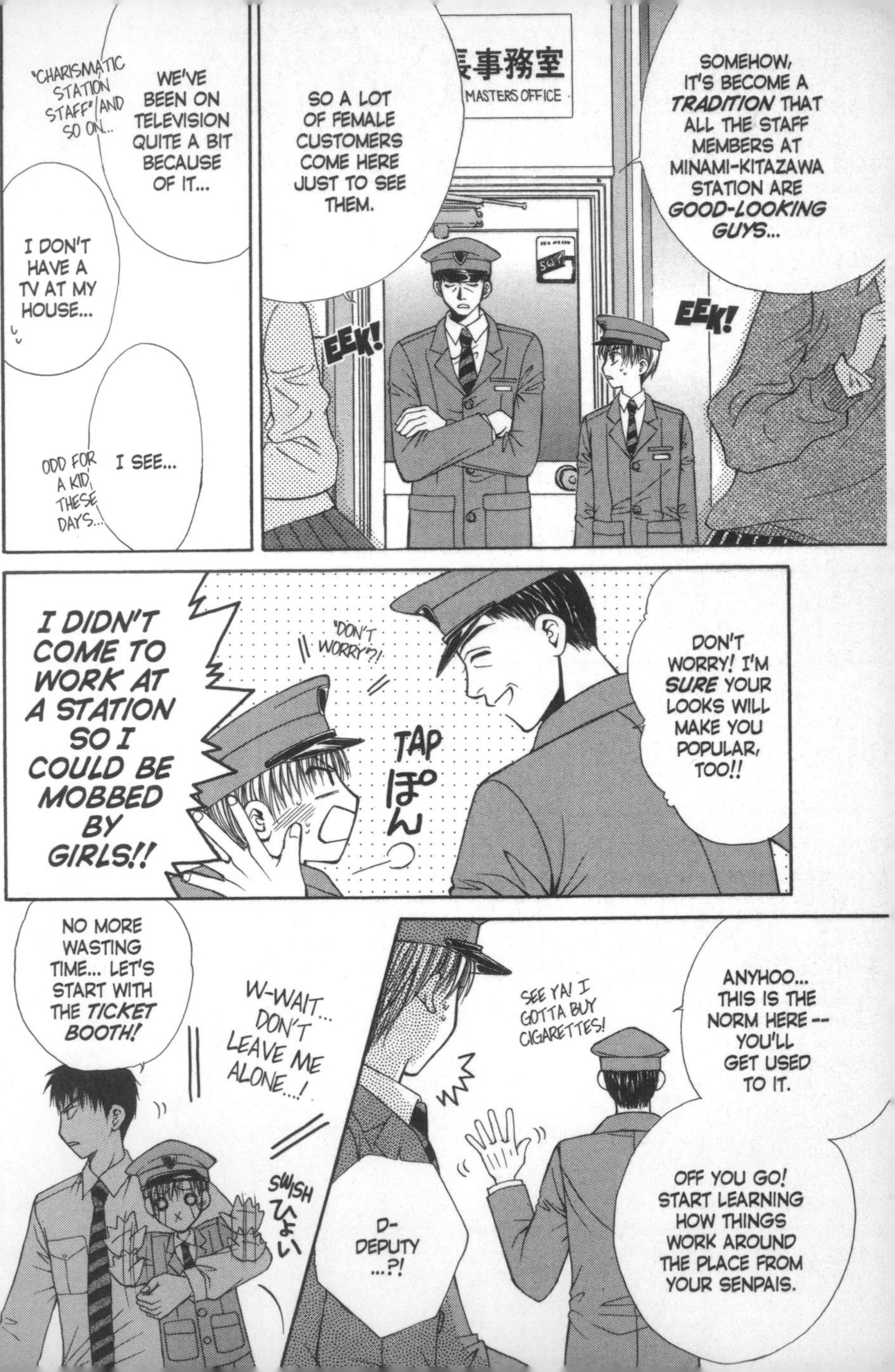
長事務室
MASTERS OFFICE
SOMEHOW, IT'S BECOME A TRADITION THAT ALL THE STAFF MEMBERS AT MINAMI-KITAZAWA STATION ARE GOOD-LOOKING GUYS...
SO A LOT OF FEMALE CUSTOMERS COME HERE JUST TO SEE THEM.
EEK!
EEK!
WE'VE BEEN ON TELEVISION QUITE A BIT BECAUSE OF IT...
"CHARISMATIC STATION STAFF" AND SO ON...
I DON'T HAVE A TV AT MY HOUSE...
I SEE...
ODD FOR A KID, THESE DAYS...
DON'T WORRY! I'M SURE YOUR LOOKS WILL MAKE YOU POPULAR, TOO!!
TAP
ぽん
"DON'T WORRY"?!
I DIDN'T COME TO WORK AT A STATION SO I COULD BE MOBBED BY GIRLS!!
ANYHOO... THIS IS THE NORM HERE -- YOU'LL GET USED TO IT.
OFF YOU GO! START LEARNING HOW THINGS WORK AROUND THE PLACE FROM YOUR SENPAIS.
SEE YA! I GOTTA BUY CIGARETTES!
D-DEPUTY ...?!
NO MORE WASTING TIME... LET'S START WITH THE TICKET BOOTH!
W-WAIT... DON'T LEAVE ME ALONE...!
SWISH
ひょい

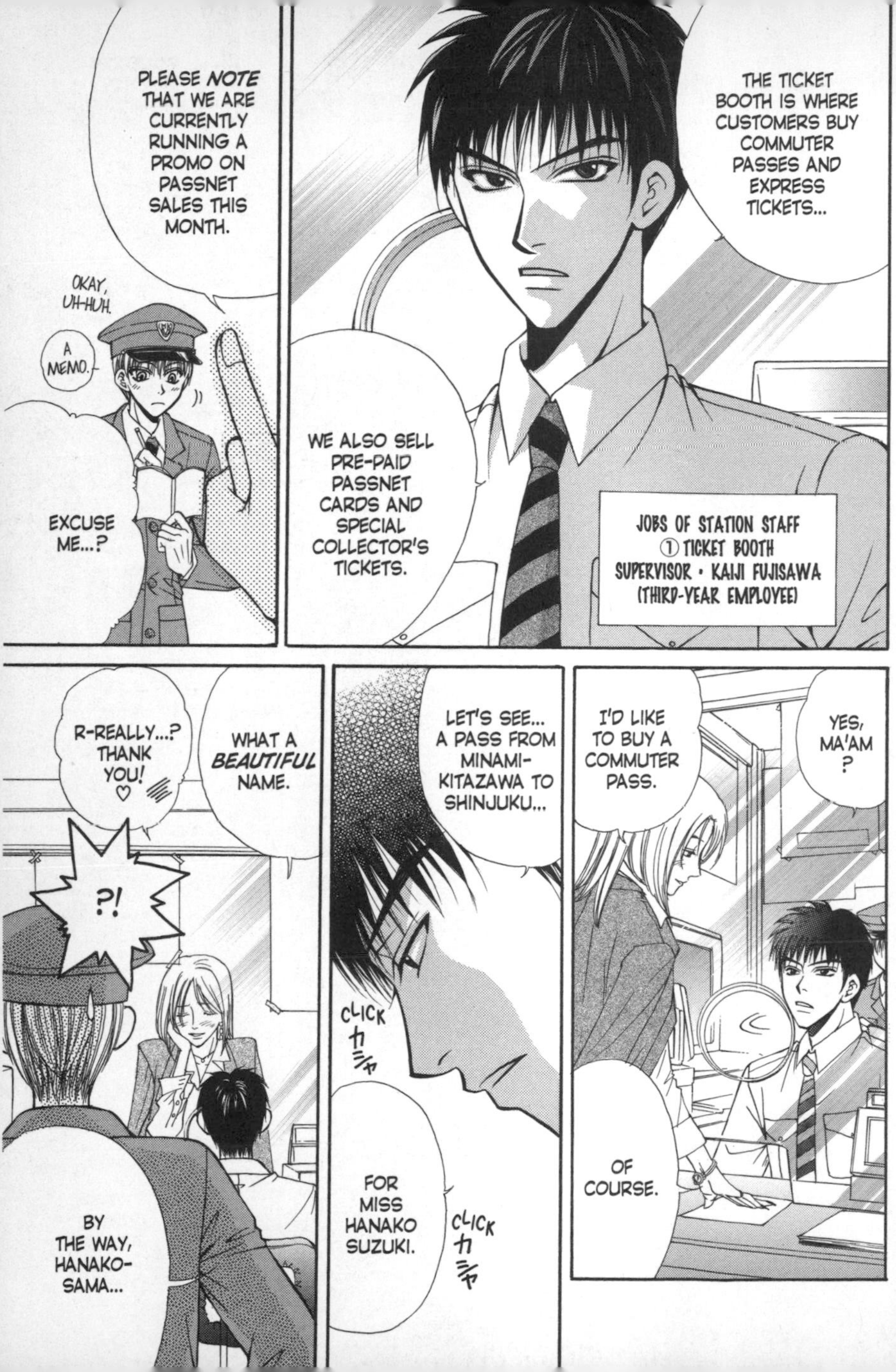
THE TICKET BOOTH IS WHERE CUSTOMERS BUY COMMUTER PASSES AND EXPRESS TICKETS...
WE ALSO SELL PRE-PAID PASSNET CARDS AND SPECIAL COLLECTOR'S TICKETS.
JOBS OF STATION STAFF ① TICKET BOOTH SUPERVISOR • KAIJI FUJISAWA (THIRD-YEAR EMPLOYEE)
PLEASE NOTE THAT WE ARE CURRENTLY RUNNING A PROMO ON PASSNET SALES THIS MONTH.
OKAY, UH-HUH.
A MEMO.
EXCUSE ME...?
YES, MA'AM?
I'D LIKE TO BUY A COMMUTER PASS.
OF COURSE.
LET'S SEE... A PASS FROM MINAMI-KITAZAWA TO SHINJUKU...
CLICK カシャ
FOR MISS HANAKO SUZUKI.
CLICK カシャ
WHAT A BEAUTIFUL NAME.
R-REALLY...? THANK YOU! ♡
?!
BY THE WAY, HANAKO-SAMA...

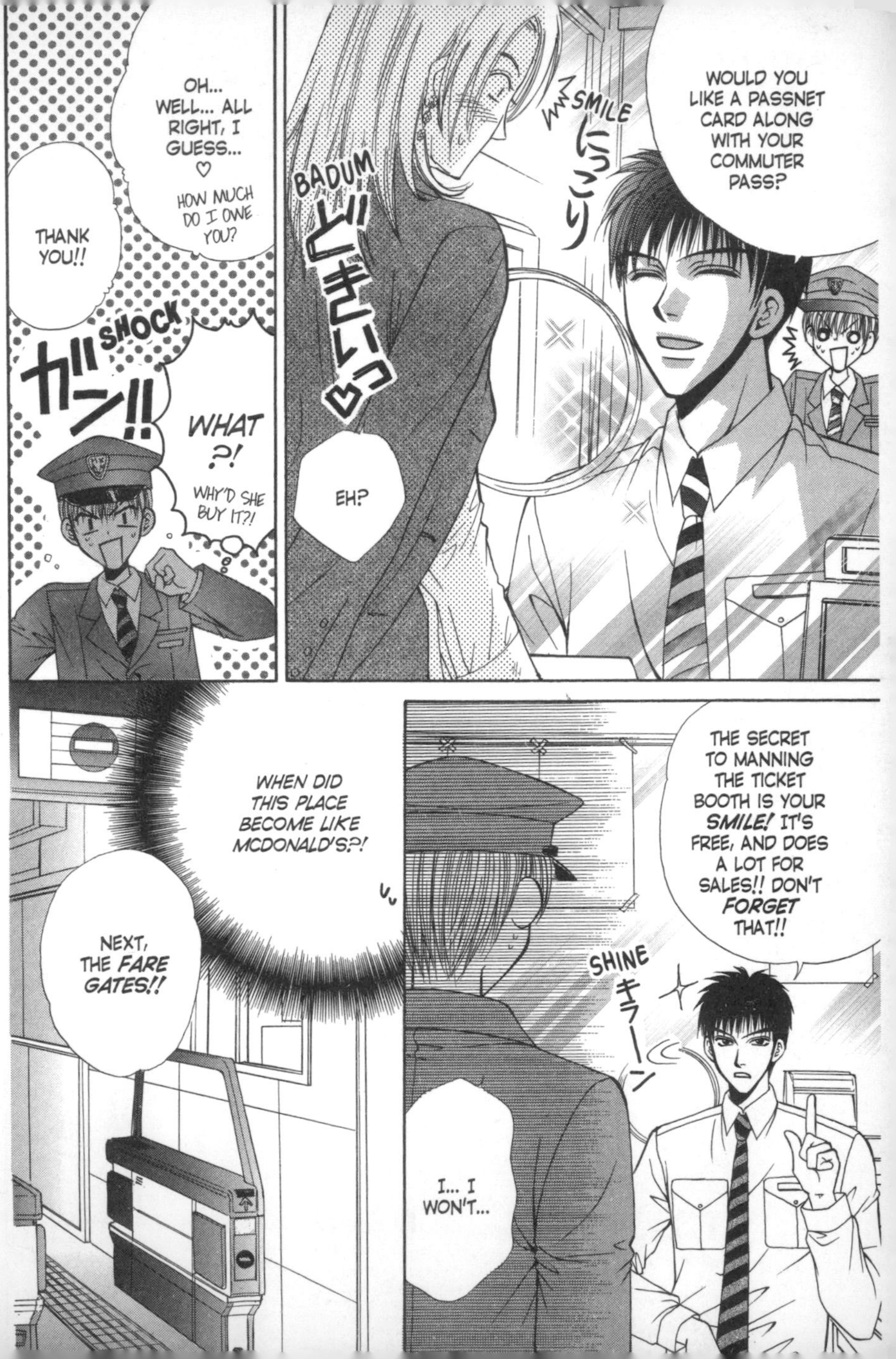

WOULD YOU LIKE A PASSNET CARD ALONG WITH YOUR COMMUTER PASS?
SMILE にっこり
BADUM どきぃっ♡
EH?
OH... WELL... ALL RIGHT, I GUESS... ♡
HOW MUCH DO I OWE YOU?
THANK YOU!!
SHOCK ガーン!!
WHAT?!
WHY'D SHE BUY IT?!
THE SECRET TO MANNING THE TICKET BOOTH IS YOUR SMILE! IT'S FREE, AND DOES A LOT FOR SALES!! DON'T FORGET THAT!!
SHINE キラーン
I... I WON'T...
WHEN DID THIS PLACE BECOME LIKE MCDONALD'S?!
NEXT, THE FARE GATES!!

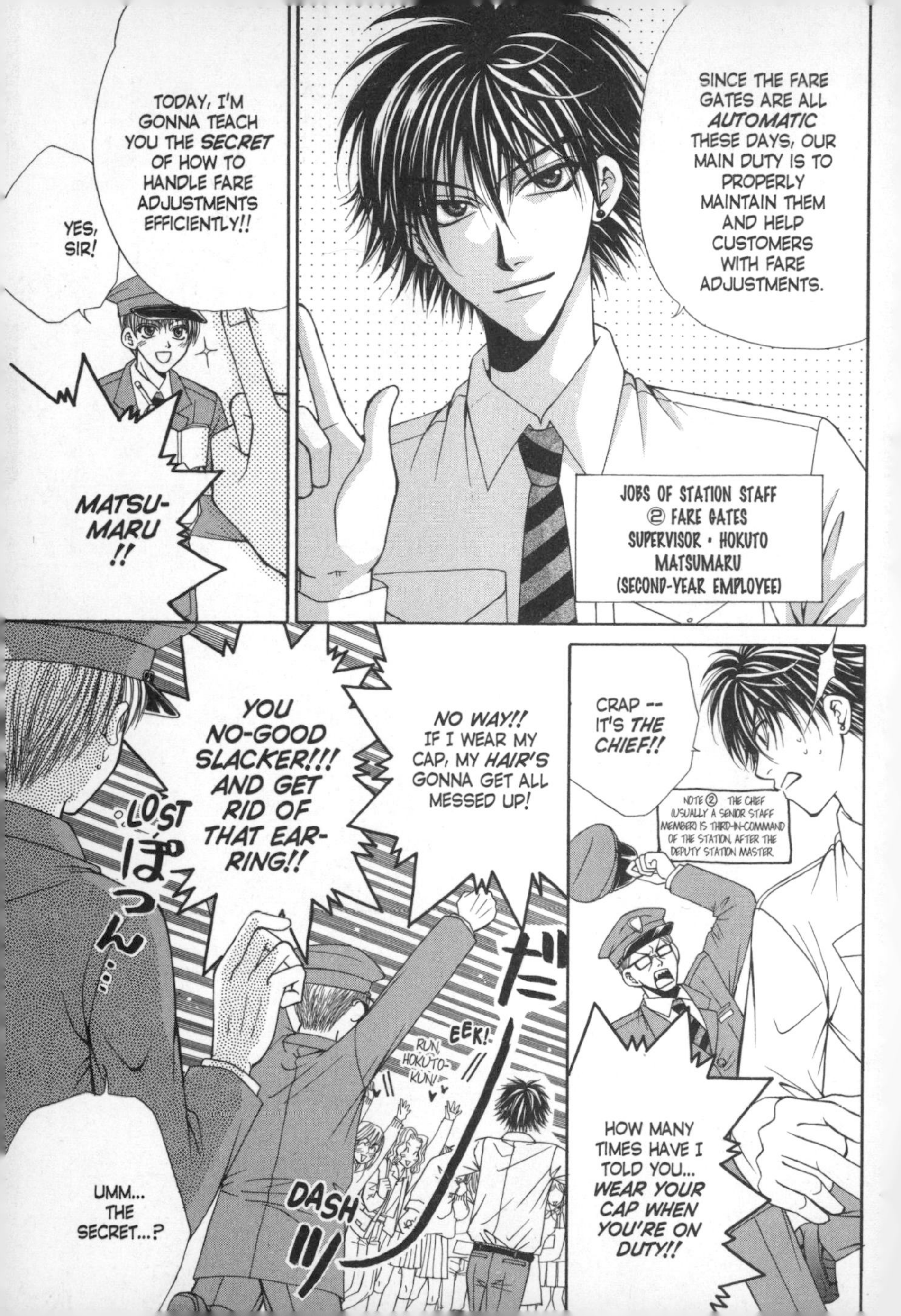
SINCE THE FARE GATES ARE ALL AUTOMATIC THESE DAYS, OUR MAIN DUTY IS TO PROPERLY MAINTAIN THEM AND HELP CUSTOMERS WITH FARE ADJUSTMENTS.
JOBS OF STATION STAFF ② FARE GATES SUPERVISOR • HOKUTO MATSUMARU (SECOND-YEAR EMPLOYEE)
TODAY, I'M GONNA TEACH YOU THE SECRET OF HOW TO HANDLE FARE ADJUSTMENTS EFFICIENTLY!!
YES, SIR!
MATSU-MARU!!
CRAP -- IT'S THE CHIEF!!
NOTE ② THE CHIEF (USUALLY A SENIOR STAFF MEMBER) IS THIRD-IN-COMMAND OF THE STATION, AFTER THE DEPUTY STATION MASTER.
HOW MANY TIMES HAVE I TOLD YOU... WEAR YOUR CAP WHEN YOU'RE ON DUTY!!
NO WAY!! IF I WEAR MY CAP, MY HAIR'S GONNA GET ALL MESSED UP!
YOU NO-GOOD SLACKER!!! AND GET RID OF THAT EAR-RING!!
だ
EEK!
RUN, HOKUTO-KUN!
DASH
LOST
ぽつん...
UMM... THE SECRET...?

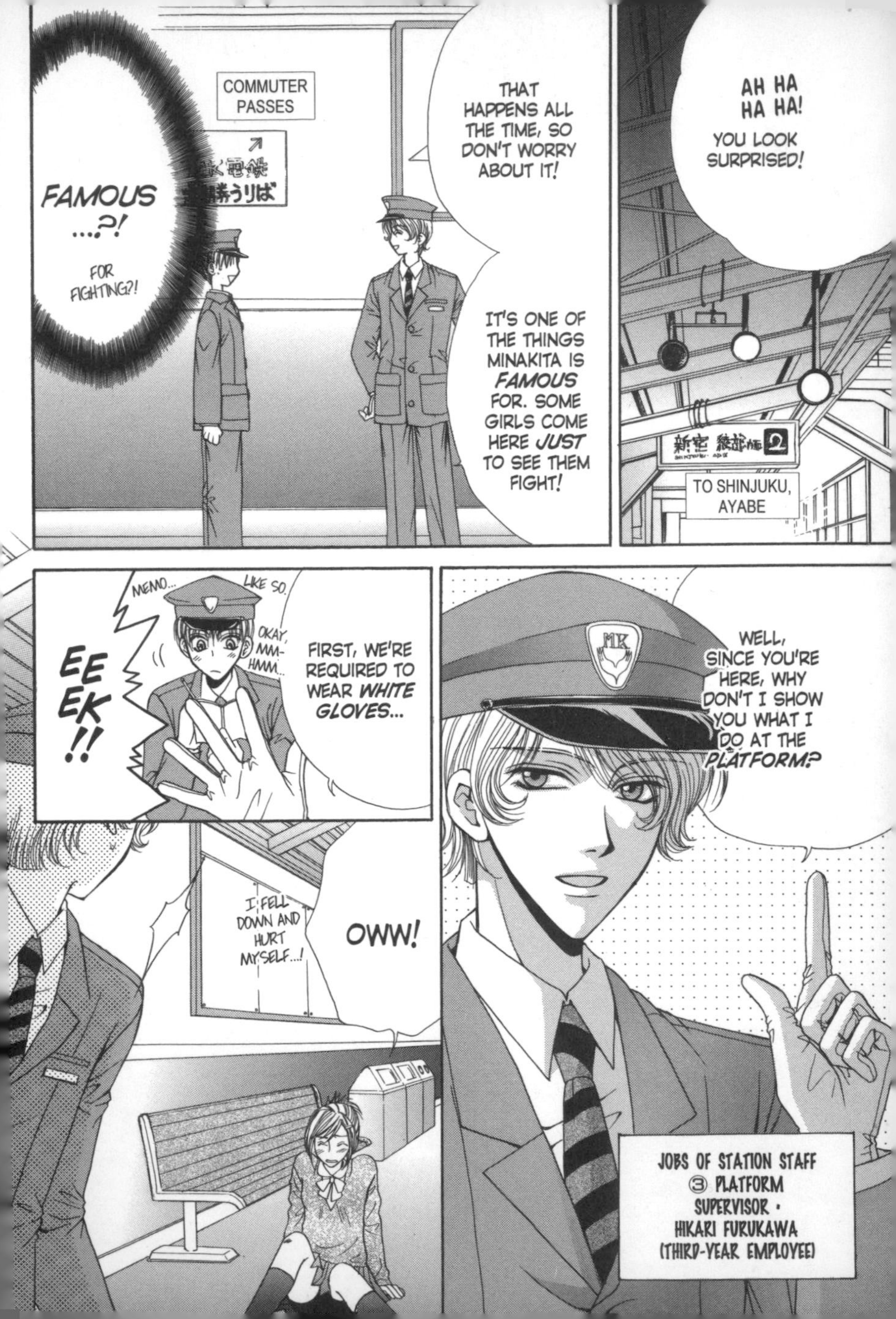
AH HA HA HA!
YOU LOOK SURPRISED!
TO SHINJUKU, AYABE
THAT HAPPENS ALL THE TIME, SO DON'T WORRY ABOUT IT!
IT'S ONE OF THE THINGS MINAKITA IS FAMOUS FOR. SOME GIRLS COME HERE JUST TO SEE THEM FIGHT!
COMMUTER PASSES
FAMOUS ...?!
FOR FIGHTING?!
WELL, SINCE YOU'RE HERE, WHY DON'T I SHOW YOU WHAT I DO AT THE PLATFORM?
JOBS OF STATION STAFF ③ PLATFORM SUPERVISOR・HIKARI FURUKAWA (THIRD-YEAR EMPLOYEE)
FIRST, WE'RE REQUIRED TO WEAR WHITE GLOVES...
LIKE SO.
OKAY, MM-HMM...
MEMO...
EEEK!!
OWW!
I FELL DOWN AND HURT MYSELF...!

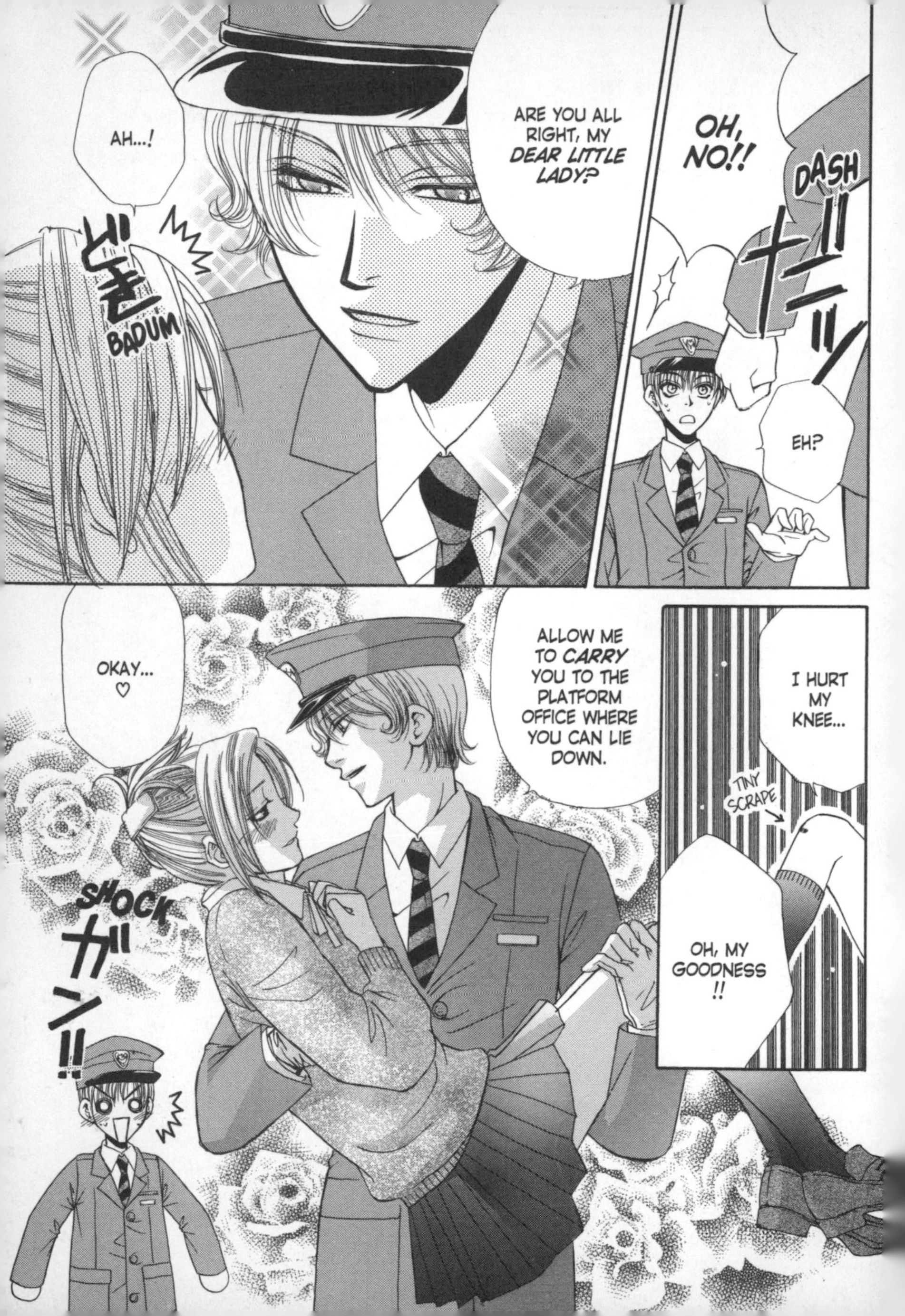
DASH
OH, NO!!
EH?
ARE YOU ALL RIGHT, MY DEAR LITTLE LADY?
AH...!
BADUM
I HURT MY KNEE...
TINY SCRAPE
OH, MY GOODNESS !!
ALLOW ME TO CARRY YOU TO THE PLATFORM OFFICE WHERE YOU CAN LIE DOWN.
OKAY... ♡
SHOCK

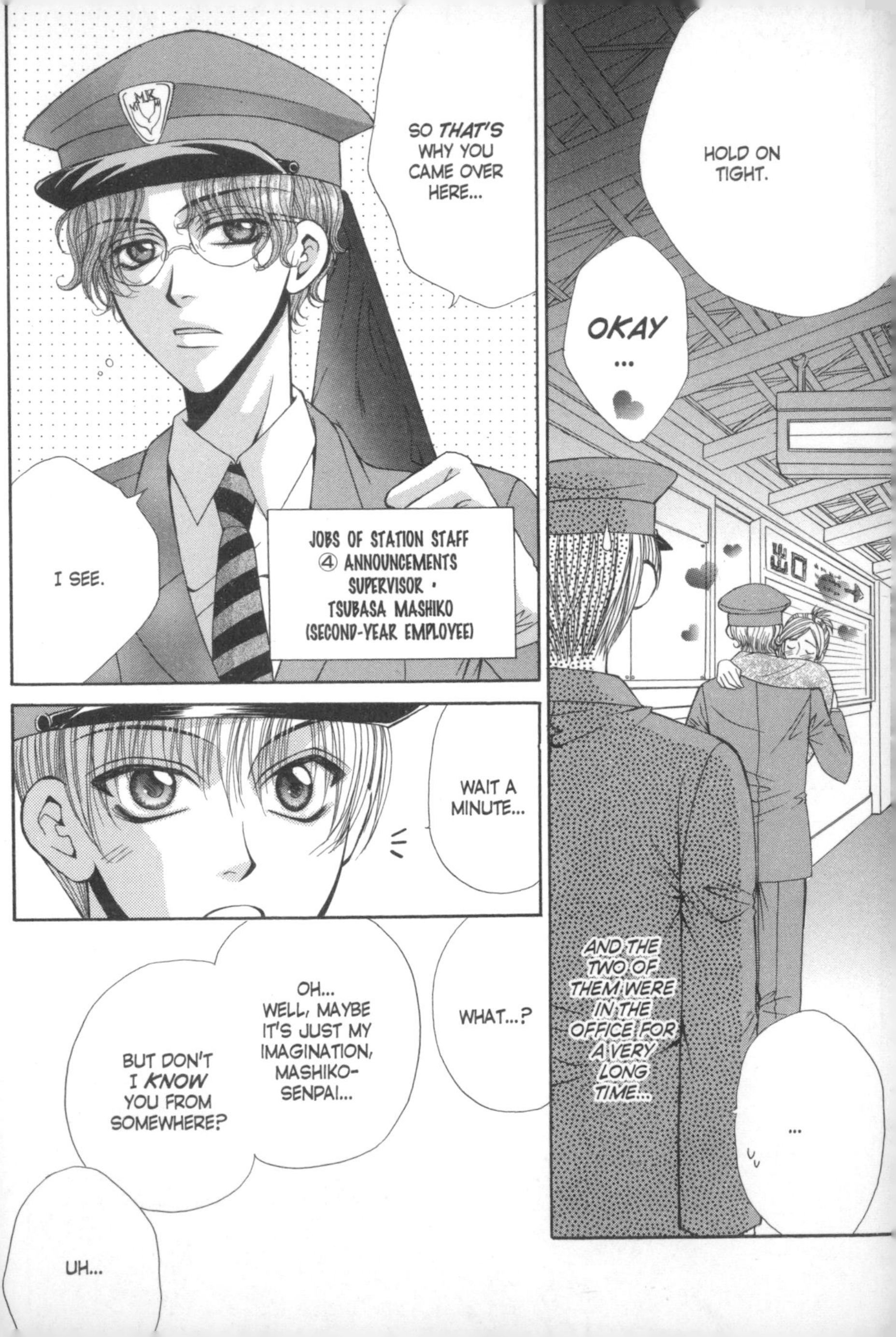
HOLD ON TIGHT.
OKAY...
AND THE TWO OF THEM WERE IN THE OFFICE FOR A VERY LONG TIME...
...
SO *THAT'S* WHY YOU CAME OVER HERE...
JOBS OF STATION STAFF ④ ANNOUNCEMENTS SUPERVISOR · TSUBASA MASHIKO (SECOND-YEAR EMPLOYEE)
I SEE.
WAIT A MINUTE...
WHAT...?
OH... WELL, MAYBE IT'S JUST MY IMAGINATION, MASHIKO-SENPAI...
BUT DON'T I *KNOW* YOU FROM SOMEWHERE?
UH...

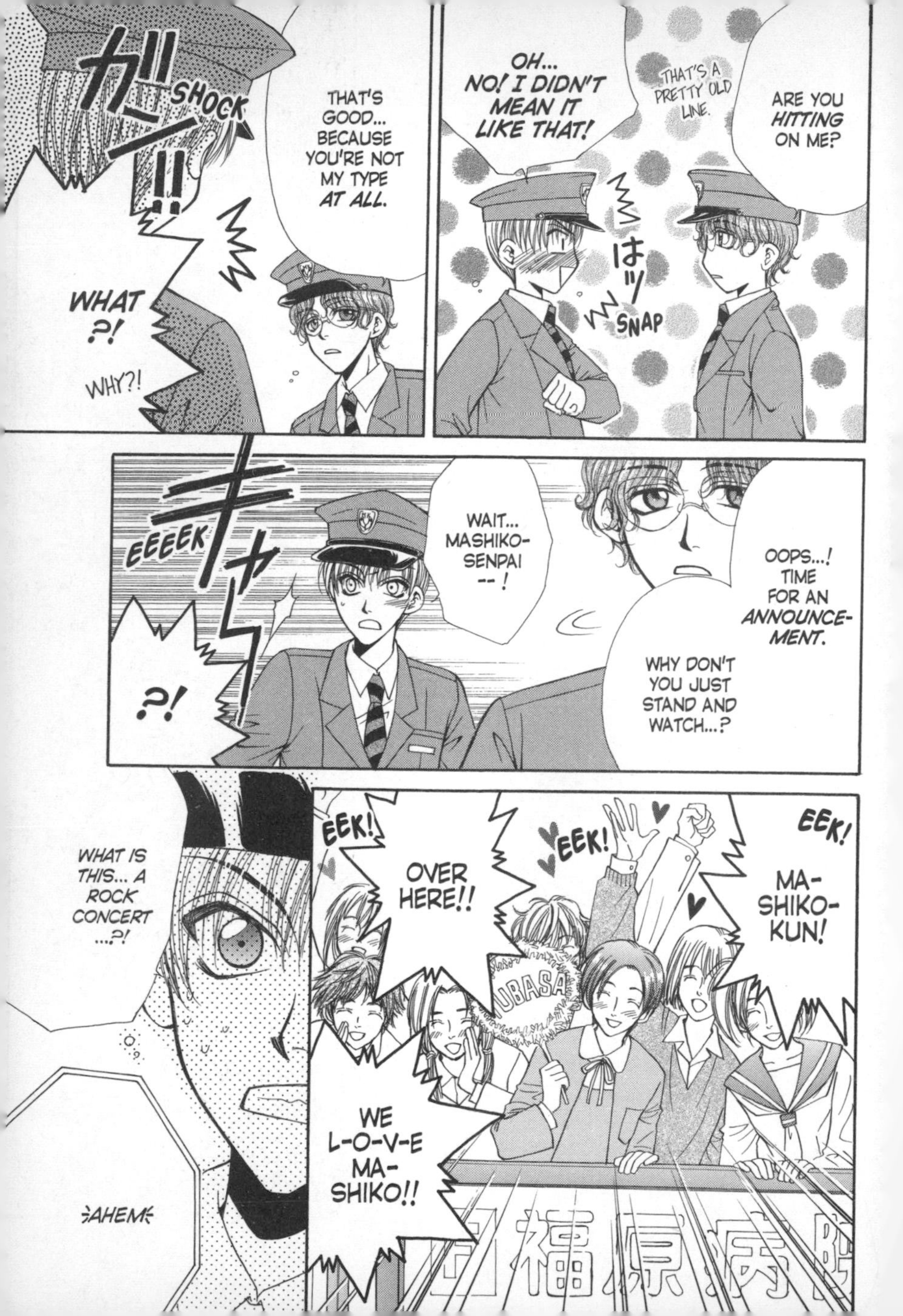
ARE YOU HITTING ON ME?
THAT'S A PRETTY OLD LINE.
OH... NO! I DIDN'T MEAN IT LIKE THAT!
はッ
SNAP
THAT'S GOOD... BECAUSE YOU'RE NOT MY TYPE AT ALL.
ガーン!!
SHOCK
WHAT?!
WHY?!
OOPS...! TIME FOR AN ANNOUNCEMENT.
WHY DON'T YOU JUST STAND AND WATCH...?
WAIT... MASHIKO-SENPAI--!
キャー
EEEEK
?!
EEK!
MA-SHIKO-KUN!
EEK!
OVER HERE!!
EEK!
WE L-O-V-E MA-SHIKO!!
WHAT IS THIS... A ROCK CONCERT...?!
AHEM

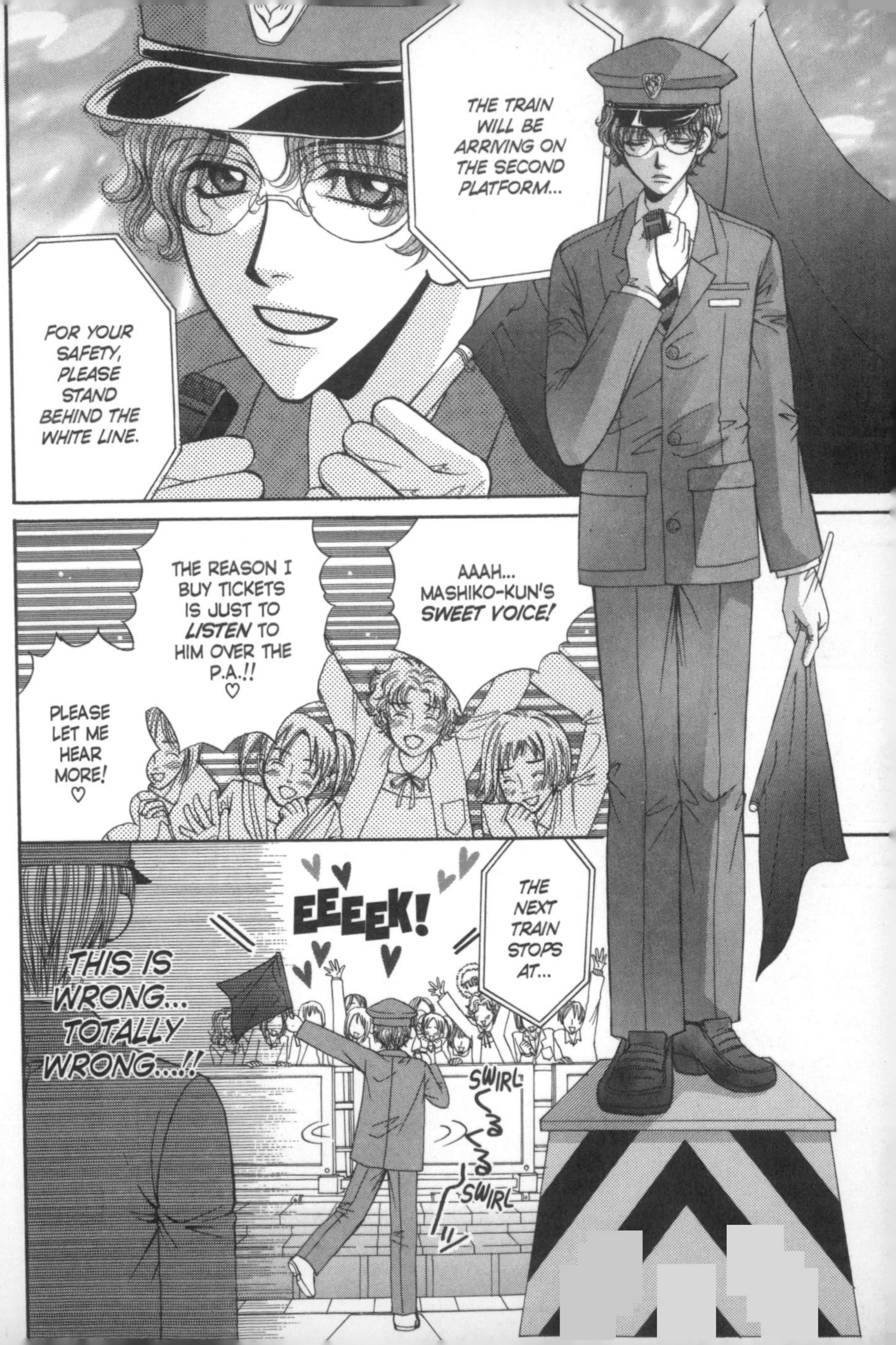
THE TRAIN WILL BE ARRIVING ON THE SECOND PLATFORM...
FOR YOUR SAFETY, PLEASE STAND BEHIND THE WHITE LINE.
AAAH... MASHIKO-KUN'S SWEET VOICE!
THE REASON I BUY TICKETS IS JUST TO LISTEN TO HIM OVER THE P.A.!! ♡
PLEASE LET ME HEAR MORE! ♡
THE NEXT TRAIN STOPS AT...
EEEEK!
THIS IS WRONG... TOTALLY WRONG...!!
SWIRL
SWIRL

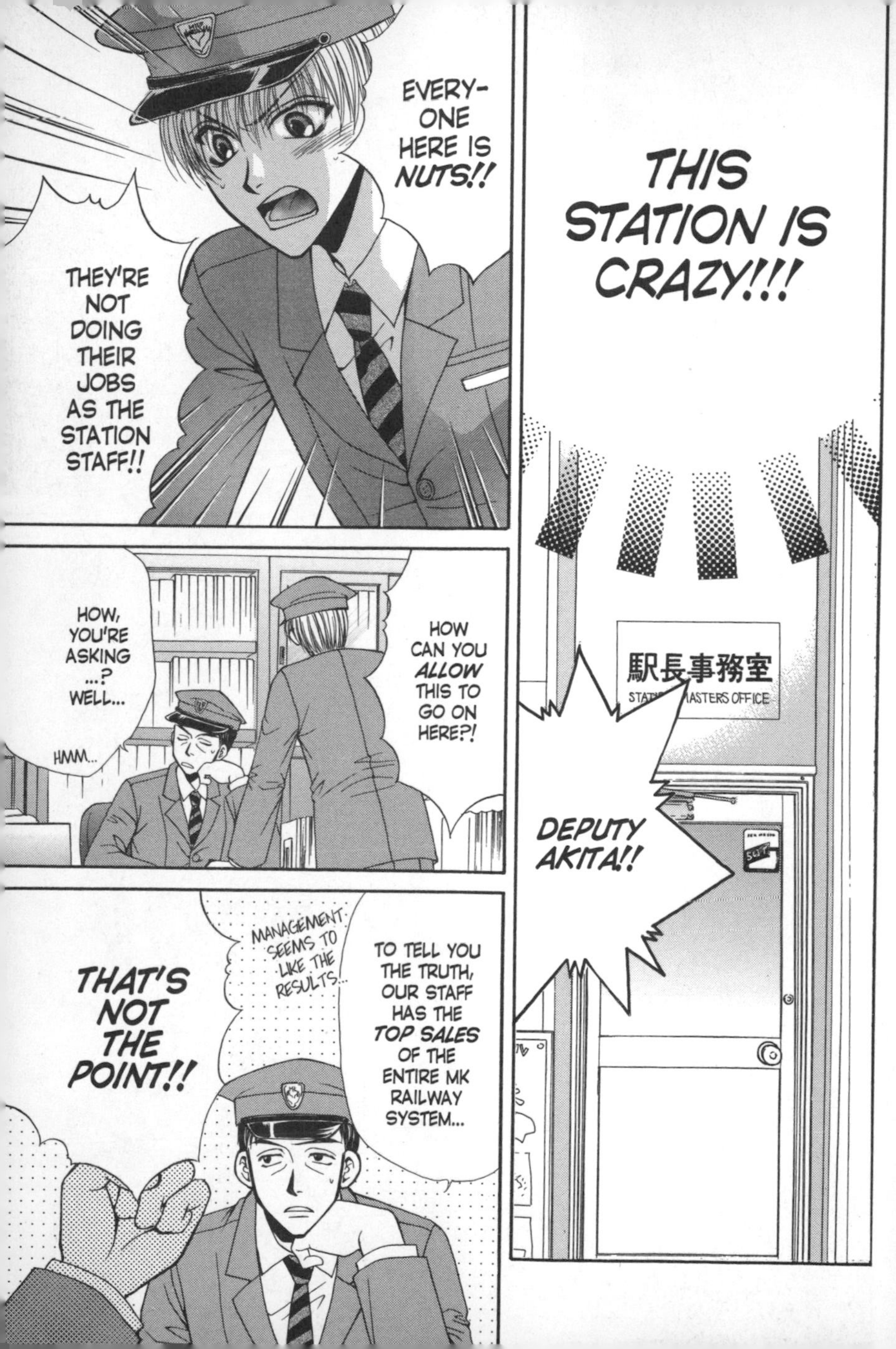
THIS STATION IS CRAZY!!!
駅長事務室
DEPUTY AKITA!!
EVERY-ONE HERE IS NUTS!!
THEY'RE NOT DOING THEIR JOBS AS THE STATION STAFF!!
HOW CAN YOU ALLOW THIS TO GO ON HERE?!
HOW, YOU'RE ASKING ...? WELL...
HMM...
TO TELL YOU THE TRUTH, OUR STAFF HAS THE TOP SALES OF THE ENTIRE MK RAILWAY SYSTEM...
MANAGEMENT SEEMS TO LIKE THE RESULTS...
THAT'S NOT THE POINT!!

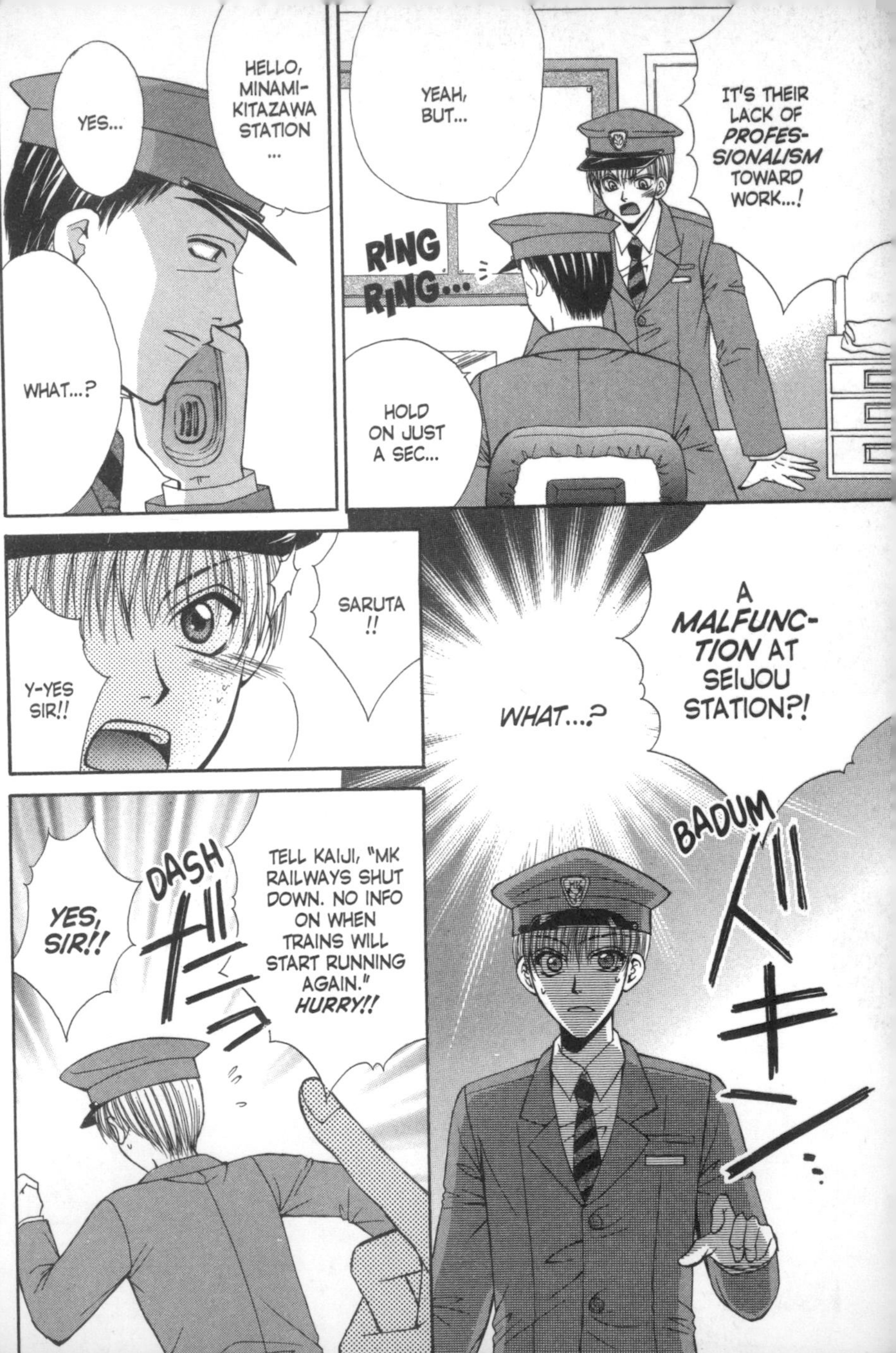
IT'S THEIR LACK OF PROFESSIONALISM TOWARD WORK...!
YEAH, BUT...
RING RING...
HOLD ON JUST A SEC...
HELLO, MINAMI-KITAZAWA STATION ...
YES...
WHAT...?
A MALFUNCTION AT SEIJOU STATION?!
WHAT...?
BADUM
SARUTA !!
Y-YES SIR!!
TELL KAIJI, "MK RAILWAYS SHUT DOWN. NO INFO ON WHEN TRAINS WILL START RUNNING AGAIN." HURRY!!
YES, SIR!!
DASH

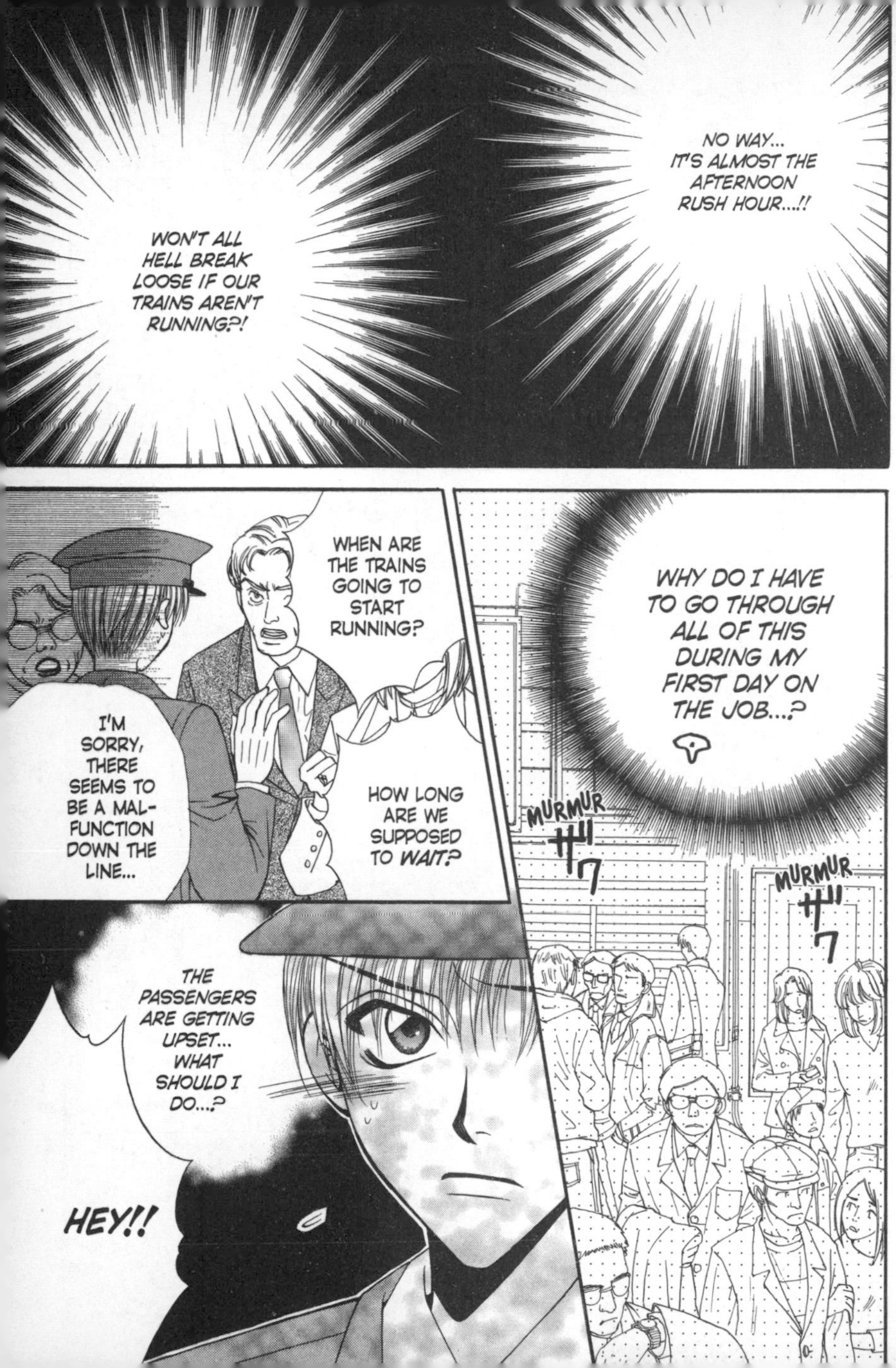
NO WAY... IT'S ALMOST THE AFTERNOON RUSH HOUR...!!
WON'T ALL HELL BREAK LOOSE IF OUR TRAINS AREN'T RUNNING?!
WHY DO I HAVE TO GO THROUGH ALL OF THIS DURING MY FIRST DAY ON THE JOB...?
MURMUR
ザワ
MURMUR
ザワ
WHEN ARE THE TRAINS GOING TO START RUNNING?
I'M SORRY, THERE SEEMS TO BE A MAL-FUNCTION DOWN THE LINE...
HOW LONG ARE WE SUPPOSED TO *WAIT?*
THE PASSENGERS ARE GETTING UPSET... WHAT SHOULD I DO...?
HEY!!

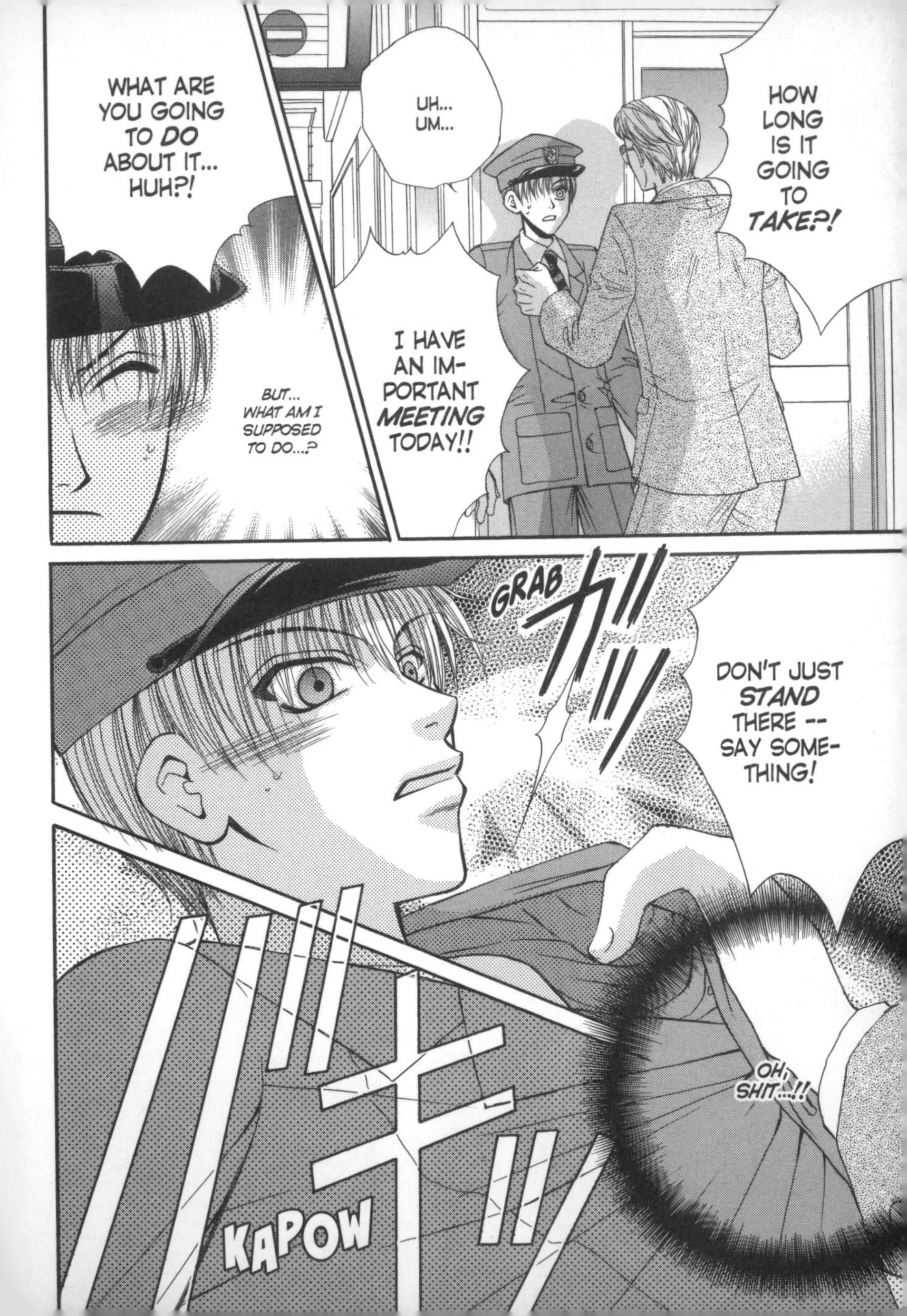
HOW LONG IS IT GOING TO TAKE?!
UH... UM...
I HAVE AN IMPORTANT MEETING TODAY!!
WHAT ARE YOU GOING TO DO ABOUT IT... HUH?!
BUT... WHAT AM I SUPPOSED TO DO...?
DON'T JUST STAND THERE -- SAY SOMETHING!
GRAB
OH, SHIT...!!
KAPOW

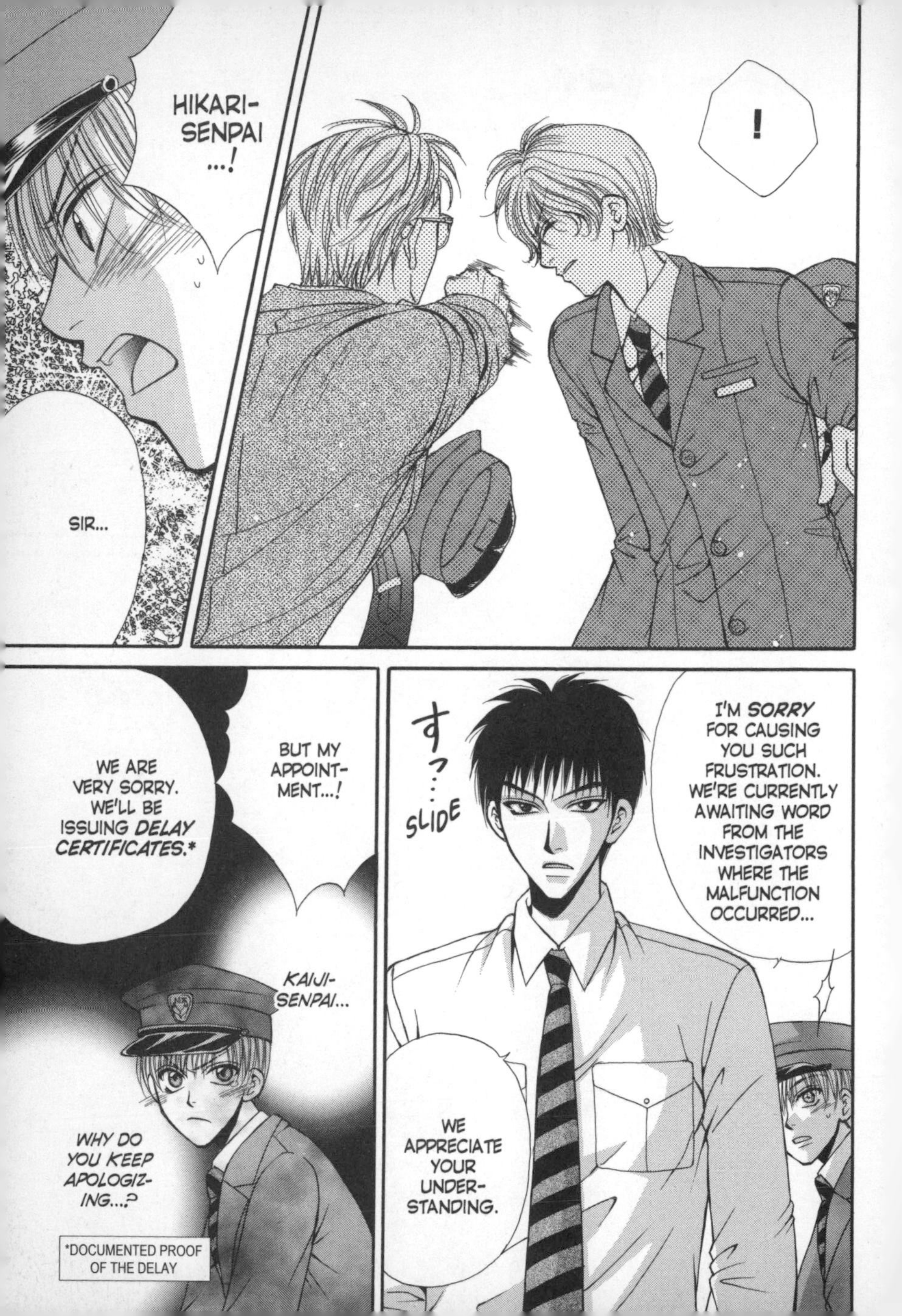
!
HIKARI-SENPAI ...!
SIR...
I'M SORRY FOR CAUSING YOU SUCH FRUSTRATION. WE'RE CURRENTLY AWAITING WORD FROM THE INVESTIGATORS WHERE THE MALFUNCTION OCCURRED...
す… SLIDE
WE APPRECIATE YOUR UNDER-STANDING.
BUT MY APPOINT-MENT...!
WE ARE VERY SORRY. WE'LL BE ISSUING DELAY CERTIFICATES.*
KAIJI-SENPAI...
WHY DO YOU KEEP APOLOGIZ-ING...?
*DOCUMENTED PROOF OF THE DELAY

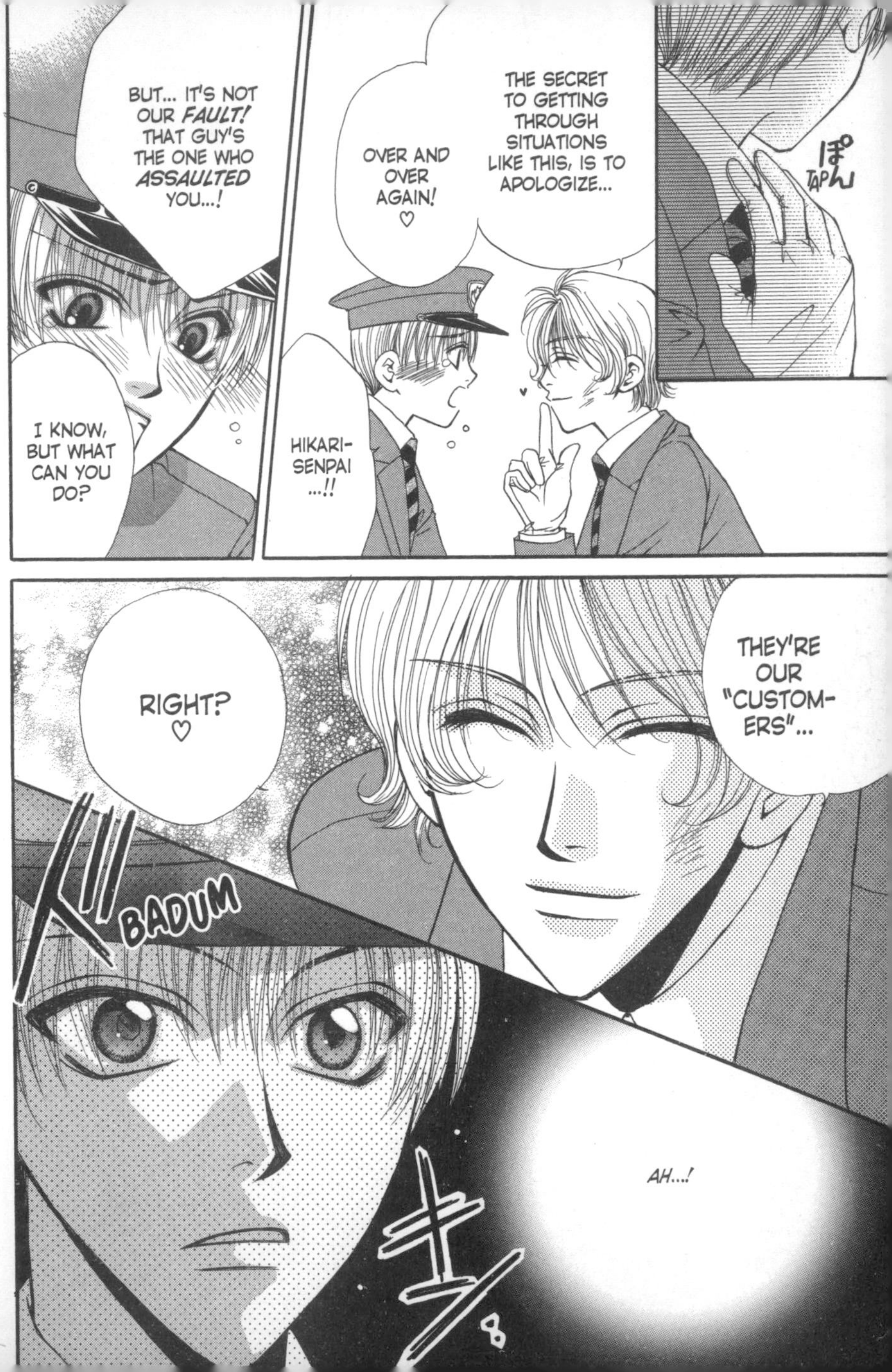
ぽん
TAP
THE SECRET TO GETTING THROUGH SITUATIONS LIKE THIS, IS TO APOLOGIZE...
OVER AND OVER AGAIN! ♡
HIKARI-SENPAI ...!!
BUT... IT'S NOT OUR *FAULT!* THAT GUY'S THE ONE WHO *ASSAULTED* YOU...!
I KNOW, BUT WHAT CAN YOU DO?
THEY'RE OUR "CUSTOMERS"...
RIGHT? ♡
BADUM
AH...!

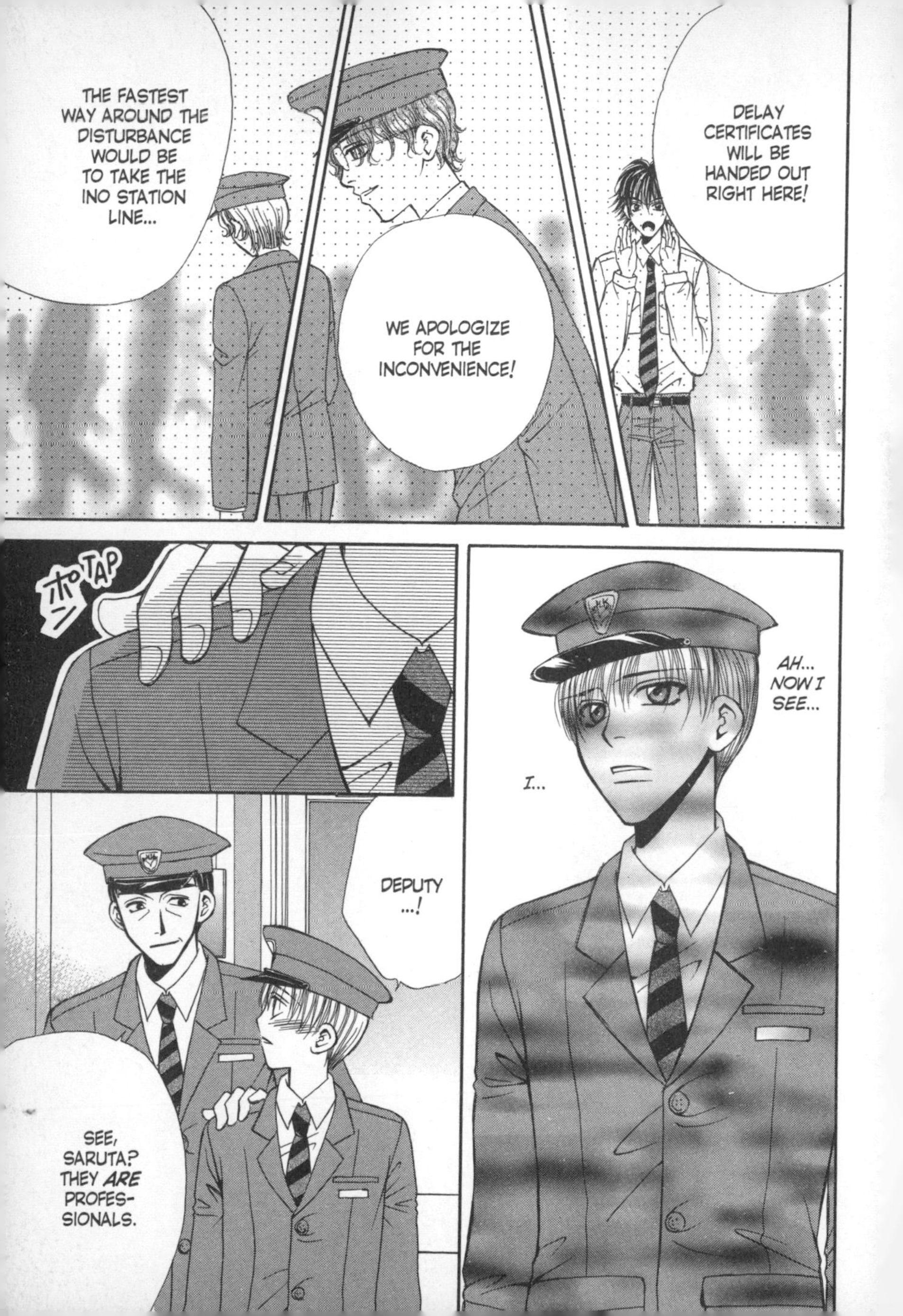
DELAY CERTIFICATES WILL BE HANDED OUT RIGHT HERE!
WE APOLOGIZE FOR THE INCONVENIENCE!
THE FASTEST WAY AROUND THE DISTURBANCE WOULD BE TO TAKE THE INO STATION LINE...
AH... NOW I SEE...
I...
TAP
DEPUTY ...!
SEE, SARUTA? THEY *ARE* PROFESSIONALS.

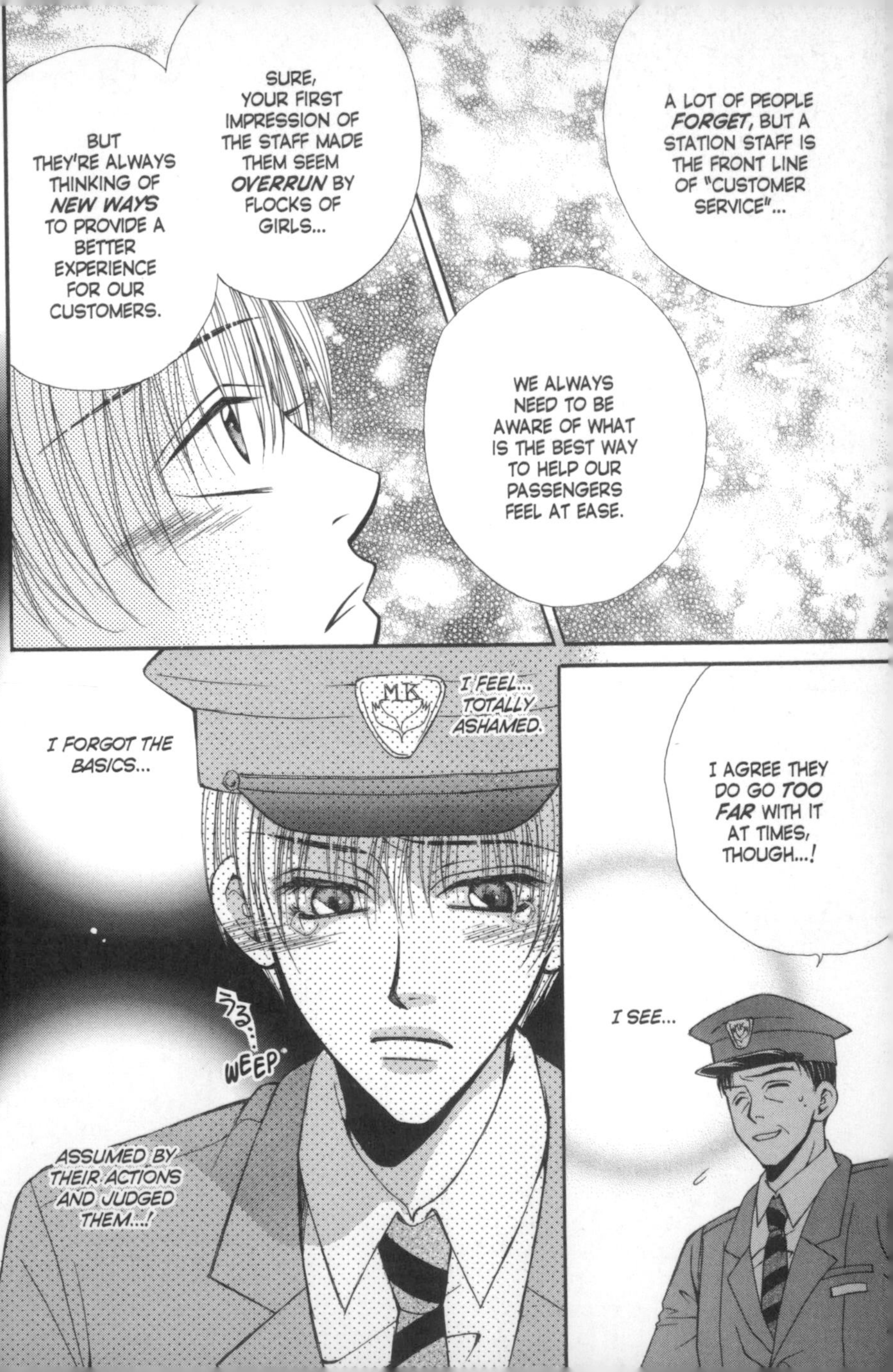
A LOT OF PEOPLE FORGET, BUT A STATION STAFF IS THE FRONT LINE OF "CUSTOMER SERVICE"...
WE ALWAYS NEED TO BE AWARE OF WHAT IS THE BEST WAY TO HELP OUR PASSENGERS FEEL AT EASE.
SURE, YOUR FIRST IMPRESSION OF THE STAFF MADE THEM SEEM OVERRUN BY FLOCKS OF GIRLS...
BUT THEY'RE ALWAYS THINKING OF NEW WAYS TO PROVIDE A BETTER EXPERIENCE FOR OUR CUSTOMERS.
I AGREE THEY DO GO TOO FAR WITH IT AT TIMES, THOUGH...!
I SEE...
I FEEL... TOTALLY ASHAMED.
I FORGOT THE BASICS...
うる... WEEP
ASSUMED BY THEIR ACTIONS AND JUDGED THEM...!

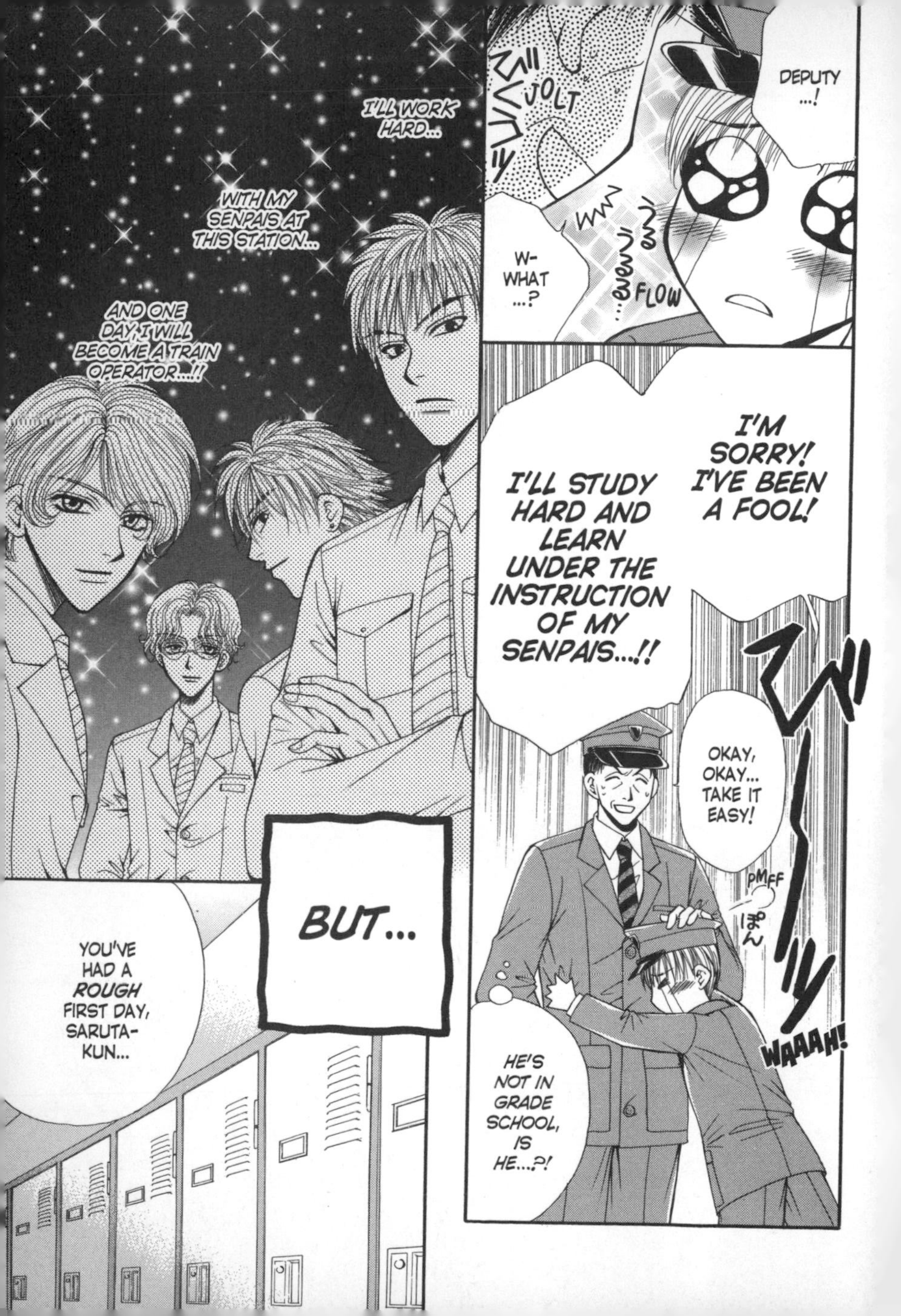

DEPUTY ...!
JOLT
W- WHAT ...?
FLOW
I'M SORRY! I'VE BEEN A FOOL!
I'LL STUDY HARD AND LEARN UNDER THE INSTRUCTION OF MY SENPAIS...!!
OKAY, OKAY... TAKE IT EASY!
PMFF
ぽん
WAAAH!
HE'S NOT IN GRADE SCHOOL, IS HE...?!
I'LL WORK HARD...
WITH MY SENPAIS AT THIS STATION...
AND ONE DAY, I WILL BECOME A TRAIN OPERATOR...!!
BUT...
YOU'VE HAD A ROUGH FIRST DAY, SARUTA-KUN...

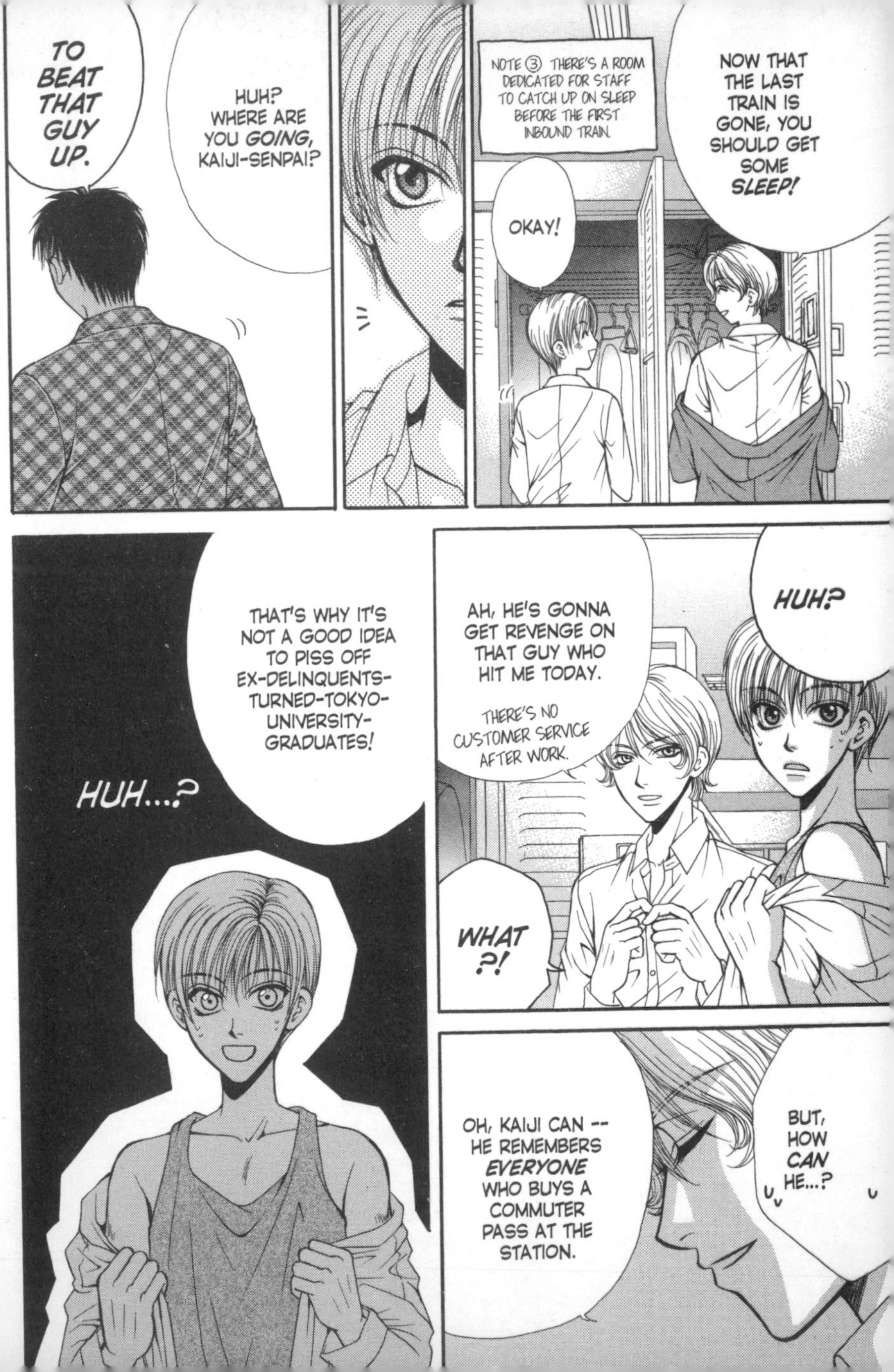
NOW THAT THE LAST TRAIN IS GONE, YOU SHOULD GET SOME SLEEP!
NOTE ③ THERE'S A ROOM DEDICATED FOR STAFF TO CATCH UP ON SLEEP BEFORE THE FIRST INBOUND TRAIN.
OKAY!
HUH? WHERE ARE YOU GOING, KAIJI-SENPAI?
TO BEAT THAT GUY UP.
HUH?
AH, HE'S GONNA GET REVENGE ON THAT GUY WHO HIT ME TODAY.
THERE'S NO CUSTOMER SERVICE AFTER WORK.
WHAT?!
BUT, HOW CAN HE...?
OH, KAIJI CAN -- HE REMEMBERS EVERYONE WHO BUYS A COMMUTER PASS AT THE STATION.
THAT'S WHY IT'S NOT A GOOD IDEA TO PISS OFF EX-DELINQUENTS-TURNED-TOKYO-UNIVERSITY-GRADUATES!
HUH...?

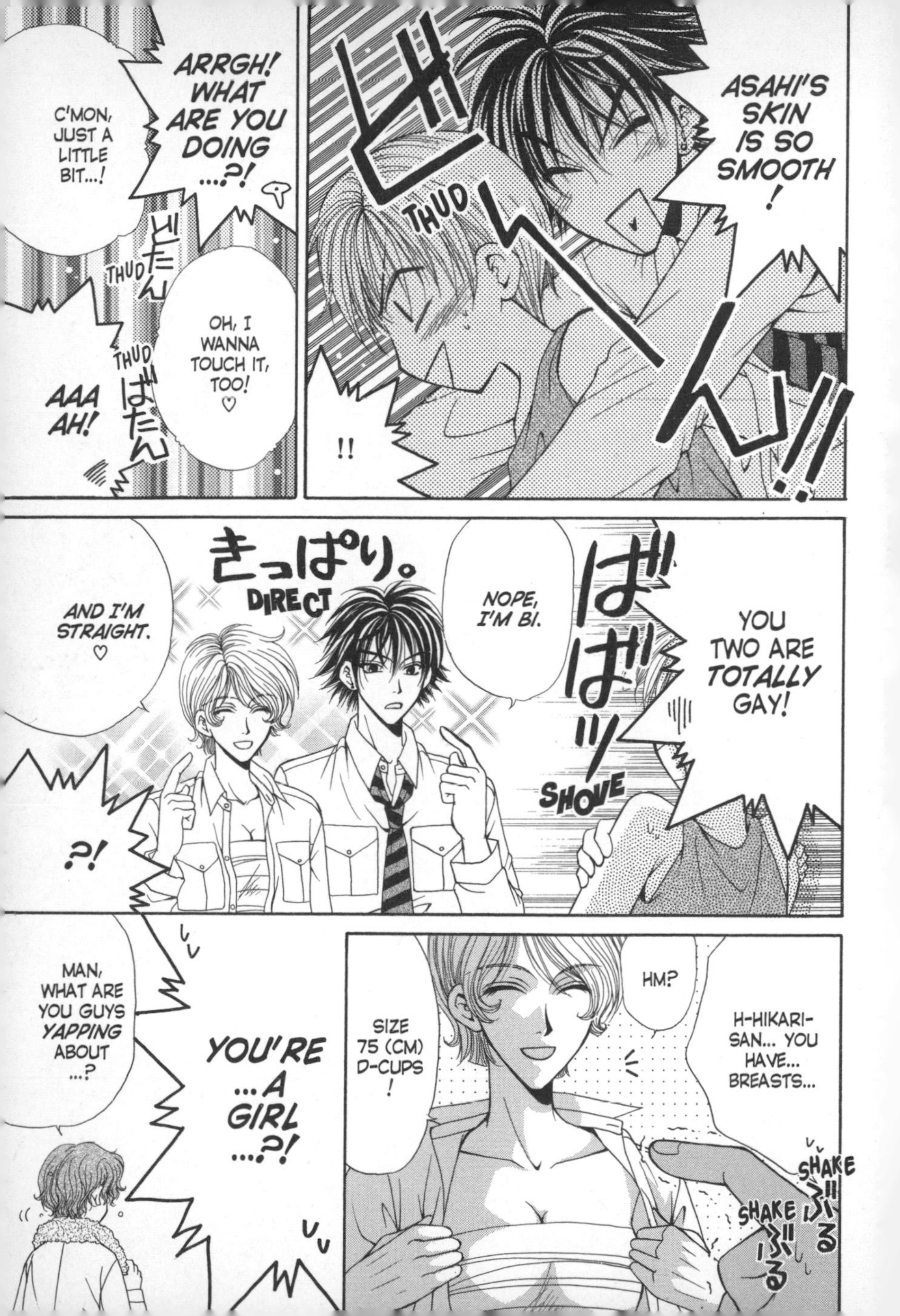
ASAHI'S SKIN IS SO SMOOTH!
THUD
!!
ARRGH! WHAT ARE YOU DOING ...?!
C'MON, JUST A LITTLE BIT...!
どたん
THUD
OH, I WANNA TOUCH IT, TOO! ♡
THUD
ばたん
AAA AH!
YOU TWO ARE TOTALLY GAY!
ばばッ
SHOVE
NOPE, I'M BI.
きっぱり。
DIRECT
AND I'M STRAIGHT. ♡
?!
H-HIKARI-SAN... YOU HAVE... BREASTS...
HM?
SIZE 75 (CM) D-CUPS!
SHAKE
ぶる
SHAKE
ぶる
YOU'RE ...A GIRL ...?!
MAN, WHAT ARE YOU GUYS YAPPING ABOUT ...?

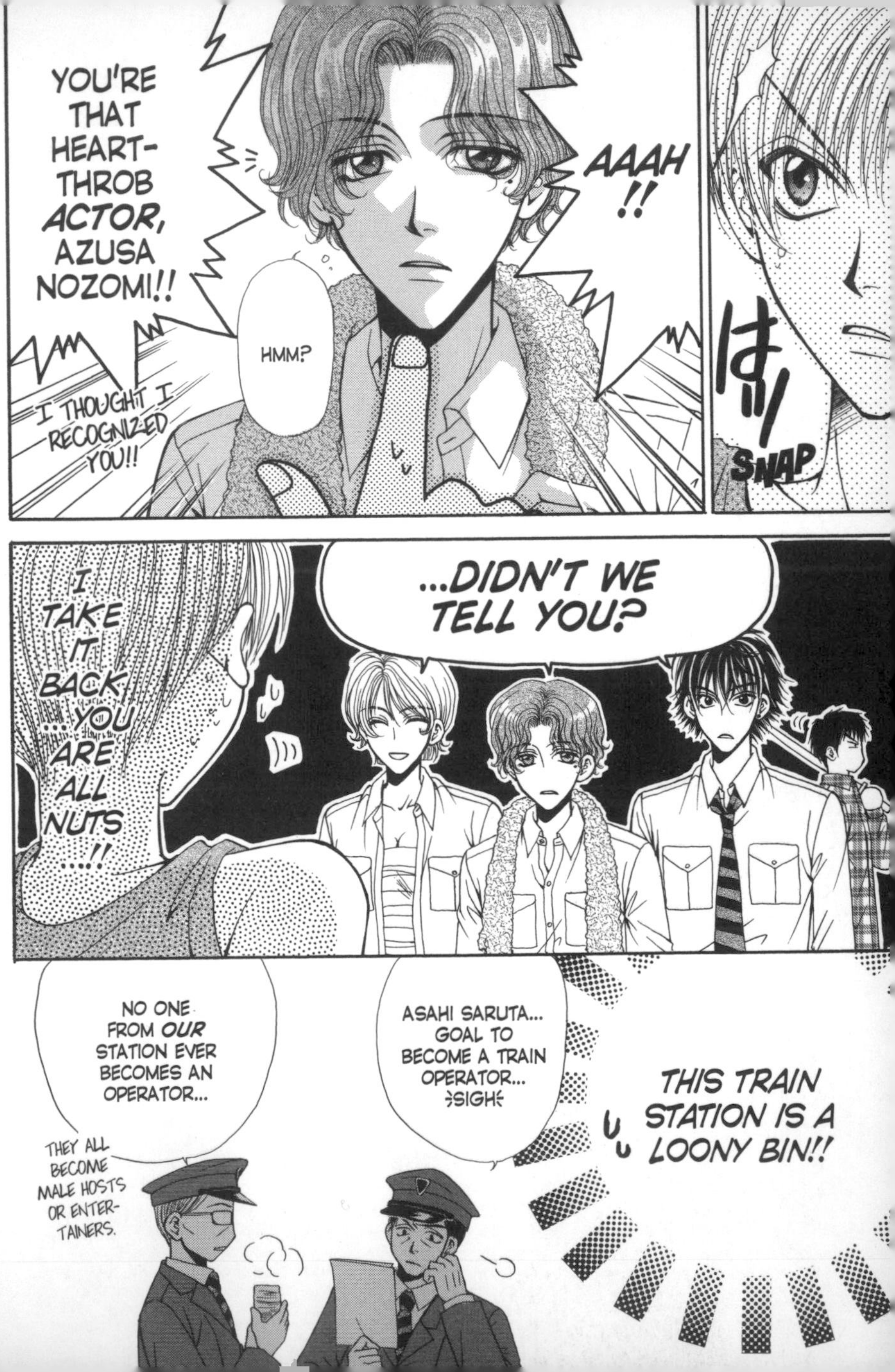
はッ
SNAP
AAAH!!
YOU'RE THAT HEART-THROB ACTOR, AZUSA NOZOMI!!
HMM?
I THOUGHT I RECOGNIZED YOU!!
...DIDN'T WE TELL YOU?
I TAKE IT BACK... YOU ARE ALL NUTS...!!
THIS TRAIN STATION IS A LOONY BIN!!
ASAHI SARUTA... GOAL TO BECOME A TRAIN OPERATOR... SIGH
NO ONE FROM OUR STATION EVER BECOMES AN OPERATOR...
THEY ALL BECOME MALE HOSTS OR ENTER-TAINERS.

## ASAHI SARUTA

MY FIRST CUDDLY-ANIMAL-TYPE MAIN CHARACTER (LOL).
BUT I THINK HE'S TURNING OUT TO BE KIND OF A CLUTZ...

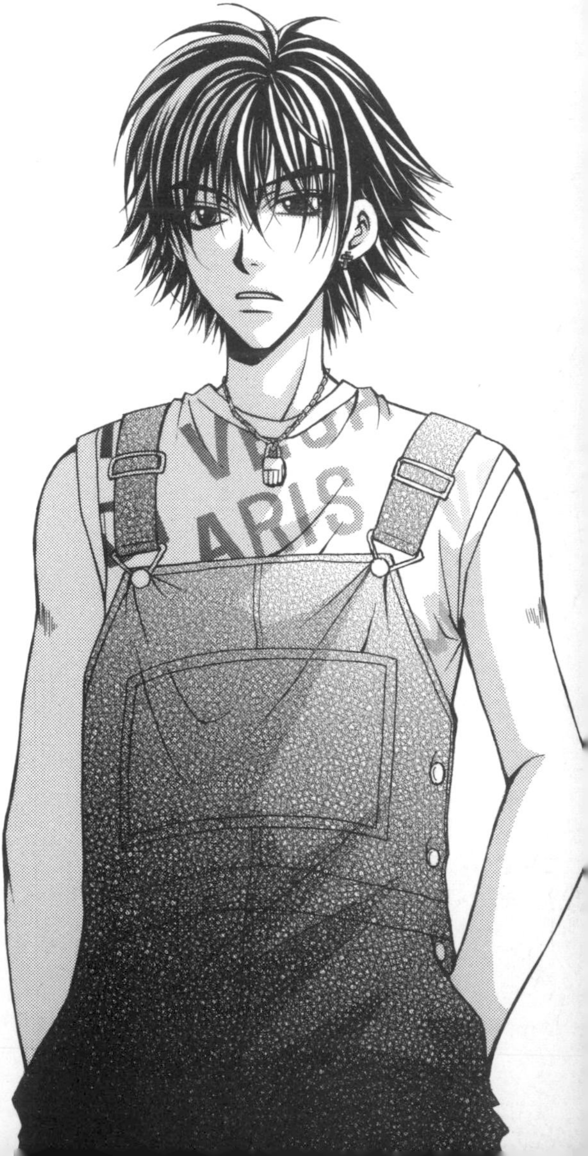

## HOKUTO MATSUMARU

THE ULTIMATE LOVE MACHINE. HIS FAVORITE WORD IS "FREEDOM."
I'LL GO IN-DEPTH INTO HIS BACKGROUND IN THE SECOND VOLUME... I HOPE?

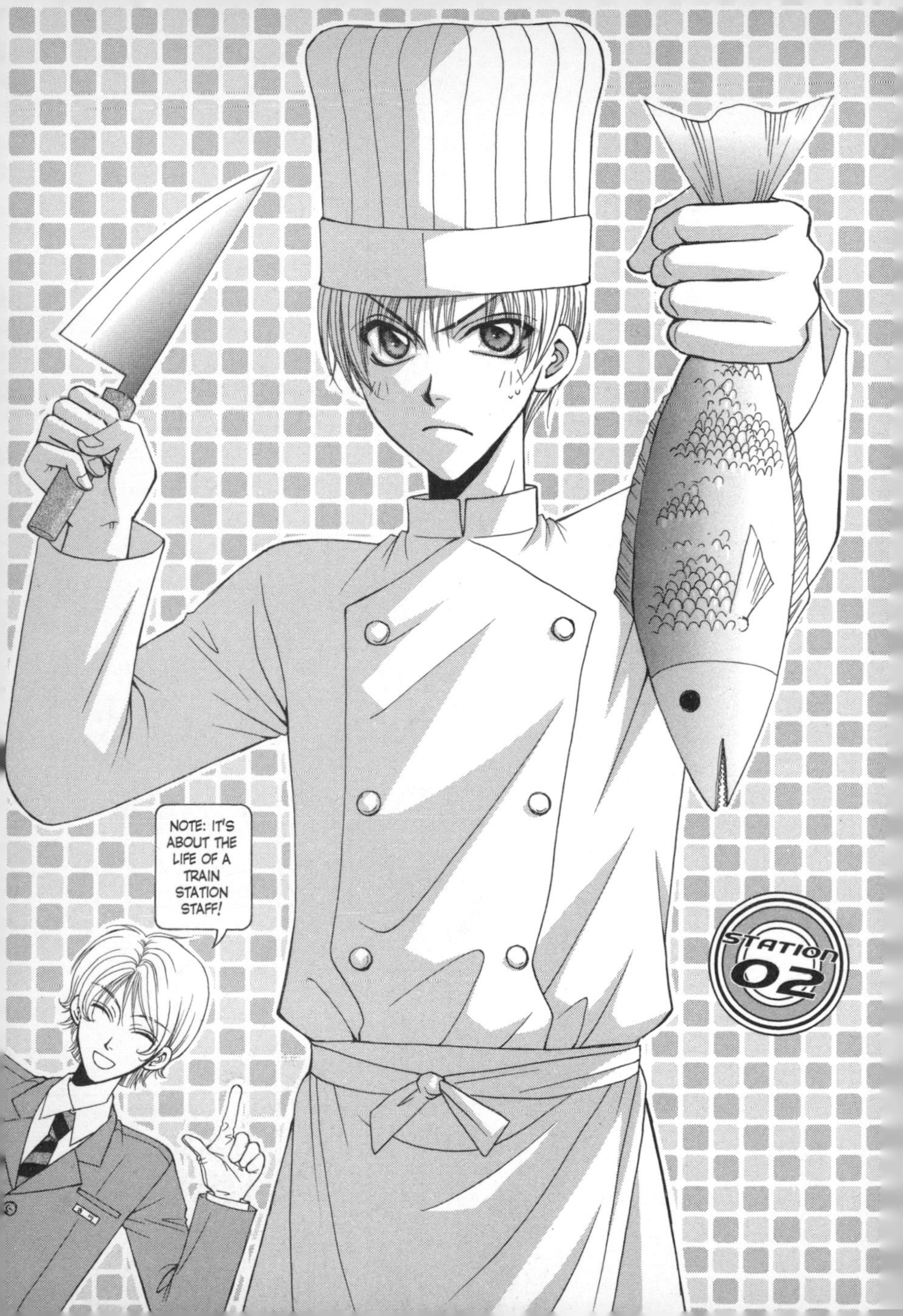
NOTE: IT'S ABOUT THE LIFE OF A TRAIN STATION STAFF!
STATION 02

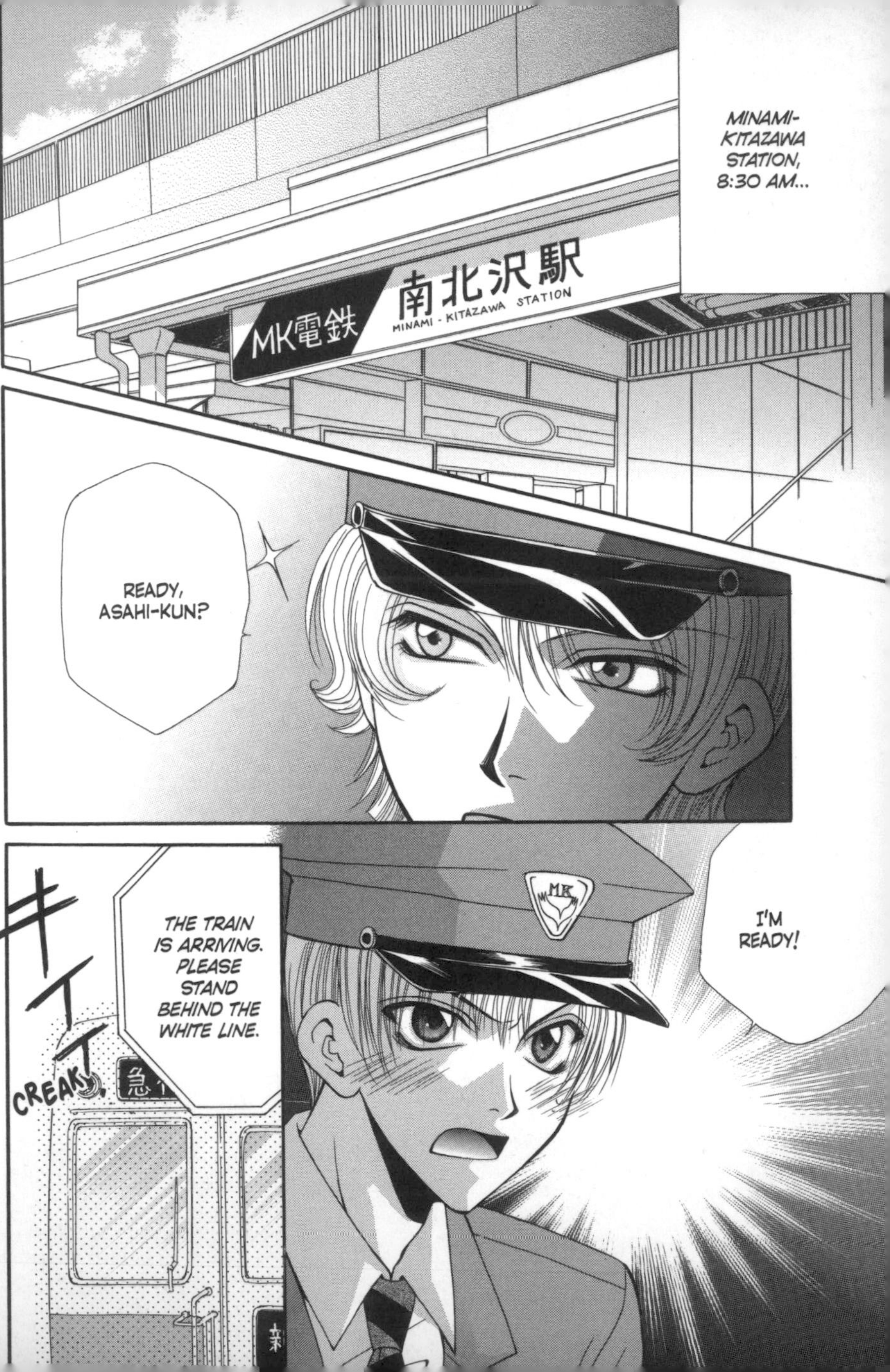
MINAMI-KITAZAWA STATION, 8:30 AM...
南北沢駅
MINAMI - KITAZAWA STATION
MK電鉄
READY, ASAHI-KUN?
I'M READY!
THE TRAIN IS ARRIVING. PLEASE STAND BEHIND THE WHITE LINE.
キイイ
CREAK

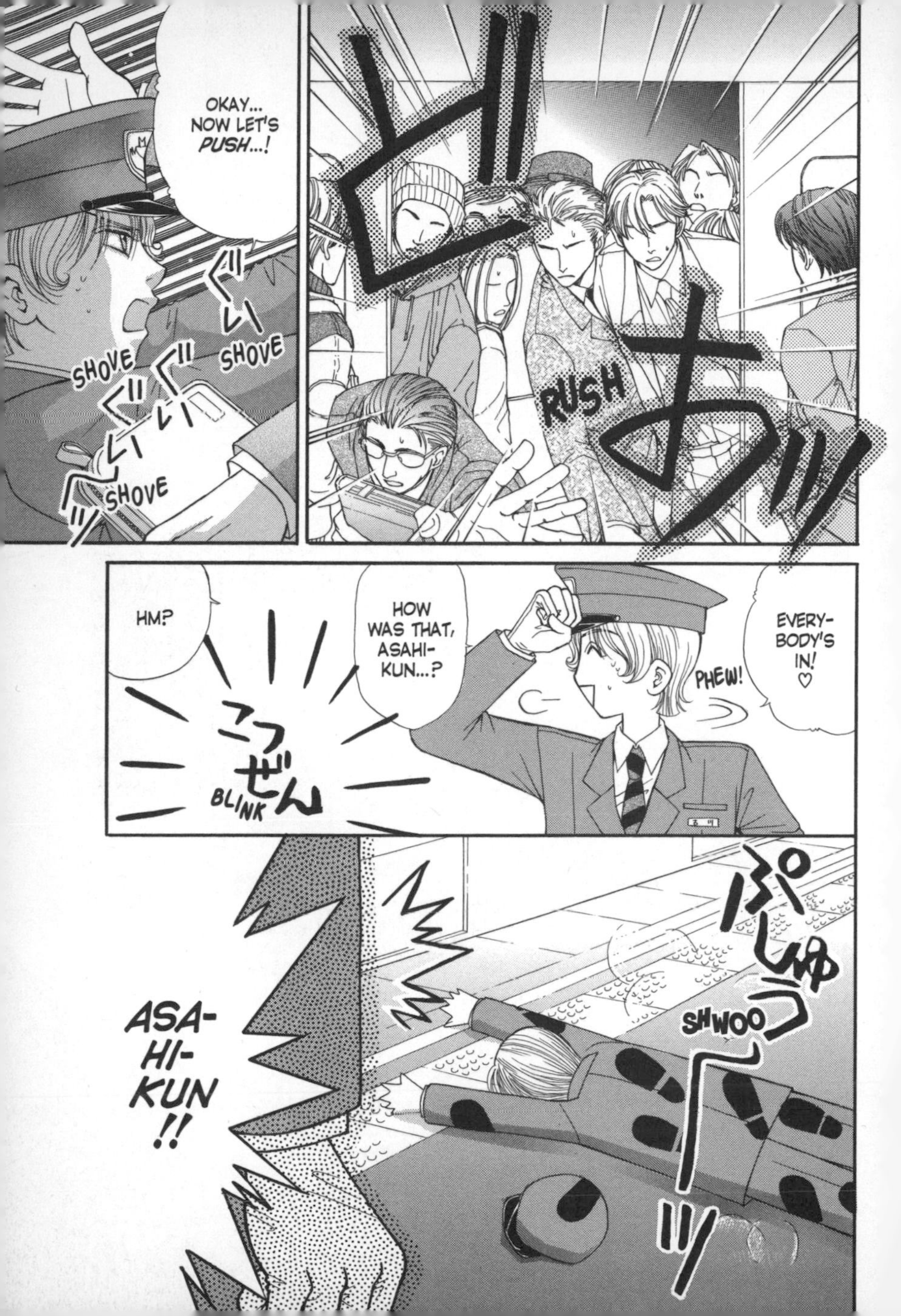

RUSH
OKAY... NOW LET'S PUSH...!
SHOVE
SHOVE
SHOVE
EVERY-BODY'S IN! ♡
PHEW!
HOW WAS THAT, ASAHI-KUN...?
HM?
BLINK
SHWOO
ASA-HI-KUN!!

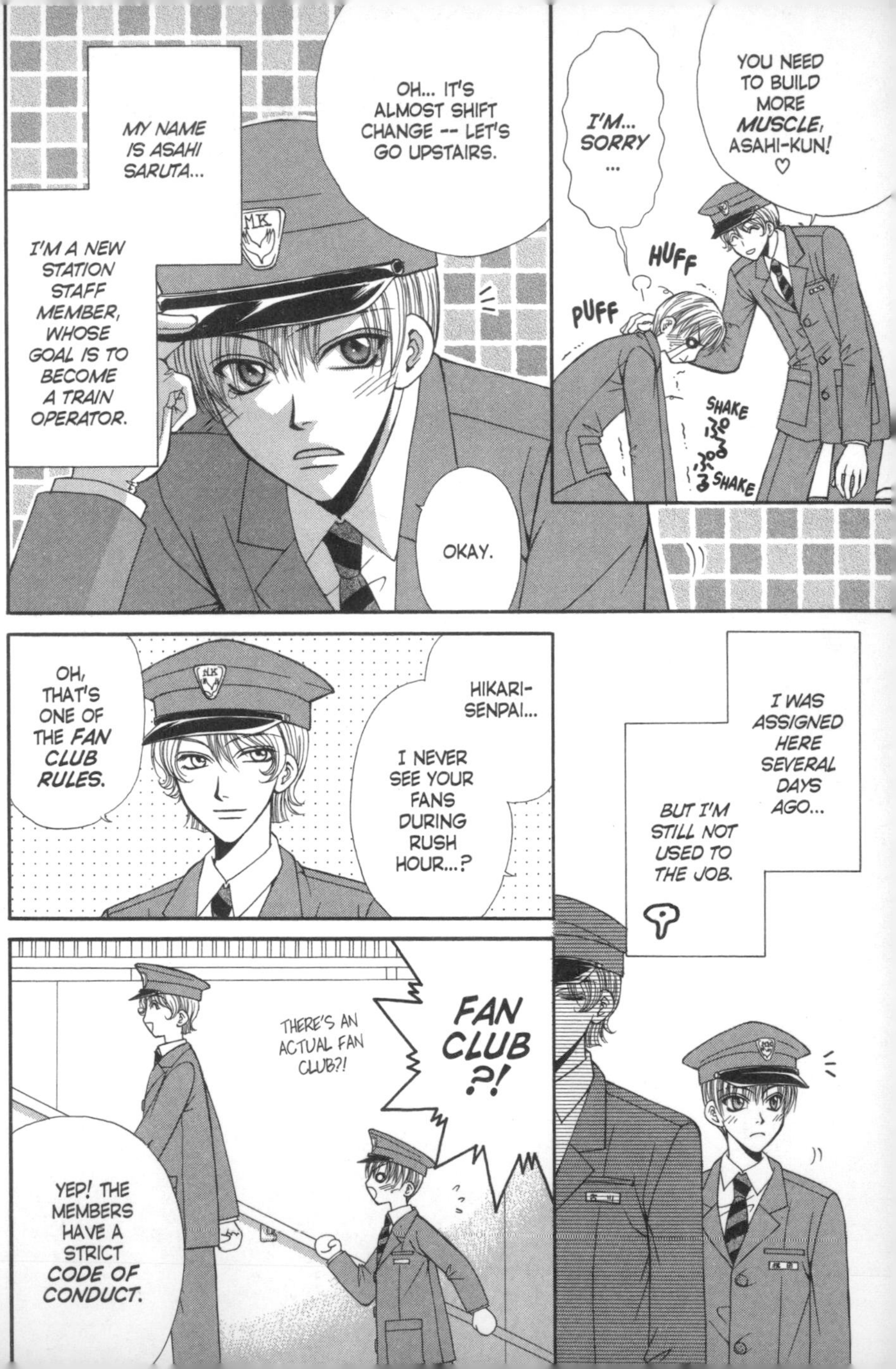
YOU NEED TO BUILD MORE MUSCLE, ASAHI-KUN! ♡
I'M... SORRY...
HUFF
PUFF
SHAKE
SHAKE
OH... IT'S ALMOST SHIFT CHANGE -- LET'S GO UPSTAIRS.
MY NAME IS ASAHI SARUTA...
I'M A NEW STATION STAFF MEMBER, WHOSE GOAL IS TO BECOME A TRAIN OPERATOR.
OKAY.
I WAS ASSIGNED HERE SEVERAL DAYS AGO...
BUT I'M STILL NOT USED TO THE JOB.
HIKARI-SENPAI...
I NEVER SEE YOUR FANS DURING RUSH HOUR...?
OH, THAT'S ONE OF THE FAN CLUB RULES.
FAN CLUB?!
THERE'S AN ACTUAL FAN CLUB?!
YEP! THE MEMBERS HAVE A STRICT CODE OF CONDUCT.

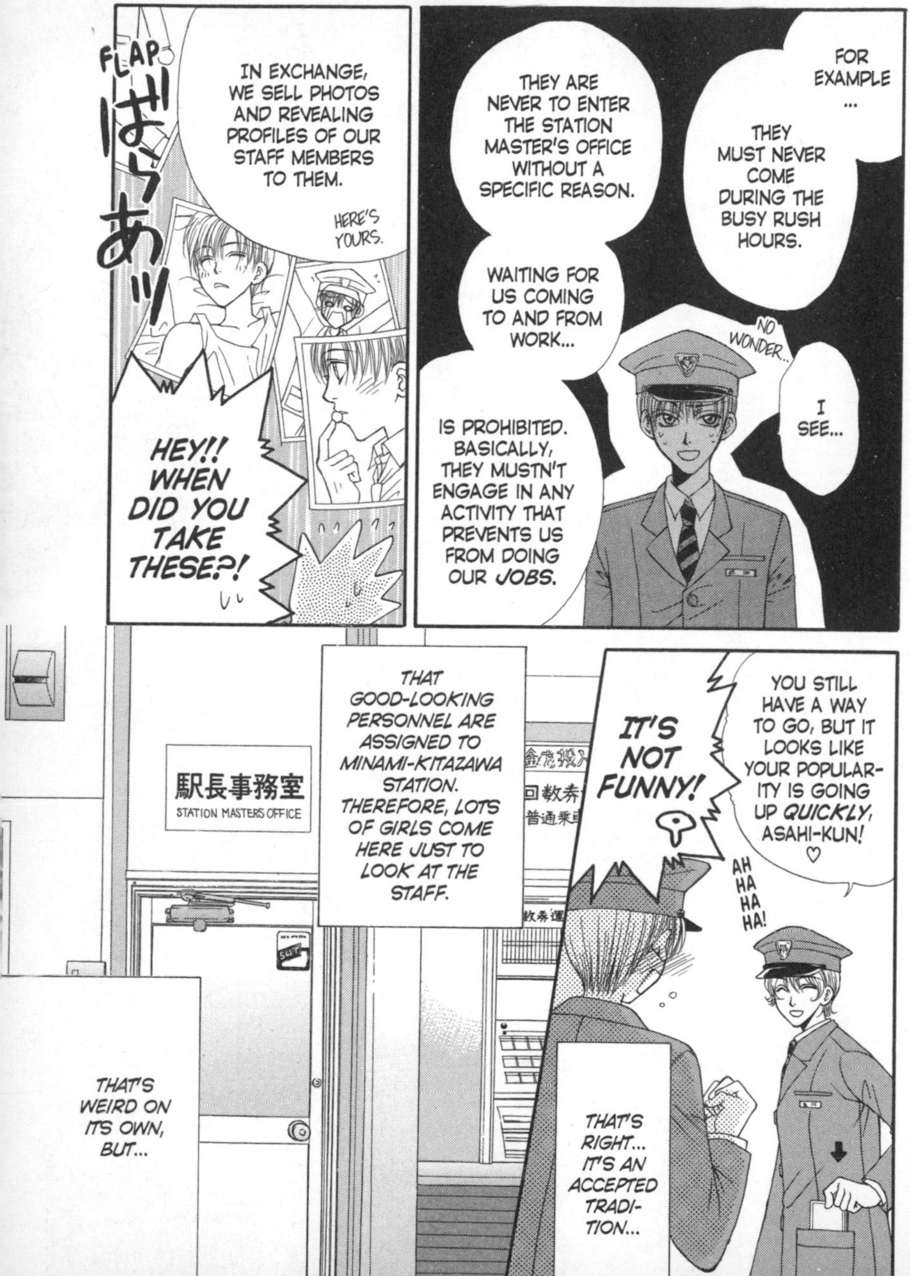

FOR EXAMPLE ...
THEY MUST NEVER COME DURING THE BUSY RUSH HOURS.
THEY ARE NEVER TO ENTER THE STATION MASTER'S OFFICE WITHOUT A SPECIFIC REASON.
WAITING FOR US COMING TO AND FROM WORK...
IS PROHIBITED. BASICALLY, THEY MUSTN'T ENGAGE IN ANY ACTIVITY THAT PREVENTS US FROM DOING OUR JOBS.
NO WONDER...
I SEE...
IN EXCHANGE, WE SELL PHOTOS AND REVEALING PROFILES OF OUR STAFF MEMBERS TO THEM.
FLAP
ばらあッ
HERE'S YOURS.
HEY!! WHEN DID YOU TAKE THESE?!
YOU STILL HAVE A WAY TO GO, BUT IT LOOKS LIKE YOUR POPULARITY IS GOING UP QUICKLY, ASAHI-KUN! ♡
IT'S NOT FUNNY!
AH HA HA HA!
THAT'S RIGHT... IT'S AN ACCEPTED TRADITION...
THAT GOOD-LOOKING PERSONNEL ARE ASSIGNED TO MINAMI-KITAZAWA STATION. THEREFORE, LOTS OF GIRLS COME HERE JUST TO LOOK AT THE STAFF.
駅長事務室
STATION MASTERS OFFICE
THAT'S WEIRD ON ITS OWN, BUT...

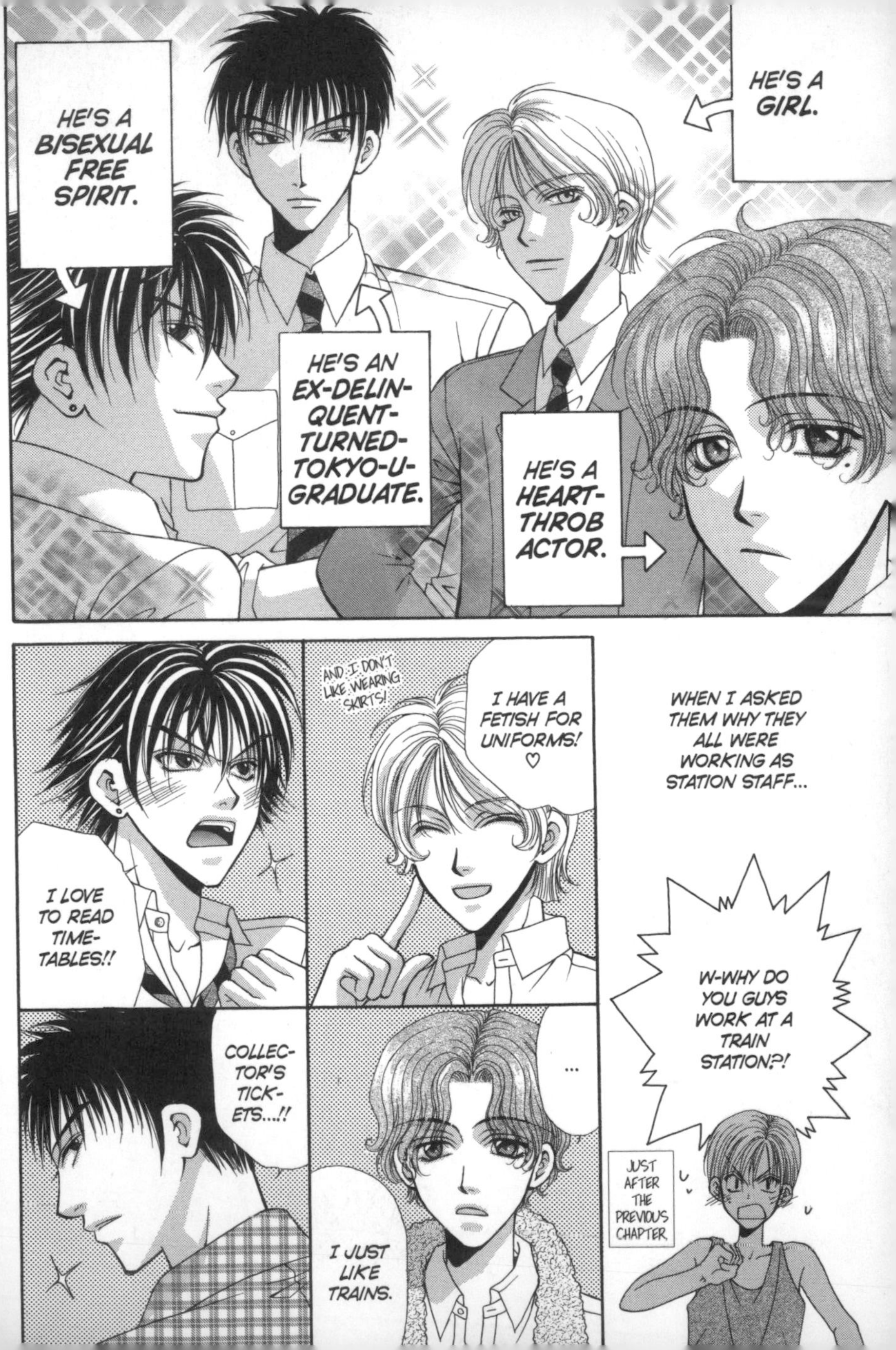
HE'S A GIRL.
HE'S A HEART-THROB ACTOR.
HE'S AN EX-DELIN-QUENT-TURNED-TOKYO-U-GRADUATE.
HE'S A BISEXUAL FREE SPIRIT.
WHEN I ASKED THEM WHY THEY ALL WERE WORKING AS STATION STAFF...
W-WHY DO YOU GUYS WORK AT A TRAIN STATION?!
JUST AFTER THE PREVIOUS CHAPTER.
I HAVE A FETISH FOR UNIFORMS! ♡
AND I DON'T LIKE WEARING SKIRTS!
I LOVE TO READ TIME-TABLES!!
...
I JUST LIKE TRAINS.
COLLEC-TOR'S TICK-ETS...!!

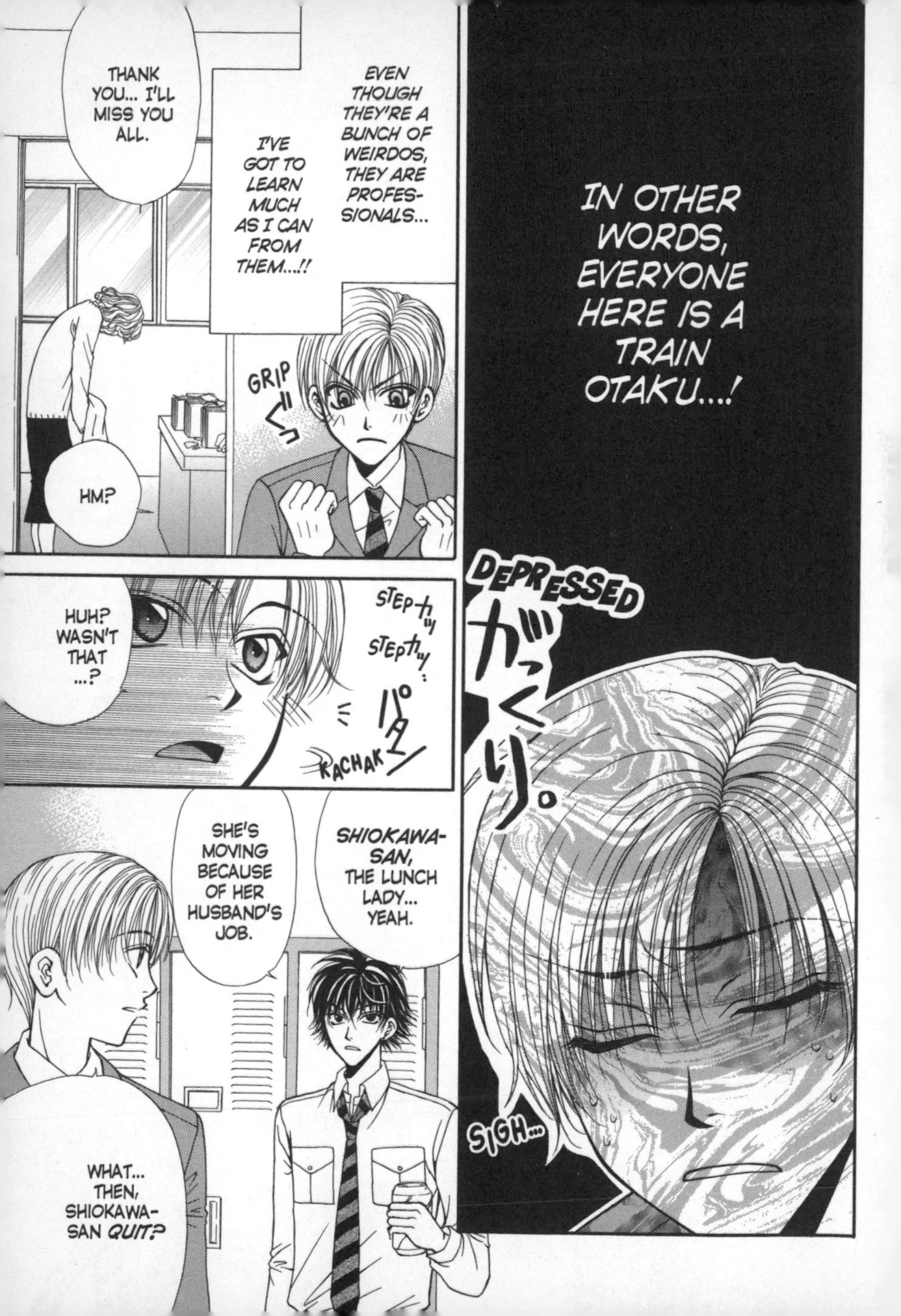
IN OTHER WORDS, EVERYONE HERE IS A TRAIN OTAKU...!
EVEN THOUGH THEY'RE A BUNCH OF WEIRDOS, THEY ARE PROFES-SIONALS...
I'VE GOT TO LEARN MUCH AS I CAN FROM THEM...!!
THANK YOU... I'LL MISS YOU ALL.
GRIP
HM?
DEPRESSED
SIGH...
STEP
STEP
KACHAK
HUH? WASN'T THAT ...?
SHIOKAWA-SAN, THE LUNCH LADY... YEAH.
SHE'S MOVING BECAUSE OF HER HUSBAND'S JOB.
WHAT... THEN, SHIOKAWA-SAN QUIT?

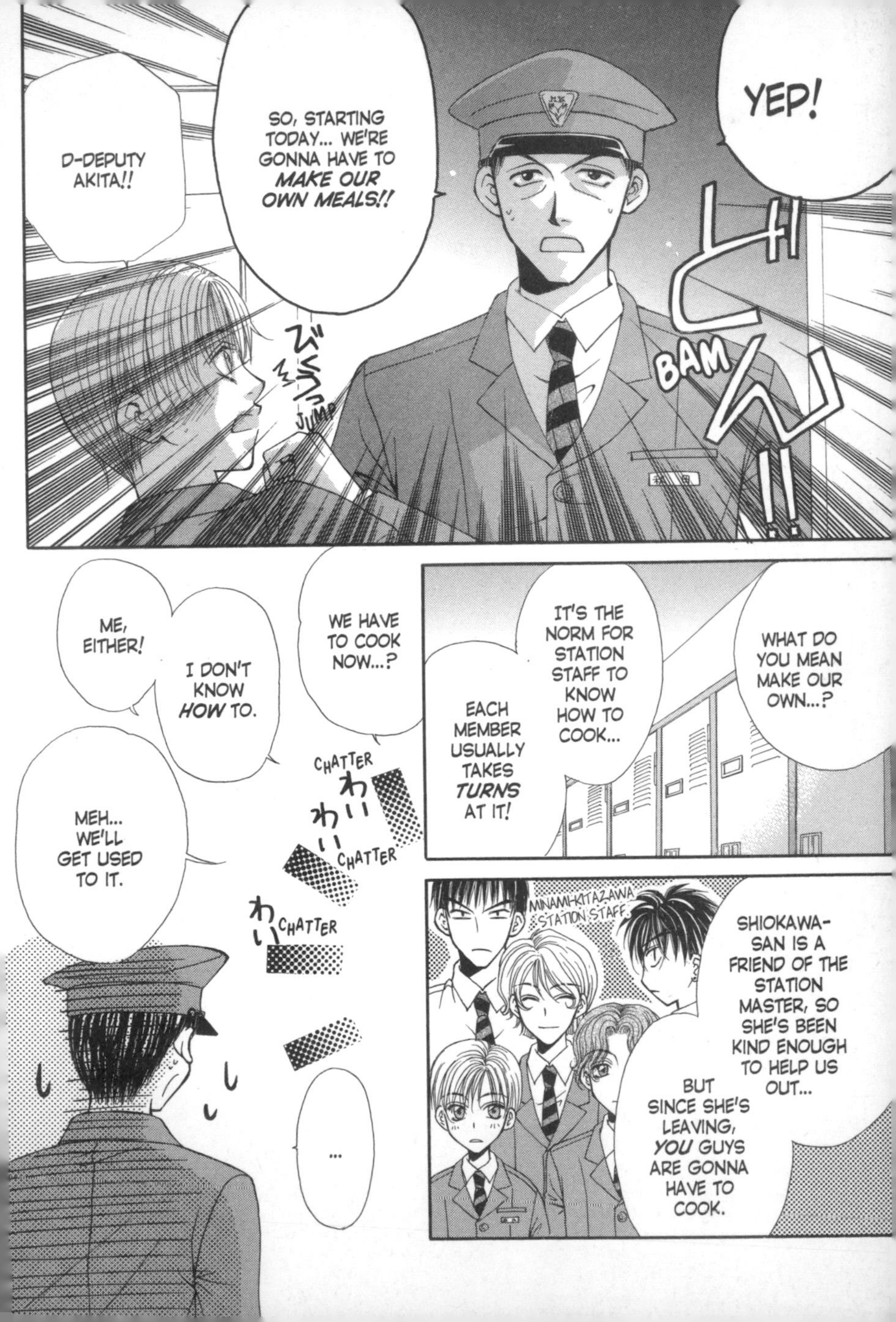
YEP!
SO, STARTING TODAY... WE'RE GONNA HAVE TO *MAKE OUR OWN MEALS!!*
D-DEPUTY AKITA!!
BAM
JUMP
WHAT DO YOU MEAN MAKE OUR OWN...?
IT'S THE NORM FOR STATION STAFF TO KNOW HOW TO COOK...
EACH MEMBER USUALLY TAKES *TURNS* AT IT!
MINAMI-KITAZAWA STATION STAFF
SHIOKAWA-SAN IS A FRIEND OF THE STATION MASTER, SO SHE'S BEEN KIND ENOUGH TO HELP US OUT...
BUT SINCE SHE'S LEAVING, *YOU* GUYS ARE GONNA HAVE TO COOK.
WE HAVE TO COOK NOW...?
I DON'T KNOW *HOW* TO.
ME, EITHER!
CHATTER
CHATTER
CHATTER
MEH... WE'LL GET USED TO IT.
...

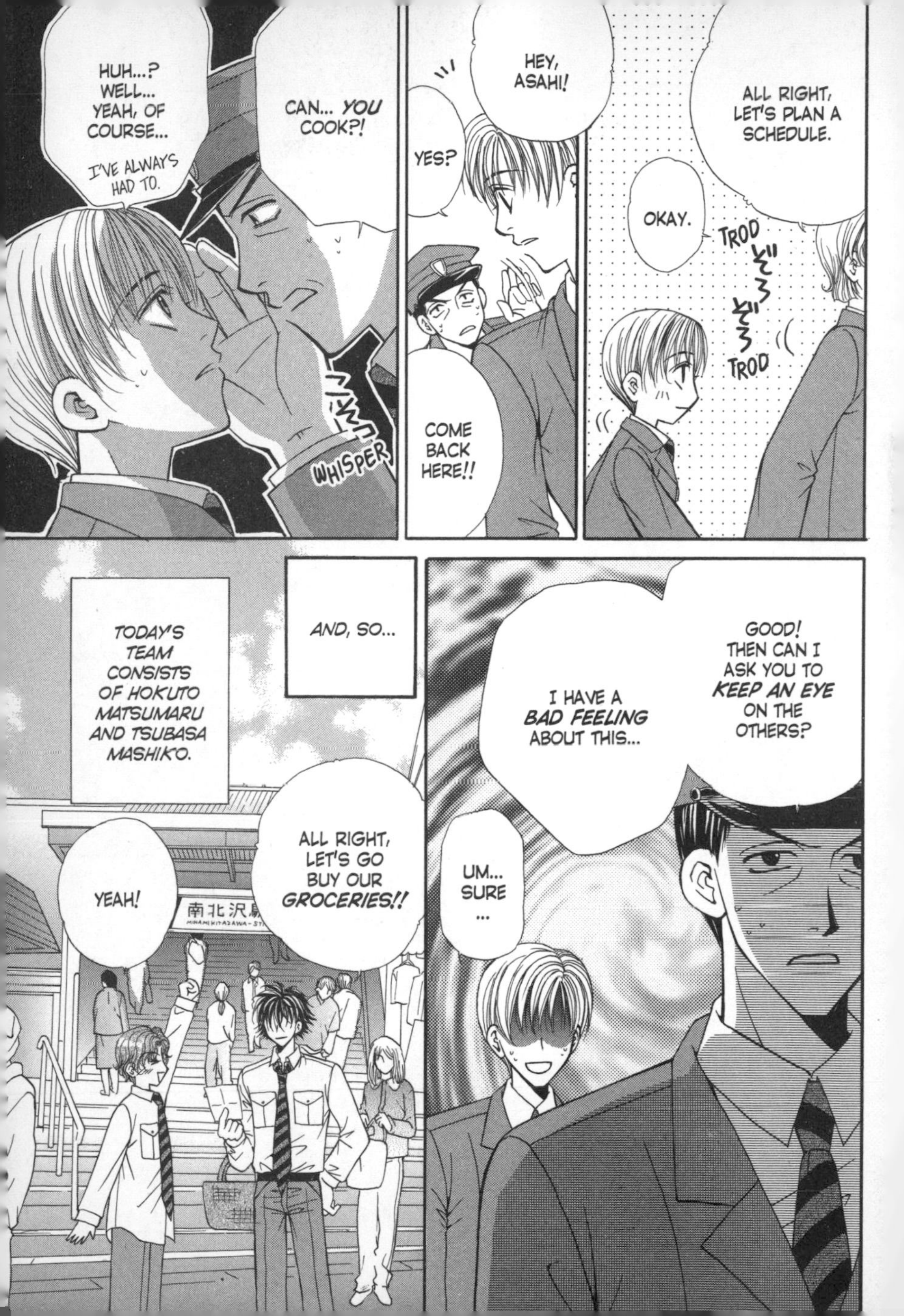
ALL RIGHT, LET'S PLAN A SCHEDULE.
OKAY.
TROD
TROD
HEY, ASAHI!
YES?
COME BACK HERE!!
CAN... *YOU* COOK?!
WHISPER
HUH...? WELL... YEAH, OF COURSE...
I'VE ALWAYS HAD TO.
GOOD! THEN CAN I ASK YOU TO ***KEEP AN EYE*** ON THE OTHERS?
I HAVE A ***BAD FEELING*** ABOUT THIS...
UM... SURE ...
*AND, SO...*
*TODAY'S TEAM CONSISTS OF HOKUTO MATSUMARU AND TSUBASA MASHIKO.*
ALL RIGHT, LET'S GO BUY OUR ***GROCERIES!!***
YEAH!

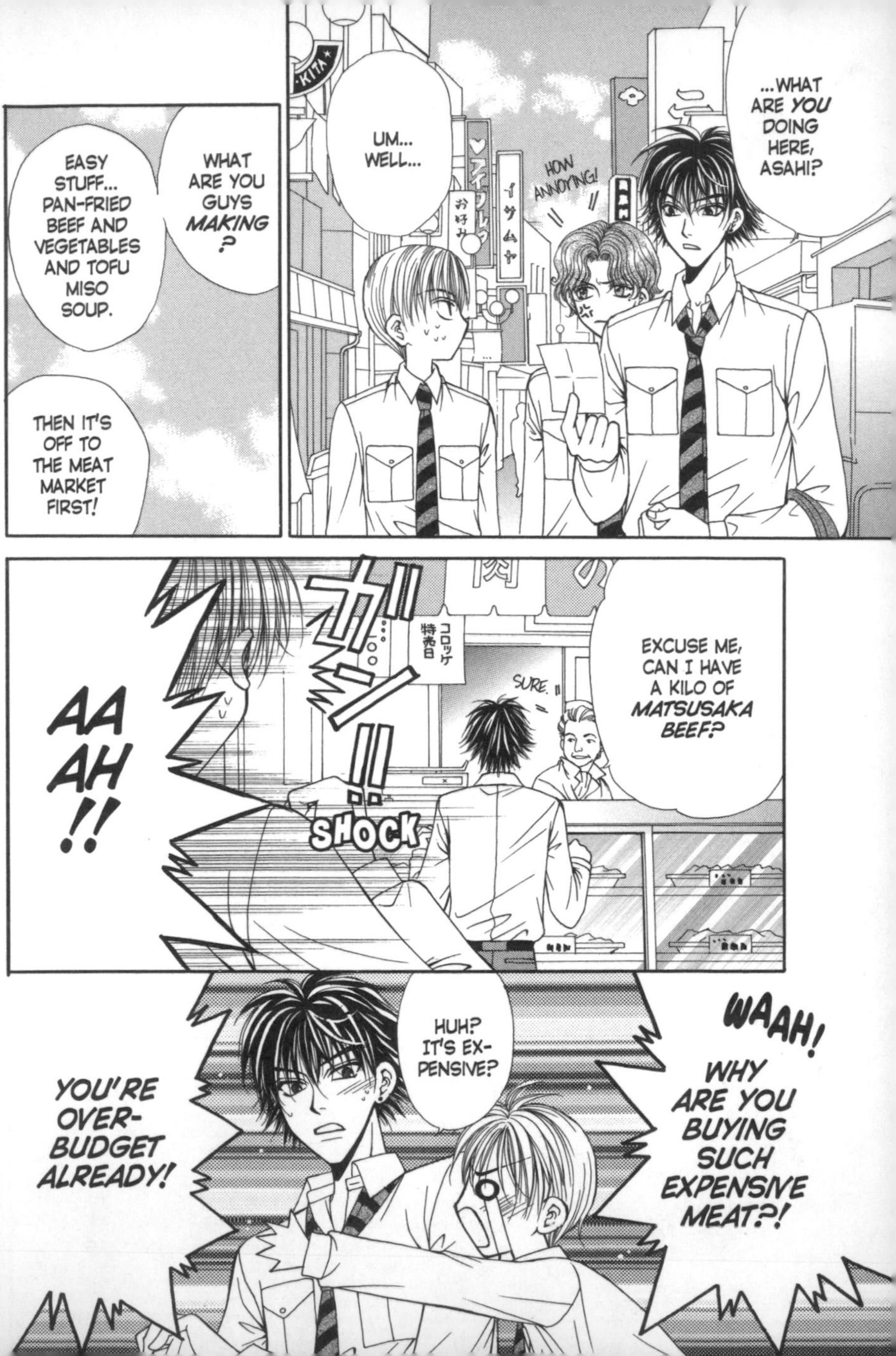
KITA
...WHAT ARE YOU DOING HERE, ASAHI?
HOW ANNOYING!
UM... WELL...
WHAT ARE YOU GUYS MAKING?
EASY STUFF... PAN-FRIED BEEF AND VEGETABLES AND TOFU MISO SOUP.
THEN IT'S OFF TO THE MEAT MARKET FIRST!
EXCUSE ME, CAN I HAVE A KILO OF MATSUSAKA BEEF?
SURE.
コロッケ 特売日
SHOCK
AAAH!!
WAAH! WHY ARE YOU BUYING SUCH EXPENSIVE MEAT?!
HUH? IT'S EX-PENSIVE?
YOU'RE OVER-BUDGET ALREADY!

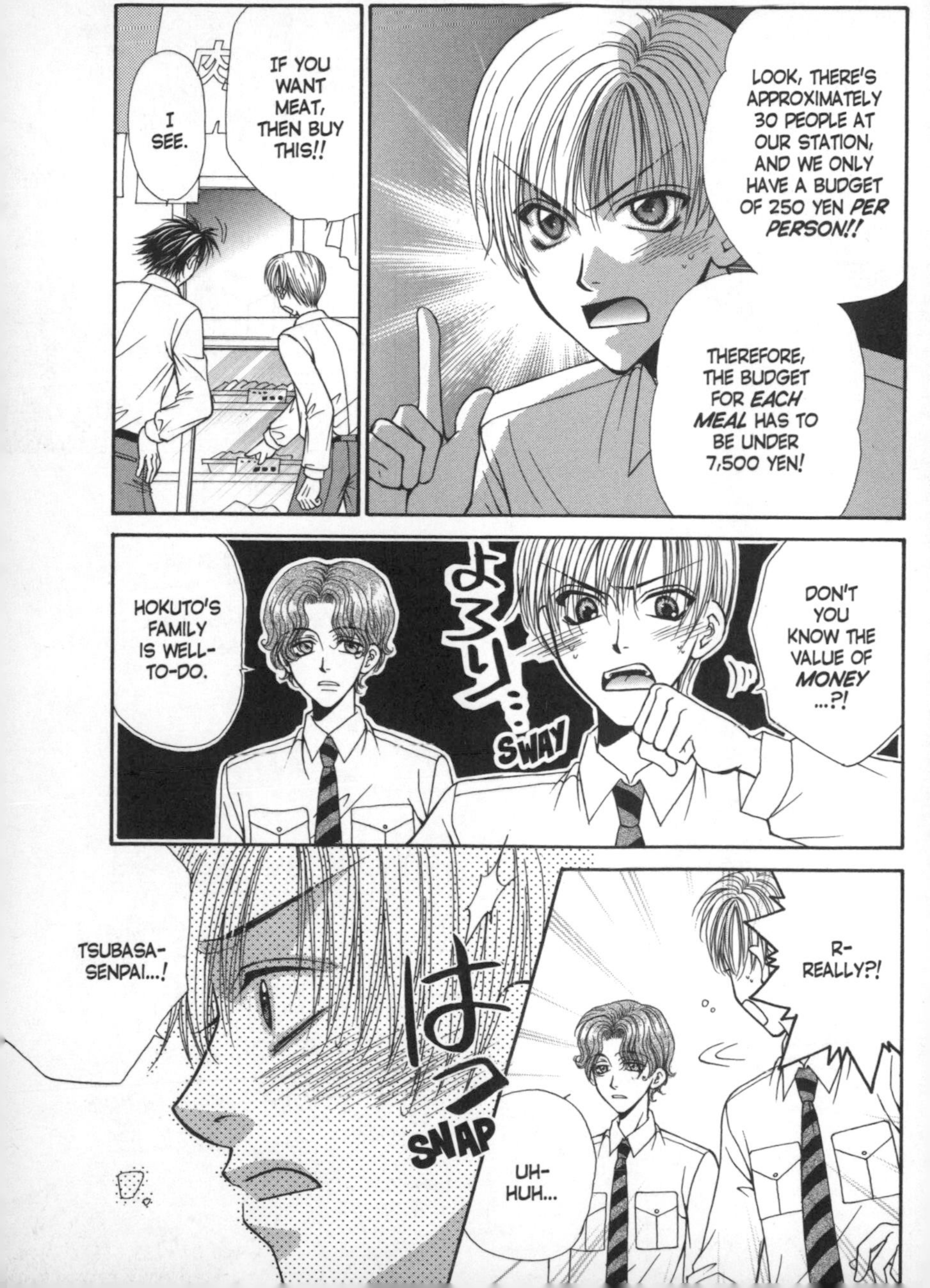
LOOK, THERE'S APPROXIMATELY 30 PEOPLE AT OUR STATION, AND WE ONLY HAVE A BUDGET OF 250 YEN PER PERSON!!
THEREFORE, THE BUDGET FOR EACH MEAL HAS TO BE UNDER 7,500 YEN!
IF YOU WANT MEAT, THEN BUY THIS!!
I SEE.
DON'T YOU KNOW THE VALUE OF MONEY ...?!
よろり
SWAY
HOKUTO'S FAMILY IS WELL-TO-DO.
R-REALLY?!
UH-HUH...
はっ
SNAP
TSUBASA-SENPAI...!

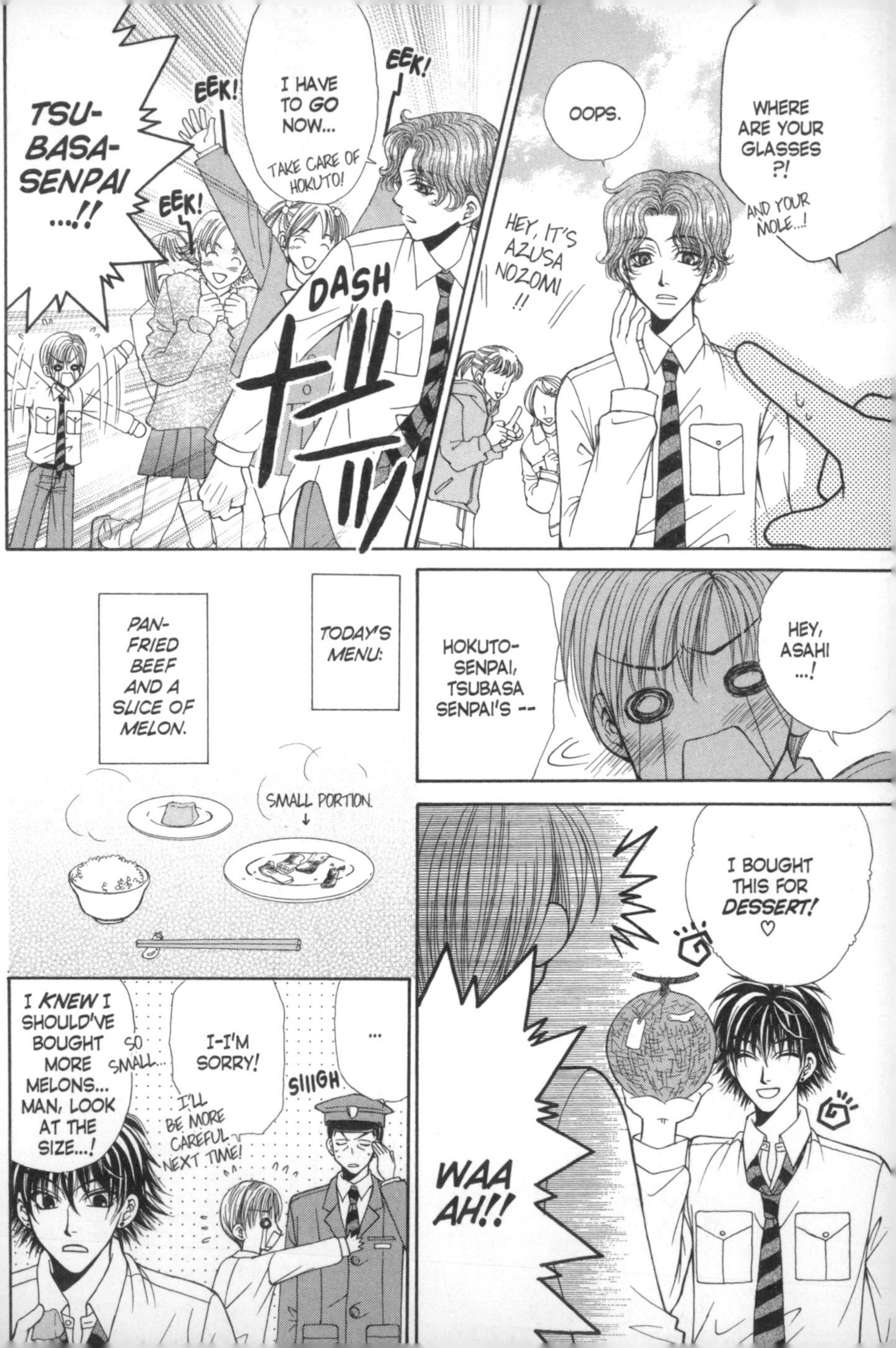
WHERE ARE YOUR GLASSES ?!
AND YOUR MOLE...!
OOPS.
HEY, IT'S AZUSA NOZOMI !!
EEK!
I HAVE TO GO NOW...
TAKE CARE OF HOKUTO!
EEK!
TSU-BASA-SENPAI ...!!
EEK!
DASH
HEY, ASAHI ...!
HOKUTO-SENPAI, TSUBASA SENPAI'S --
I BOUGHT THIS FOR DESSERT! ♡
WAA AH!!
TODAY'S MENU:
PAN-FRIED BEEF AND A SLICE OF MELON.
SMALL PORTION.
...
SIIIGH
I-I'M SORRY!
I'LL BE MORE CAREFUL NEXT TIME!
SO SMALL...
I KNEW I SHOULD'VE BOUGHT MORE MELONS... MAN, LOOK AT THE SIZE...!

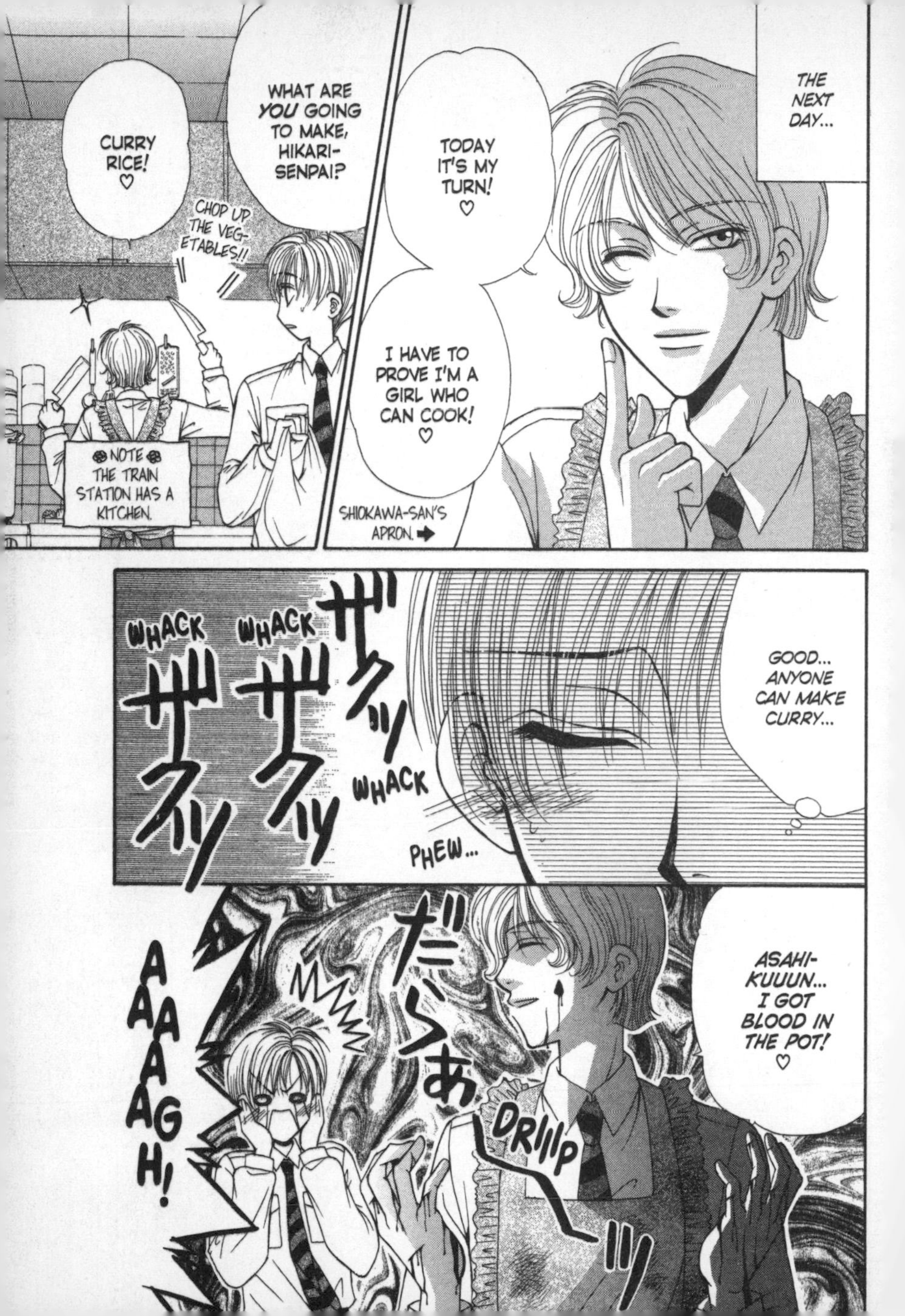
THE NEXT DAY...
TODAY IT'S MY TURN! ♡
I HAVE TO PROVE I'M A GIRL WHO CAN COOK! ♡
SHIOKAWA-SAN'S APRON. ➡
WHAT ARE YOU GOING TO MAKE, HIKARI-SENPAI?
CURRY RICE! ♡
CHOP UP THE VEGETABLES!!
NOTE THE TRAIN STATION HAS A KITCHEN.
GOOD... ANYONE CAN MAKE CURRY...
PHEW...
ザクッ
WHACK
ザクッ
WHACK
ザクッ
WHACK
ASAHI-KUUUN... I GOT BLOOD IN THE POT! ♡
DRIIIP
だらあ
AAAAAGH!

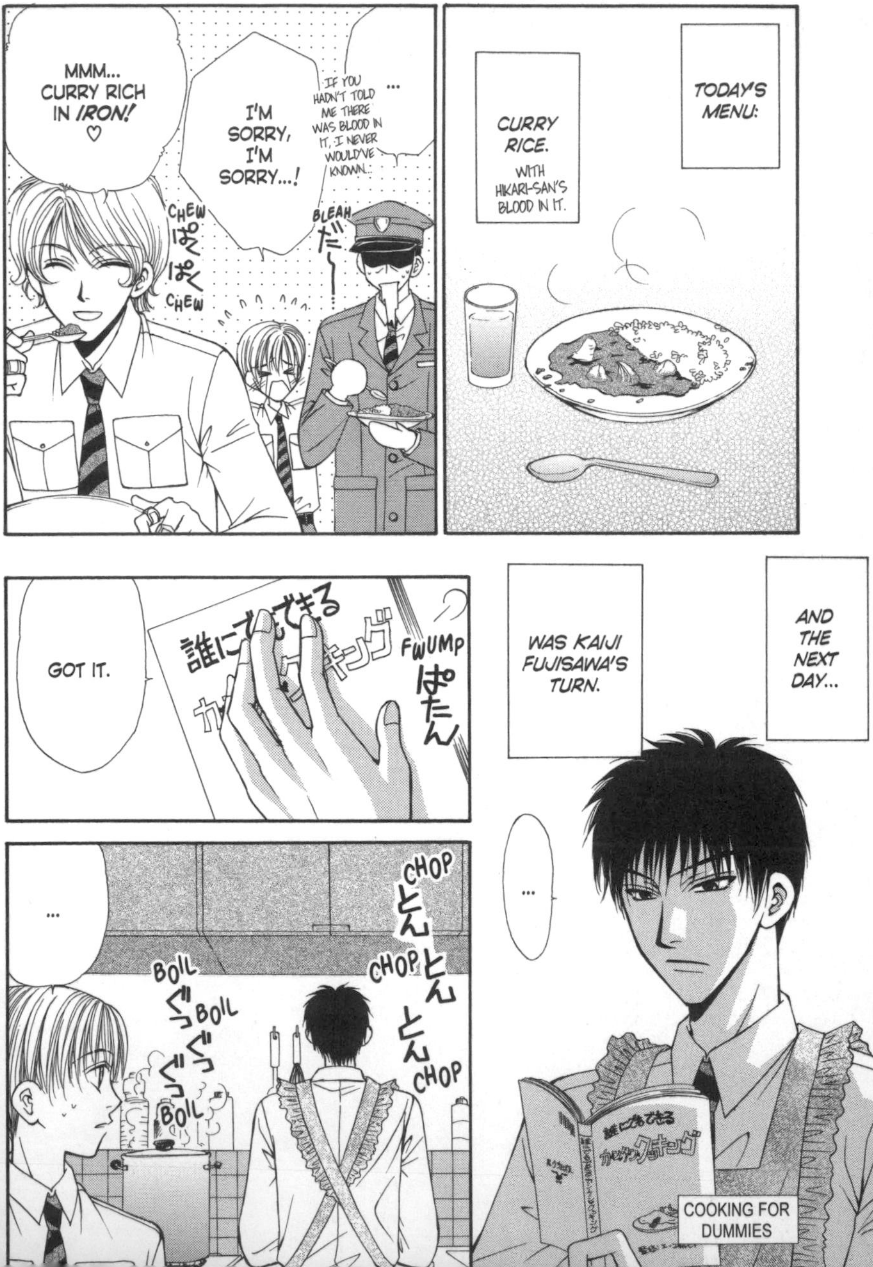

TODAY'S MENU:
CURRY RICE.
WITH HIKARI-SAN'S BLOOD IN IT.
...
IF YOU HADN'T TOLD ME THERE WAS BLOOD IN IT, I NEVER WOULD'VE KNOWN...
BLEAH
だ～
I'M SORRY, I'M SORRY...!
MMM... CURRY RICH IN IRON! ♡
CHEW
ぱく
ぱく
CHEW
AND THE NEXT DAY...
WAS KAIJI FUJISAWA'S TURN.
...
誰にでもできる
COOKING FOR DUMMIES
FWUMP
ぱたん
GOT IT.
CHOP
とん
CHOP
とん
とん
CHOP
BOIL
ぐつ
BOIL
ぐつ
ぐつ
BOIL
...

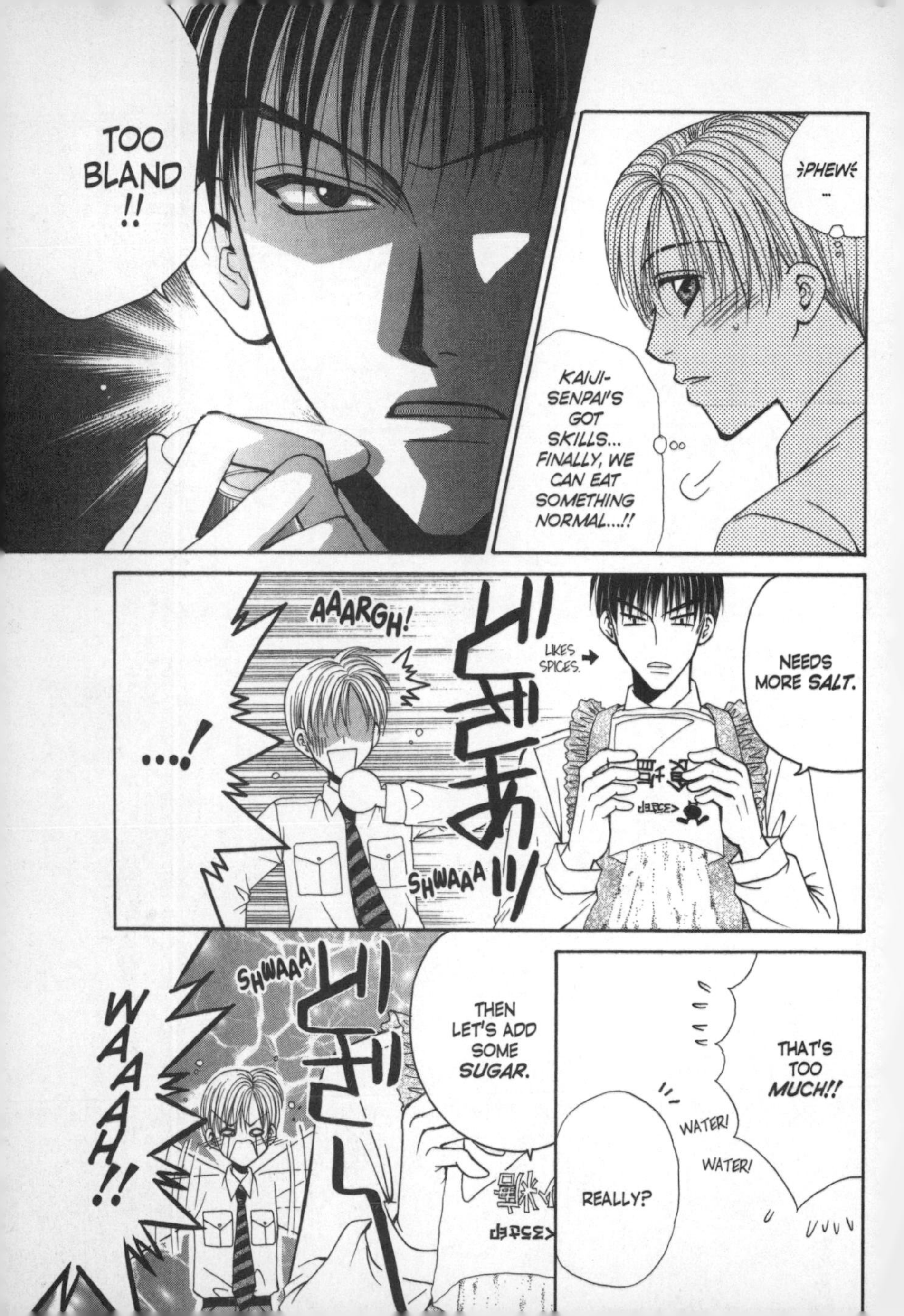
PHEW ...
KAIJI-SENPAI'S GOT SKILLS... FINALLY, WE CAN EAT SOMETHING NORMAL...!!
TOO BLAND !!
NEEDS MORE SALT.
LIKES SPICES.
AAARGH!
...!
SHWAAA
THAT'S TOO MUCH!!
WATER!
WATER!
REALLY?
THEN LET'S ADD SOME SUGAR.
SHWAAA
WAAAAH!!

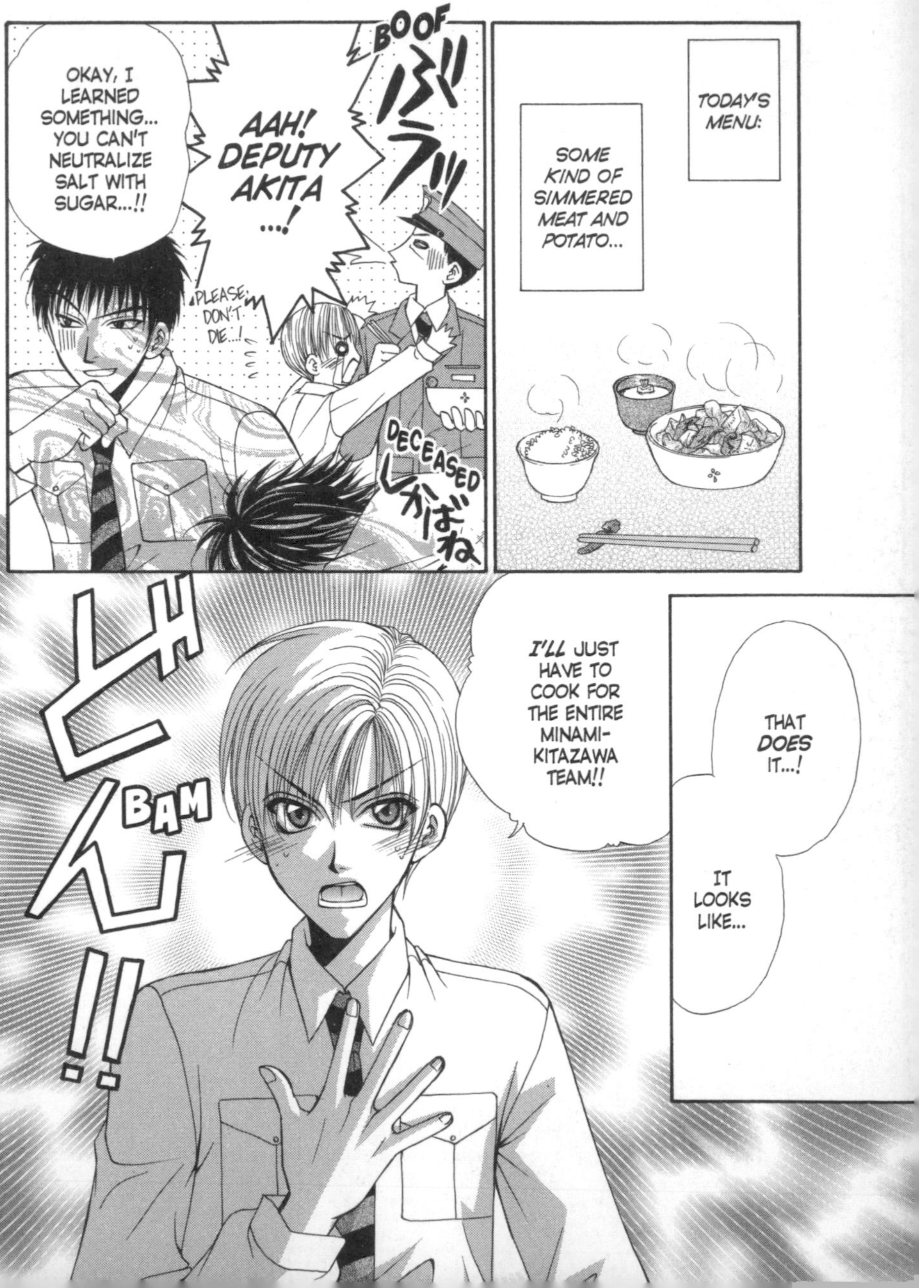
TODAY'S MENU:
SOME KIND OF SIMMERED MEAT AND POTATO...
BOOF
AAH! DEPUTY AKITA ...!
OKAY, I LEARNED SOMETHING... YOU CAN'T NEUTRALIZE SALT WITH SUGAR...!!
PLEASE, DON'T DIE...!
DECEASED
THAT DOES IT...!
IT LOOKS LIKE...
I'LL JUST HAVE TO COOK FOR THE ENTIRE MINAMI-KITAZAWA TEAM!!
BAM

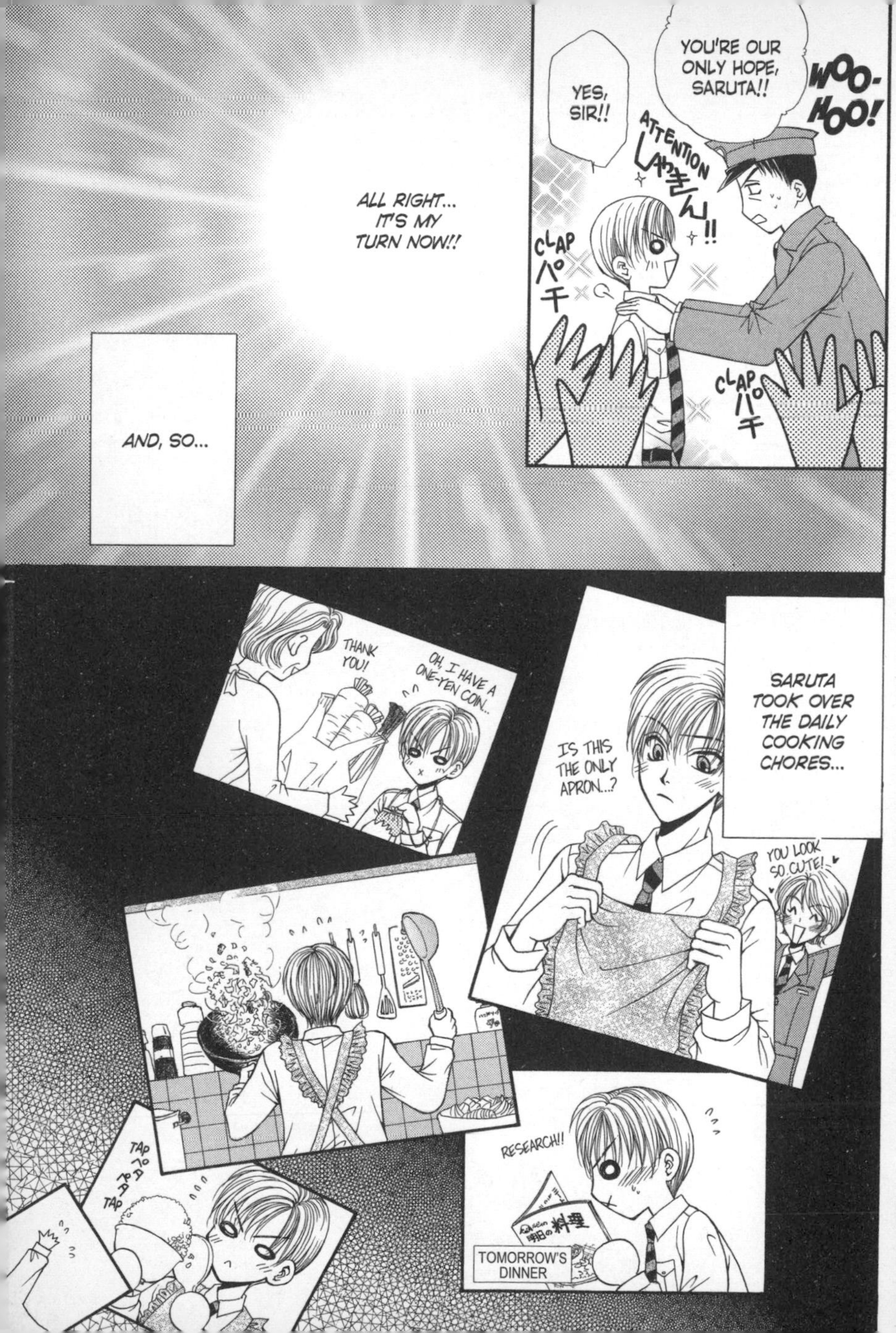
WOO-HOO!
YOU'RE OUR ONLY HOPE, SARUTA!!
YES, SIR!!
ATTENTION
しゃきん!!
CLAP
パチ
CLAP
パチ
ALL RIGHT... IT'S MY TURN NOW!!
AND, SO...
SARUTA TOOK OVER THE DAILY COOKING CHORES...
YOU LOOK SO CUTE!
IS THIS THE ONLY APRON...?
OH, I HAVE A ONE-YEN COIN...
THANK YOU!
RESEARCH!!
明日の料理
TOMORROW'S DINNER
TAP TAP TAP

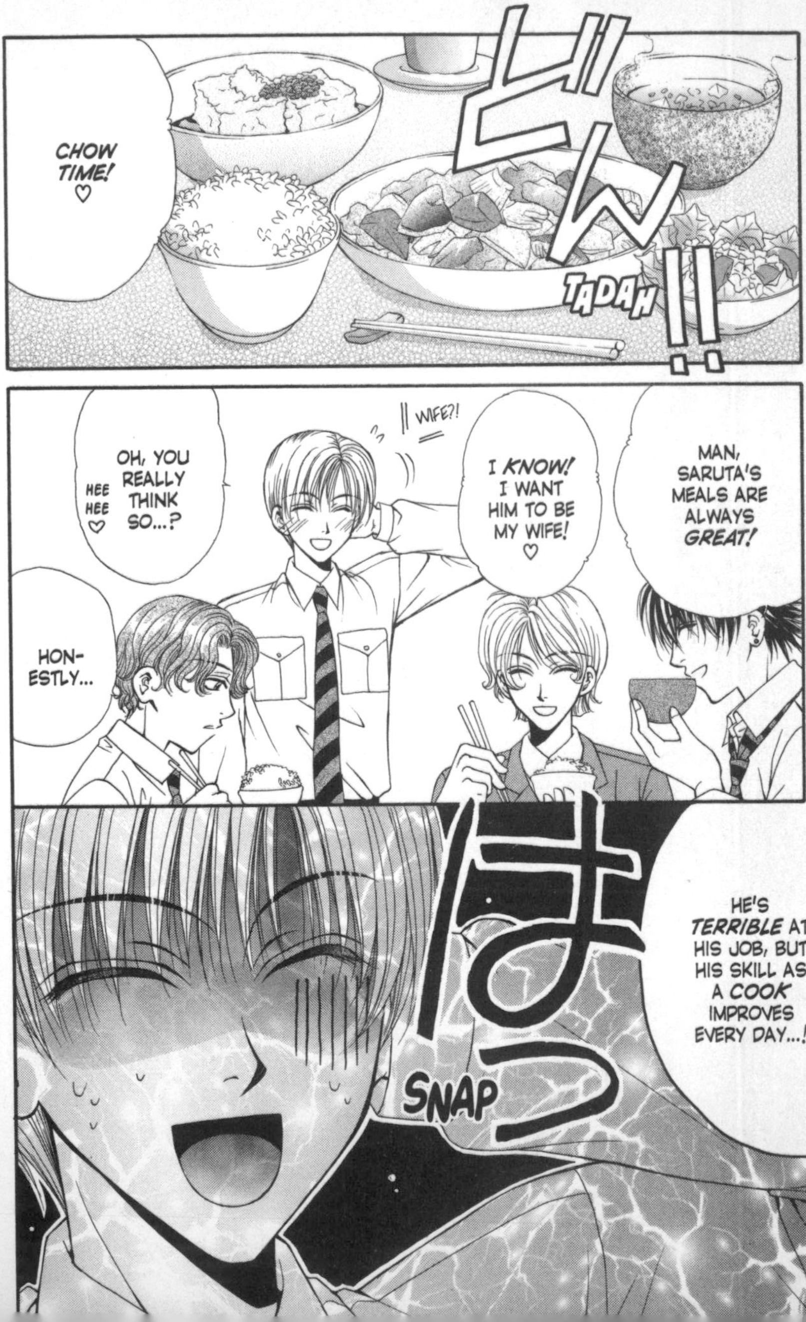
CHOW TIME! ♡
TADAH!!
MAN, SARUTA'S MEALS ARE ALWAYS GREAT!
I KNOW! I WANT HIM TO BE MY WIFE! ♡
WIFE?!
OH, YOU REALLY THINK SO...?
HEE HEE ♡
HON-ESTLY...
HE'S TERRIBLE AT HIS JOB, BUT HIS SKILL AS A COOK IMPROVES EVERY DAY...!
SNAP

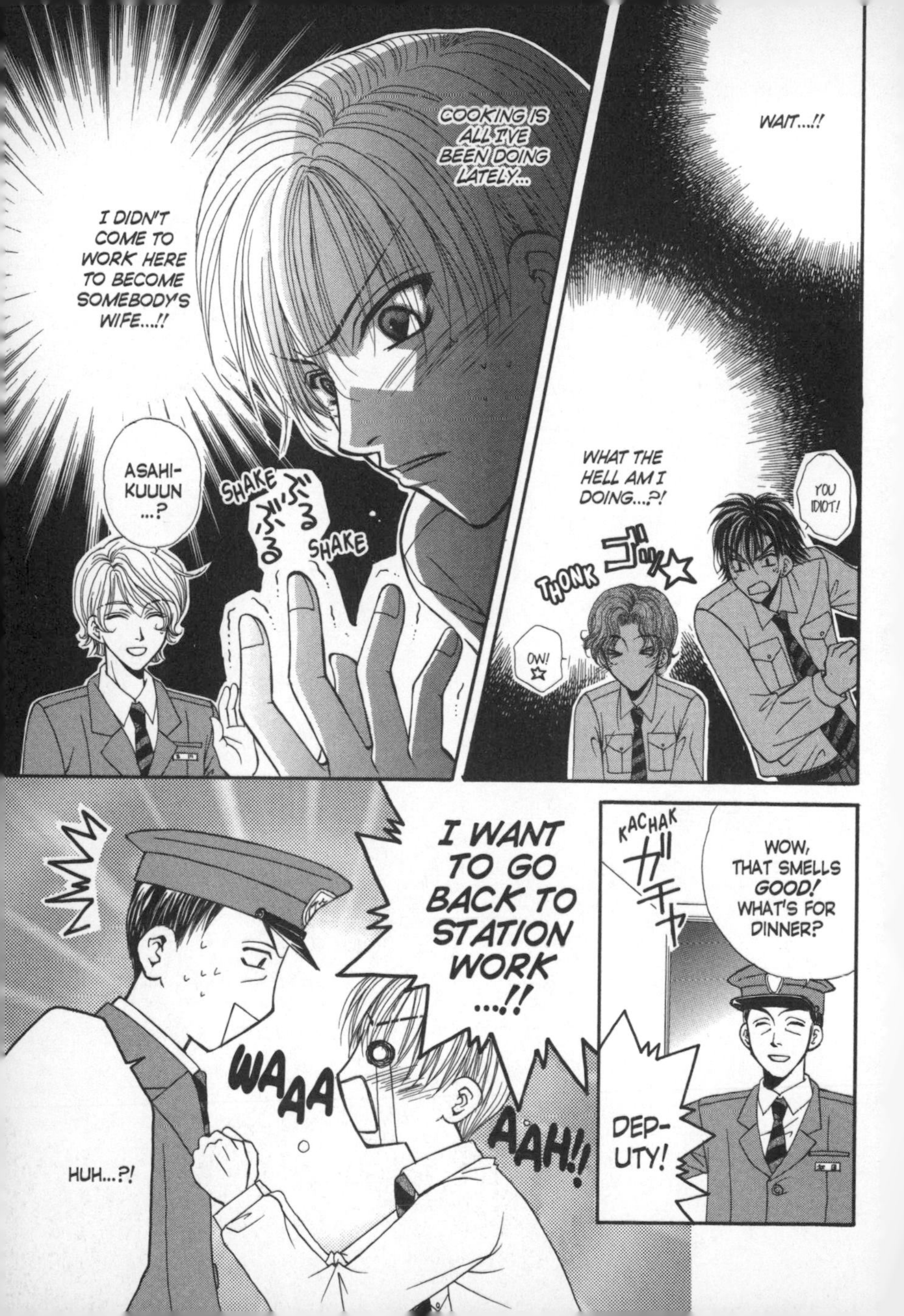

WAIT...!!
WHAT THE HELL AM I DOING...?!
YOU IDIOT!
THONK
OW! ☆
COOKING IS ALL I'VE BEEN DOING LATELY...
I DIDN'T COME TO WORK HERE TO BECOME SOMEBODY'S WIFE...!!
ASAHI-KUUUN ...?
SHAKE ぶるぶる SHAKE
KACHAK ガチャ
WOW, THAT SMELLS GOOD! WHAT'S FOR DINNER?
DEP-UTY!
I WANT TO GO BACK TO STATION WORK ...!!
WAAAAAH!!
HUH...?!

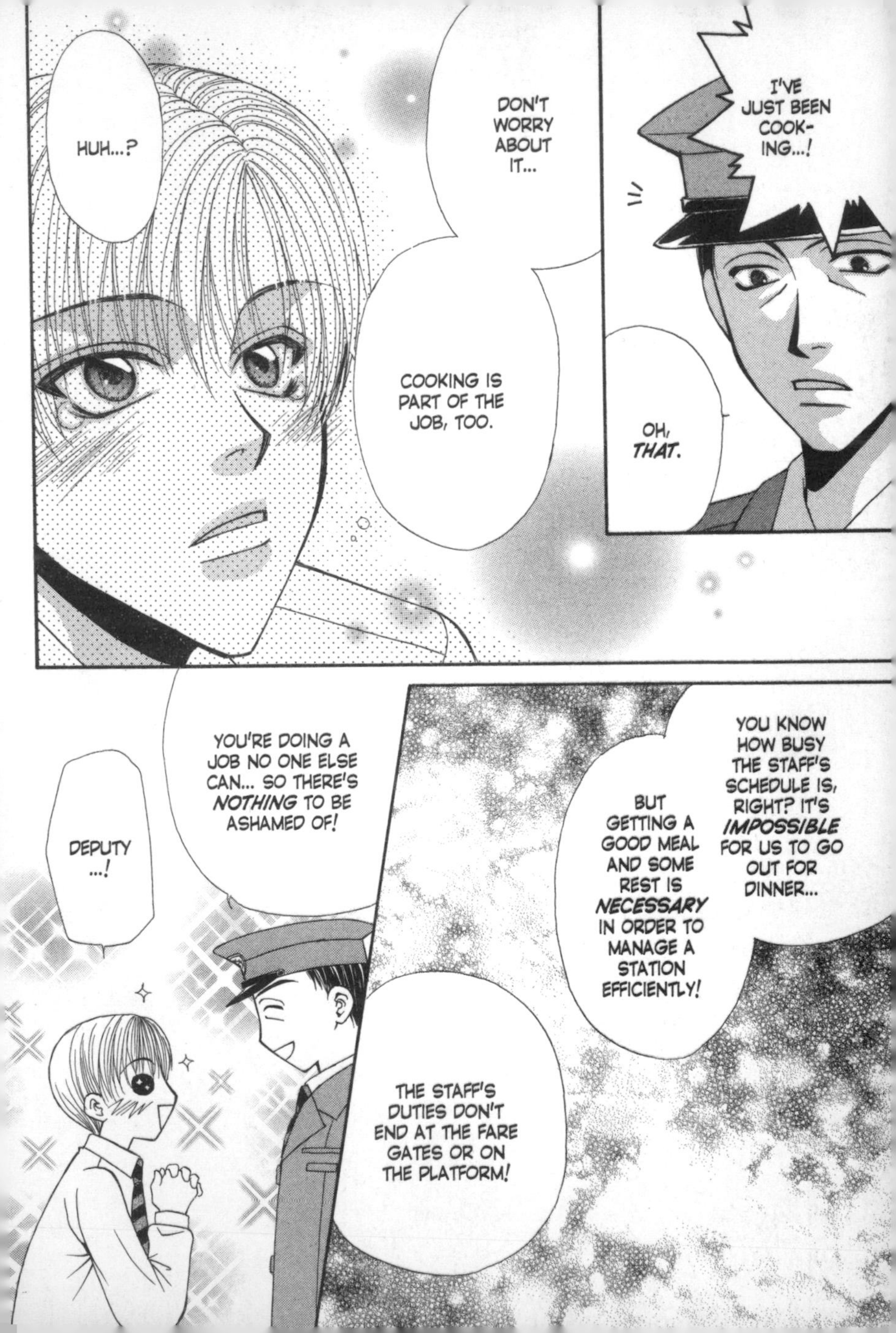
I'VE JUST BEEN COOKING...!
OH, THAT.
DON'T WORRY ABOUT IT...
HUH...?
COOKING IS PART OF THE JOB, TOO.
YOU KNOW HOW BUSY THE STAFF'S SCHEDULE IS, RIGHT? IT'S IMPOSSIBLE FOR US TO GO OUT FOR DINNER...
BUT GETTING A GOOD MEAL AND SOME REST IS NECESSARY IN ORDER TO MANAGE A STATION EFFICIENTLY!
THE STAFF'S DUTIES DON'T END AT THE FARE GATES OR ON THE PLATFORM!
YOU'RE DOING A JOB NO ONE ELSE CAN... SO THERE'S NOTHING TO BE ASHAMED OF!
DEPUTY ...!

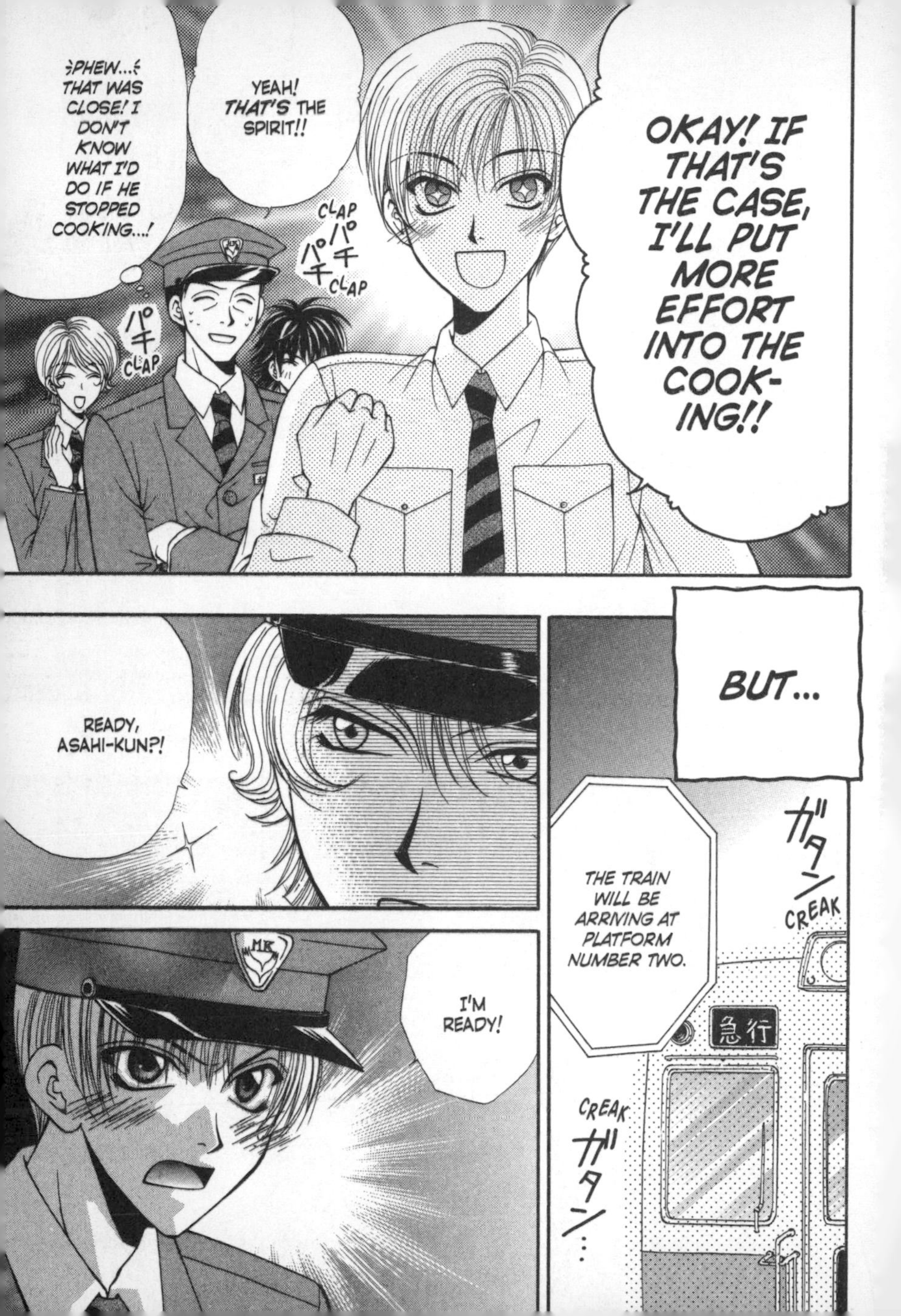
OKAY! IF THAT'S THE CASE, I'LL PUT MORE EFFORT INTO THE COOK-ING!!
YEAH! THAT'S THE SPIRIT!!
CLAP パチ
パチ CLAP
パチ CLAP
PHEW... THAT WAS CLOSE! I DON'T KNOW WHAT I'D DO IF HE STOPPED COOKING...!
BUT...
THE TRAIN WILL BE ARRIVING AT PLATFORM NUMBER TWO.
ガタン CREAK
急行
CREAK ガタン...
READY, ASAHI-KUN?!
I'M READY!

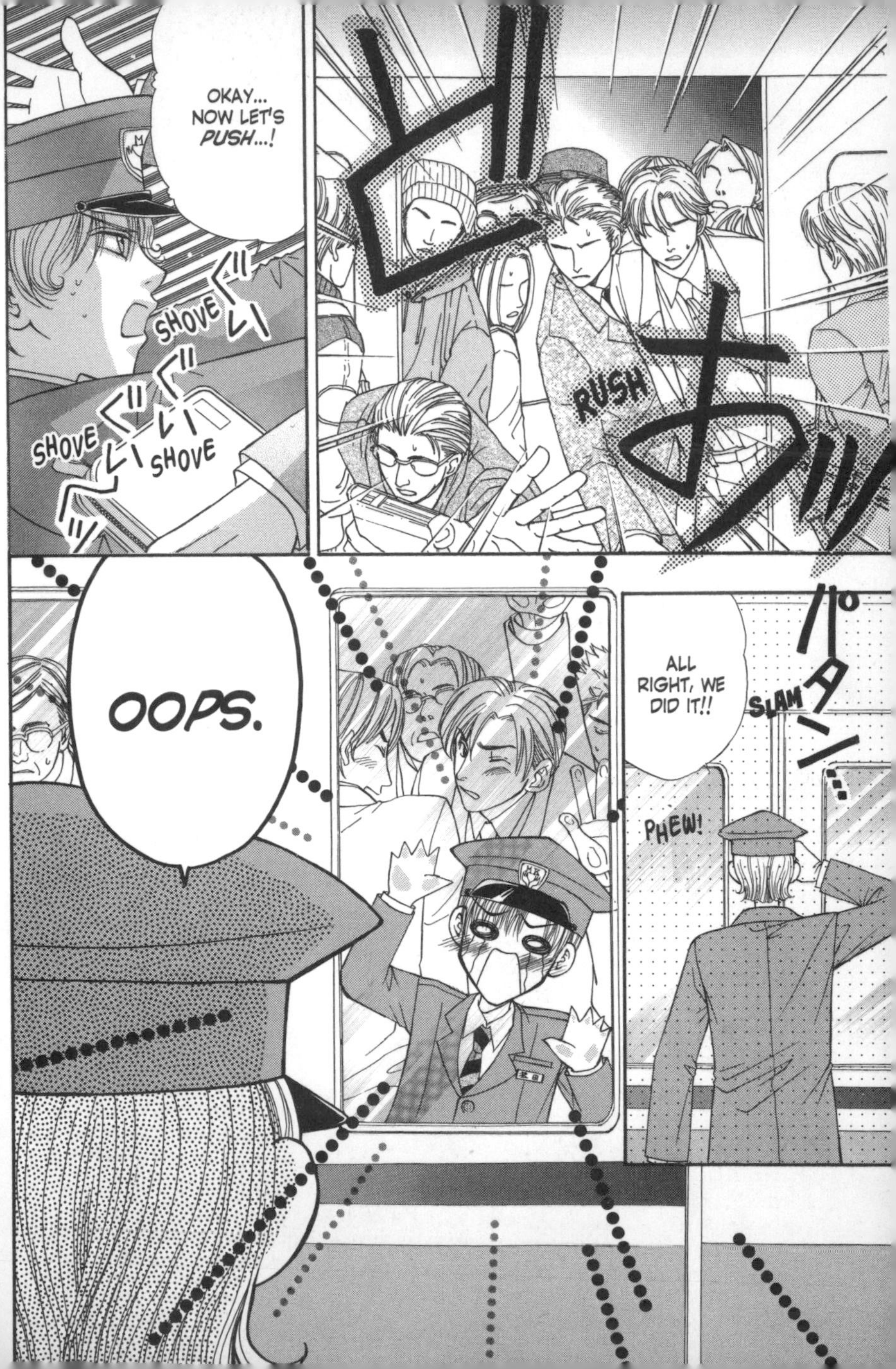
RUSH
OKAY... NOW LET'S *PUSH*...!
SHOVE
SHOVE
SHOVE
ALL RIGHT, WE DID IT!!
SLAM
パタン…
PHEW!
OOPS.

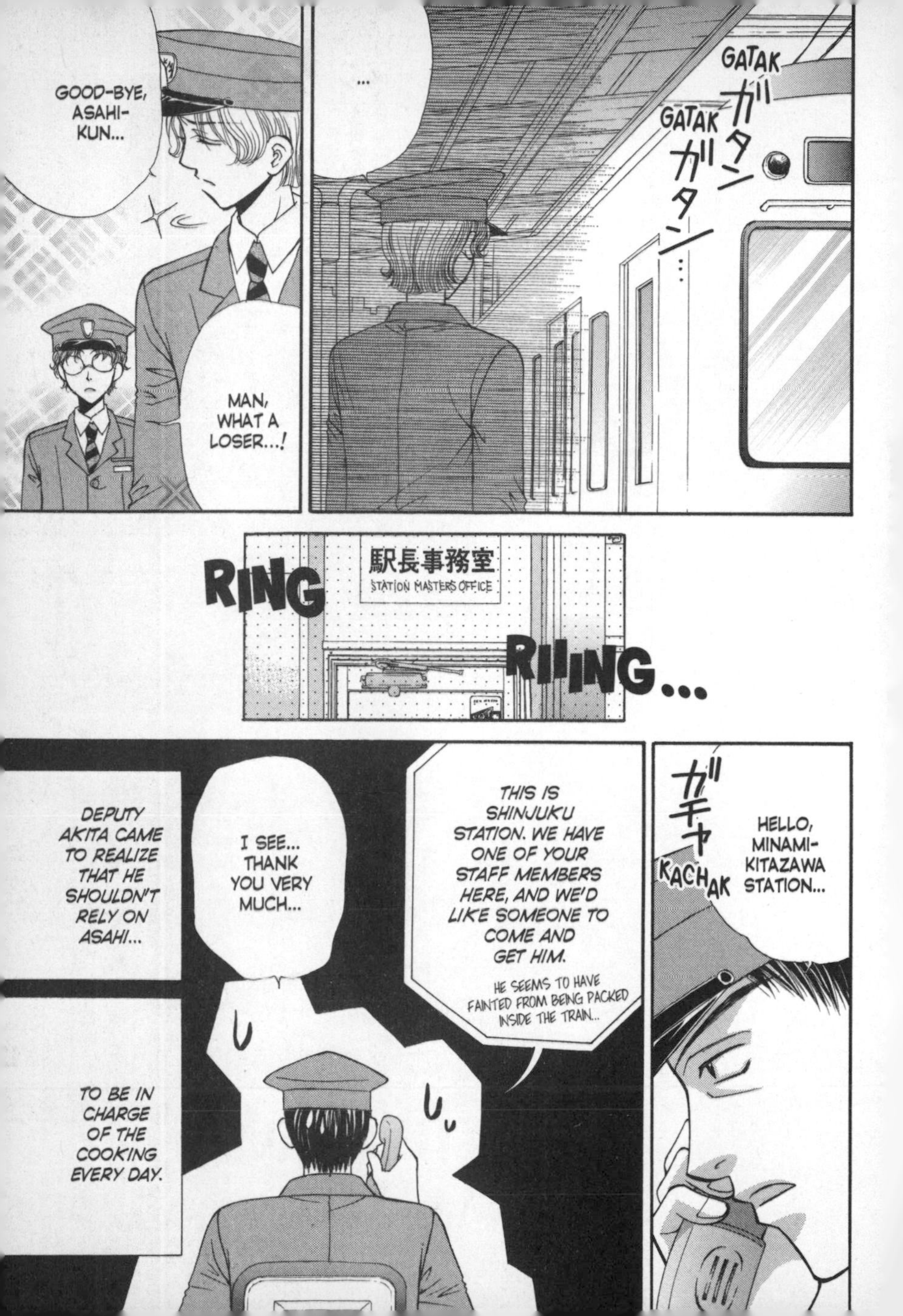
GATAK
ガタン
GATAK
ガタン…
...
GOOD-BYE, ASAHI-KUN...
MAN, WHAT A LOSER...!
駅長事務室
STATION MASTERS OFFICE
RING
RIIING...
ガチャ
KACHAK
HELLO, MINAMI-KITAZAWA STATION...
THIS IS SHINJUKU STATION. WE HAVE ONE OF YOUR STAFF MEMBERS HERE, AND WE'D LIKE SOMEONE TO COME AND GET HIM.
HE SEEMS TO HAVE FAINTED FROM BEING PACKED INSIDE THE TRAIN...
I SEE... THANK YOU VERY MUCH...
DEPUTY AKITA CAME TO REALIZE THAT HE SHOULDN'T RELY ON ASAHI...
TO BE IN CHARGE OF THE COOKING EVERY DAY.

# TSUBASA MASHIKO

SINCE HE HAS TWO NAMES, STATION CO-WORKERS REFER TO
HIM AS "IDOL-KUN." HE'S IN CHARGE OF DARK HUMOR

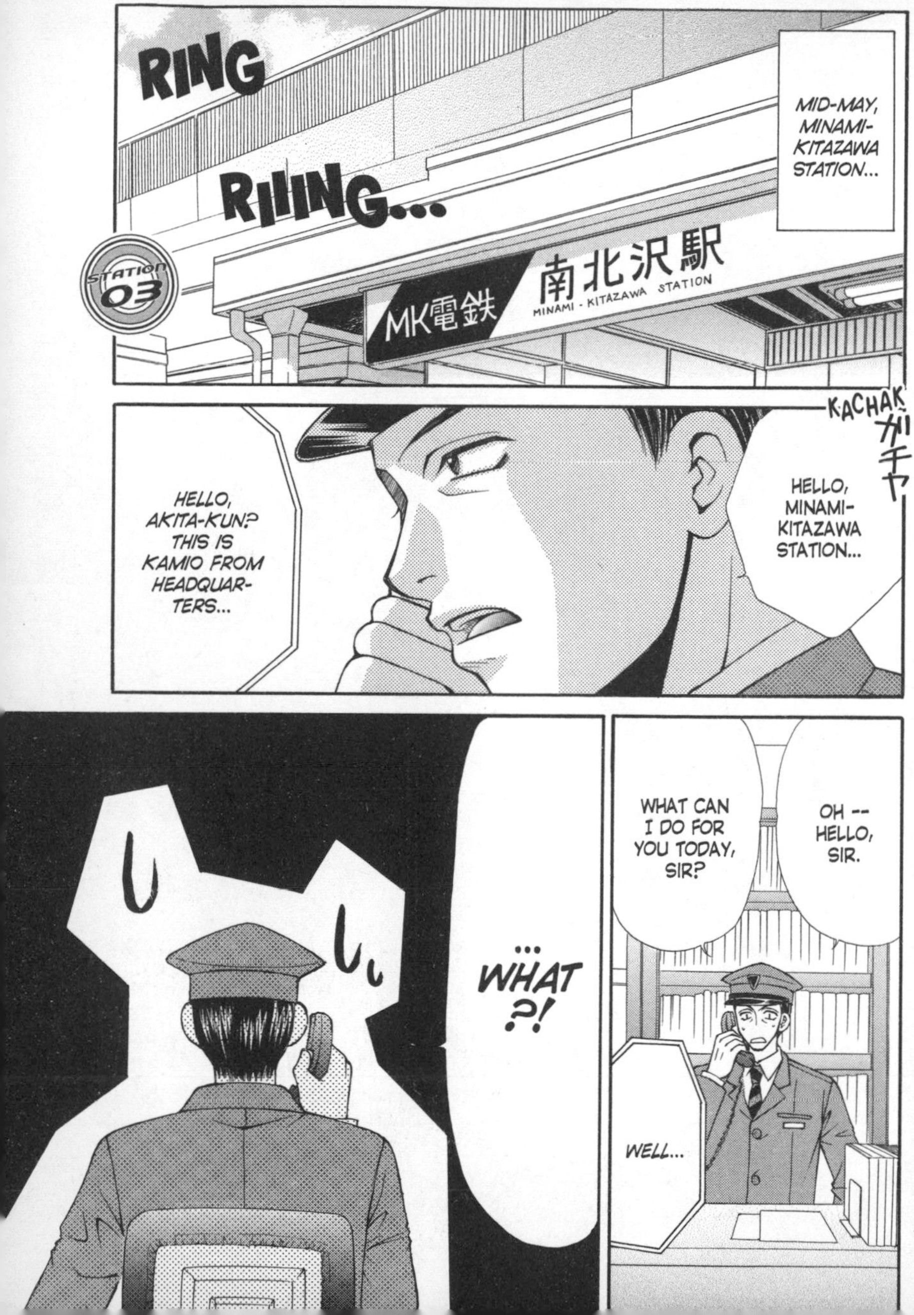
MID-MAY, MINAMI-KITAZAWA STATION...
RING
RIIING...
STATION 03
MK電鉄
南北沢駅
MINAMI - KITAZAWA STATION
KACHAK ガチャ
HELLO, MINAMI-KITAZAWA STATION...
HELLO, AKITA-KUN? THIS IS KAMIO FROM HEADQUAR-TERS...
OH -- HELLO, SIR.
WHAT CAN I DO FOR YOU TODAY, SIR?
WELL...
... WHAT ?!

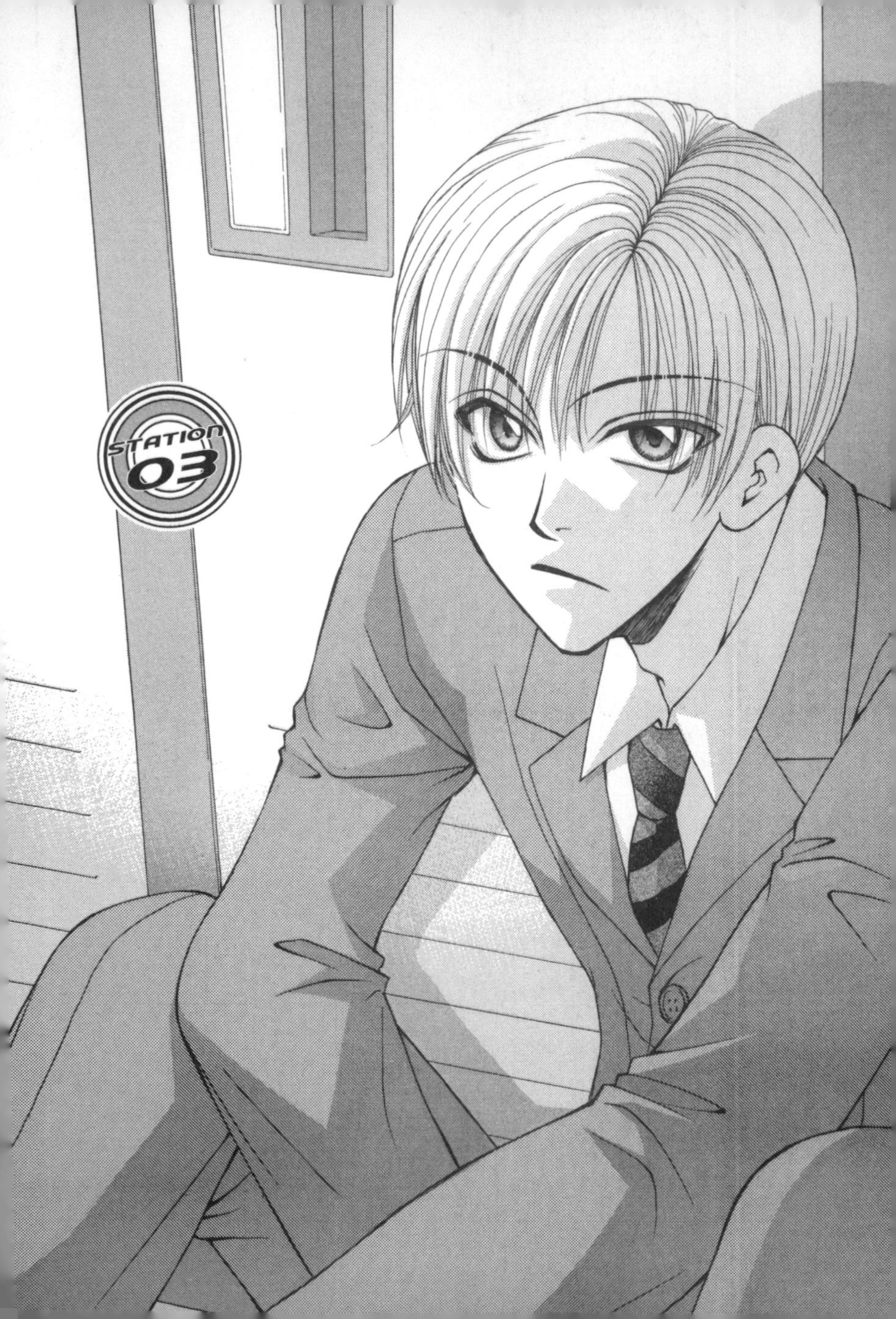
STATION
03

EXCUSE ME!

バタ TROMP

YES?

TROMP バタ TROMP

バタ TROMP バ

WHAT?! OH, NO!!

I'M SORRY -- MY DAUGHTER *FELL* OFF THE PLATFORM!

MAMA!

HERE YOU GO, MA'AM!

THERE SHE IS!

THANK YOU! I'M SO SORRY!

TIPTOE

B A A A H!

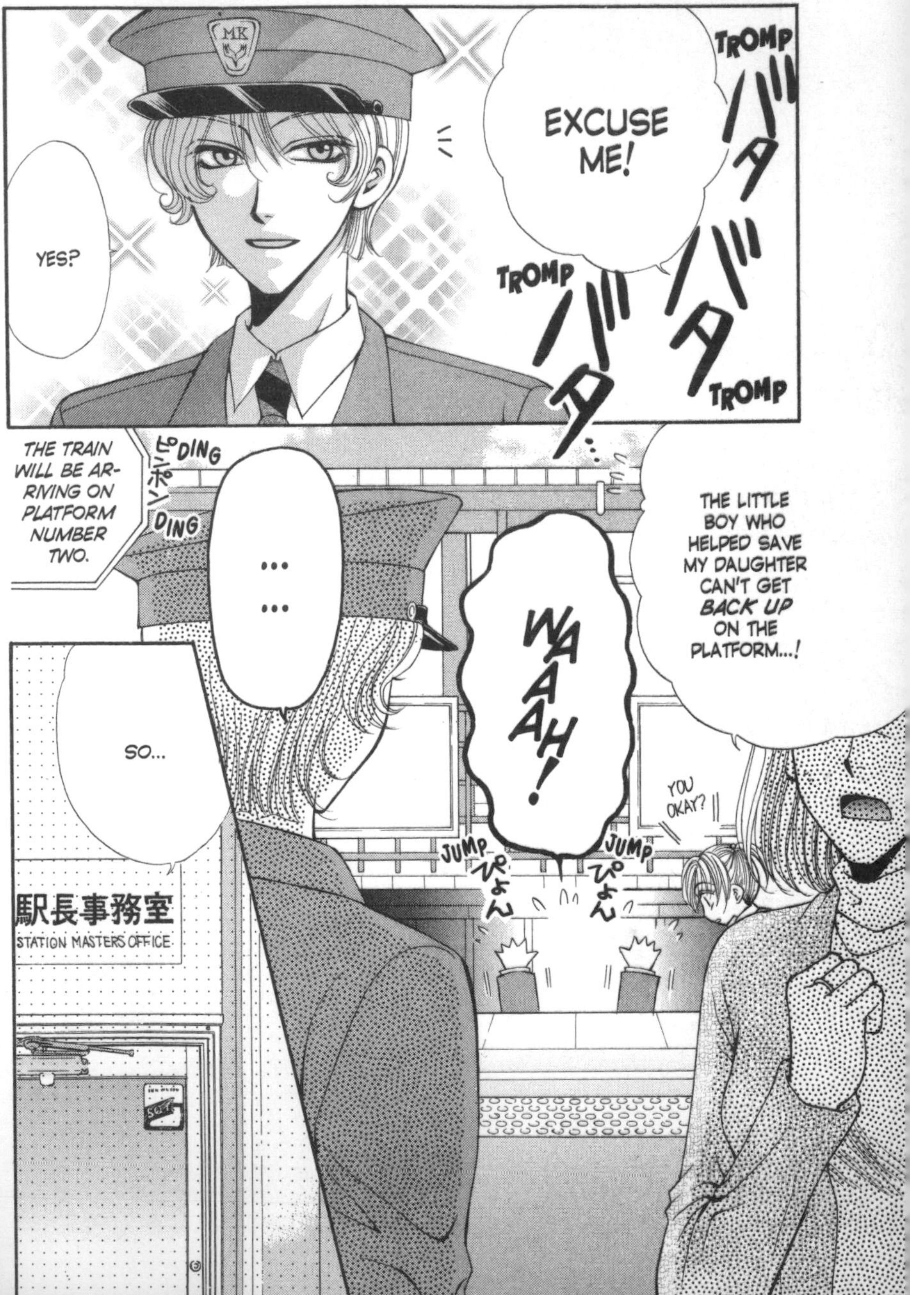
TROMP
バタ
TROMP
バタ
TROMP
バタ
EXCUSE ME!
YES?
THE LITTLE BOY WHO HELPED SAVE MY DAUGHTER CAN'T GET BACK UP ON THE PLATFORM...!
YOU OKAY?
WAAAH!
JUMP ぴょん
JUMP ぴょん
......
DING ピンポン DING
THE TRAIN WILL BE AR-RIVING ON PLATFORM NUMBER TWO.
SO...
駅長事務室
STATION MASTERS OFFICE

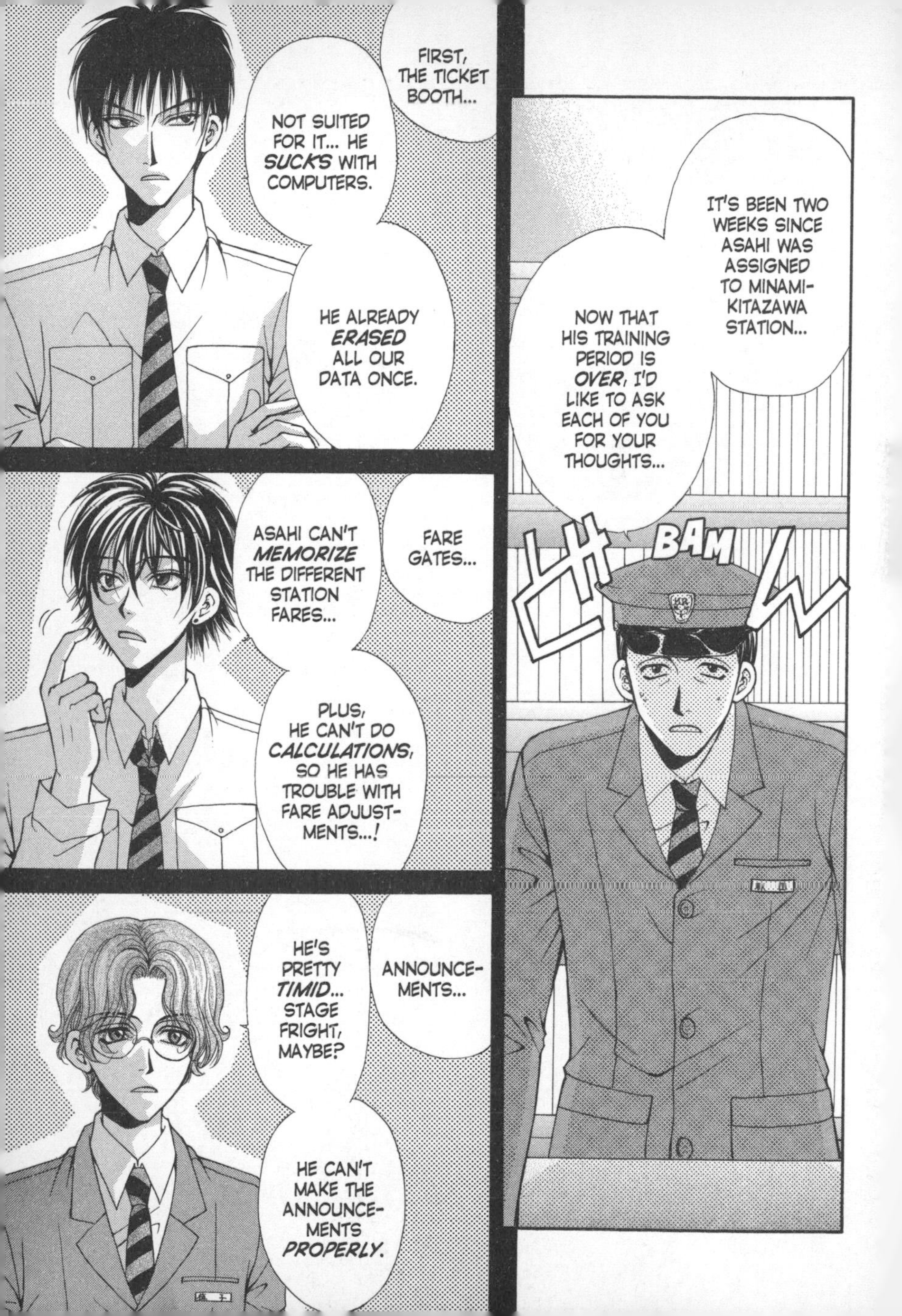
IT'S BEEN TWO WEEKS SINCE ASAHI WAS ASSIGNED TO MINAMI-KITAZAWA STATION...
NOW THAT HIS TRAINING PERIOD IS OVER, I'D LIKE TO ASK EACH OF YOU FOR YOUR THOUGHTS...
BAM
FIRST, THE TICKET BOOTH...
NOT SUITED FOR IT... HE SUCKS WITH COMPUTERS.
HE ALREADY ERASED ALL OUR DATA ONCE.
FARE GATES...
ASAHI CAN'T MEMORIZE THE DIFFERENT STATION FARES...
PLUS, HE CAN'T DO CALCULATIONS, SO HE HAS TROUBLE WITH FARE ADJUSTMENTS...!
ANNOUNCEMENTS...
HE'S PRETTY TIMID... STAGE FRIGHT, MAYBE?
HE CAN'T MAKE THE ANNOUNCEMENTS PROPERLY.

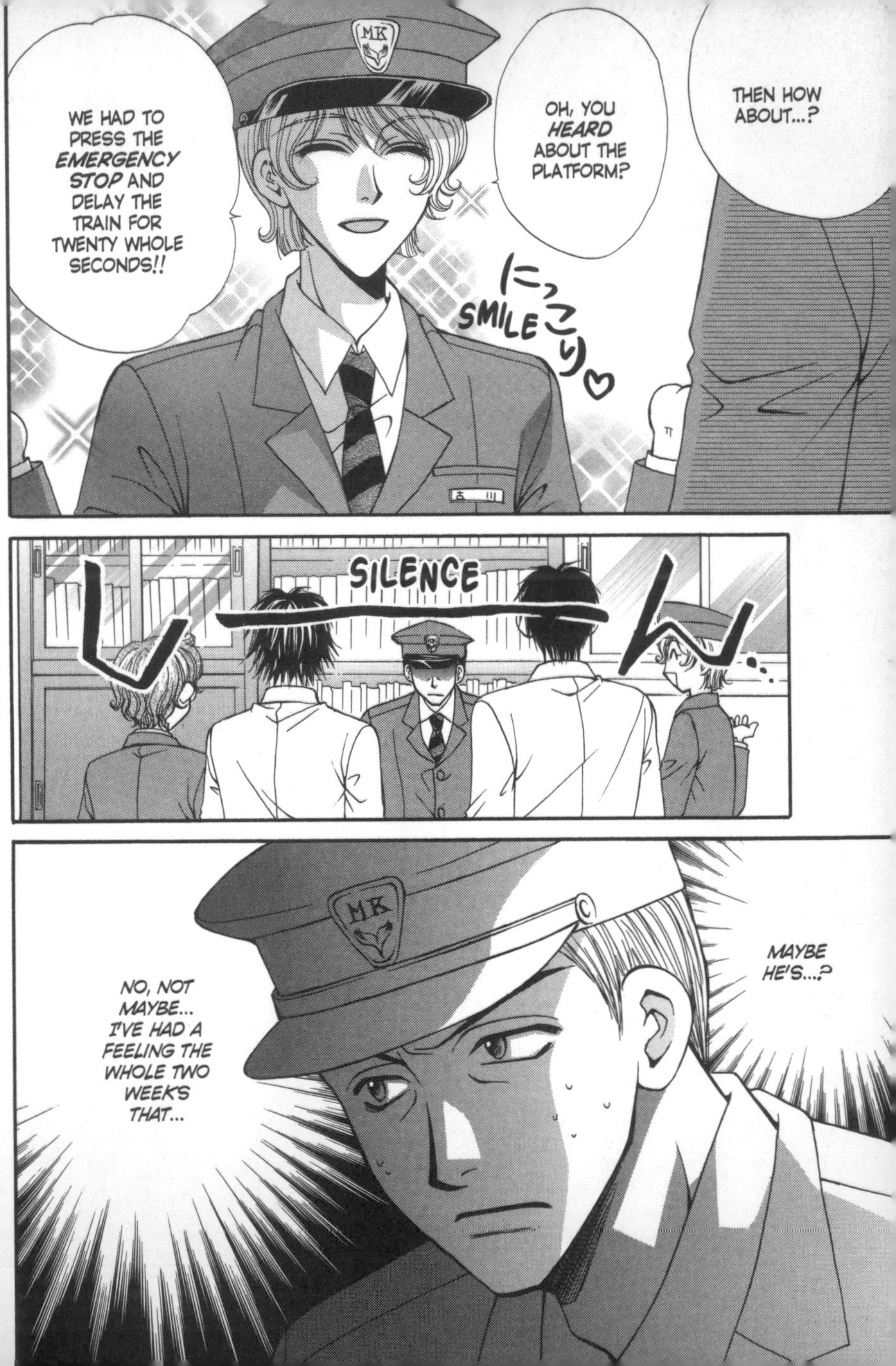
THEN HOW ABOUT...?
OH, YOU HEARD ABOUT THE PLATFORM?
WE HAD TO PRESS THE EMERGENCY STOP AND DELAY THE TRAIN FOR TWENTY WHOLE SECONDS!!
にっこり SMILE
しーーーん SILENCE
MAYBE HE'S...?
NO, NOT MAYBE... I'VE HAD A FEELING THE WHOLE TWO WEEKS THAT...

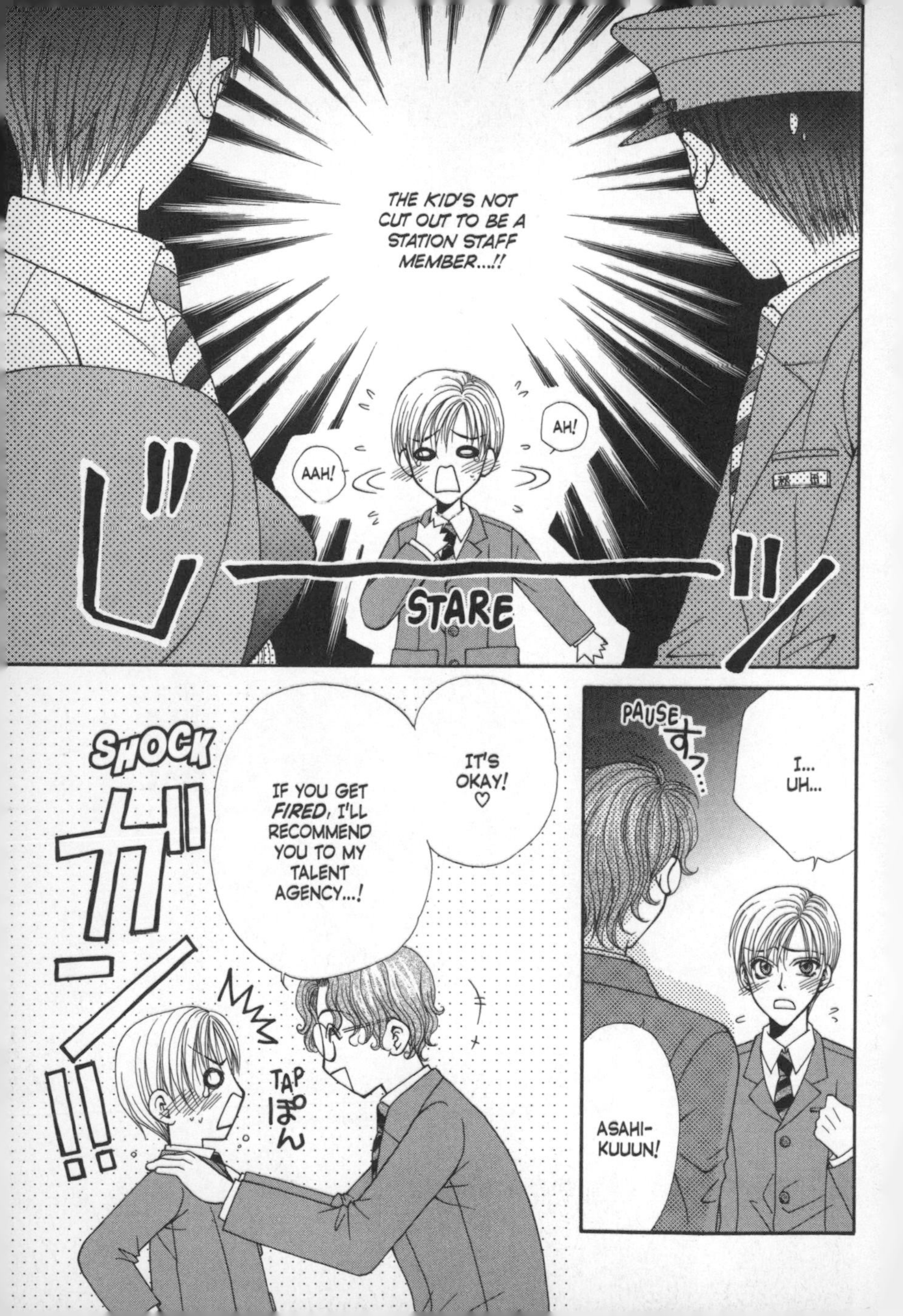
THE KID'S NOT CUT OUT TO BE A STATION STAFF MEMBER...!!
AH!
AAH!
STARE
PAUSE
すっ...
I... UH...
ASAHI-KUUUN!
IT'S OKAY! ♡
IF YOU GET *FIRED*, I'LL RECOMMEND YOU TO MY TALENT AGENCY...!
SHOCK
TAP
ぽん

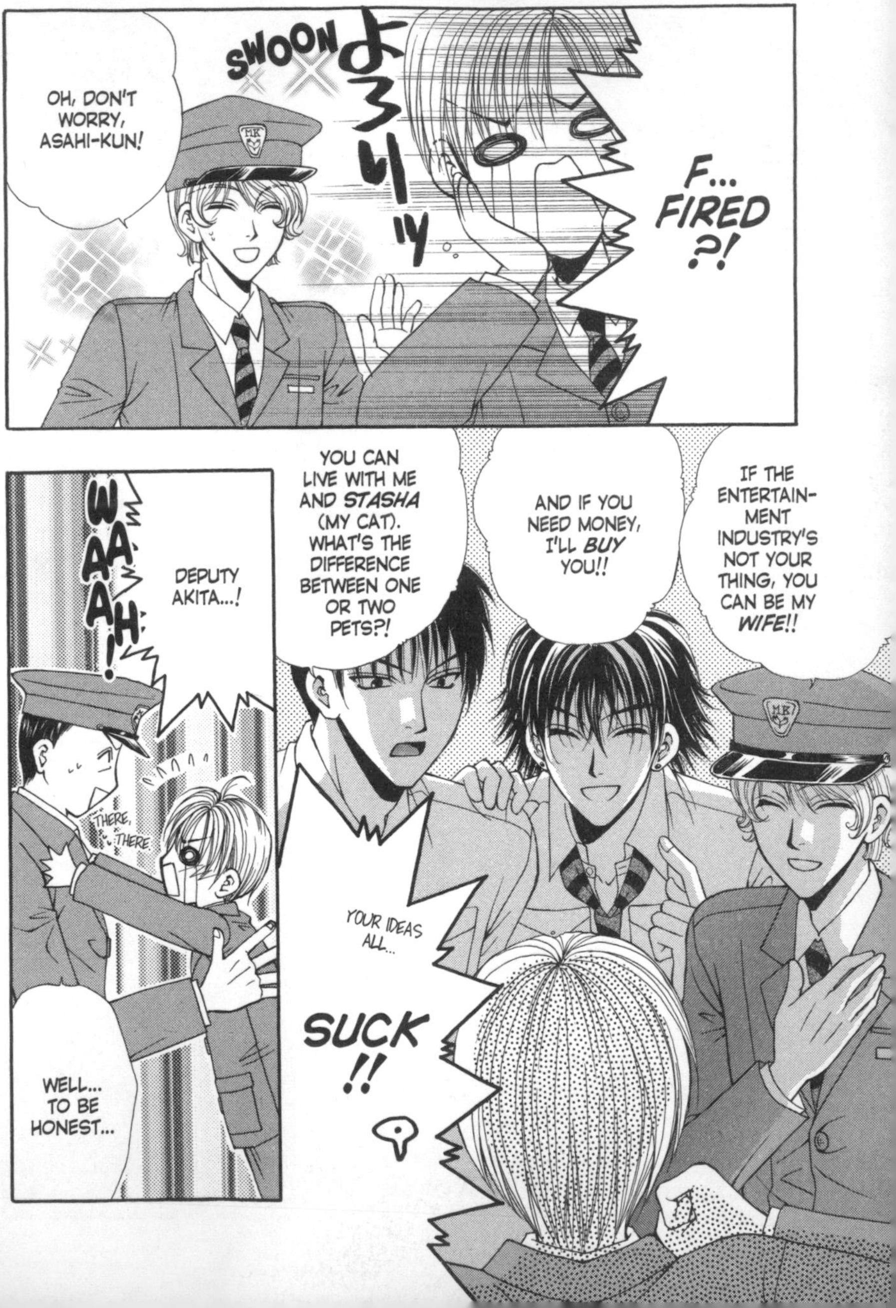
F... FIRED?!
SWOON
よろりッ
OH, DON'T WORRY, ASAHI-KUN!
IF THE ENTERTAINMENT INDUSTRY'S NOT YOUR THING, YOU CAN BE MY *WIFE*!!
AND IF YOU NEED MONEY, I'LL *BUY* YOU!!
YOU CAN LIVE WITH ME AND *STASHA* (MY CAT). WHAT'S THE DIFFERENCE BETWEEN ONE OR TWO PETS?!
YOUR IDEAS ALL...
SUCK!!
WAAAH!
DEPUTY AKITA...!
THERE, THERE.
WELL... TO BE HONEST...

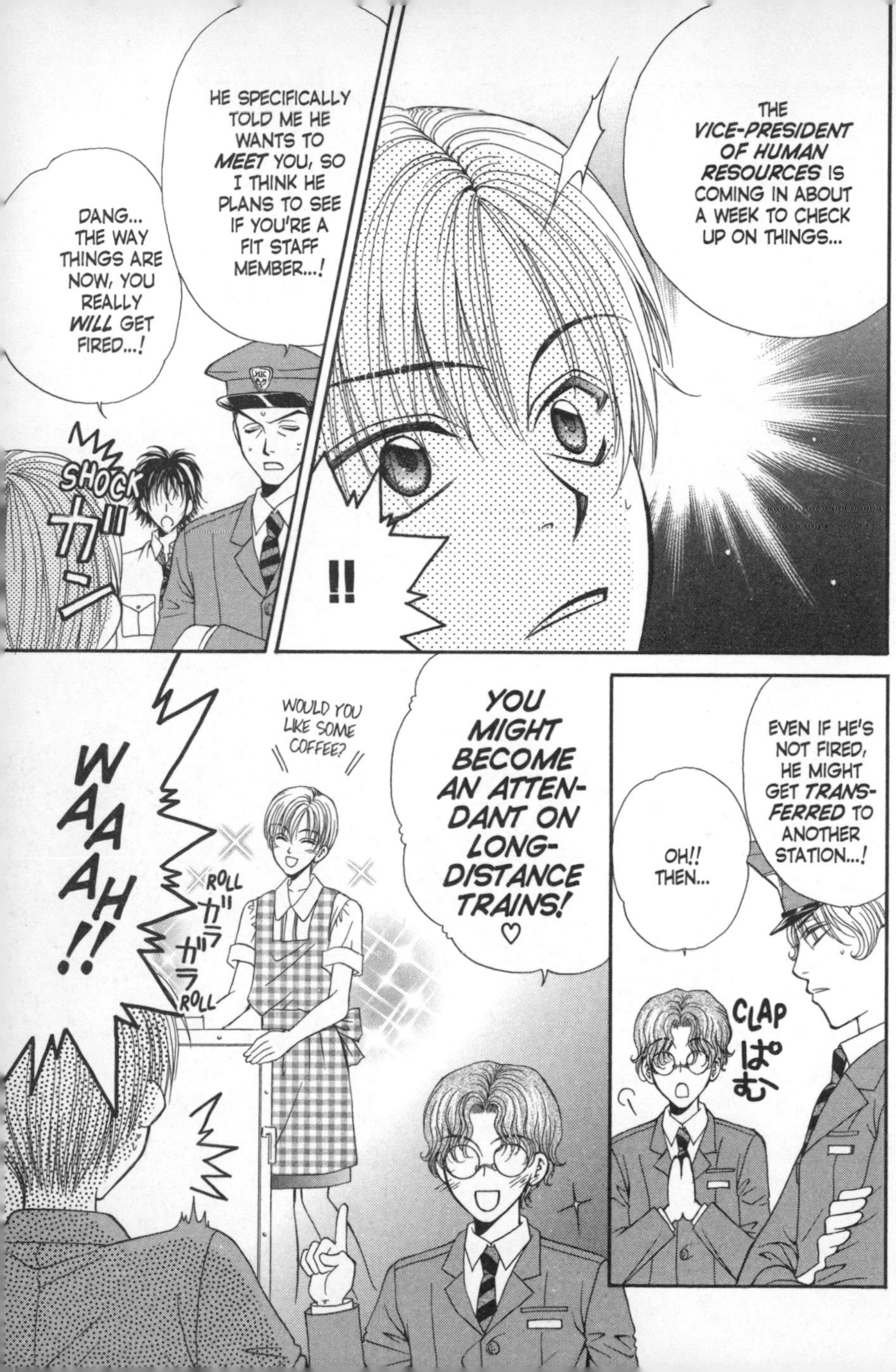
THE VICE-PRESIDENT OF HUMAN RESOURCES IS COMING IN ABOUT A WEEK TO CHECK UP ON THINGS...
!!
HE SPECIFICALLY TOLD ME HE WANTS TO MEET YOU, SO I THINK HE PLANS TO SEE IF YOU'RE A FIT STAFF MEMBER...!
DANG... THE WAY THINGS ARE NOW, YOU REALLY WILL GET FIRED...!
SHOCK
ガーン
EVEN IF HE'S NOT FIRED, HE MIGHT GET TRANSFERRED TO ANOTHER STATION...!
OH!! THEN...
CLAP
ぱむ
YOU MIGHT BECOME AN ATTENDANT ON LONG-DISTANCE TRAINS! ♡
WOULD YOU LIKE SOME COFFEE?
ROLL
ガラ
ガラ
ROLL
WAAAAH!!

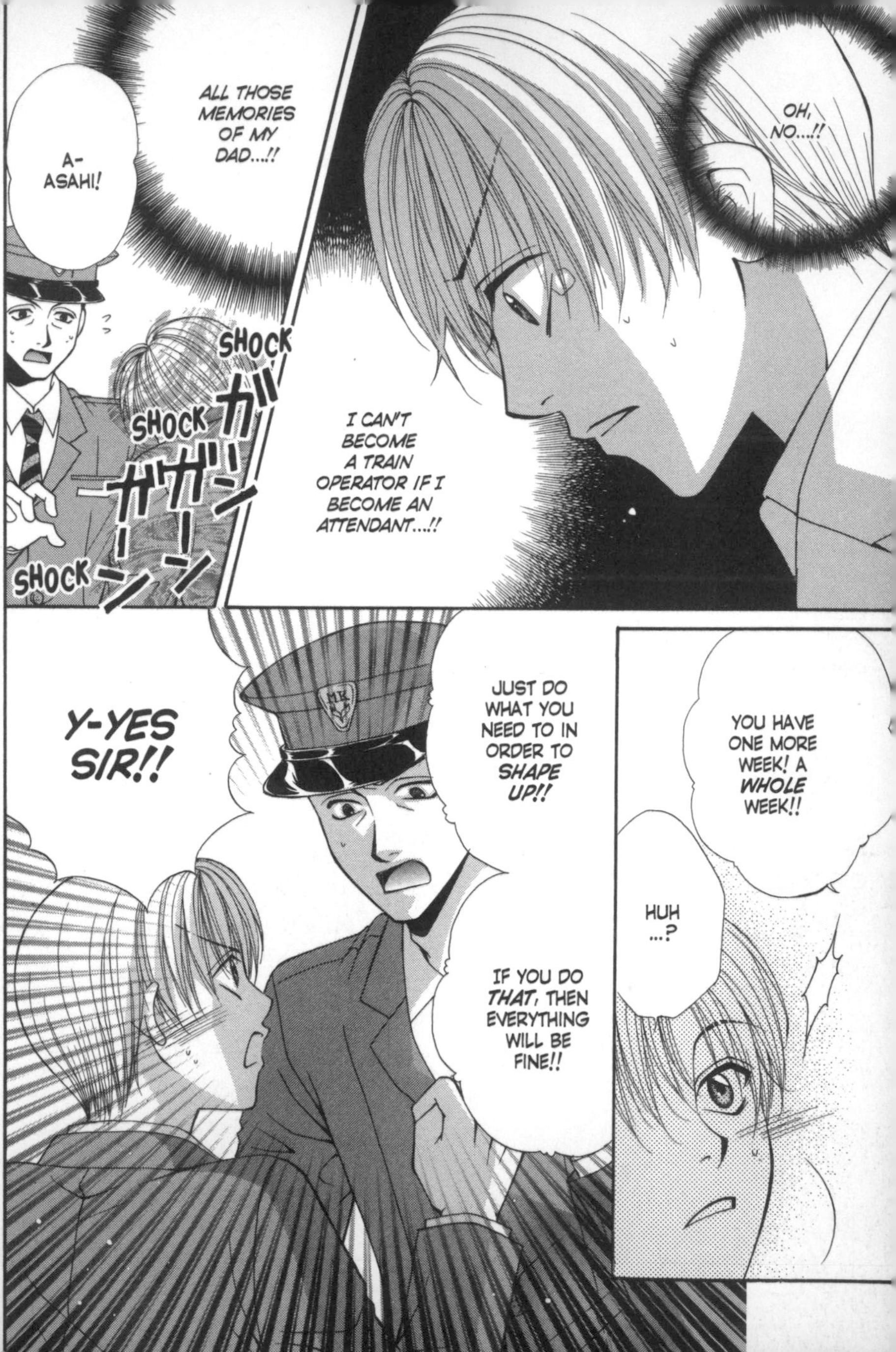
OH, NO...!!
I CAN'T BECOME A TRAIN OPERATOR IF I BECOME AN ATTENDANT...!!
ALL THOSE MEMORIES OF MY DAD...!!
A-ASAHI!
SHOCK
SHOCK
SHOCK
ガガーン
ガーン
YOU HAVE ONE MORE WEEK! A WHOLE WEEK!!
HUH ...?
JUST DO WHAT YOU NEED TO IN ORDER TO SHAPE UP!!
IF YOU DO THAT, THEN EVERYTHING WILL BE FINE!!
Y-YES SIR!!

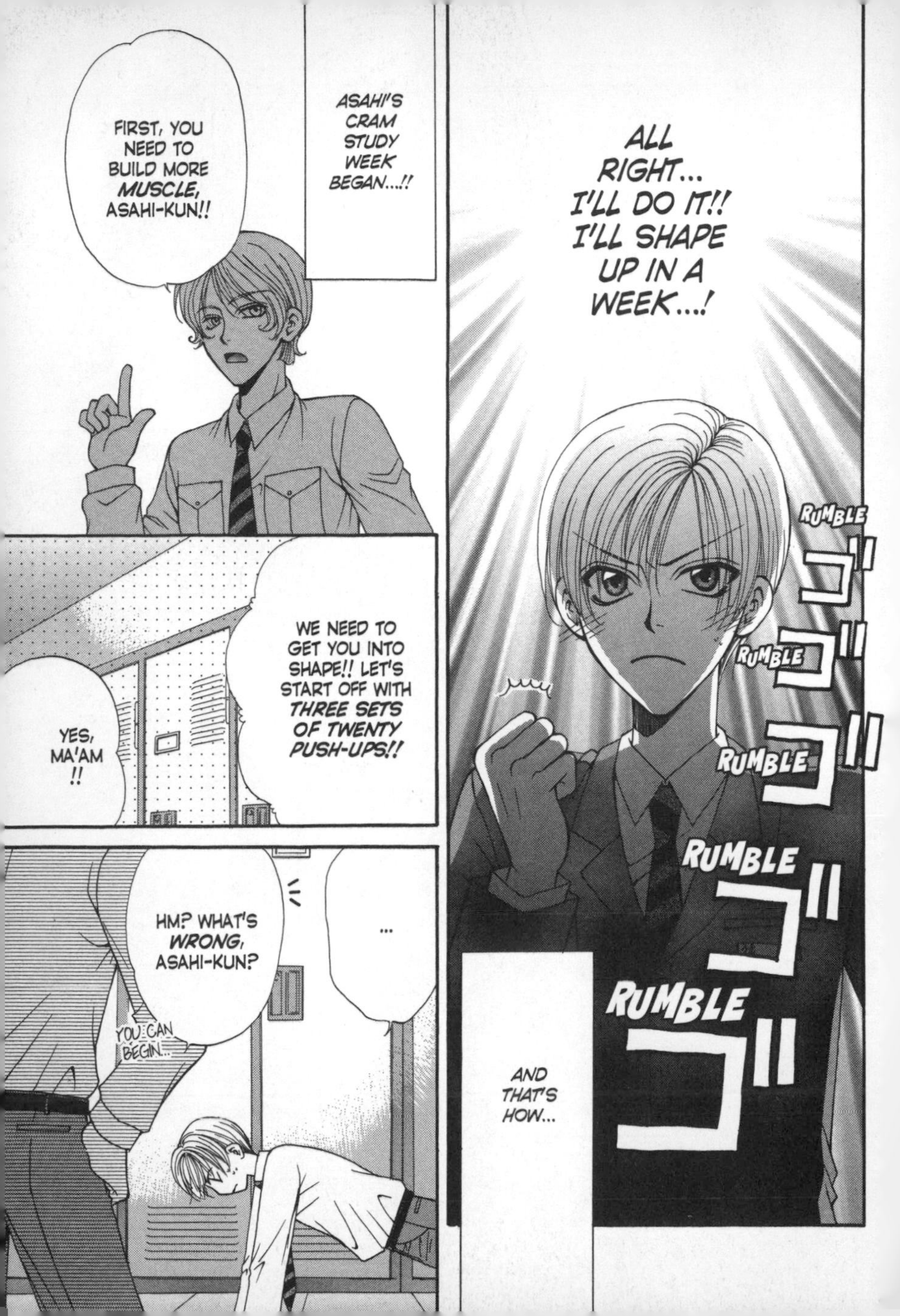
ALL RIGHT... I'LL DO IT!! I'LL SHAPE UP IN A WEEK...!
RUMBLE
RUMBLE
RUMBLE
RUMBLE
RUMBLE
AND THAT'S HOW...
ASAHI'S CRAM STUDY WEEK BEGAN...!!
FIRST, YOU NEED TO BUILD MORE *MUSCLE*, ASAHI-KUN!!
WE NEED TO GET YOU INTO SHAPE!! LET'S START OFF WITH *THREE SETS OF TWENTY PUSH-UPS!!*
YES, MA'AM!!
...
HM? WHAT'S *WRONG*, ASAHI-KUN?
YOU CAN BEGIN...

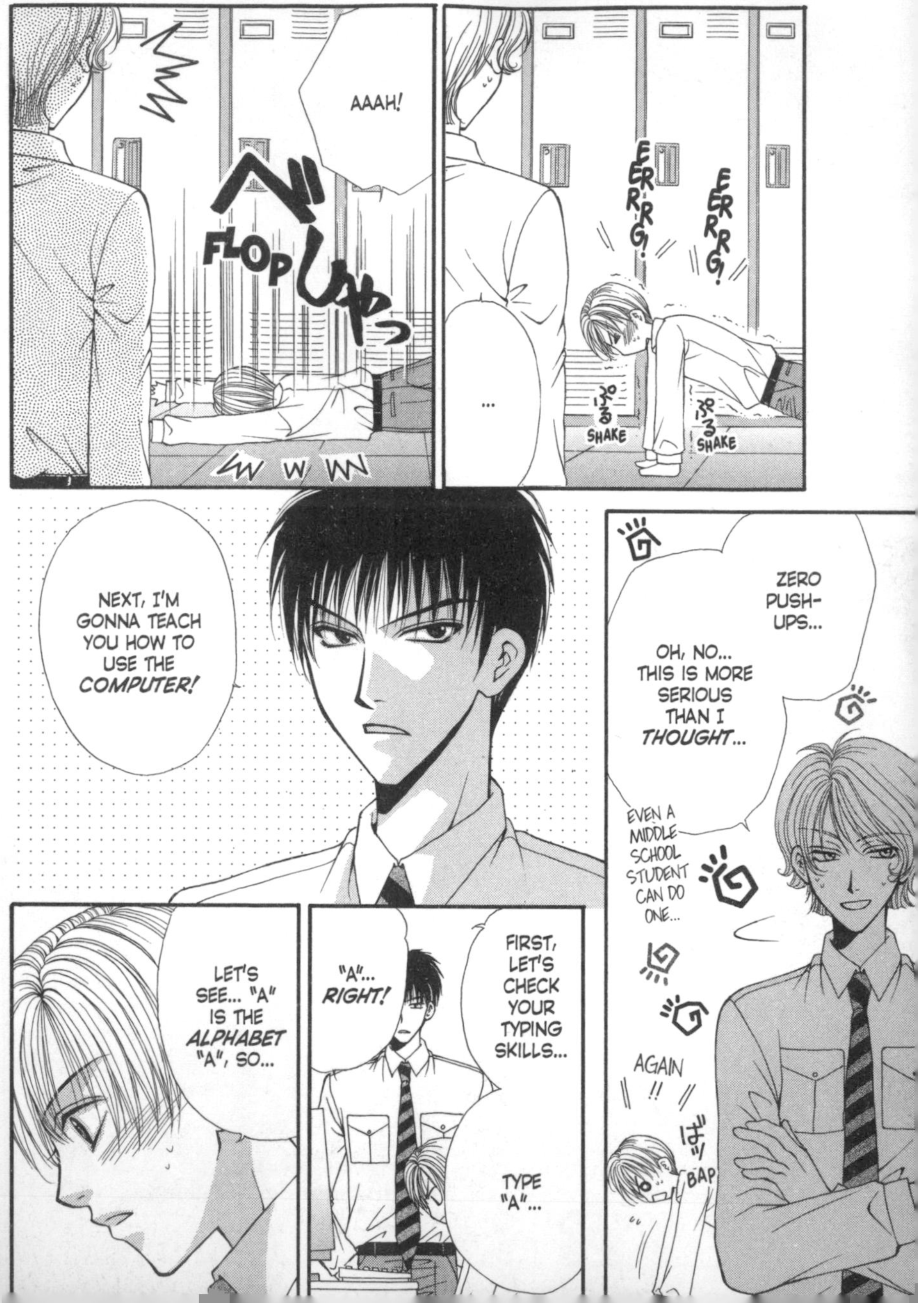
...
EERRRG!
EERRRG!
ぷる
SHAKE
ぷる
SHAKE
AAAH!
べ
FLOP
ひゃっ
ZERO PUSH-UPS...
OH, NO... THIS IS MORE SERIOUS THAN I *THOUGHT*...
EVEN A MIDDLE SCHOOL STUDENT CAN DO ONE...
AGAIN!!
ばッ
BAP
NEXT, I'M GONNA TEACH YOU HOW TO USE THE *COMPUTER!*
FIRST, LET'S CHECK YOUR TYPING SKILLS...
"A"... *RIGHT!*
TYPE "A"...
LET'S SEE... "A" IS THE *ALPHABET* "A", SO...

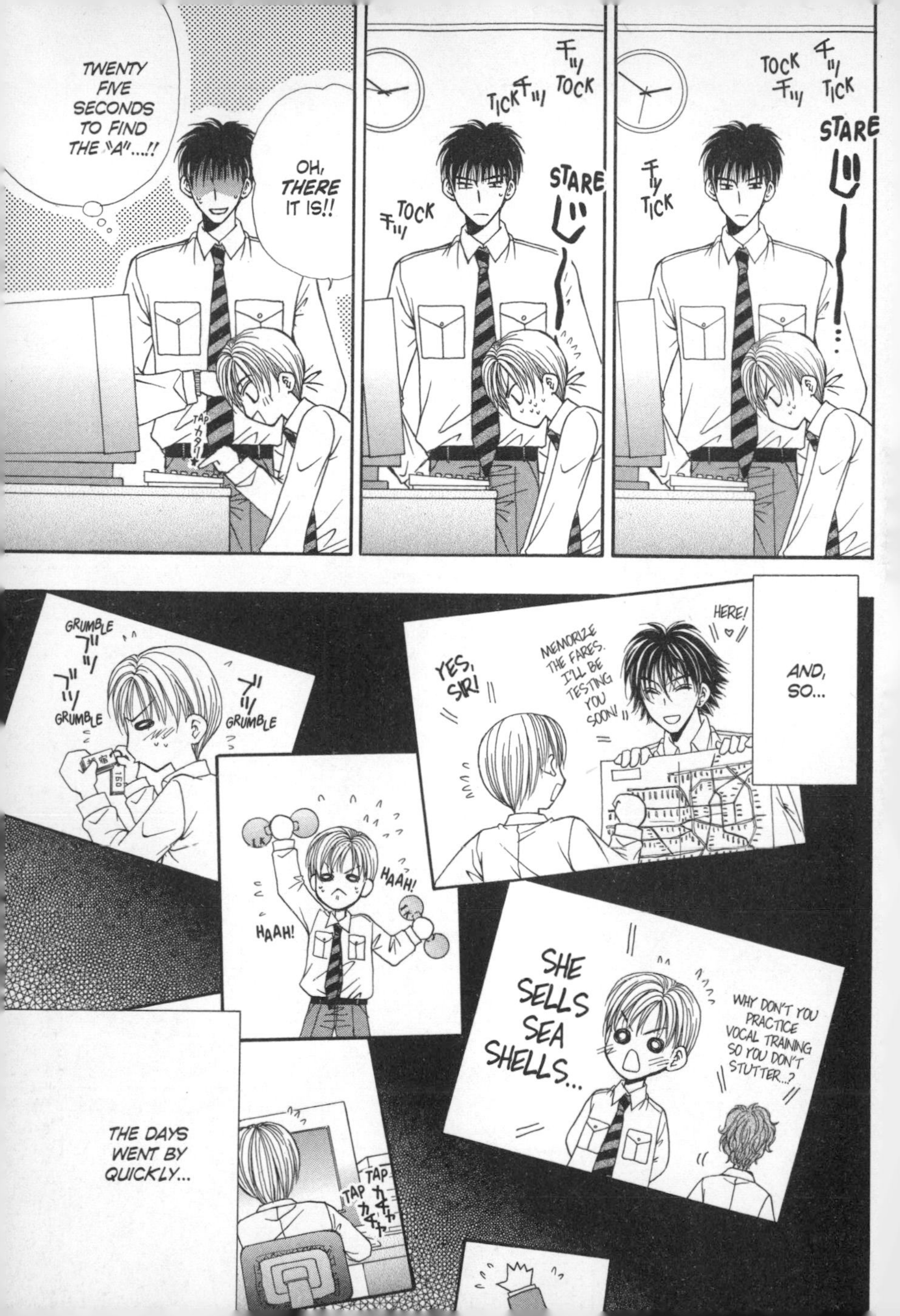

TOCK チッ
チッ TICK
STARE じ
チッ TICK
TICK チッ
チッ TOCK
STARE じ
TOCK チッ
TWENTY FIVE SECONDS TO FIND THE "A"...!!
OH, THERE IT IS!!
TAP カタ
AND, SO...
HERE!
MEMORIZE THE FARES. I'LL BE TESTING YOU SOON!
YES, SIR!
GRUMBLE ブツ
GRUMBLE ブツ
GRUMBLE ブツ
HAAH!
HAAH!
WHY DON'T YOU PRACTICE VOCAL TRAINING SO YOU DON'T STUTTER...?
SHE SELLS SEA SHELLS...
THE DAYS WENT BY QUICKLY...
TAP カチャ
TAP カチャ

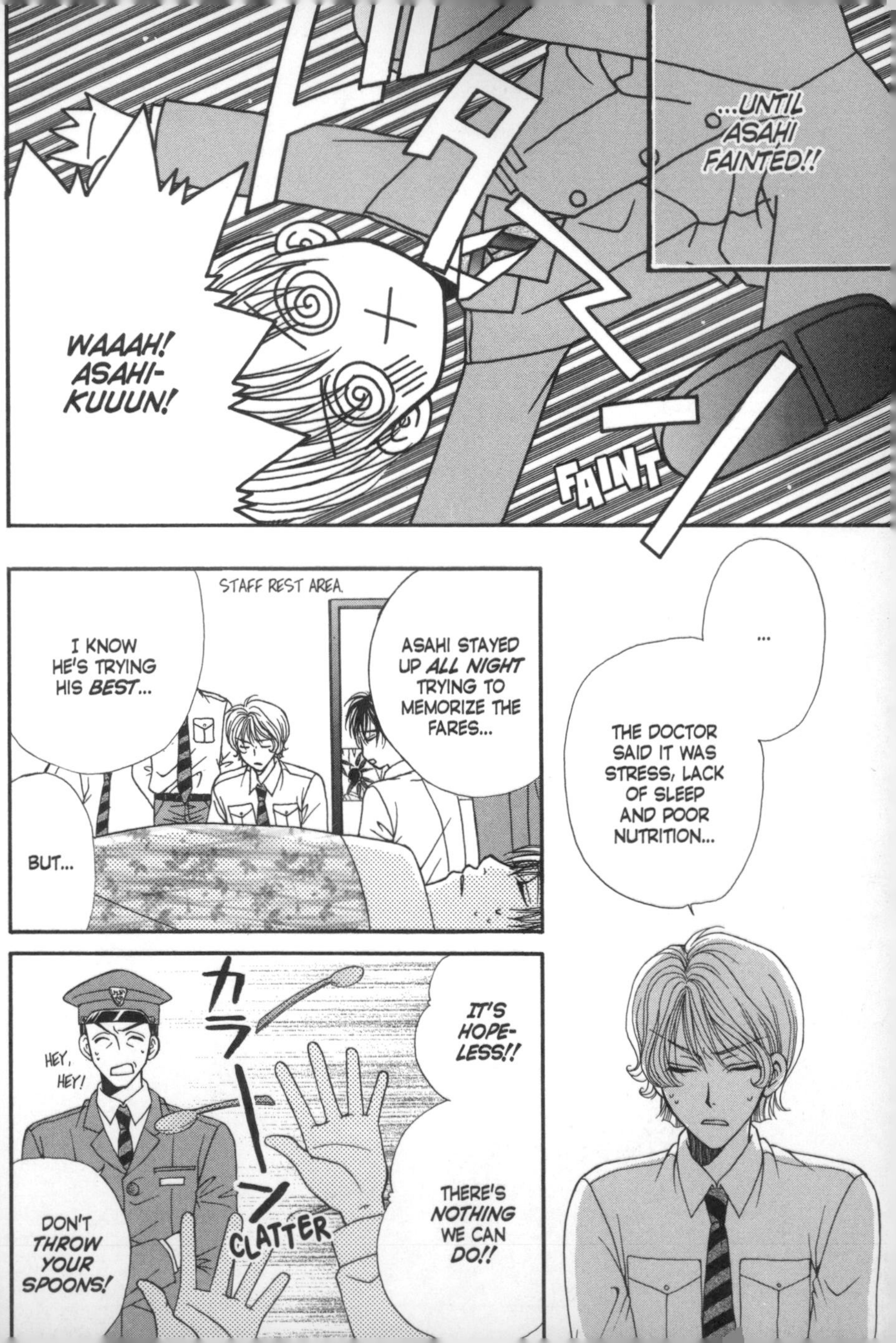
...UNTIL ASAHI FAINTED!!
WAAAH! ASAHI-KUUUN!
FAINT
...
THE DOCTOR SAID IT WAS STRESS, LACK OF SLEEP AND POOR NUTRITION...
STAFF REST AREA.
ASAHI STAYED UP ALL NIGHT TRYING TO MEMORIZE THE FARES...
I KNOW HE'S TRYING HIS BEST...
BUT...
IT'S HOPE-LESS!!
THERE'S NOTHING WE CAN DO!!
カラーン
CLATTER
HEY, HEY!
DON'T THROW YOUR SPOONS!

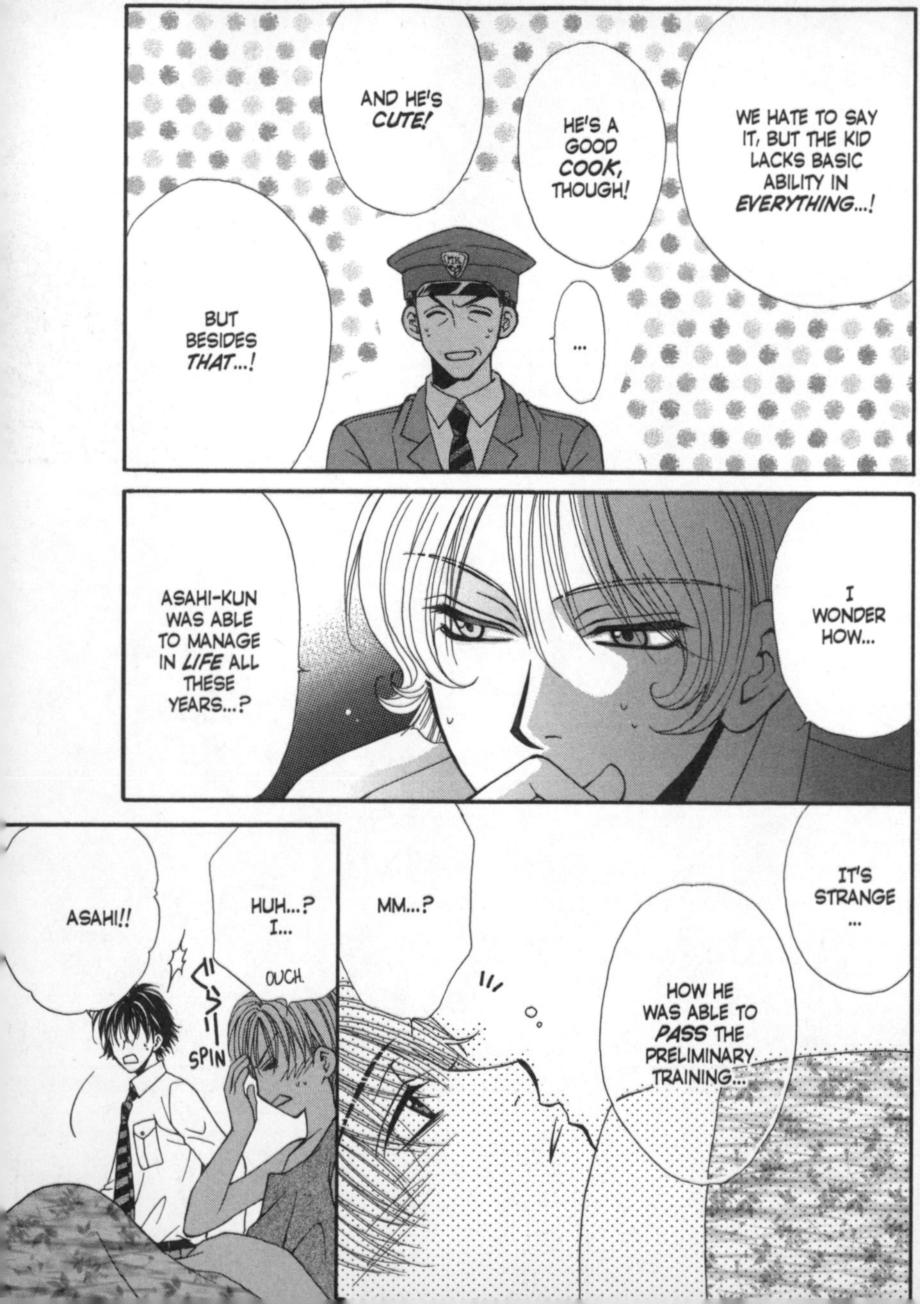
WE HATE TO SAY IT, BUT THE KID LACKS BASIC ABILITY IN EVERYTHING...!
HE'S A GOOD COOK, THOUGH!
AND HE'S CUTE!
...
BUT BESIDES THAT...!
I WONDER HOW...
ASAHI-KUN WAS ABLE TO MANAGE IN LIFE ALL THESE YEARS...?
IT'S STRANGE...
HOW HE WAS ABLE TO PASS THE PRELIMINARY TRAINING...
MM...?
HUH...? I...
OUCH.
SPIN
ASAHI!!

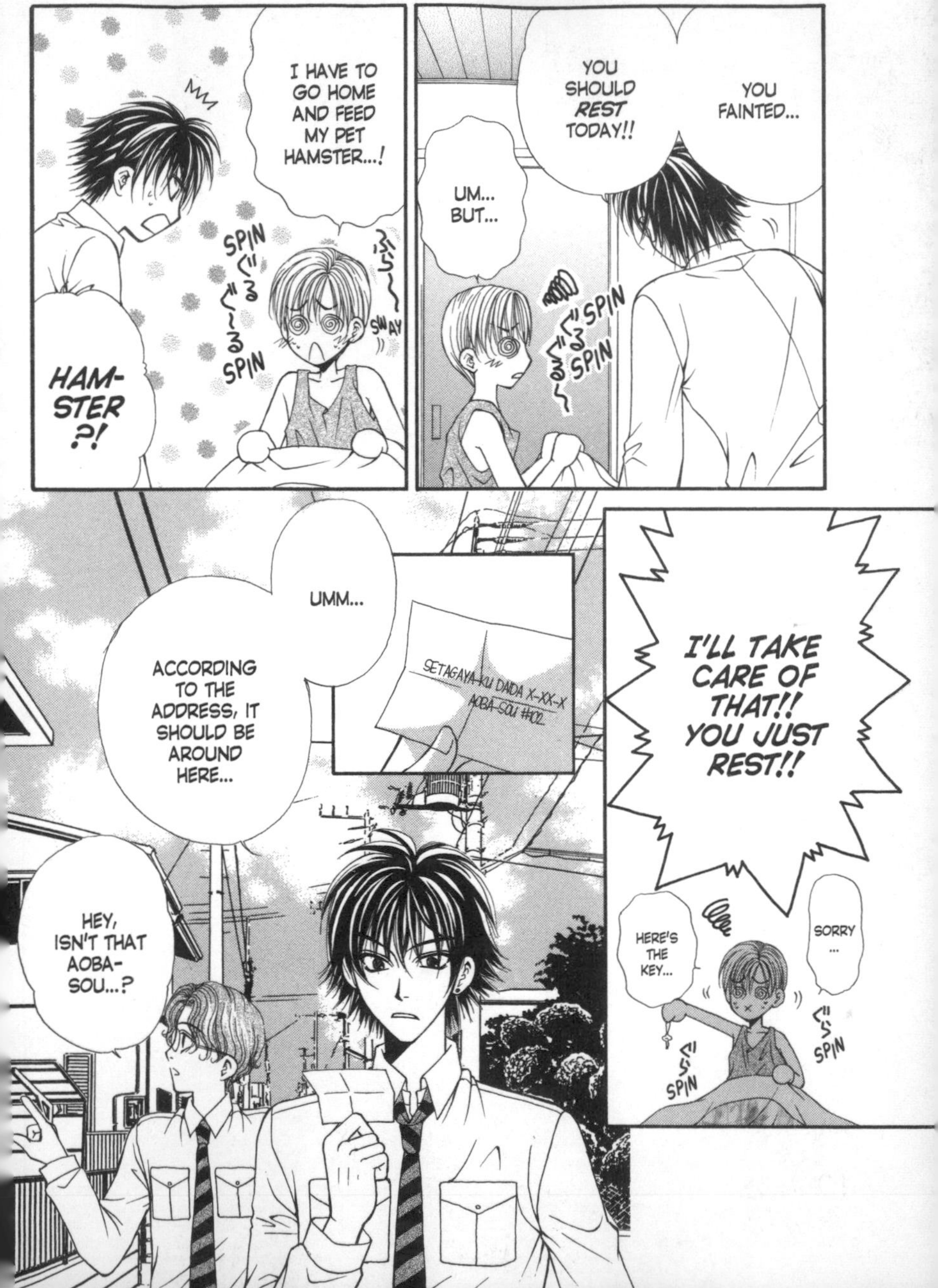
YOU FAINTED...
YOU SHOULD REST TODAY!!
UM... BUT...
SPIN SPIN
I HAVE TO GO HOME AND FEED MY PET HAMSTER...!
SWAY
SPIN
SPIN
HAM-STER ?!
I'LL TAKE CARE OF THAT!! YOU JUST REST!!
SORRY ...
HERE'S THE KEY...
SPIN
SPIN
SETAGAYA-KU DAIDA X-XX-X AOBA-SOU #102
UMM...
ACCORDING TO THE ADDRESS, IT SHOULD BE AROUND HERE...
HEY, ISN'T THAT AOBA-SOU...?

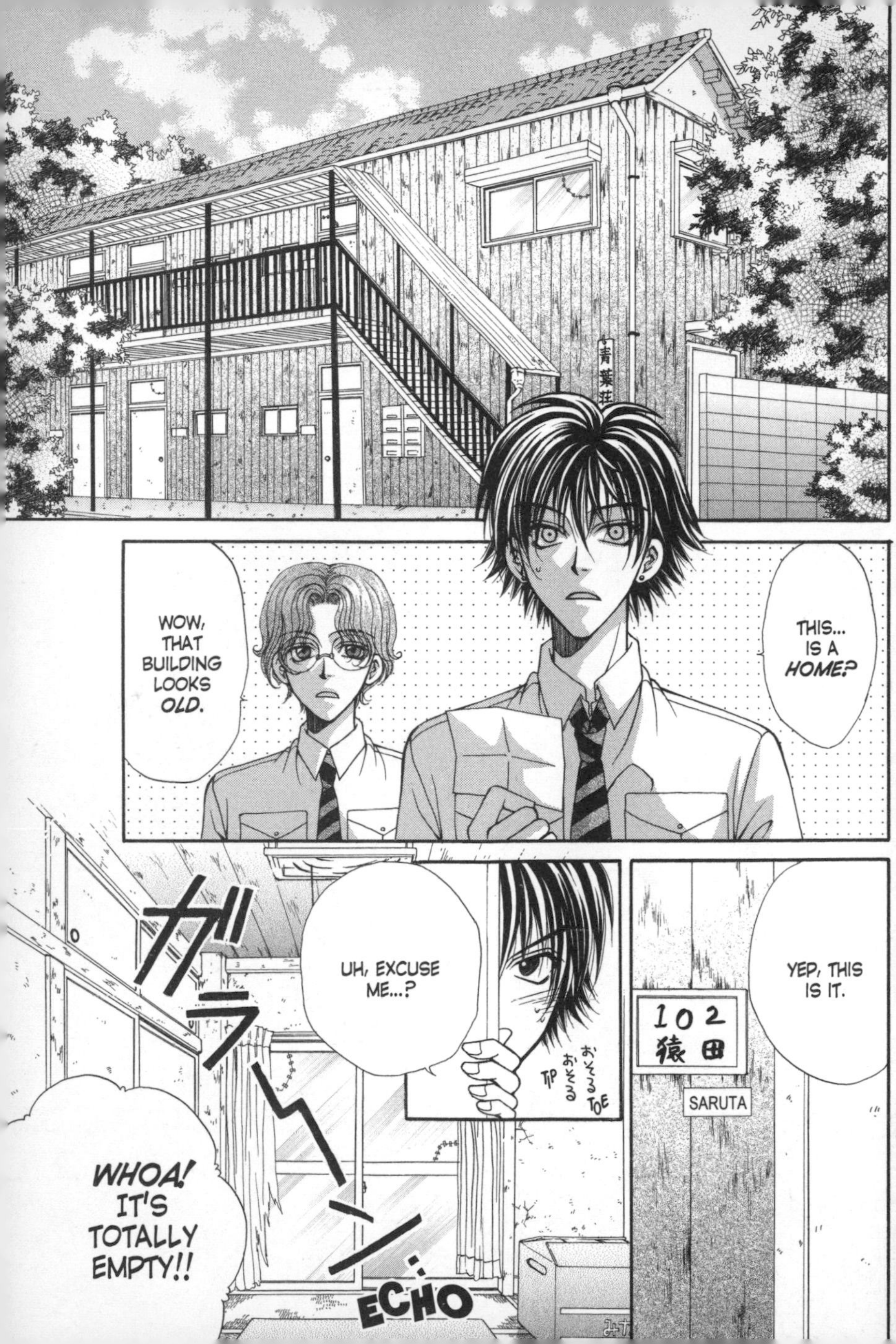
青葉荘
THIS... IS A HOME?
WOW, THAT BUILDING LOOKS OLD.
YEP, THIS IS IT.
102 猿田
SARUTA
UH, EXCUSE ME...?
おそる おそる
TOE TIP
ガラ〜ン
ECHO
WHOA! IT'S TOTALLY EMPTY!!

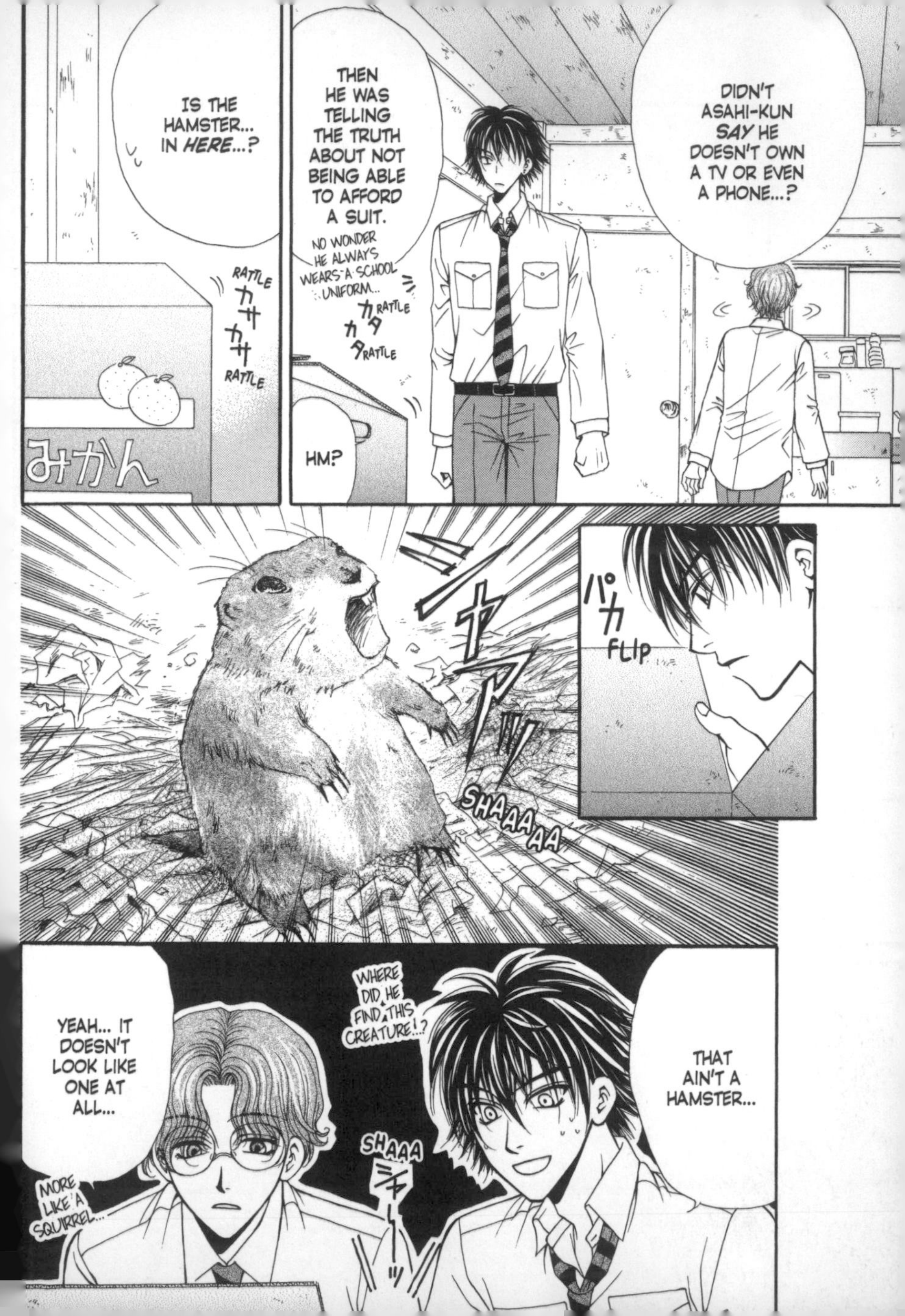
DIDN'T ASAHI-KUN SAY HE DOESN'T OWN A TV OR EVEN A PHONE...?
THEN HE WAS TELLING THE TRUTH ABOUT NOT BEING ABLE TO AFFORD A SUIT.
NO WONDER HE ALWAYS WEARS A SCHOOL UNIFORM...
カタ RATTLE
カタ RATTLE
HM?
IS THE HAMSTER... IN HERE...?
RATTLE
カサ
カサ
RATTLE
みかん
パカ
FLIP
シャァ
SHAAAAAA
THAT AIN'T A HAMSTER...
WHERE DID HE FIND THIS CREATURE!?
YEAH... IT DOESN'T LOOK LIKE ONE AT ALL...
SHAAA
シャー
MORE LIKE A SQUIRREL...

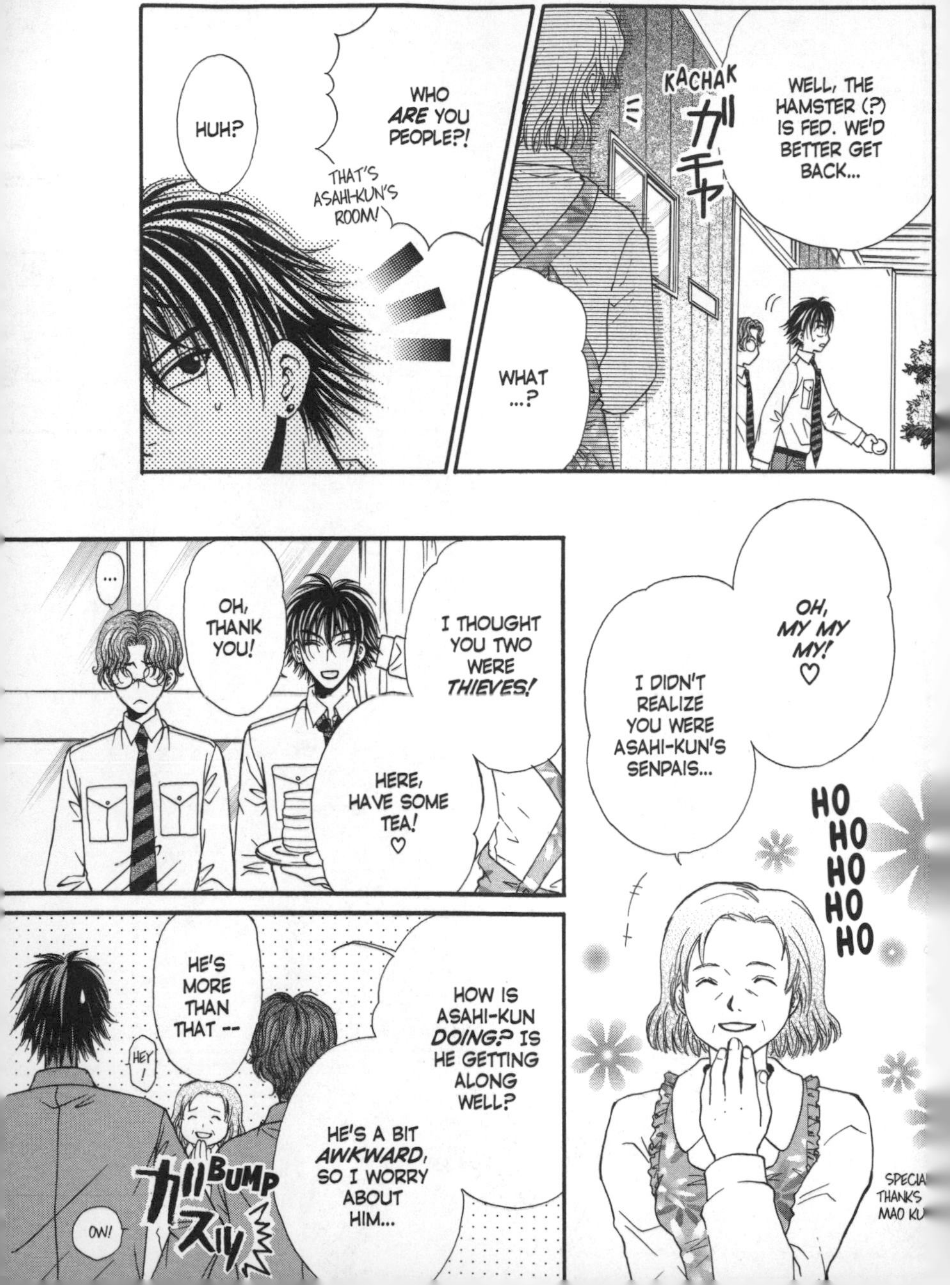
KACHAK
WELL, THE HAMSTER (?) IS FED. WE'D BETTER GET BACK...
WHAT ...?
WHO ARE YOU PEOPLE?!
HUH?
THAT'S ASAHI-KUN'S ROOM!
OH, MY MY MY! ♡
I DIDN'T REALIZE YOU WERE ASAHI-KUN'S SENPAIS...
HO HO HO HO HO HO HO
I THOUGHT YOU TWO WERE THIEVES!
HERE, HAVE SOME TEA! ♡
OH, THANK YOU!
...
HOW IS ASAHI-KUN DOING? IS HE GETTING ALONG WELL?
HE'S A BIT AWKWARD, SO I WORRY ABOUT HIM...
HE'S MORE THAN THAT --
HEY!
BUMP
OW!
SPECIA THANKS MAO KU

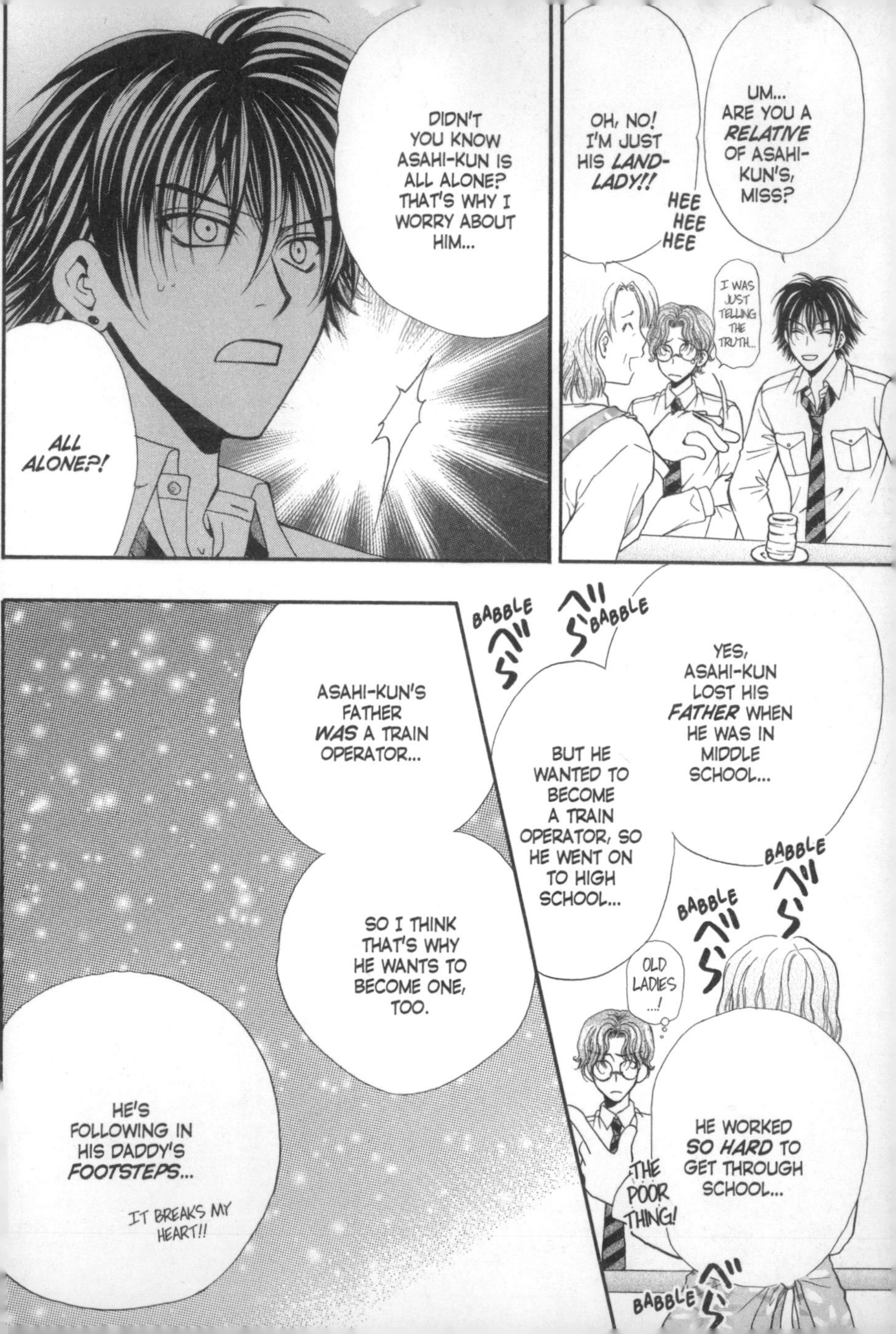
UM... ARE YOU A *RELATIVE* OF ASAHI-KUN'S, MISS?
OH, NO! I'M JUST HIS *LANDLADY!!*
HEE HEE HEE
I WAS JUST TELLING THE TRUTH...
DIDN'T YOU KNOW ASAHI-KUN IS ALL ALONE? THAT'S WHY I WORRY ABOUT HIM...
*ALL ALONE?!*
BABBLE
BABBLE
YES, ASAHI-KUN LOST HIS *FATHER* WHEN HE WAS IN MIDDLE SCHOOL...
BUT HE WANTED TO BECOME A TRAIN OPERATOR, SO HE WENT ON TO HIGH SCHOOL...
BABBLE
BABBLE
OLD LADIES ...!
HE WORKED *SO HARD* TO GET THROUGH SCHOOL...
THE POOR THING!
BABBLE
ASAHI-KUN'S FATHER *WAS* A TRAIN OPERATOR...
SO I THINK THAT'S WHY HE WANTS TO BECOME ONE, TOO.
HE'S FOLLOWING IN HIS DADDY'S *FOOTSTEPS*...
IT BREAKS MY HEART!!

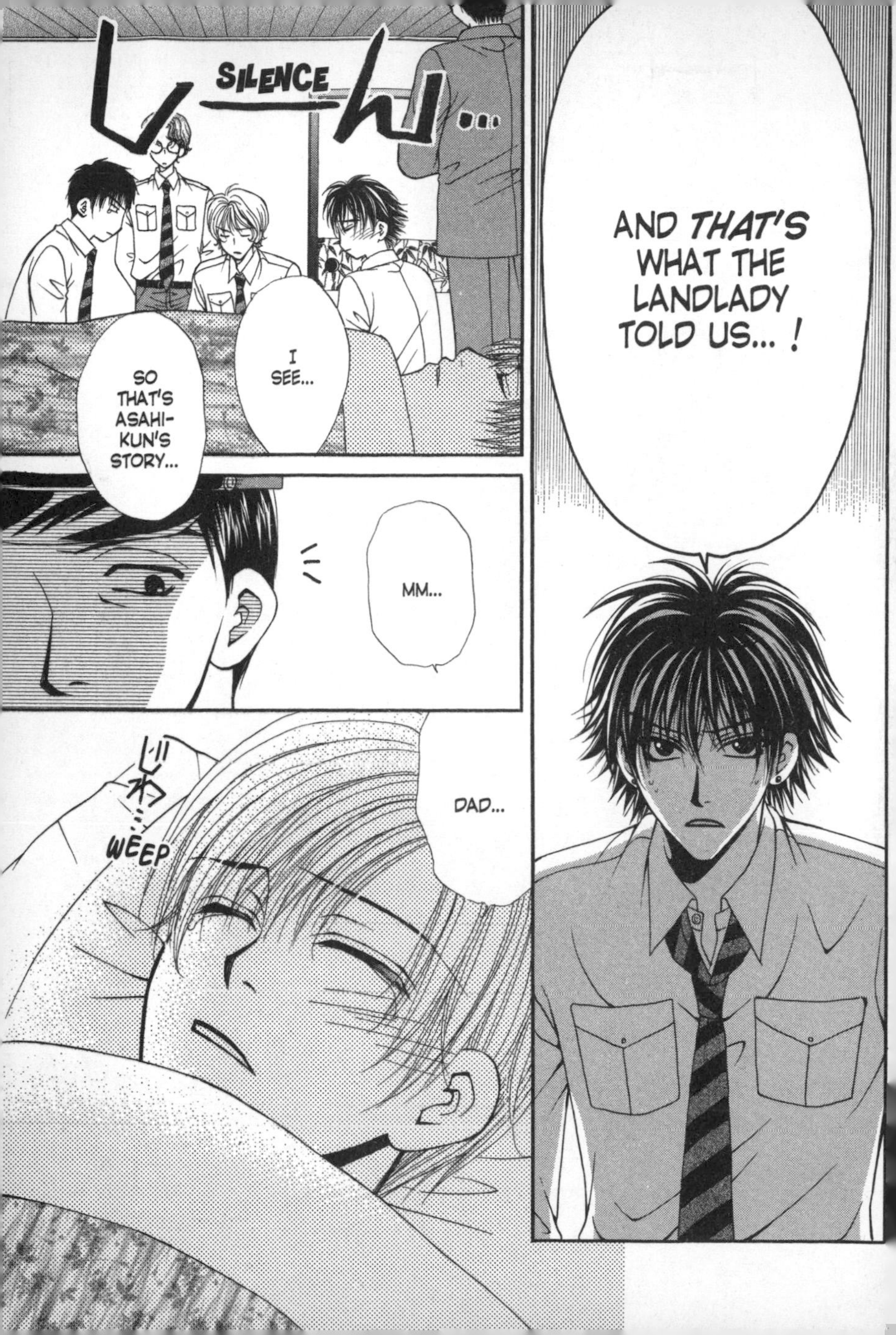

AND *THAT'S* WHAT THE LANDLADY TOLD US...!
SILENCE
I SEE...
SO THAT'S ASAHI-KUN'S STORY...
MM...
DAD...
WEEP

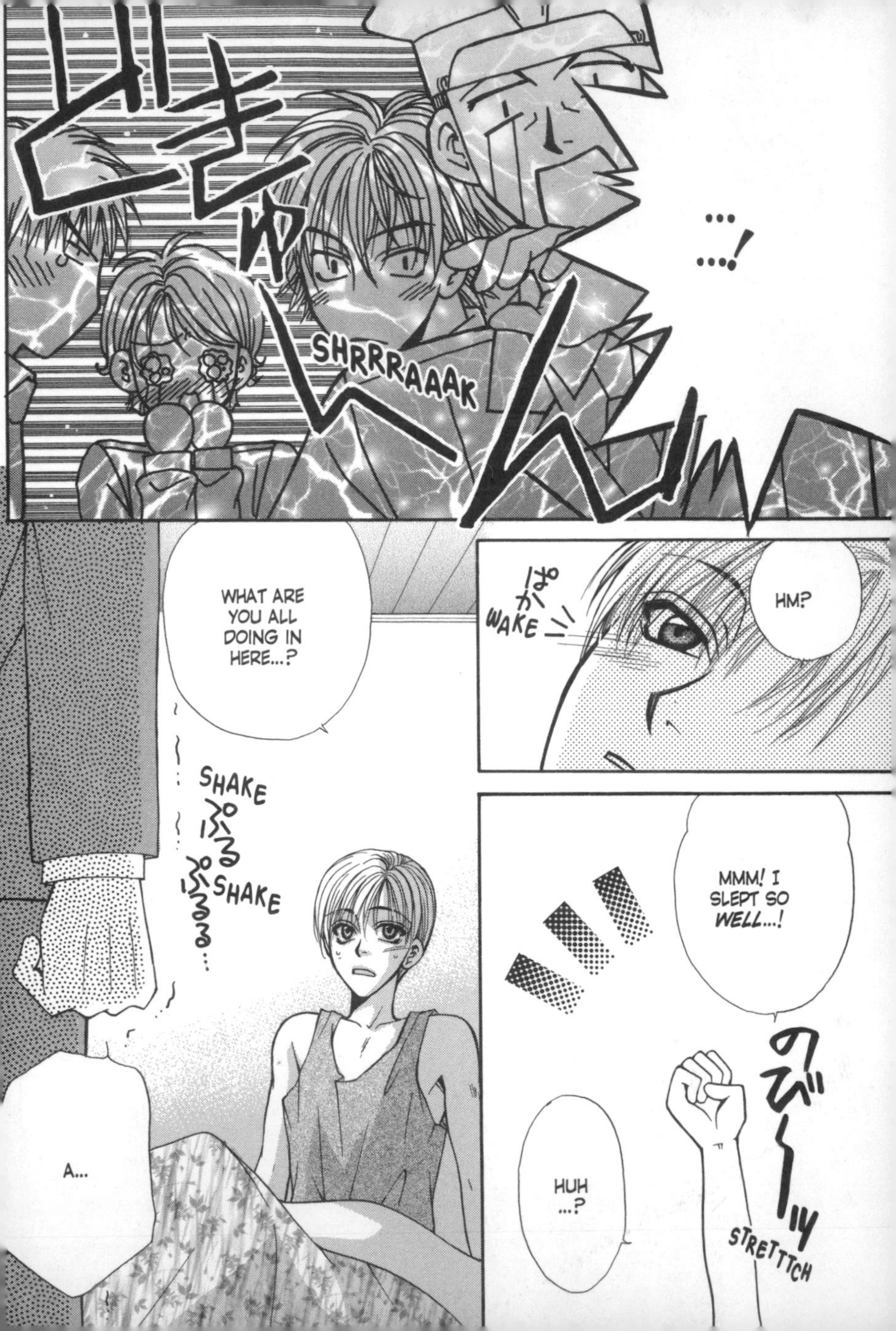
……
……!
SHRRRAAAK
ぱか
WAKE
HM?
WHAT ARE YOU ALL DOING IN HERE...?
MMM! I SLEPT SO WELL...!
のび～～っ
STRETTTCH
HUH ...?
SHAKE
ぷるぷる
SHAKE
A...

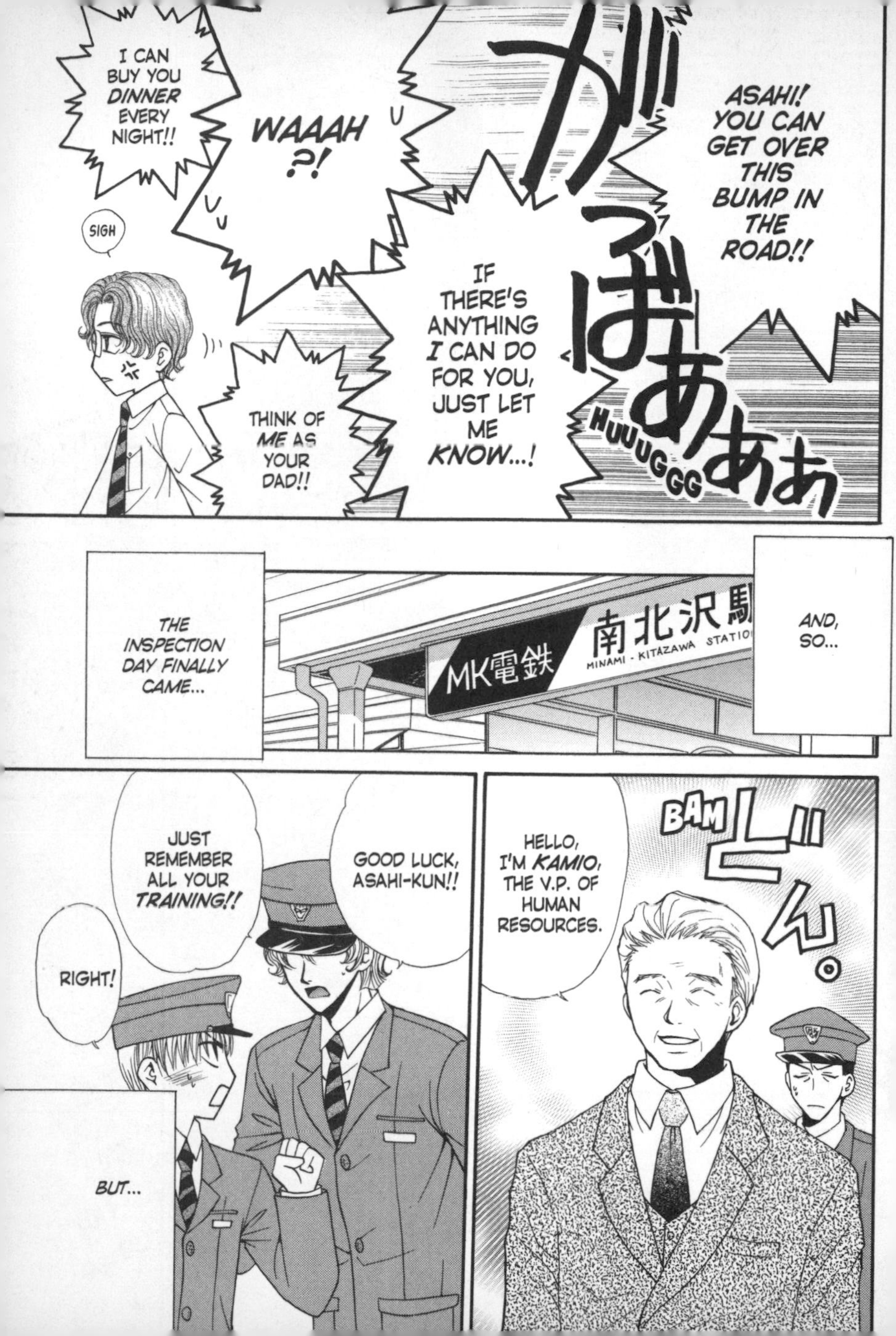
ASAHI! YOU CAN GET OVER THIS BUMP IN THE ROAD!!
がっばあぁぁ
HUUUGGG
IF THERE'S ANYTHING I CAN DO FOR YOU, JUST LET ME KNOW...!
THINK OF ME AS YOUR DAD!!
WAAAH ?!
I CAN BUY YOU DINNER EVERY NIGHT!!
SIGH
AND, SO...
南北沢駅
MINAMI - KITAZAWA STATIO
MK電鉄
THE INSPECTION DAY FINALLY CAME...
BAM
どん。
HELLO, I'M KAMIO, THE V.P. OF HUMAN RESOURCES.
GOOD LUCK, ASAHI-KUN!!
JUST REMEMBER ALL YOUR TRAINING!!
RIGHT!
BUT...

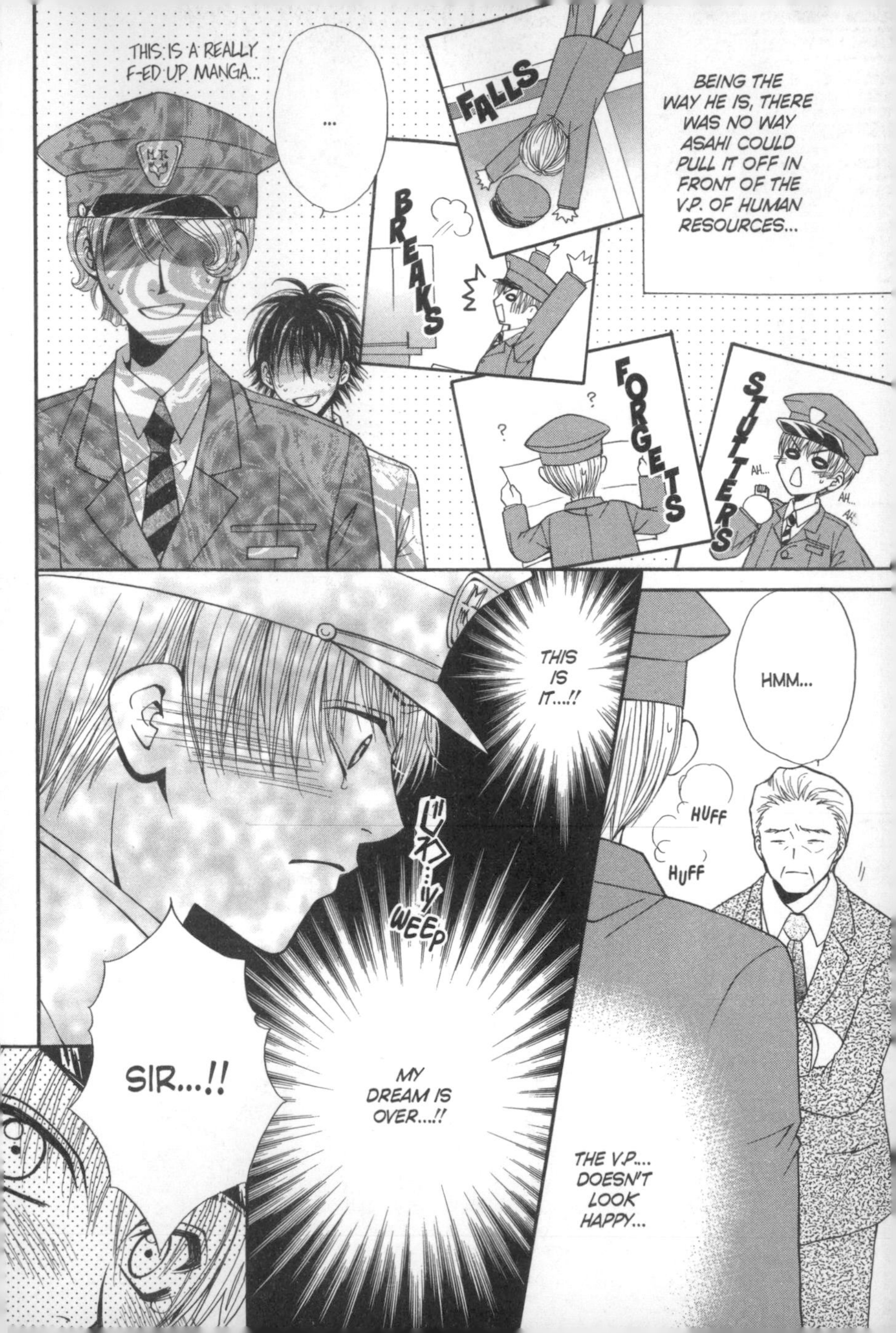
BEING THE WAY HE IS, THERE WAS NO WAY ASAHI COULD PULL IT OFF IN FRONT OF THE V.P. OF HUMAN RESOURCES...
FALLS
BREAKS
STUTTERS
AH...
AH...
AH...
FORGETS
?
?
...
THIS IS A REALLY F-ED UP MANGA...
HMM...
HUFF
HUFF
THE V.P.... DOESN'T LOOK HAPPY...
THIS IS IT...!!
WEEP
MY DREAM IS OVER...!!
SIR...!!

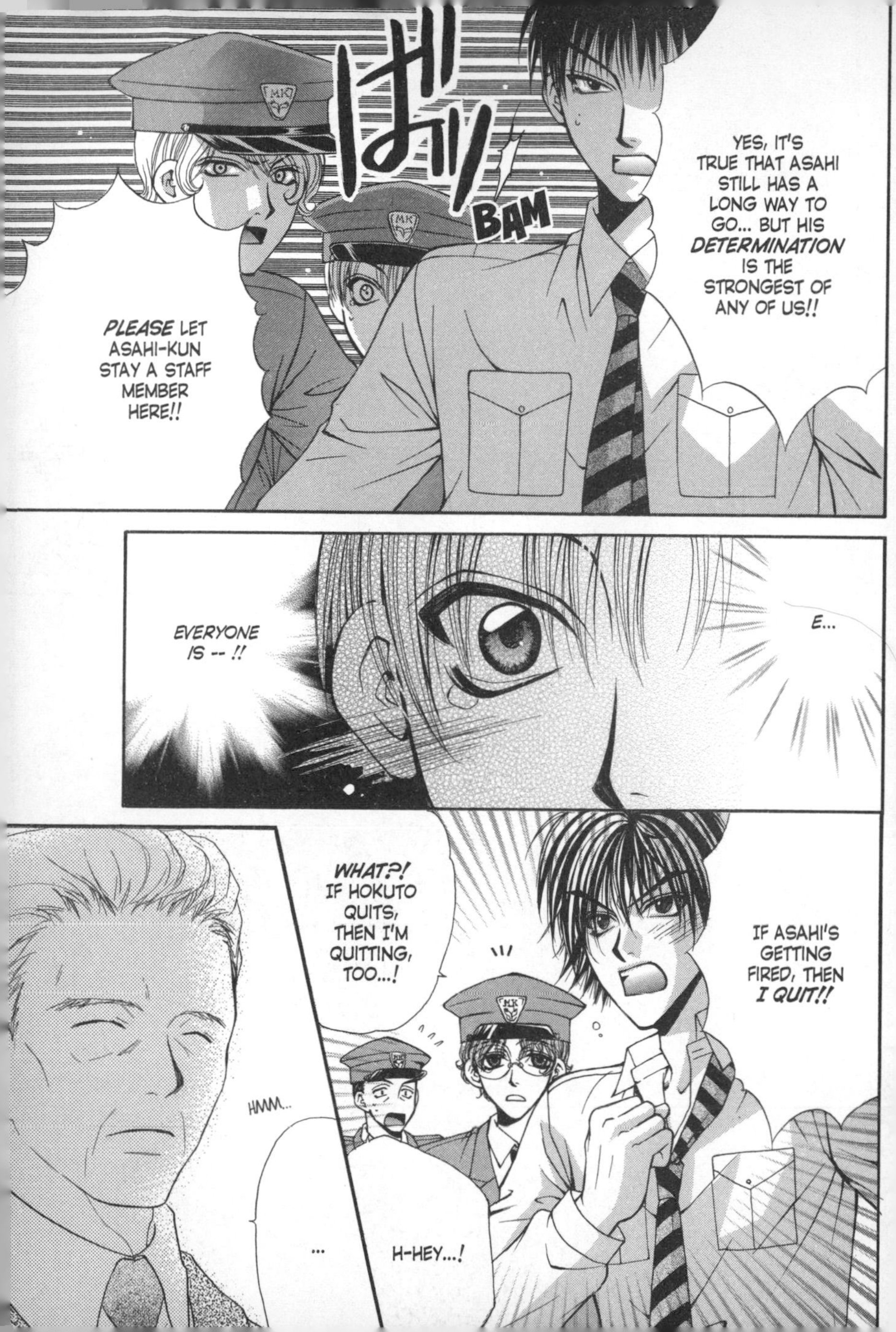
ばん
BAM
YES, IT'S TRUE THAT ASAHI STILL HAS A LONG WAY TO GO... BUT HIS *DETERMINATION* IS THE STRONGEST OF ANY OF US!!
*PLEASE* LET ASAHI-KUN STAY A STAFF MEMBER HERE!!
E...
*EVERYONE IS -- !!*
IF ASAHI'S GETTING FIRED, THEN *I QUIT!!*
*WHAT?!* IF HOKUTO QUITS, THEN I'M QUITTING, TOO...!
H-HEY...!
HMM...
...

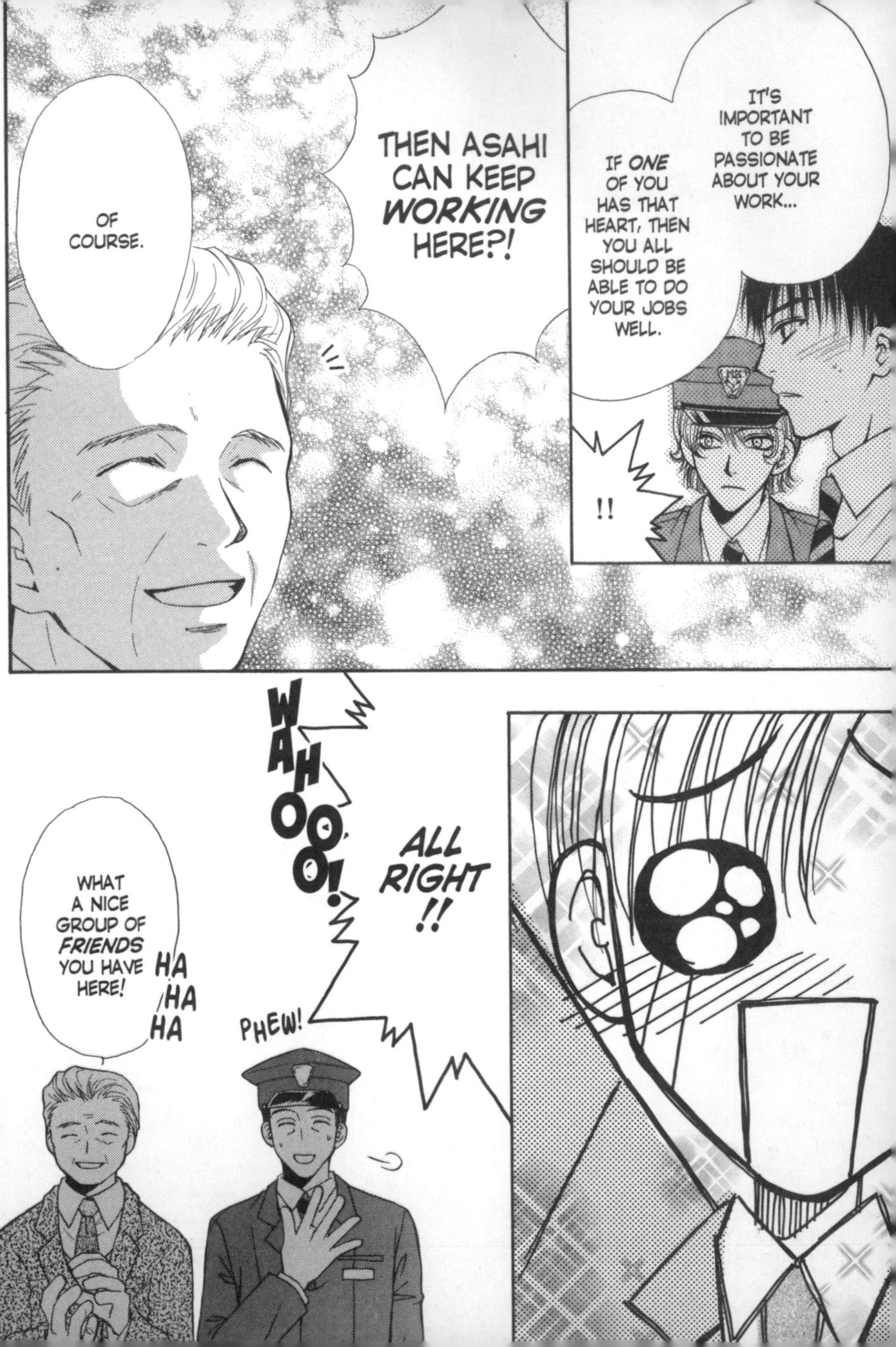
IT'S IMPORTANT TO BE PASSIONATE ABOUT YOUR WORK...
IF *ONE* OF YOU HAS THAT HEART, THEN YOU ALL SHOULD BE ABLE TO DO YOUR JOBS WELL.
!!
THEN ASAHI CAN KEEP *WORKING* HERE?!
OF COURSE.
WAHOOO!
ALL RIGHT!!
PHEW!
WHAT A NICE GROUP OF *FRIENDS* YOU HAVE HERE!
HA HA HA

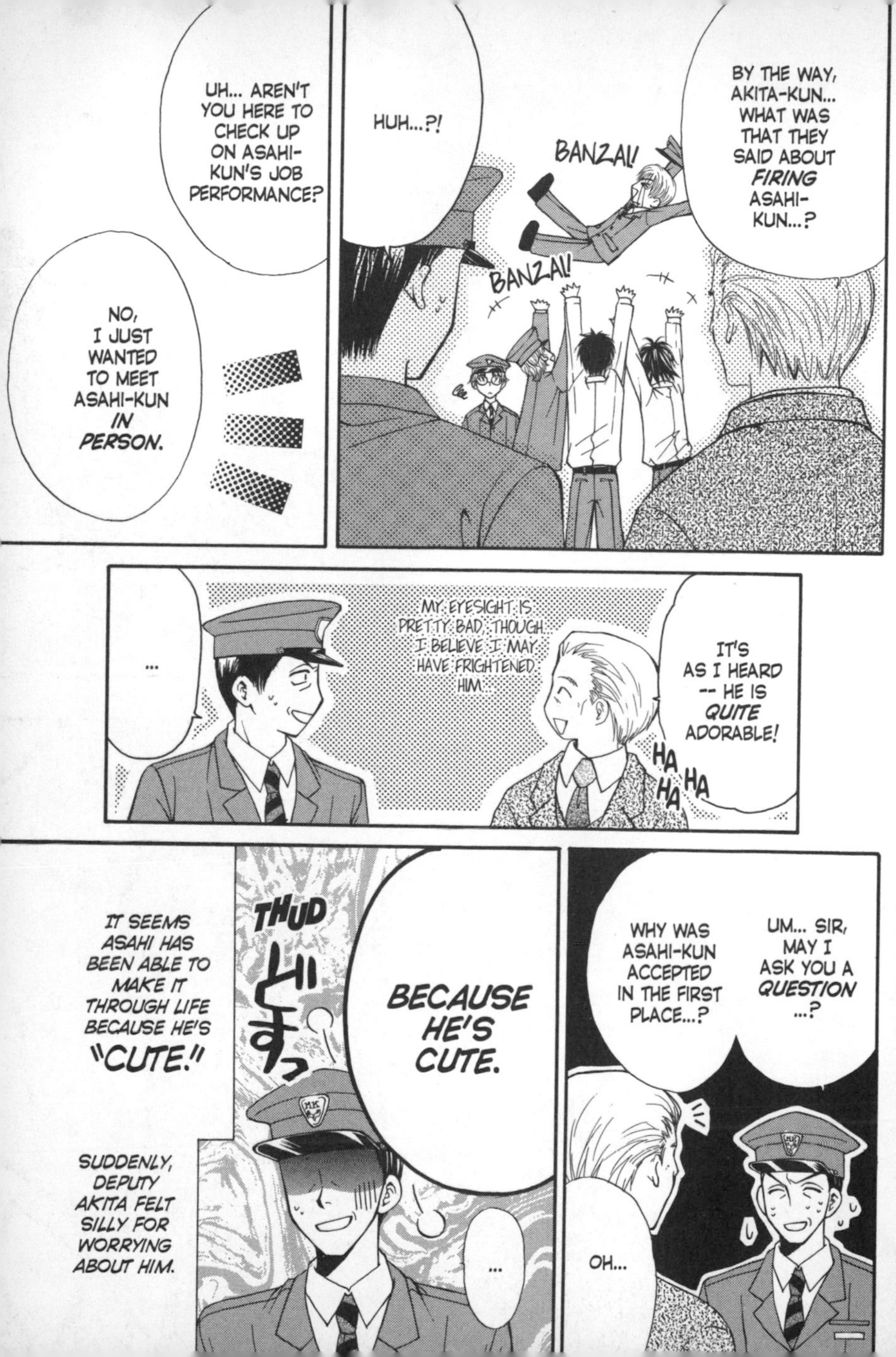
BY THE WAY, AKITA-KUN... WHAT WAS THAT THEY SAID ABOUT FIRING ASAHI-KUN...?
BANZAI!
HUH...?!
BANZAI!
UH... AREN'T YOU HERE TO CHECK UP ON ASAHI-KUN'S JOB PERFORMANCE?
NO, I JUST WANTED TO MEET ASAHI-KUN IN PERSON.
IT'S AS I HEARD -- HE IS QUITE ADORABLE!
HA HA HA
MY EYESIGHT IS PRETTY BAD, THOUGH. I BELIEVE I MAY HAVE FRIGHTENED HIM.
...
UM... SIR, MAY I ASK YOU A QUESTION ...?
WHY WAS ASAHI-KUN ACCEPTED IN THE FIRST PLACE...?
OH...
BECAUSE HE'S CUTE.
THUD
どすっ
...
IT SEEMS ASAHI HAS BEEN ABLE TO MAKE IT THROUGH LIFE BECAUSE HE'S "CUTE."
SUDDENLY, DEPUTY AKITA FELT SILLY FOR WORRYING ABOUT HIM.

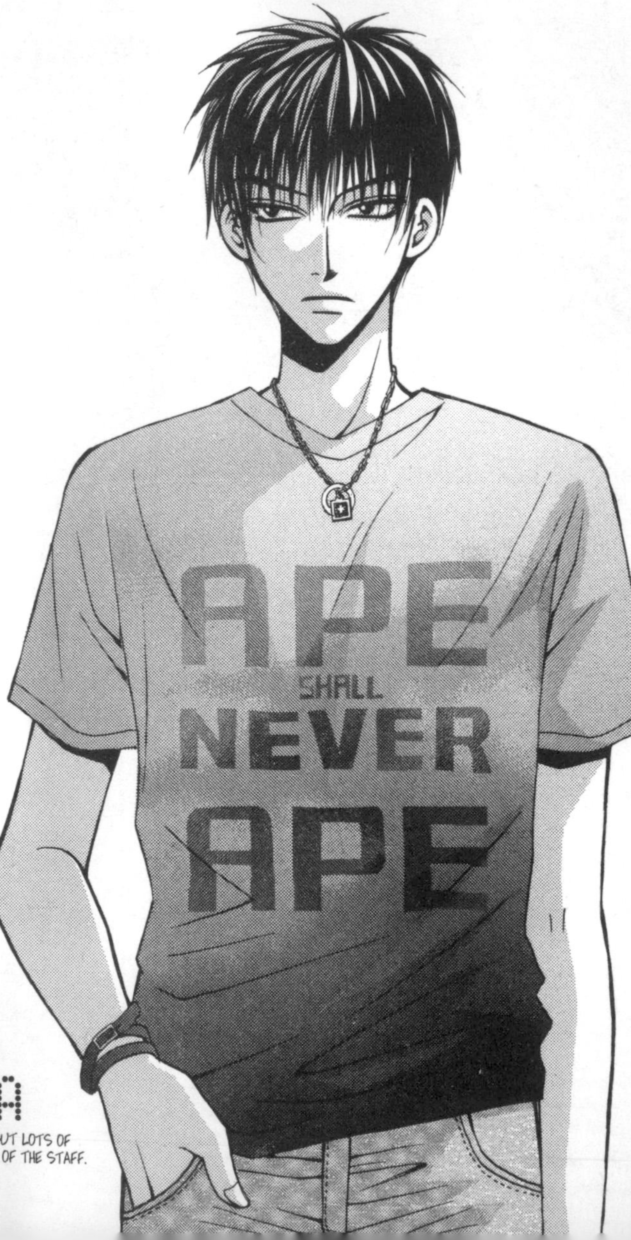
APE
SHALL
NEVER
APE

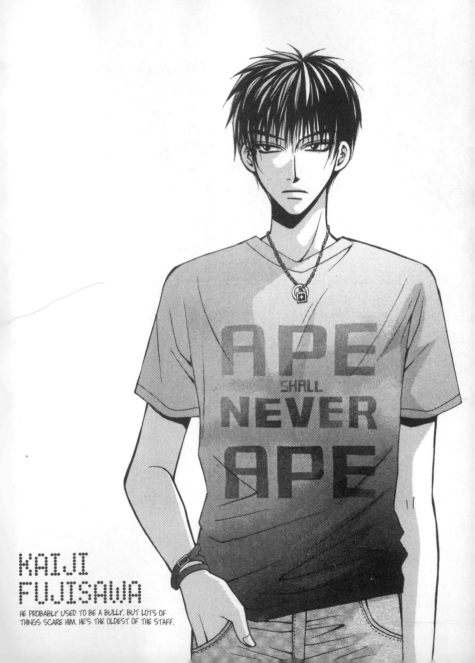

KAIJI FUJISAWA

HE PROBABLY USED TO BE A BULLY, BUT LOTS OF THINGS SCARE HIM. HE'S THE OLDEST OF THE STAFF.

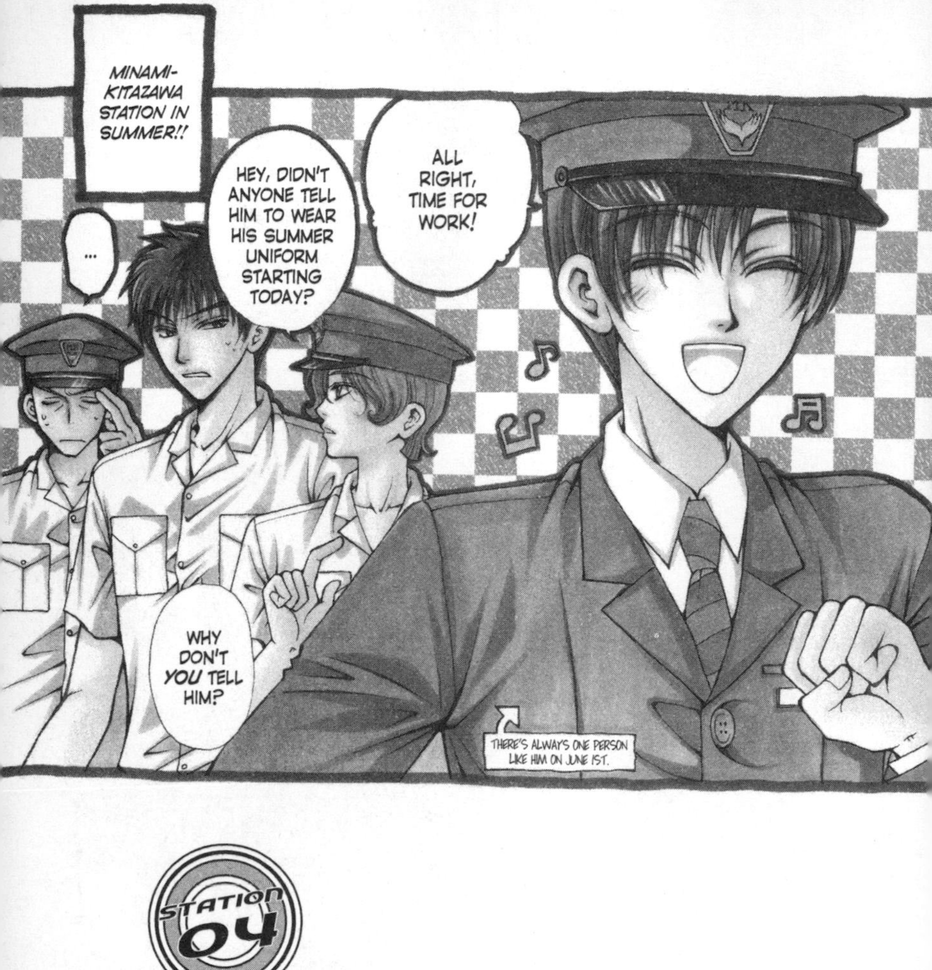
MINAMI-KITAZAWA STATION IN SUMMER!!
ALL RIGHT, TIME FOR WORK!
HEY, DIDN'T ANYONE TELL HIM TO WEAR HIS SUMMER UNIFORM STARTING TODAY?
...
WHY DON'T *YOU* TELL HIM?
THERE'S ALWAYS ONE PERSON LIKE HIM ON JUNE 1ST.

# STATION 04

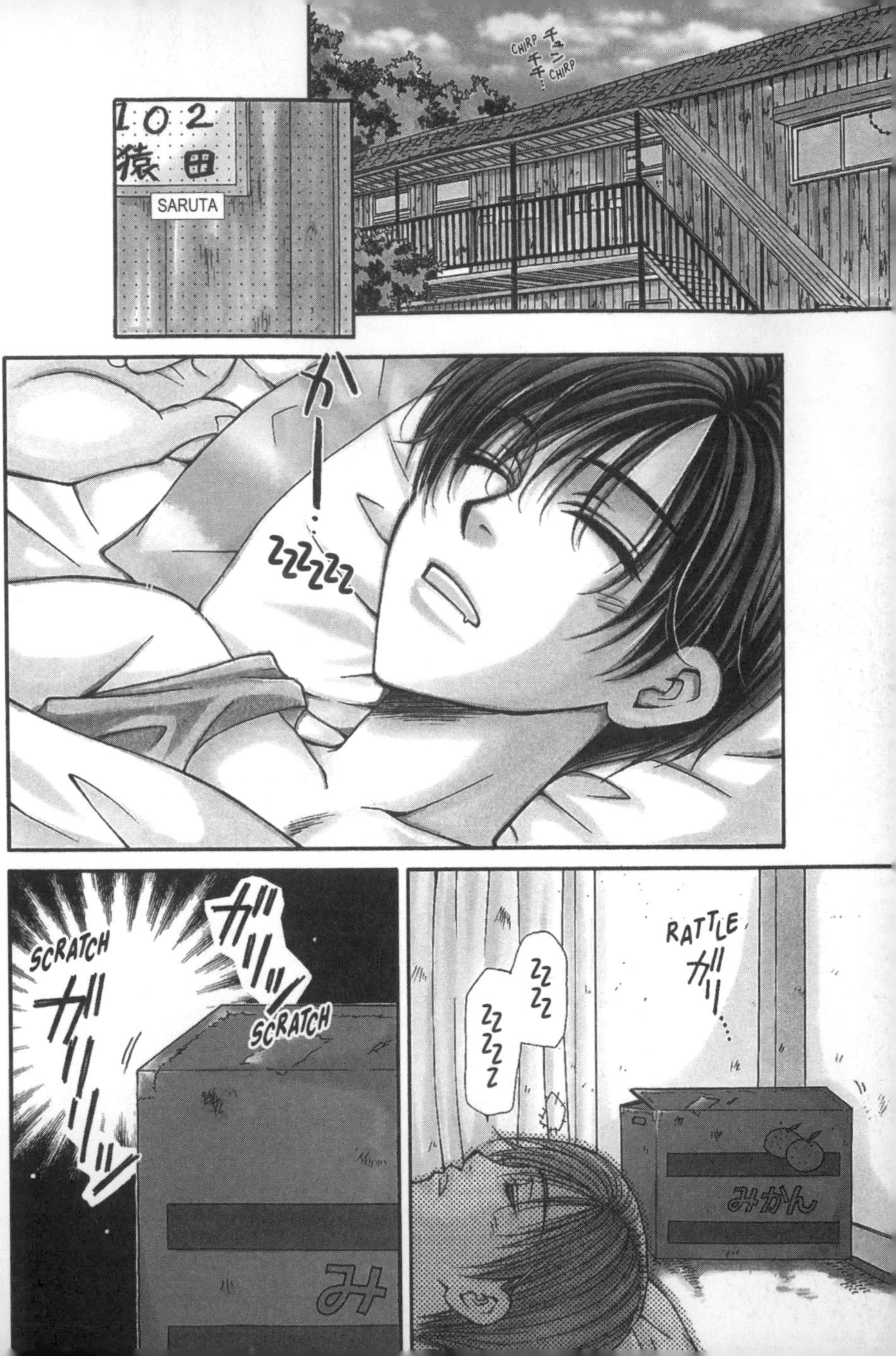
CHIRP チュン
CHIRP チチ…
102
猿田
SARUTA
がー…!
ZZZZZZ
RATTLE
ガリ…
ZZZ
ZZZZ
みかん
ガリッ
SCRATCH
SCRATCH
ガリリリッ
み

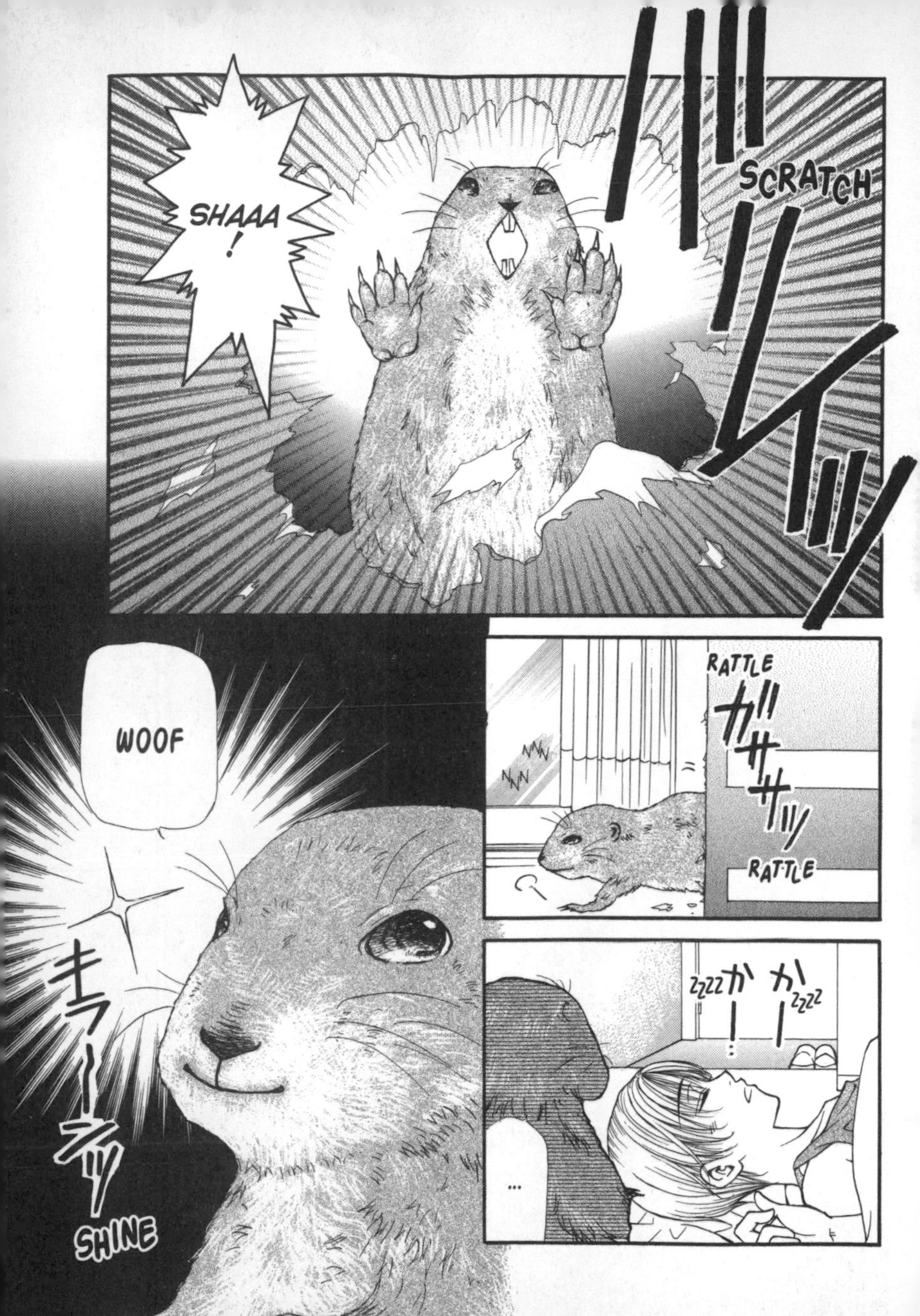
SCRATCH
SHAAA!
RATTLE
ガサササッ
RATTLE
かー
ZZZZ
かー!!
ZZZZ
...
WOOF
キラーンッ
SHINE

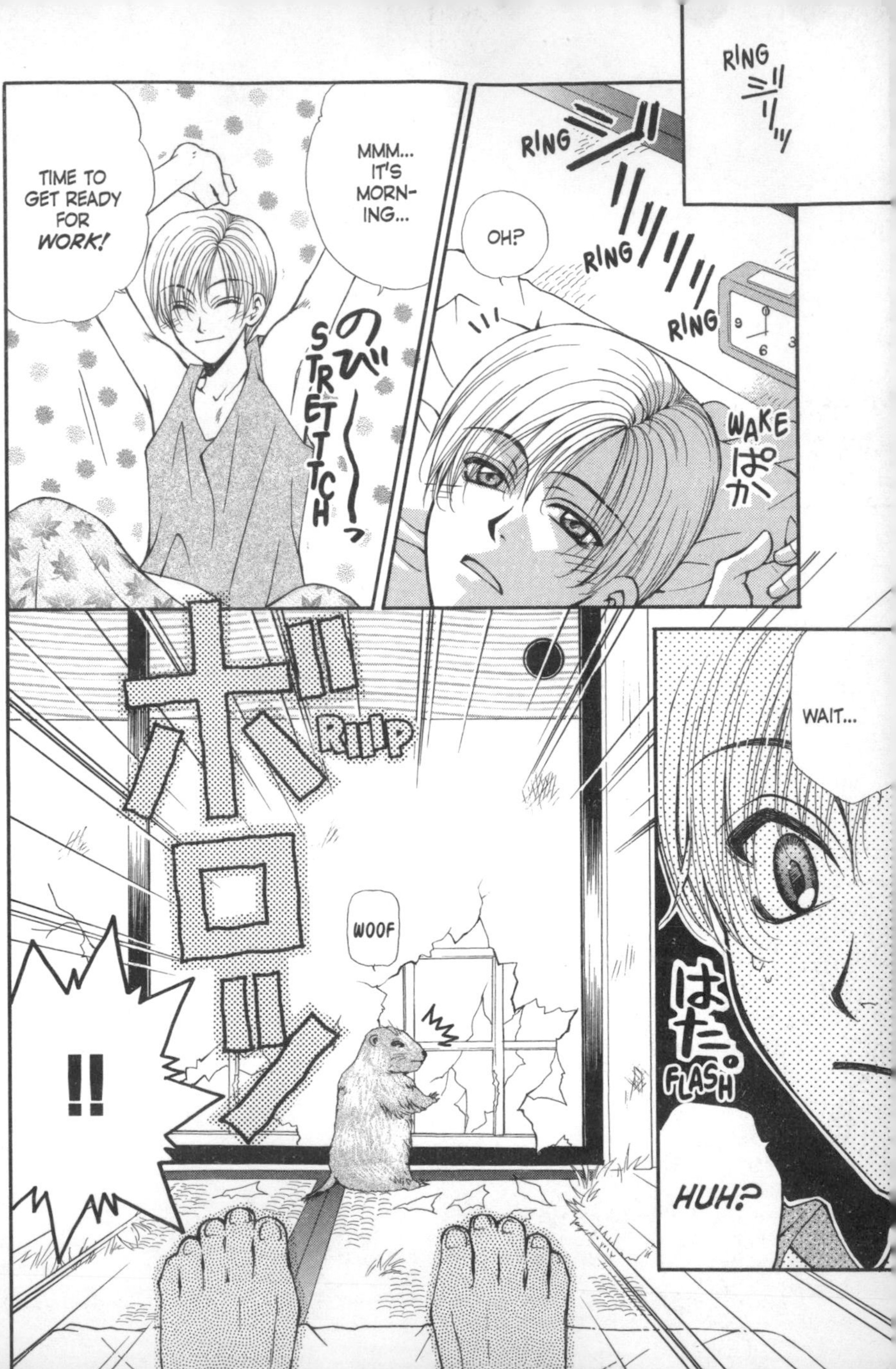
RING
ジリッ
RING
RING
RING
RING
OH?
WAKE
ぱか
MMM... IT'S MORNING...
TIME TO GET READY FOR WORK!
のびーっ
STRETTTCH
WAIT...
はた。
FLASH
HUH?
ボロッ
RIIIP
WOOF
!!

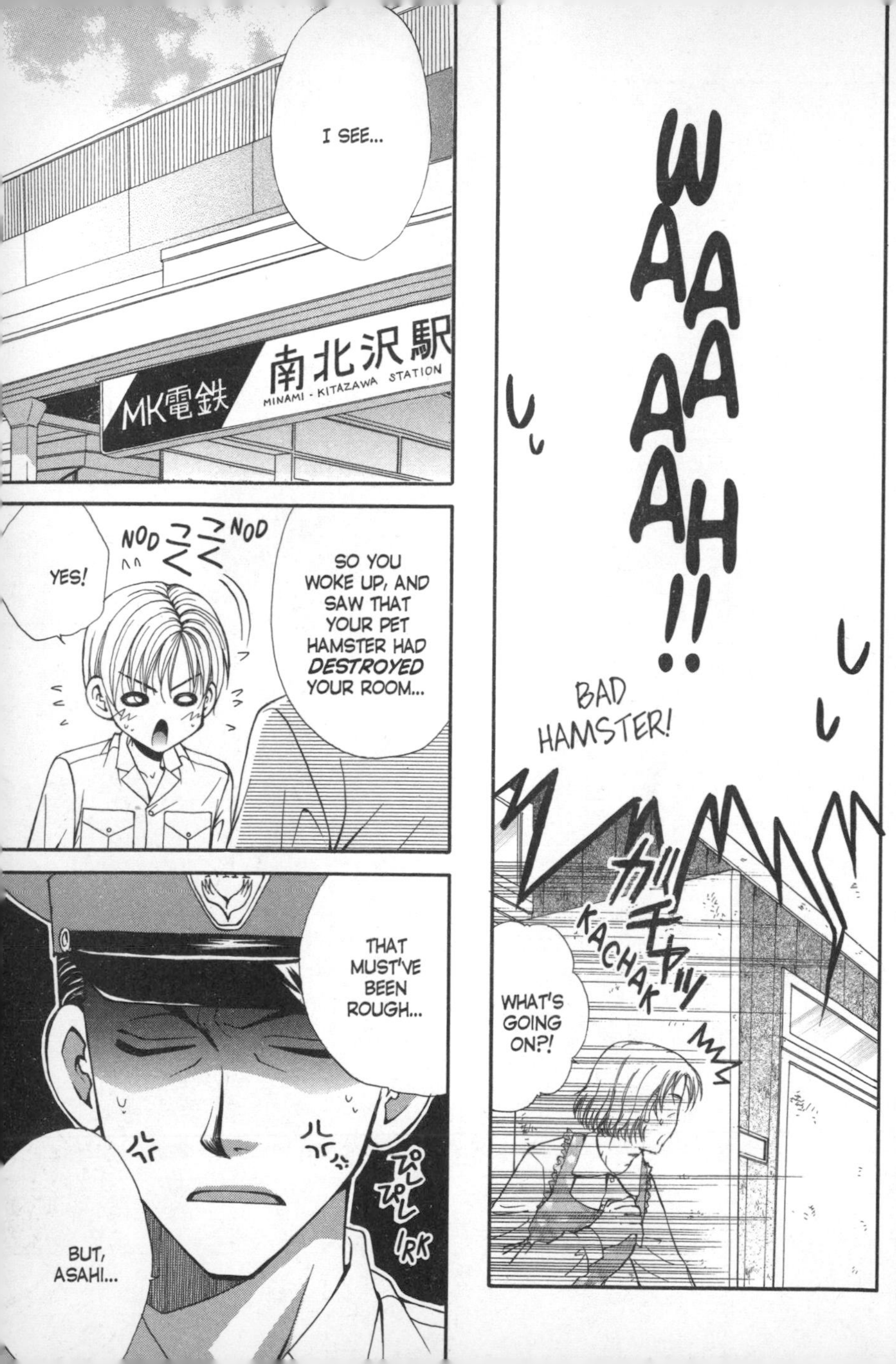
WAAAAAH!!
BAD HAMSTER!
KACHAK
WHAT'S GOING ON?!
南北沢駅
MINAMI - KITAZAWA STATION
MK電鉄
I SEE...
SO YOU WOKE UP, AND SAW THAT YOUR PET HAMSTER HAD *DESTROYED* YOUR ROOM...
NOD NOD
YES!
THAT MUST'VE BEEN ROUGH...
IRK
BUT, ASAHI...

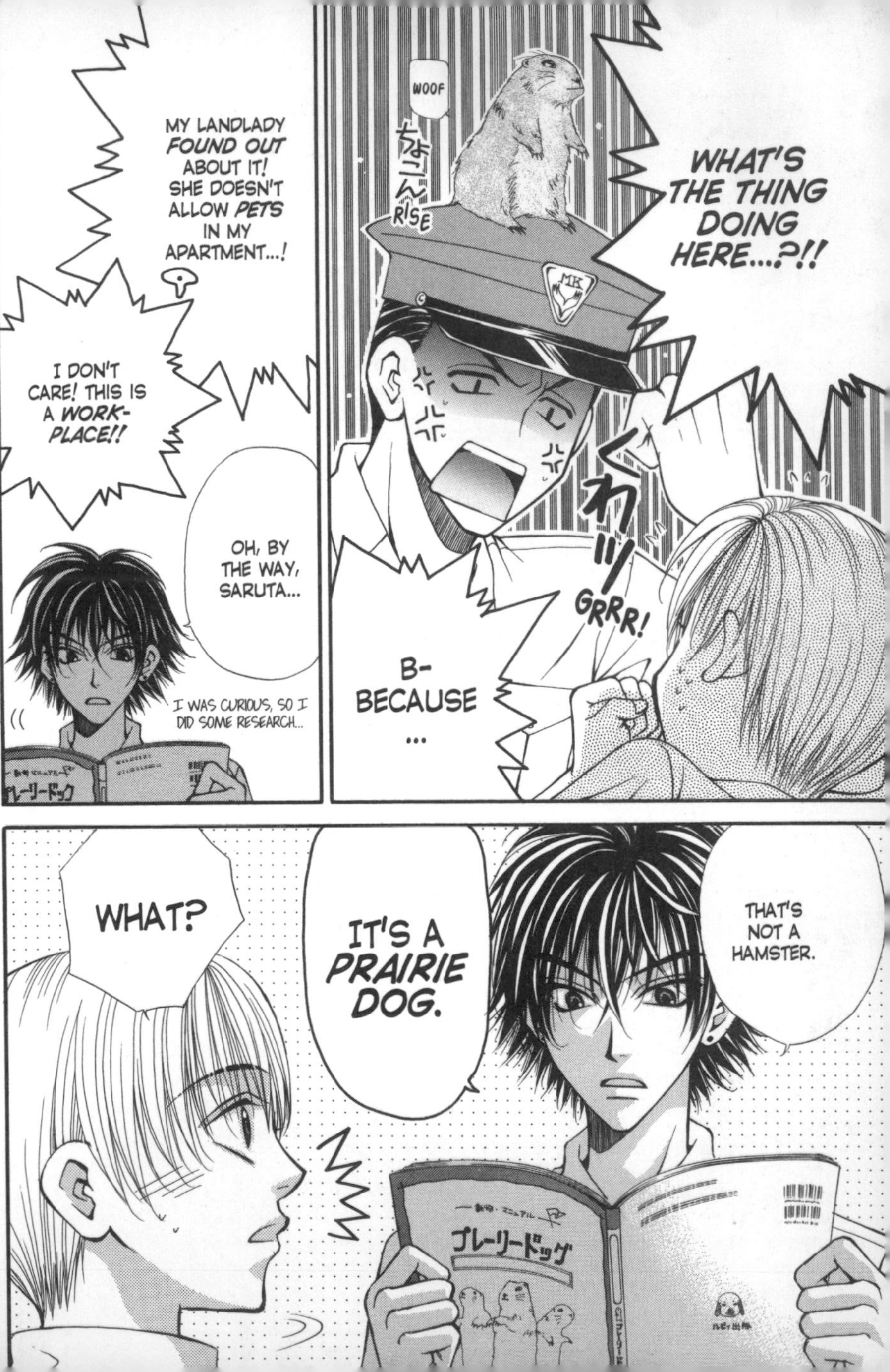
WHAT'S THE THING DOING HERE...?!!
WOOF
ちょこん RISE
くわッ GRRR!
B-BECAUSE ...
MY LANDLADY FOUND OUT ABOUT IT! SHE DOESN'T ALLOW PETS IN MY APARTMENT...!
I DON'T CARE! THIS IS A WORK-PLACE!!
OH, BY THE WAY, SARUTA...
I WAS CURIOUS, SO I DID SOME RESEARCH...
THAT'S NOT A HAMSTER.
IT'S A PRAIRIE DOG.
WHAT?
プレーリードッグ

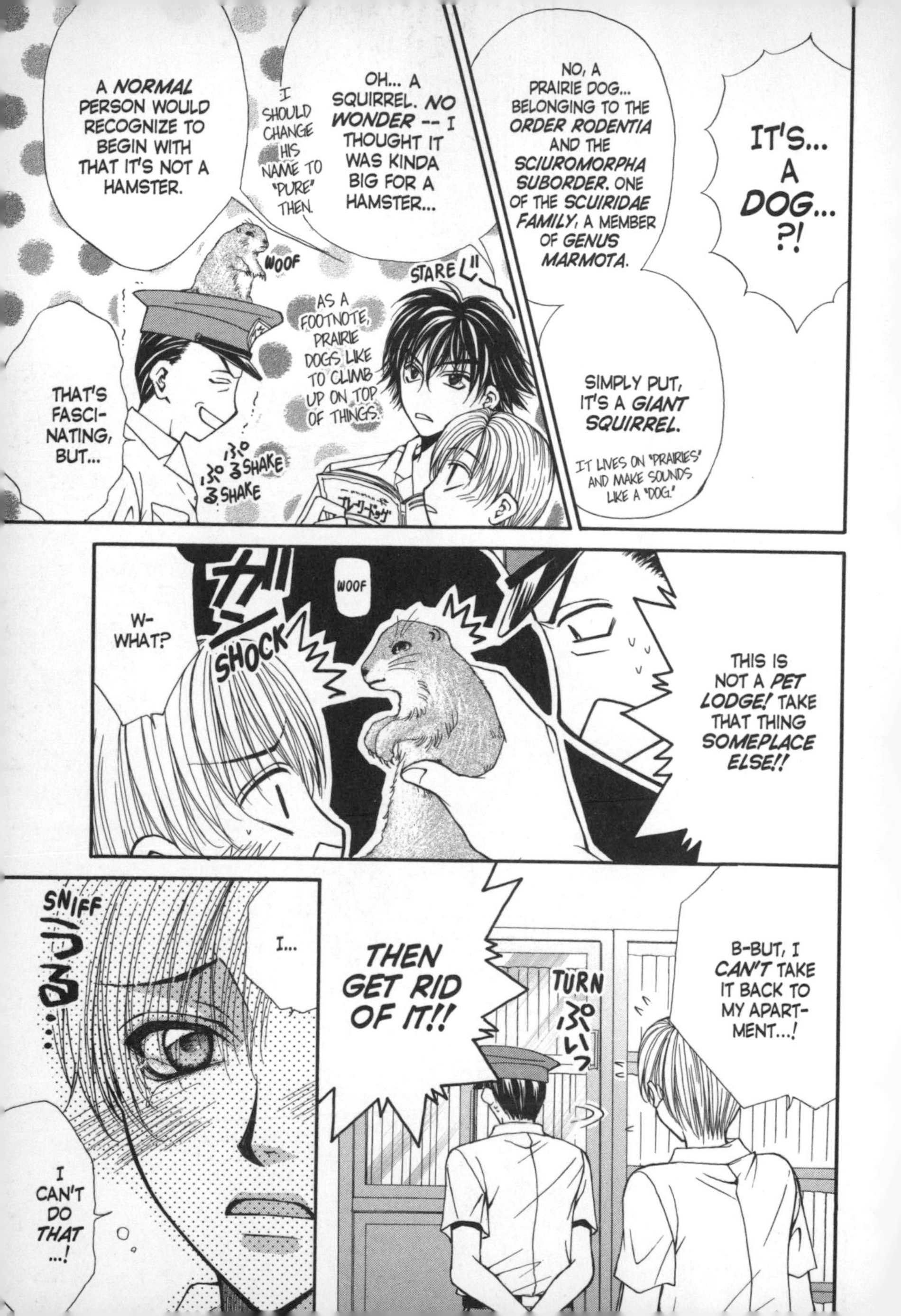
IT'S... A DOG...?!
NO, A PRAIRIE DOG... BELONGING TO THE ORDER RODENTIA AND THE SCIUROMORPHA SUBORDER. ONE OF THE SCUIRIDAE FAMILY, A MEMBER OF GENUS MARMOTA.
SIMPLY PUT, IT'S A GIANT SQUIRREL.
IT LIVES ON "PRAIRIES" AND MAKE SOUNDS LIKE A "DOG."
OH... A SQUIRREL. NO WONDER -- I THOUGHT IT WAS KINDA BIG FOR A HAMSTER...
I SHOULD CHANGE HIS NAME TO "PURE" THEN.
A NORMAL PERSON WOULD RECOGNIZE TO BEGIN WITH THAT IT'S NOT A HAMSTER.
STARE
WOOF
AS A FOOTNOTE, PRAIRIE DOGS LIKE TO CLIMB UP ON TOP OF THINGS.
THAT'S FASCINATING, BUT...
SHAKE SHAKE
THIS IS NOT A PET LODGE! TAKE THAT THING SOMEPLACE ELSE!!
WOOF
SHOCK
W-WHAT?
B-BUT, I CAN'T TAKE IT BACK TO MY APARTMENT...!
TURN
THEN GET RID OF IT!!
I...
SNIFF
I CAN'T DO THAT...!

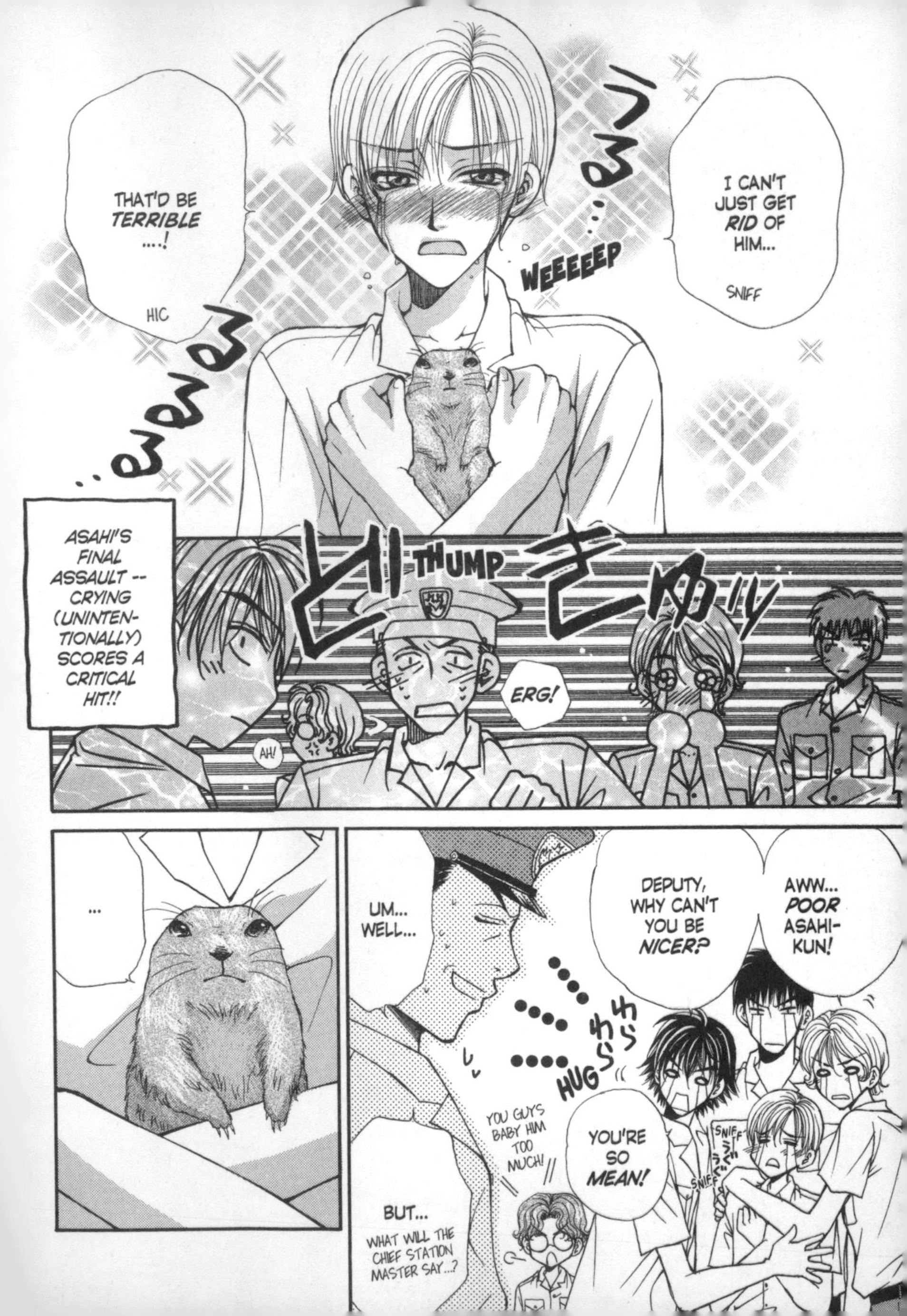
I CAN'T JUST GET RID OF HIM...
SNIFF
WEEEEEP
THAT'D BE TERRIBLE ....!
HIC
THUMP
ERG!
AH!
ASAHI'S FINAL ASSAULT -- CRYING (UNINTENTIONALLY) SCORES A CRITICAL HIT!!
AWW... POOR ASAHI-KUN!
DEPUTY, WHY CAN'T YOU BE NICER?
UM... WELL...
HUG
YOU'RE SO MEAN!
SNIFF
SNIFF
YOU GUYS BABY HIM TOO MUCH!
BUT... WHAT WILL THE CHIEF STATION MASTER SAY...?
...

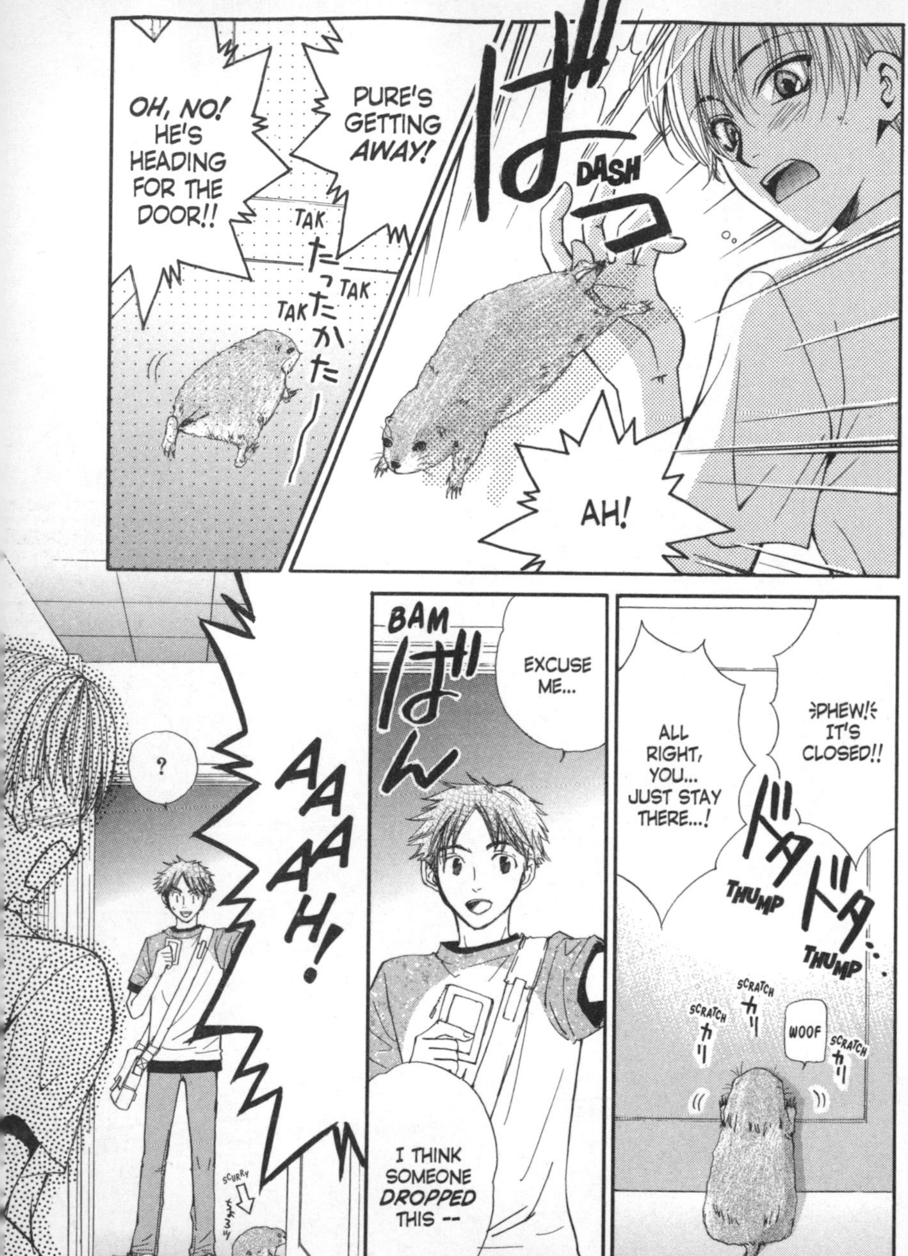
ばっ
DASH
AH!
PURE'S GETTING AWAY!
OH, NO! HE'S HEADING FOR THE DOOR!!
TAK
TAK
TAK
たったかたー
PHEW! IT'S CLOSED!!
ALL RIGHT, YOU... JUST STAY THERE...!
ドタドタ
THUMP
THUMP
SCRATCH
カリ
SCRATCH
カリ
WOOF
SCRATCH
カリ
BAM
ばばん
EXCUSE ME...
I THINK SOMEONE DROPPED THIS --
AAAAAH!
?
SCURRY

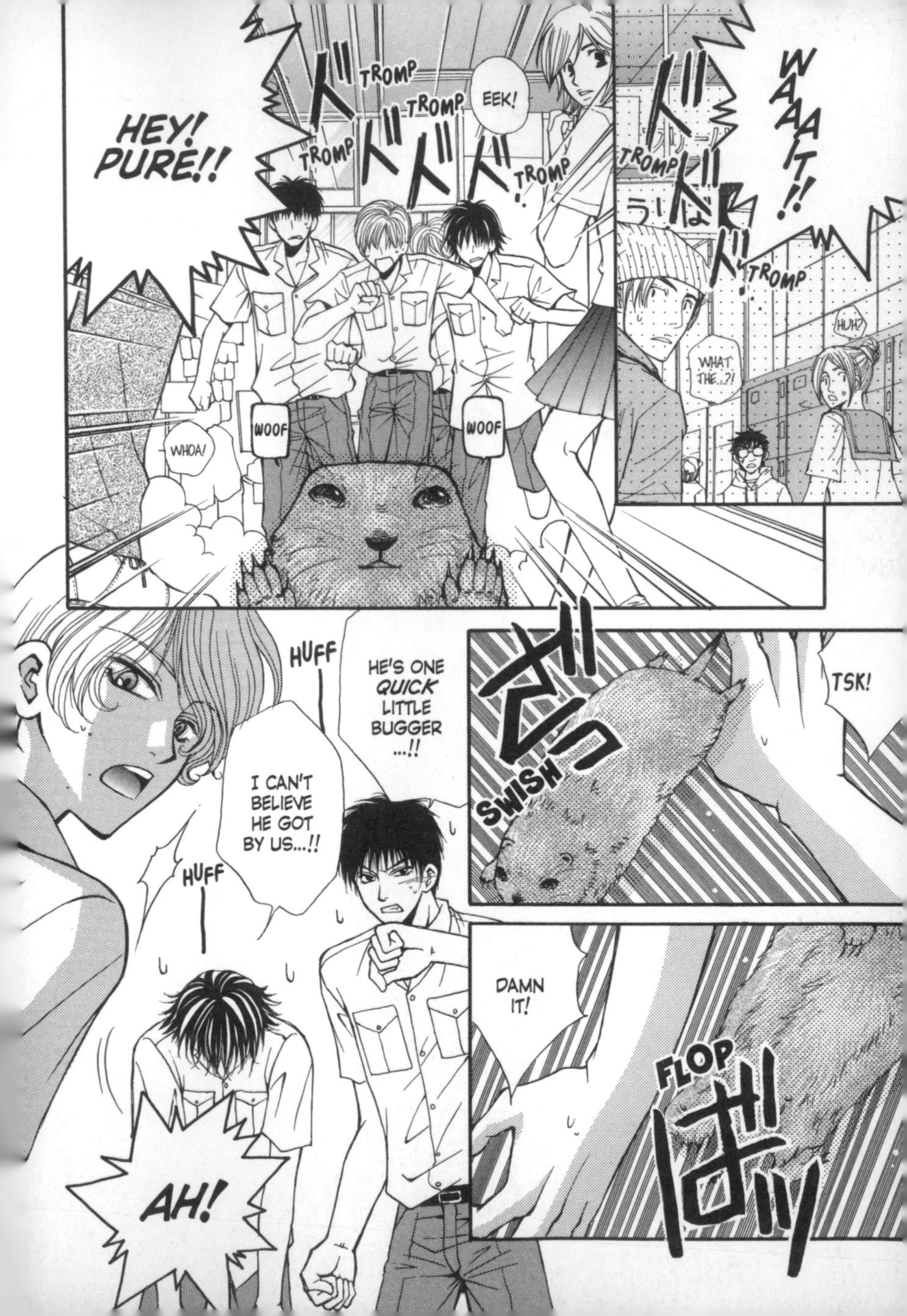

WAAAIT!!
TROMP
TROMP
HUH?
WHAT THE...?!
HEY! PURE!!
TROMP
TROMP
TROMP
EEK!
TROMP
WOOF
WOOF
WHOA!
TSK!
SWISH
DAMN IT!
FLOP
HUFF
HE'S ONE QUICK LITTLE BUGGER...!!
I CAN'T BELIEVE HE GOT BY US...!!
HUFF
AH!

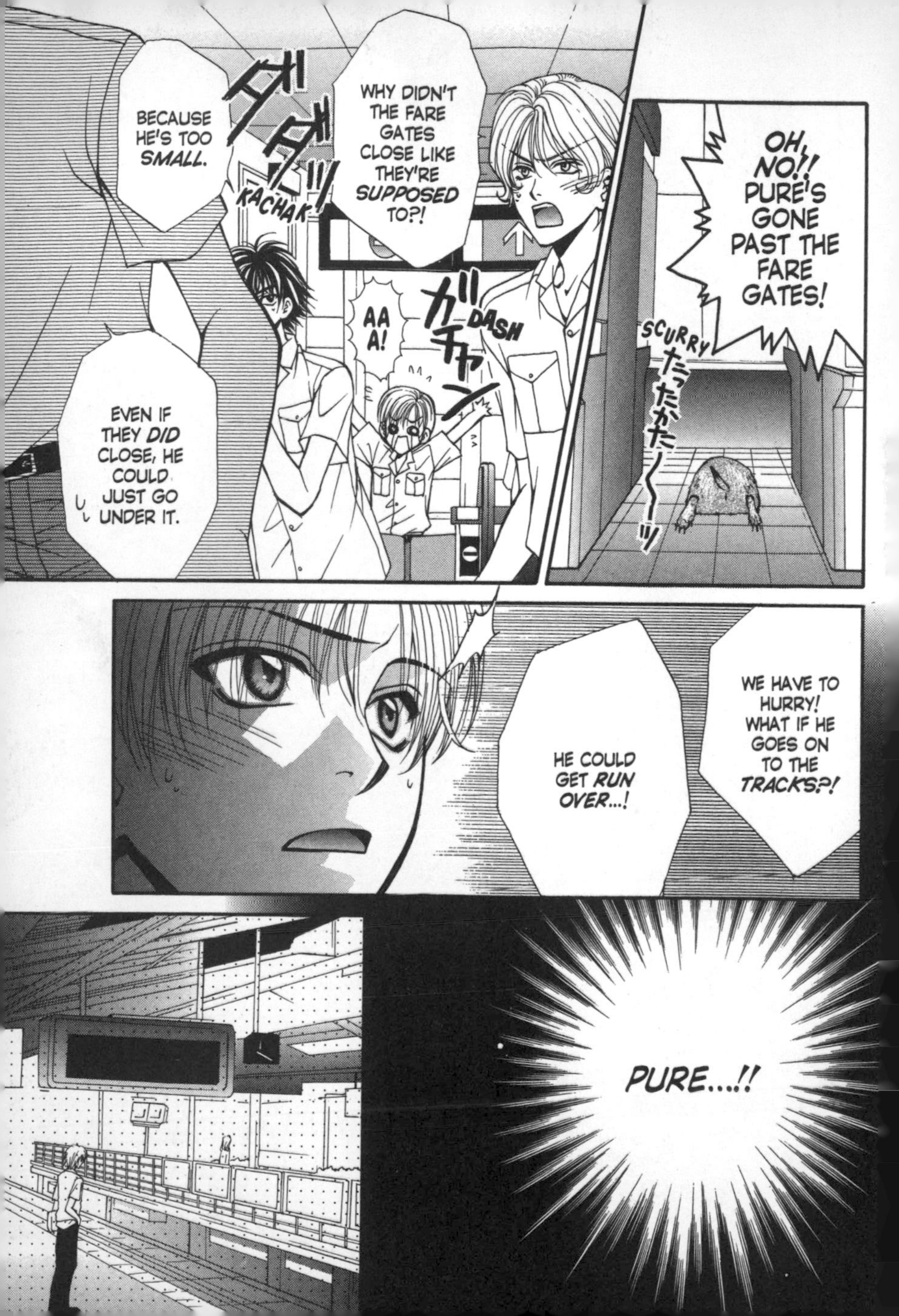
OH, NO!! PURE'S GONE PAST THE FARE GATES!
SCURRY
たったかた～～ッ
WHY DIDN'T THE FARE GATES CLOSE LIKE THEY'RE SUPPOSED TO?!
BECAUSE HE'S TOO SMALL.
ダダッ
KACHAK
DASH
ガチャン
AA A!
EVEN IF THEY DID CLOSE, HE COULD JUST GO UNDER IT.
WE HAVE TO HURRY! WHAT IF HE GOES ON TO THE TRACKS?!
HE COULD GET RUN OVER...!
PURE...!!

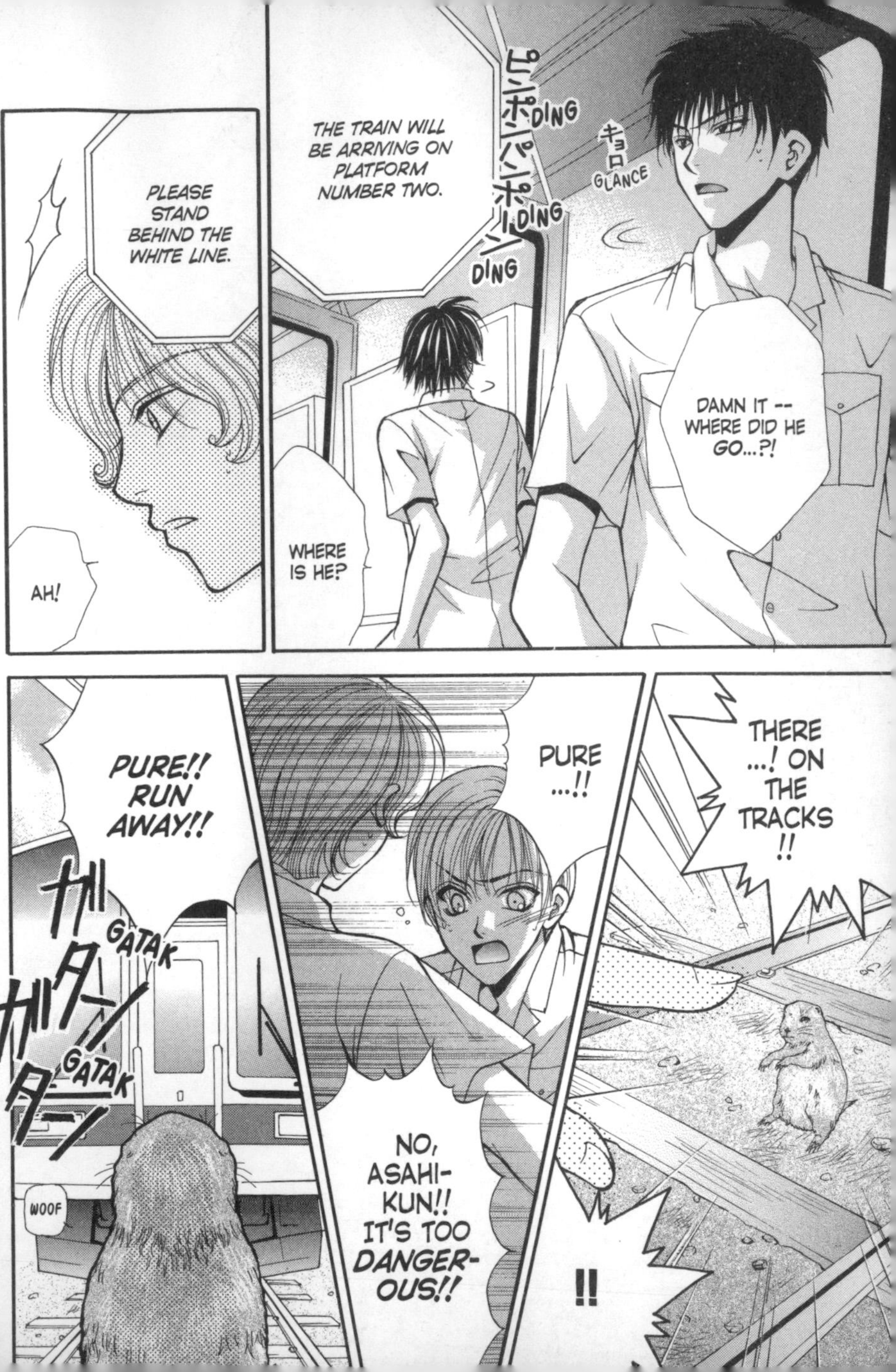
キョロ
GLANCE
ピンポンパンポーン
DING
DING
DING
THE TRAIN WILL BE ARRIVING ON PLATFORM NUMBER TWO.
DAMN IT -- WHERE DID HE GO...?!
WHERE IS HE?
PLEASE STAND BEHIND THE WHITE LINE.
AH!
THERE ...! ON THE TRACKS !!
!!
PURE ...!!
NO, ASAHI-KUN!! IT'S TOO DANGER-OUS!!
PURE!! RUN AWAY!!
GATAK
GATAK
WOOF

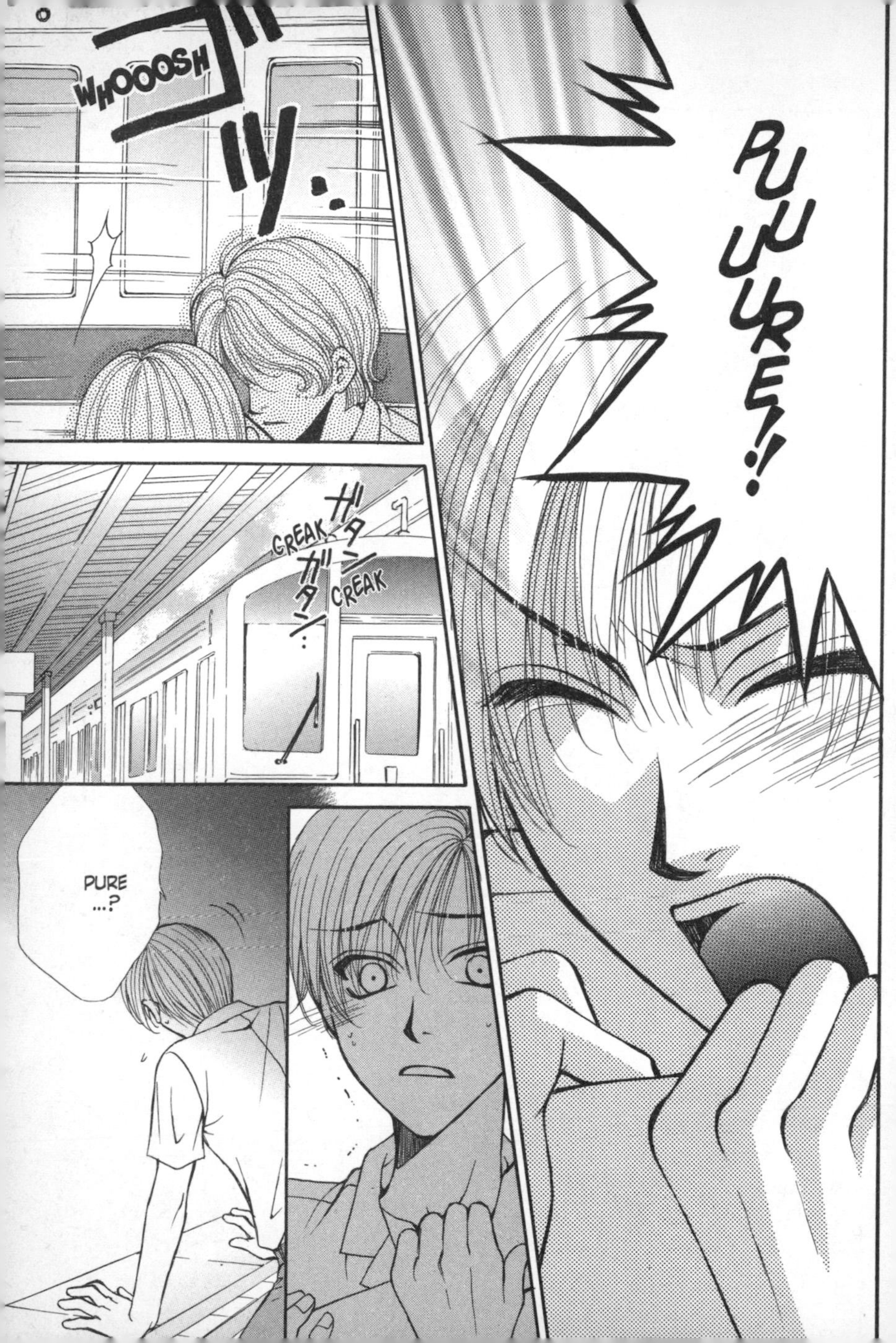
PUUUURE!!
WHOOOSH
CREAK
ガタン
ガタン
CREAK
PURE ...?

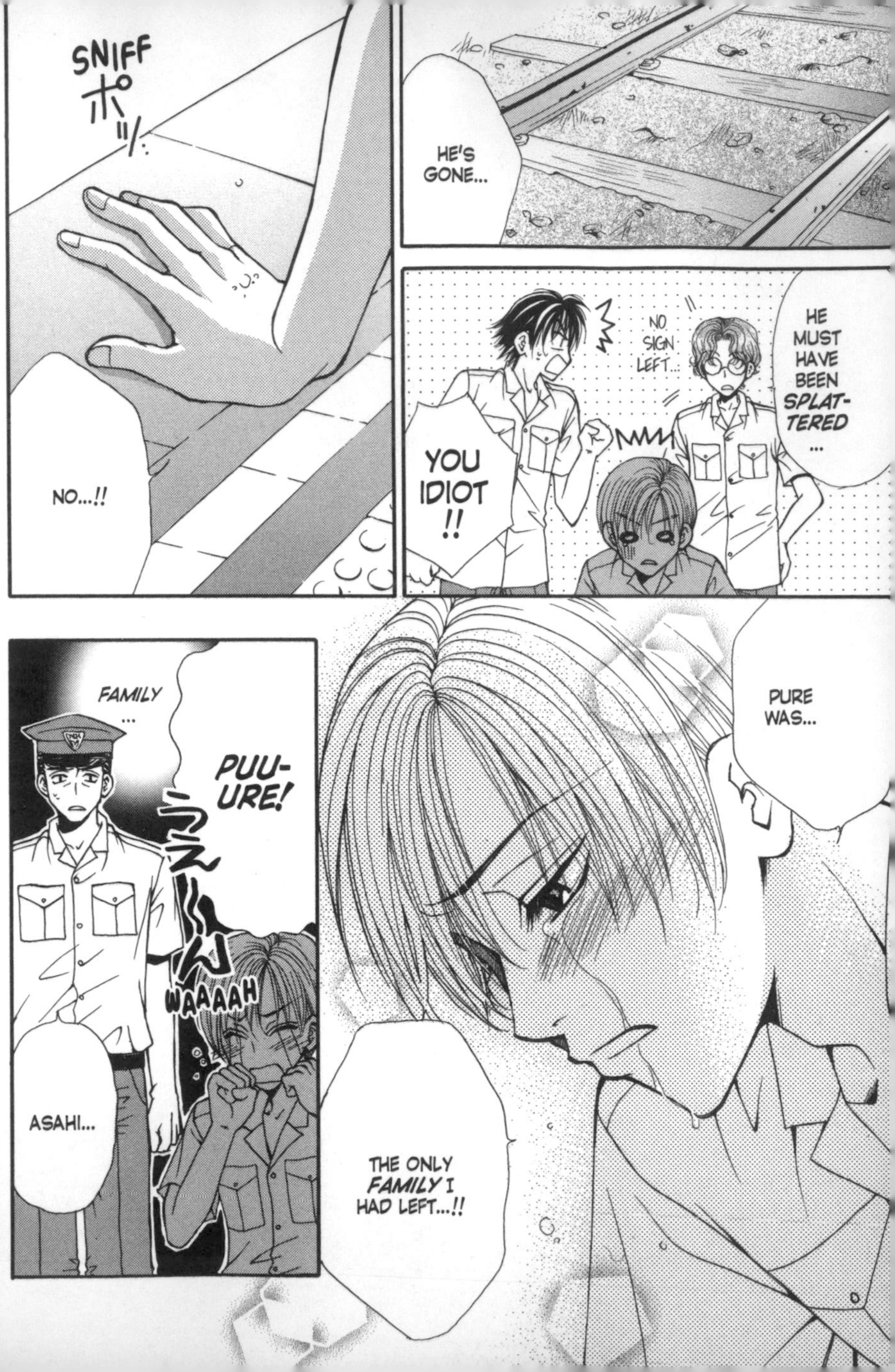
HE'S GONE...
HE MUST HAVE BEEN SPLAT-TERED...
NO SIGN LEFT...
YOU IDIOT!!
SNIFF
ポッ
NO...!!
PURE WAS...
THE ONLY *FAMILY* I HAD LEFT...!!
*FAMILY*...
*PUUU-URE!*
WAAAAH
ASAHI...

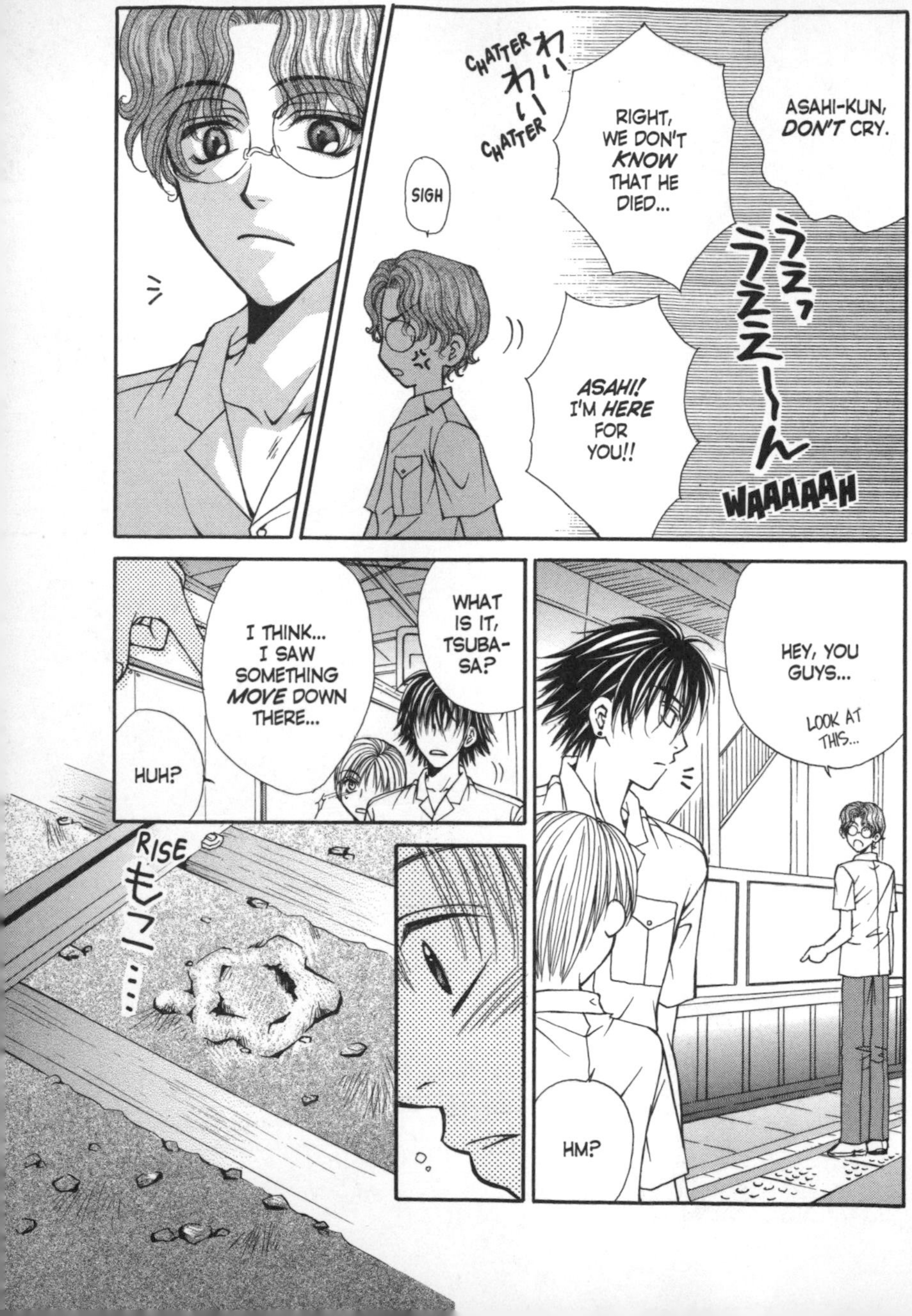
ASAHI-KUN, *DON'T* CRY.
ううっ うええ～ん
WAAAAAH
RIGHT, WE DON'T *KNOW* THAT HE DIED...
*ASAHI!* I'M *HERE* FOR YOU!!
CHATTER わいわい CHATTER
SIGH
HEY, YOU GUYS...
LOOK AT THIS...
HM?
WHAT IS IT, TSUBASA?
I THINK... I SAW SOMETHING *MOVE* DOWN THERE...
HUH?
RISE もこー…

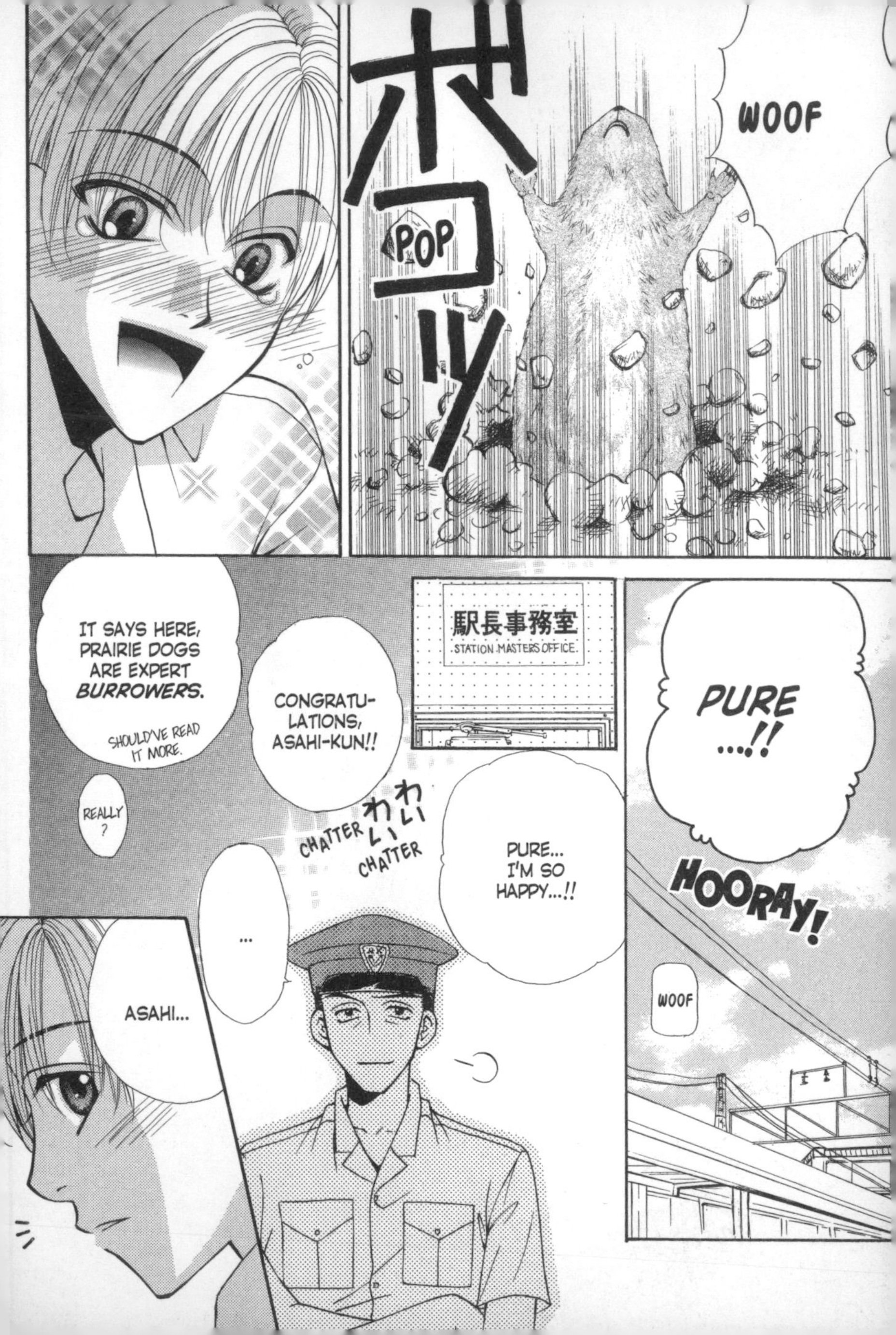
WOOF
ポコッ
POP
PURE ...!!
HOORAY!
WOOF
駅長事務室
STATION MASTERS OFFICE
CONGRATULATIONS, ASAHI-KUN!!
IT SAYS HERE, PRAIRIE DOGS ARE EXPERT **BURROWERS**.
SHOULD'VE READ IT MORE.
REALLY ?
わいわい
CHATTER CHATTER
PURE... I'M SO HAPPY...!!
...
ASAHI...

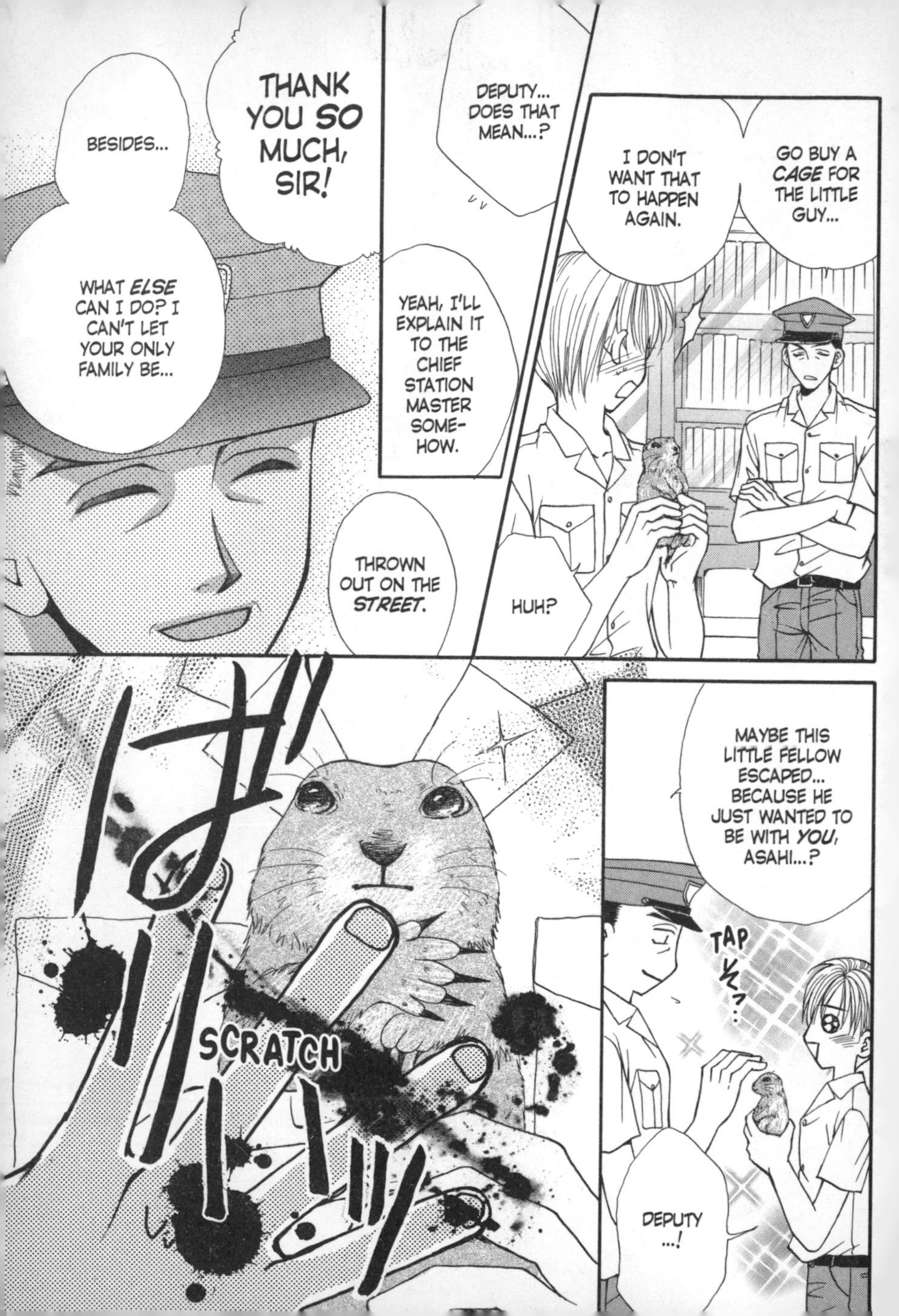
GO BUY A *CAGE* FOR THE LITTLE GUY...
I DON'T WANT THAT TO HAPPEN AGAIN.
HUH?
DEPUTY... DOES THAT MEAN...?
YEAH, I'LL EXPLAIN IT TO THE CHIEF STATION MASTER SOME-HOW.
THANK YOU SO MUCH, SIR!
BESIDES...
WHAT *ELSE* CAN I DO? I CAN'T LET YOUR ONLY FAMILY BE...
THROWN OUT ON THE *STREET*.
MAYBE THIS LITTLE FELLOW ESCAPED... BECAUSE HE JUST WANTED TO BE WITH *YOU*, ASAHI...?
TAP
DEPUTY ...!
SCRATCH

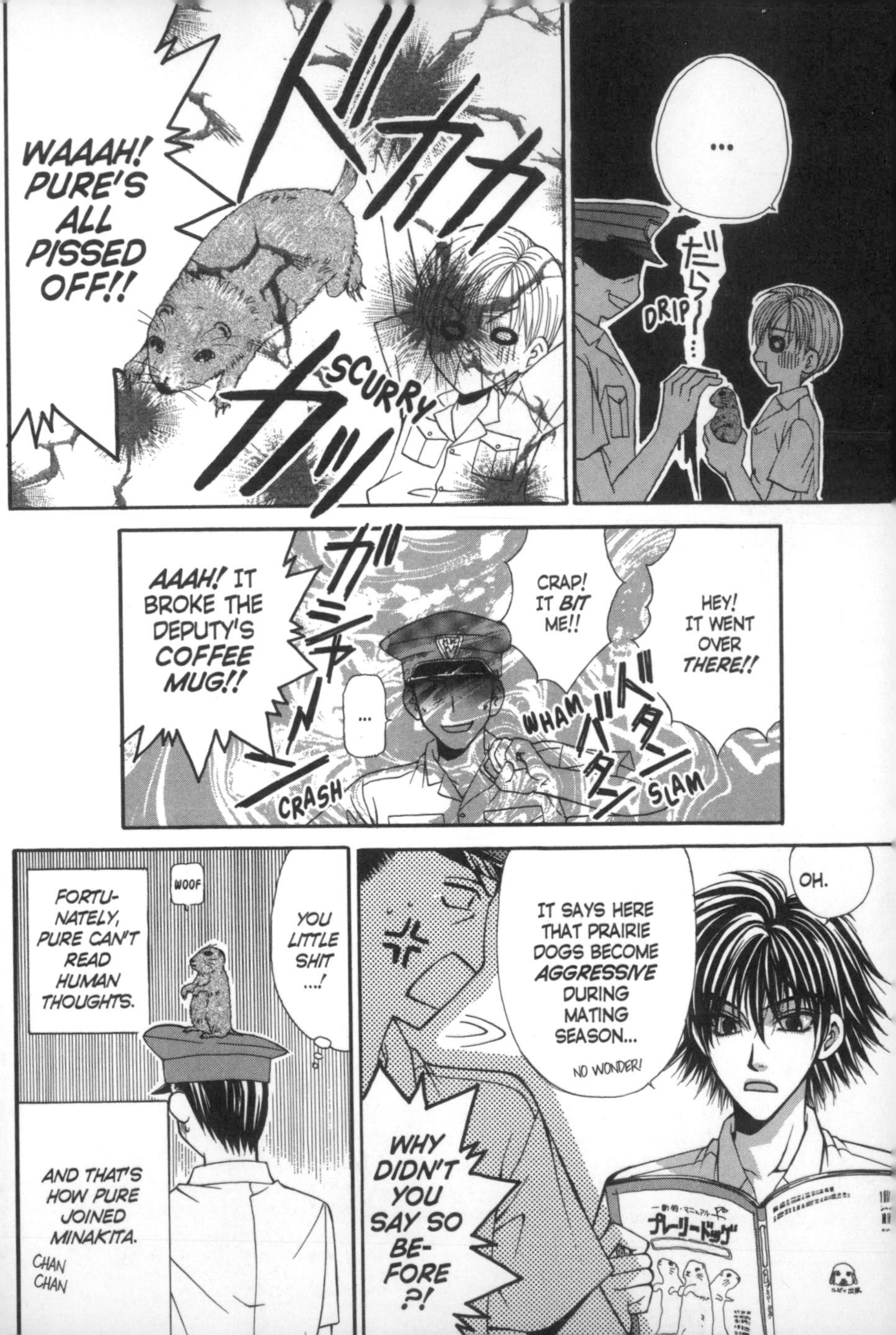
...
DRIP
WAAAH! PURE'S ALL PISSED OFF!!
SCURRY
HEY! IT WENT OVER THERE!!
SLAM
WHAM
CRAP! IT BIT ME!!
...
CRASH
AAAH! IT BROKE THE DEPUTY'S COFFEE MUG!!
OH.
IT SAYS HERE THAT PRAIRIE DOGS BECOME AGGRESSIVE DURING MATING SEASON...
NO WONDER!
WHY DIDN'T YOU SAY SO BEFORE?!
YOU LITTLE SHIT ...!
WOOF
FORTUNATELY, PURE CAN'T READ HUMAN THOUGHTS.
AND THAT'S HOW PURE JOINED MINAKITA.
CHAN CHAN

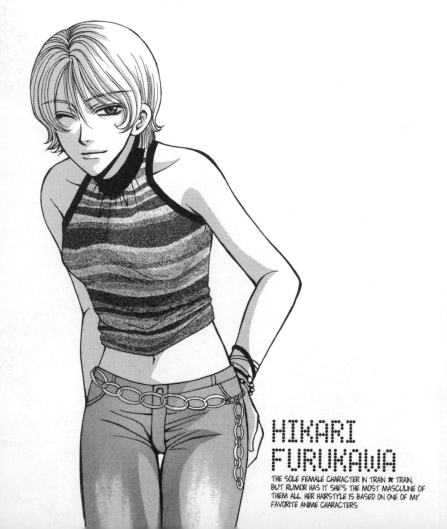

# HIKARI FURUKAWA

THE SOLE FEMALE CHARACTER IN TRAIN ★ TRAIN,
BUT RUMOR HAS IT SHE'S THE MOST MASCULINE OF
THEM ALL. HER HAIRSTYLE IS BASED ON ONE OF MY
FAVORITE ANIME CHARACTERS.

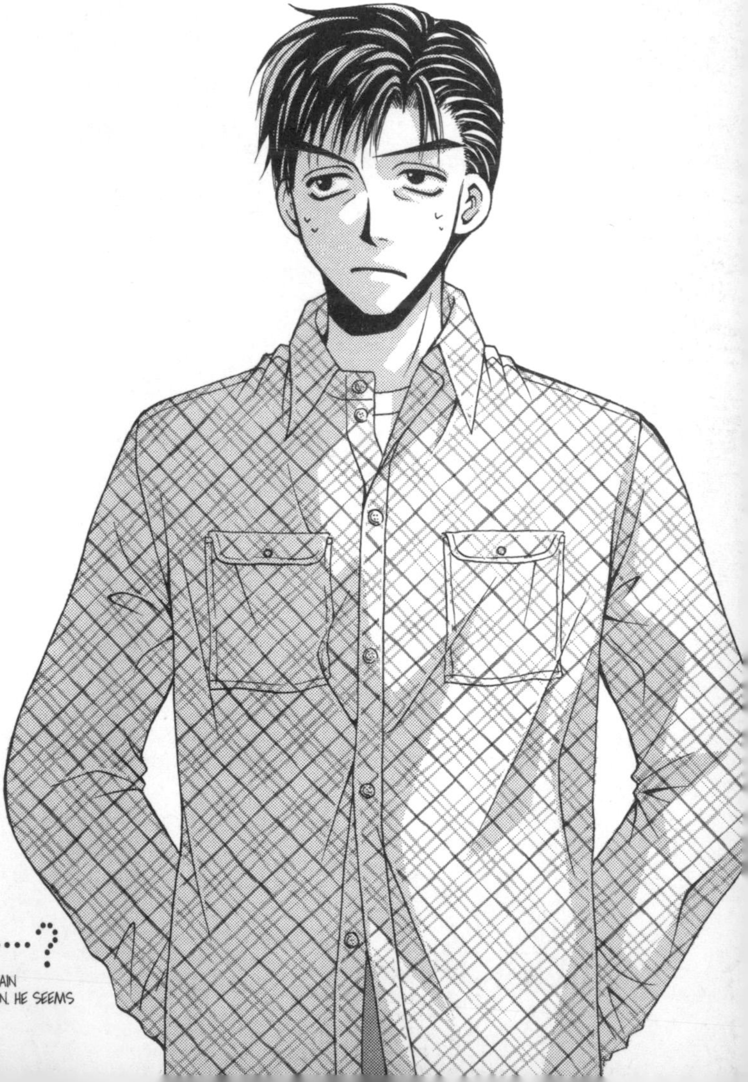

AKITA·····?

SUPPOSEDLY, THE "OTHER" MAIN CHARACTER OF TRAIN ☆ TRAIN. HE SEEMS TO BE VERY POPULAR..

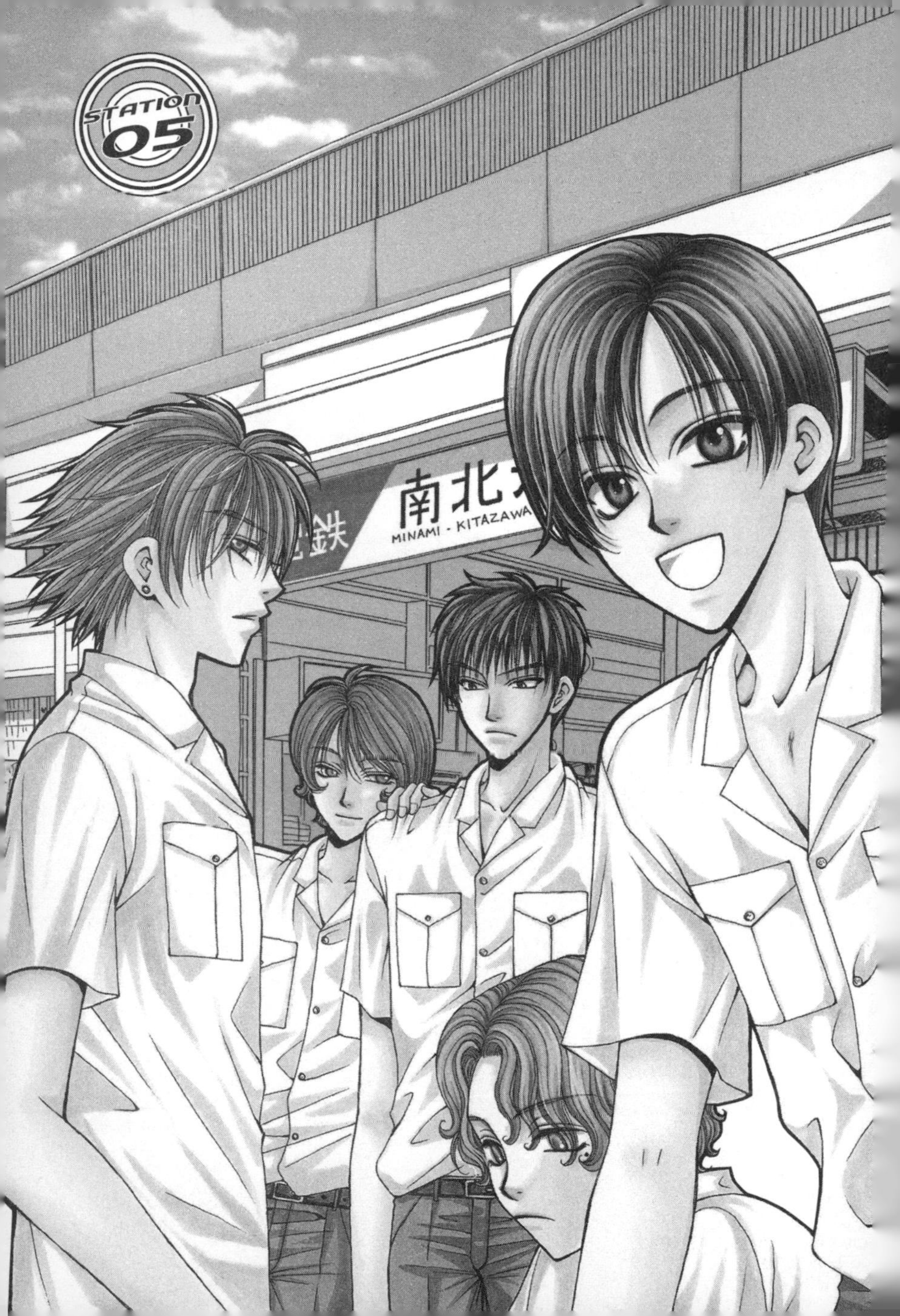
STATION 05
南北
MINAMI - KITAZAWA
鉄

PURE

MALE PRAIRIE DOG. FOUND BY
ASAHI WHEN HE WAS JUST A CUB.

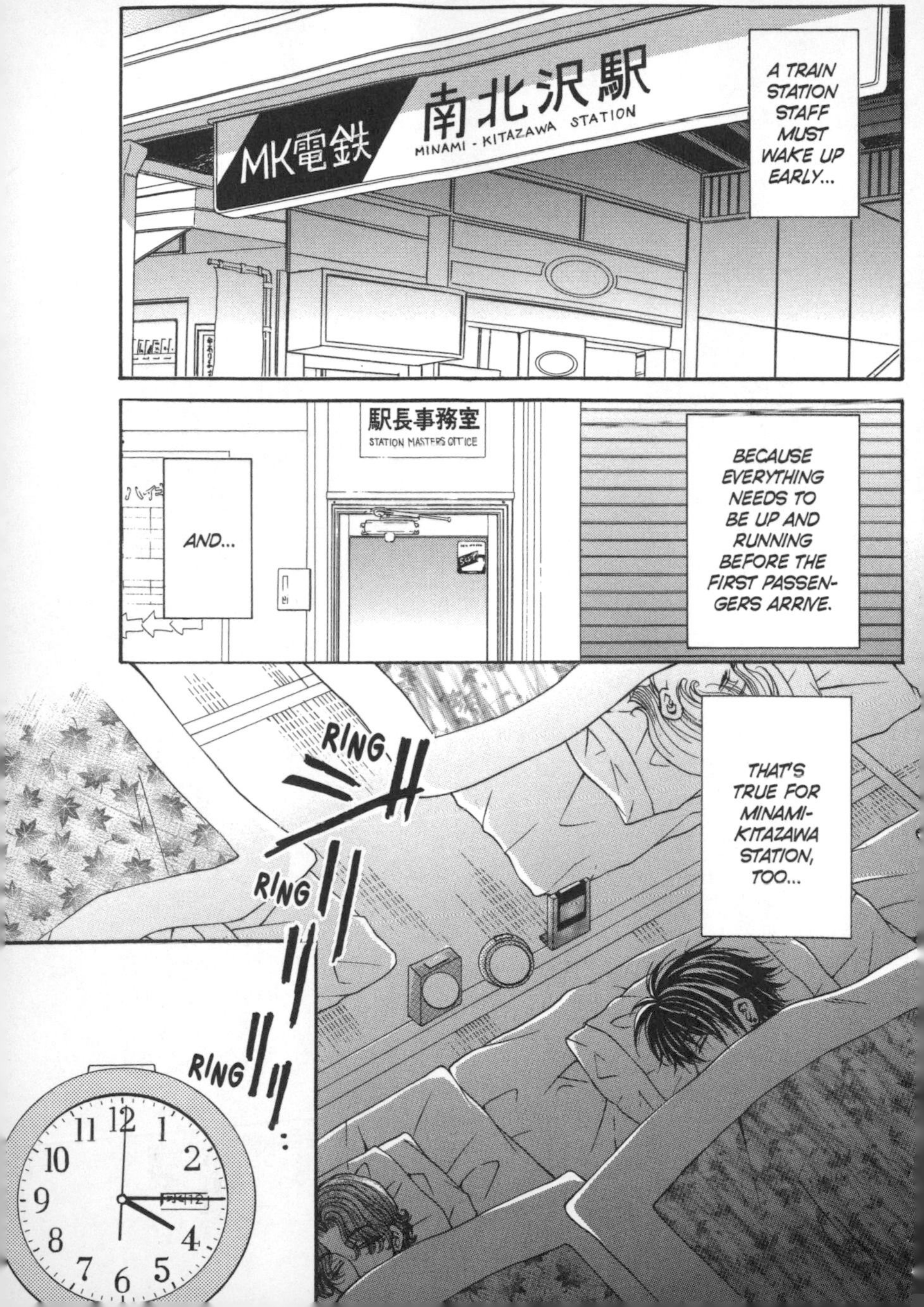
MK電鉄
南北沢駅
MINAMI - KITAZAWA STATION
A TRAIN STATION STAFF MUST WAKE UP EARLY...
BECAUSE EVERYTHING NEEDS TO BE UP AND RUNNING BEFORE THE FIRST PASSEN-GERS ARRIVE.
駅長事務室
STATION MASTERS OFFICE
AND...
THAT'S TRUE FOR MINAMI-KITAZAWA STATION, TOO...
RING
RING
RING

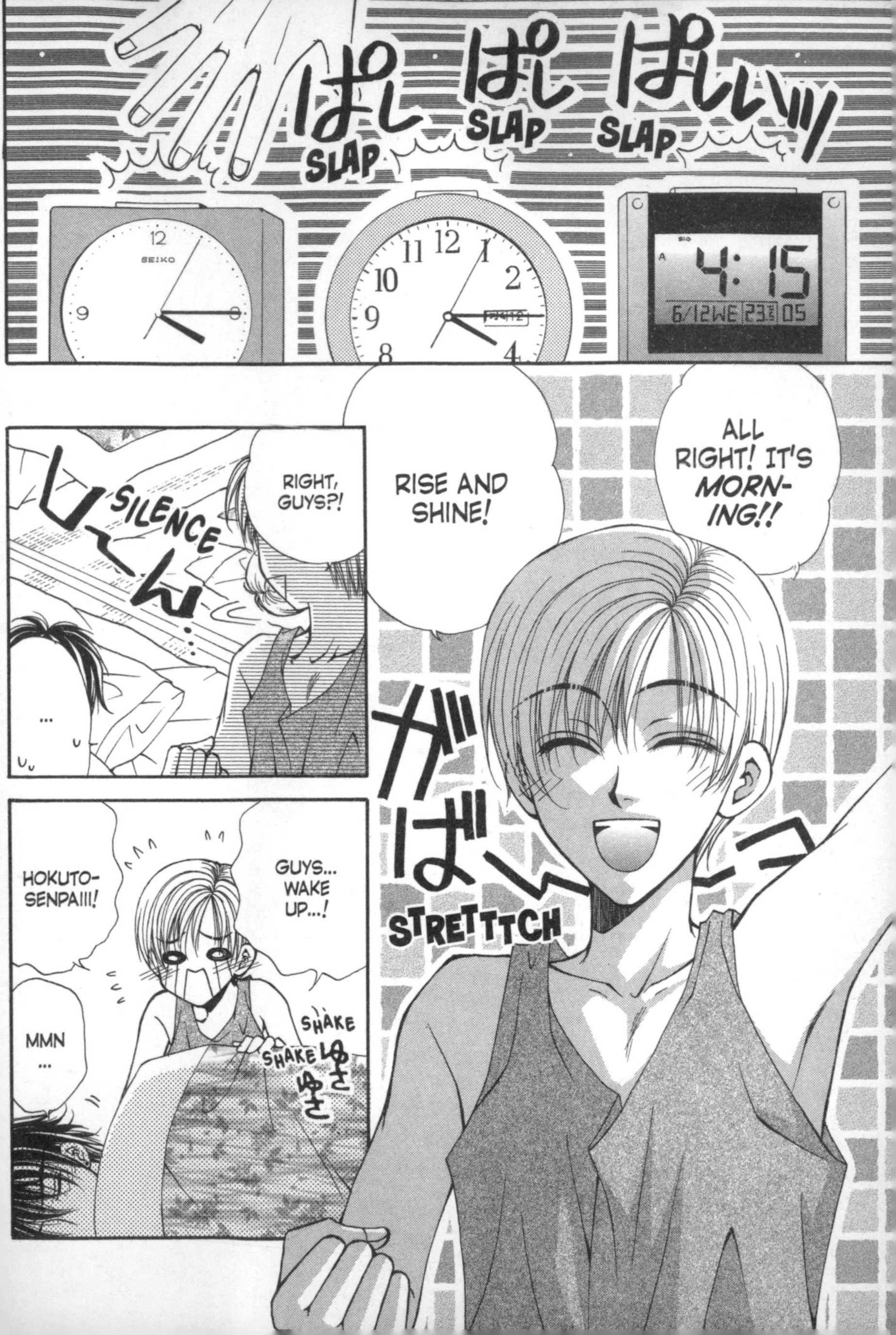

ぱしいッ
SLAP
ぱし
SLAP
ぱし
SLAP
SEIKO
4:15
ALL RIGHT! IT'S MORNING!!
RISE AND SHINE!
がば〜っ
STRETTTCH
RIGHT, GUYS?!
しーん
SILENCE
...
GUYS... WAKE UP...!
HOKUTO-SENPAIII!
ゆさ ゆさ
SHAKE
SHAKE
MMN ...

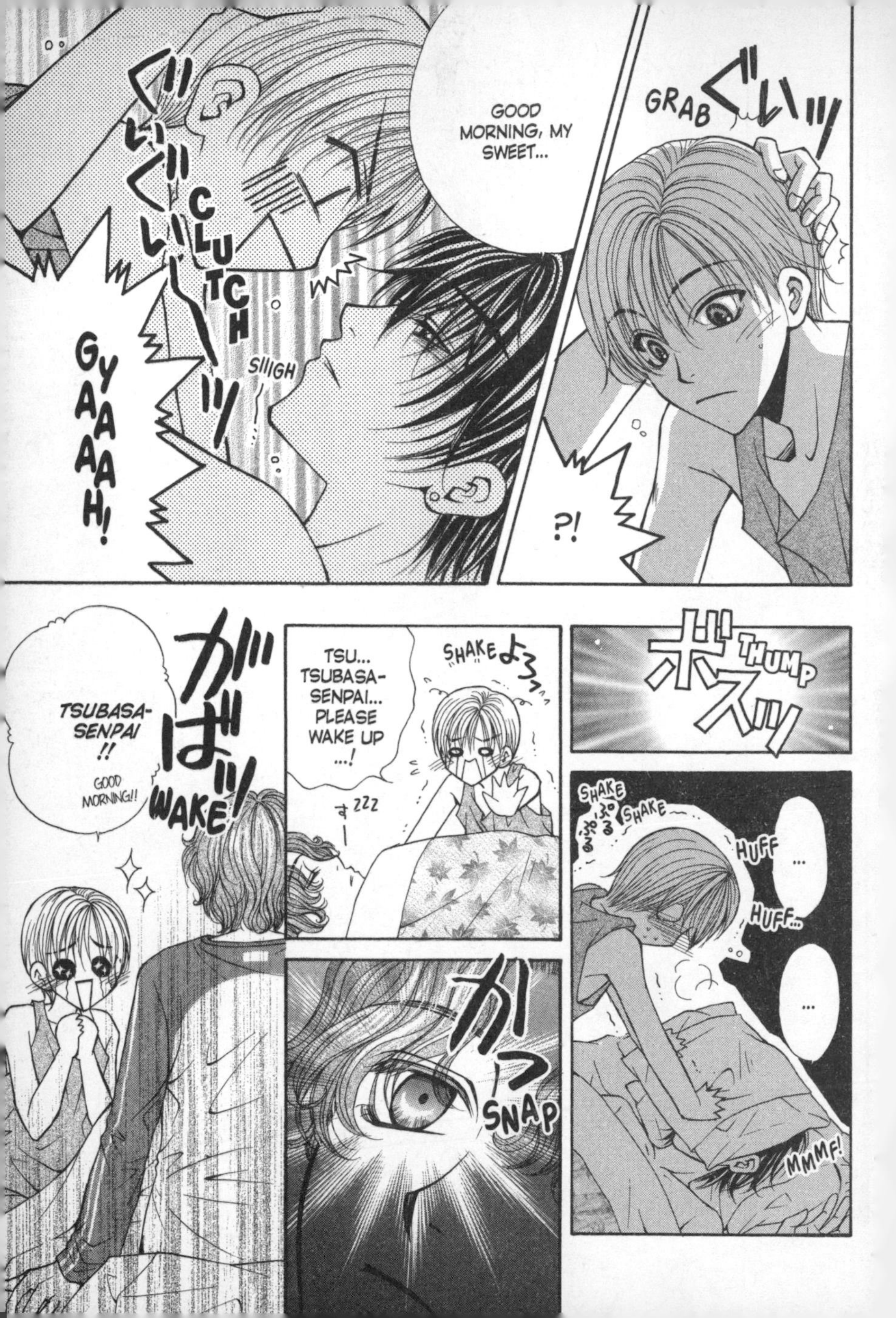
GRAB
?!
GOOD MORNING, MY SWEET...
CLUTCH
SIIIGH
GYAAAAH!
THUMP
SHAKE SHAKE
HUFF...
HUFF...
...
...
MMMF!
TSU... TSUBASA-SENPAI... PLEASE WAKE UP ...!
SHAKE
ZZZ
SNAP
TSUBASA-SENPAI!!
GOOD MORNING!!
WAKE

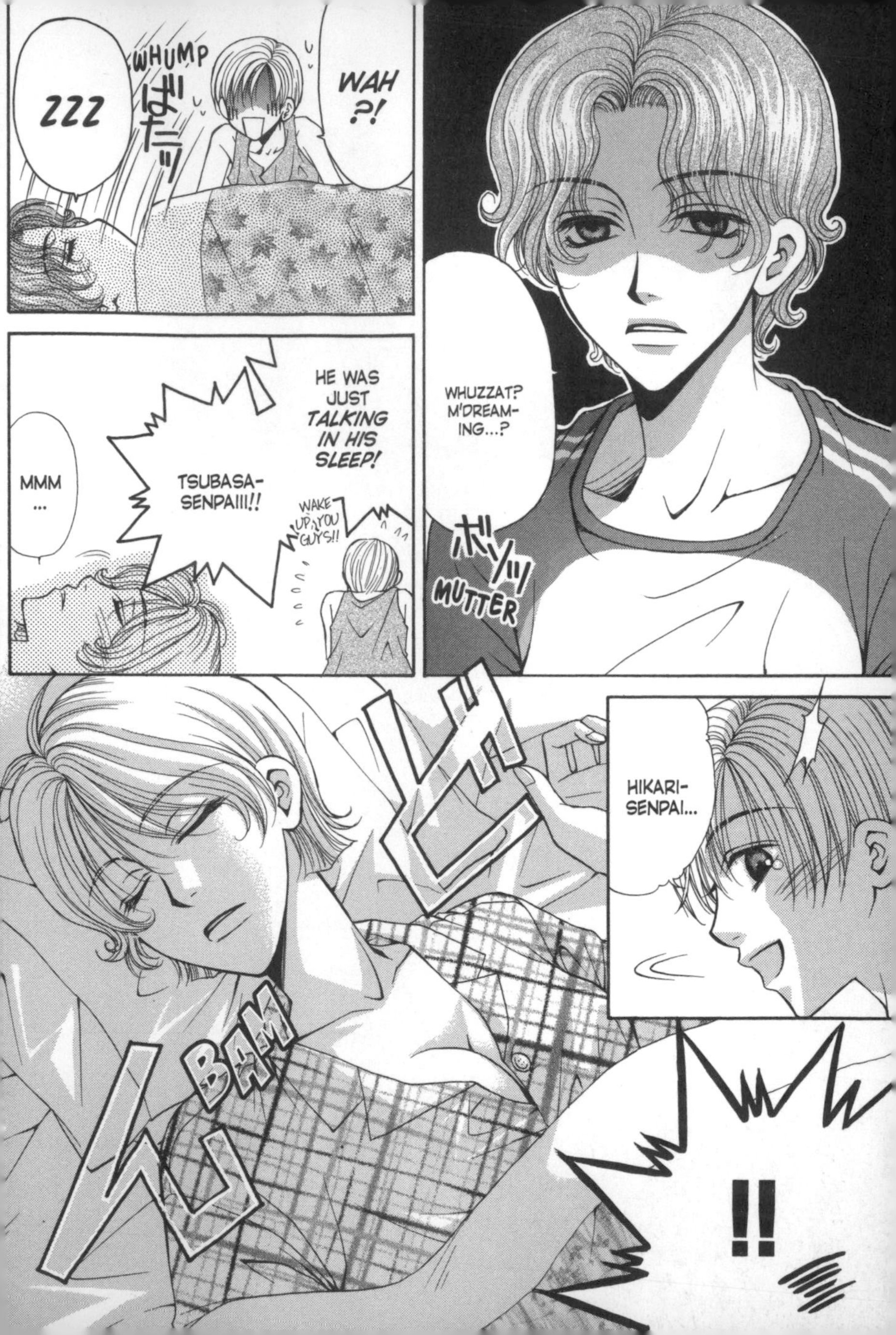

WHUZZAT? M'DREAMING...?
ボソッ
MUTTER
WAH ?!
WHUMP
ばたッ
ZZZ
HE WAS JUST TALKING IN HIS SLEEP!
WAKE UP, YOU GUYS!!
TSUBASA-SENPAI!!!
MMM ...
HIKARI-SENPAI...
!!
BAM

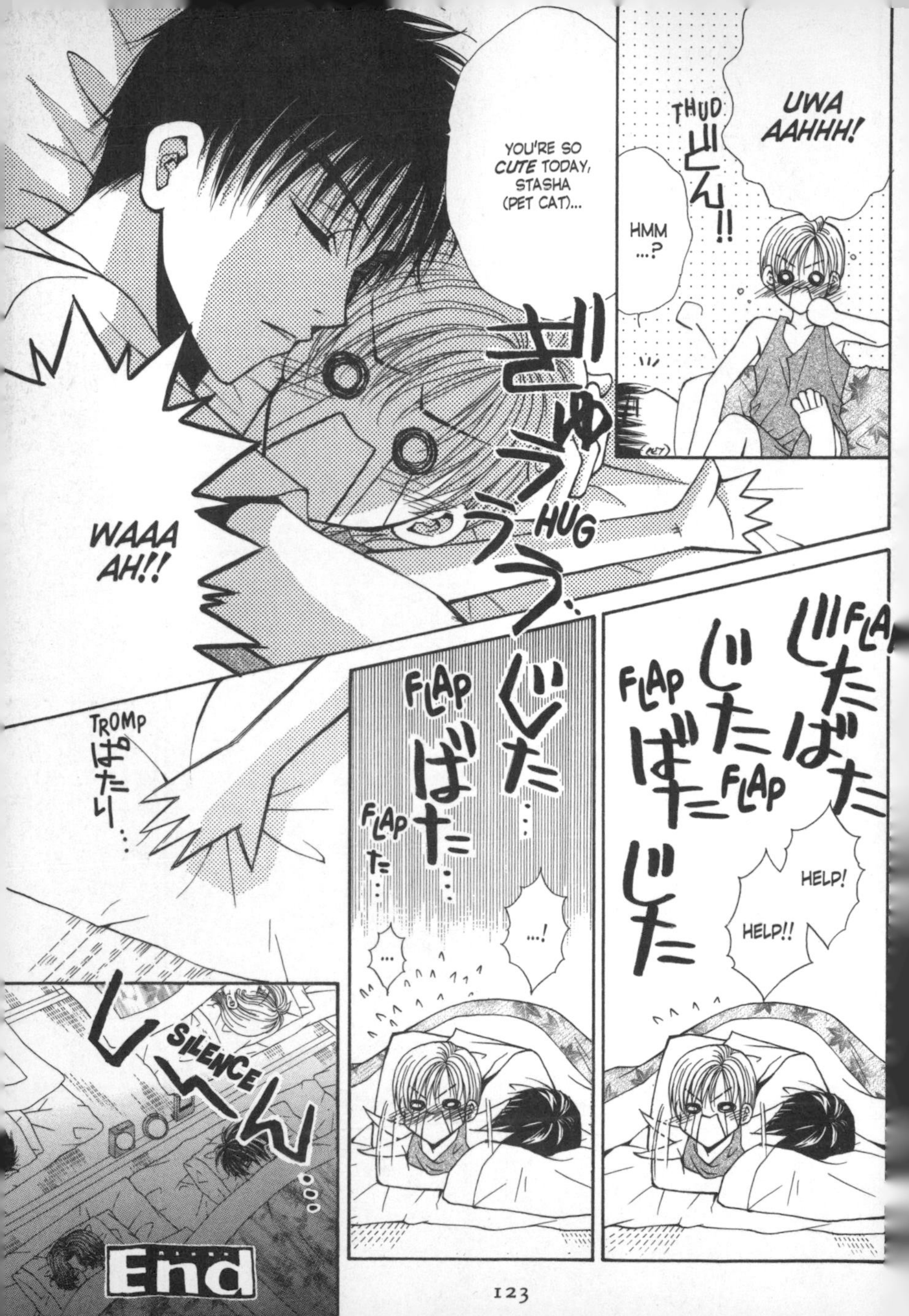
UWA AAHHH!
THUD
どん!!
HMM ...?
PET
YOU'RE SO CUTE TODAY, STASHA (PET CAT)...
ぎゅううう
HUG
WAAAAH!!
じたばた
FLAP
じたばた
FLAP
じたばた
FLAP
HELP!
HELP!!
じた...
FLAP
ばた...
FLAP
た...
...!
...
TROMP
ぱたり...
しーん...
SILENCE
End

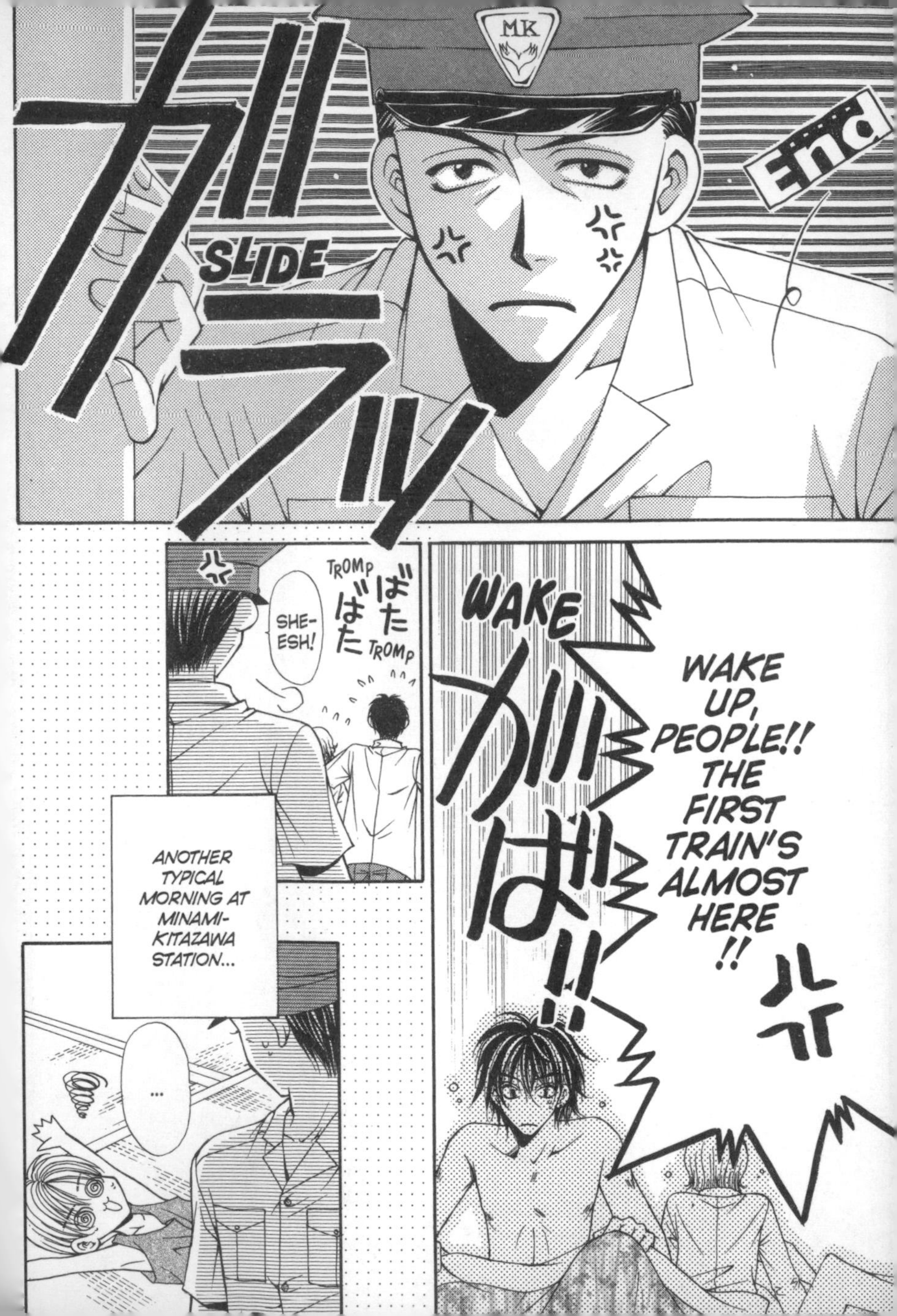
End
ガラッ
SLIDE
WAKE
がばっ!!
WAKE UP, PEOPLE!! THE FIRST TRAIN'S ALMOST HERE!!
ばたばた
TROMP TROMP
SHE-ESH!
ANOTHER TYPICAL MORNING AT MINAMI-KITAZAWA STATION...
...

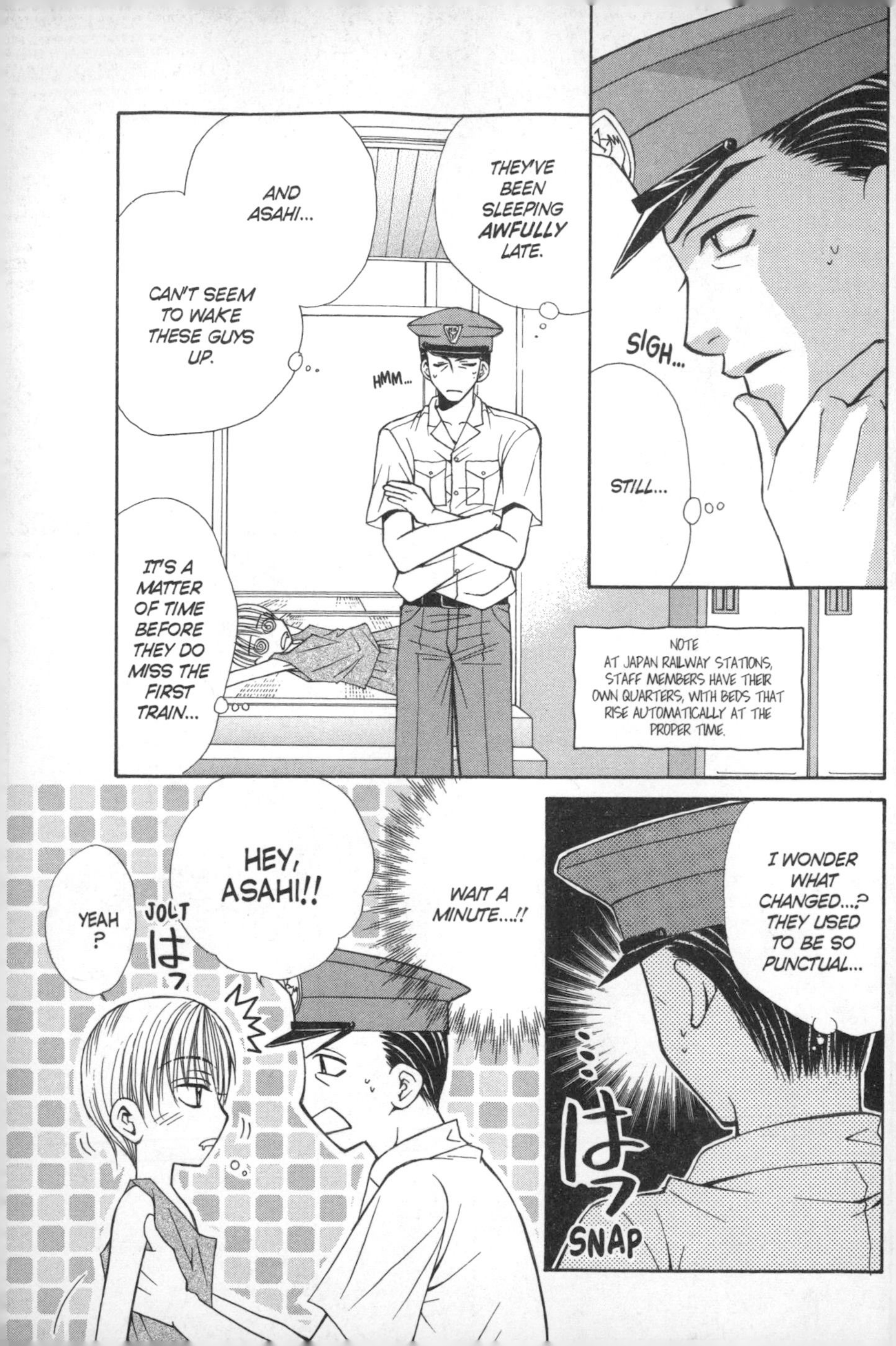
SIGH...
STILL...
THEY'VE BEEN SLEEPING AWFULLY LATE.
AND ASAHI...
CAN'T SEEM TO WAKE THESE GUYS UP.
HMM...
IT'S A MATTER OF TIME BEFORE THEY DO MISS THE FIRST TRAIN...
NOTE
AT JAPAN RAILWAY STATIONS, STAFF MEMBERS HAVE THEIR OWN QUARTERS, WITH BEDS THAT RISE AUTOMATICALLY AT THE PROPER TIME.
I WONDER WHAT CHANGED...? THEY USED TO BE SO PUNCTUAL...
はっ
SNAP
WAIT A MINUTE...!!
HEY, ASAHI!!
JOLT
はっ
YEAH ?

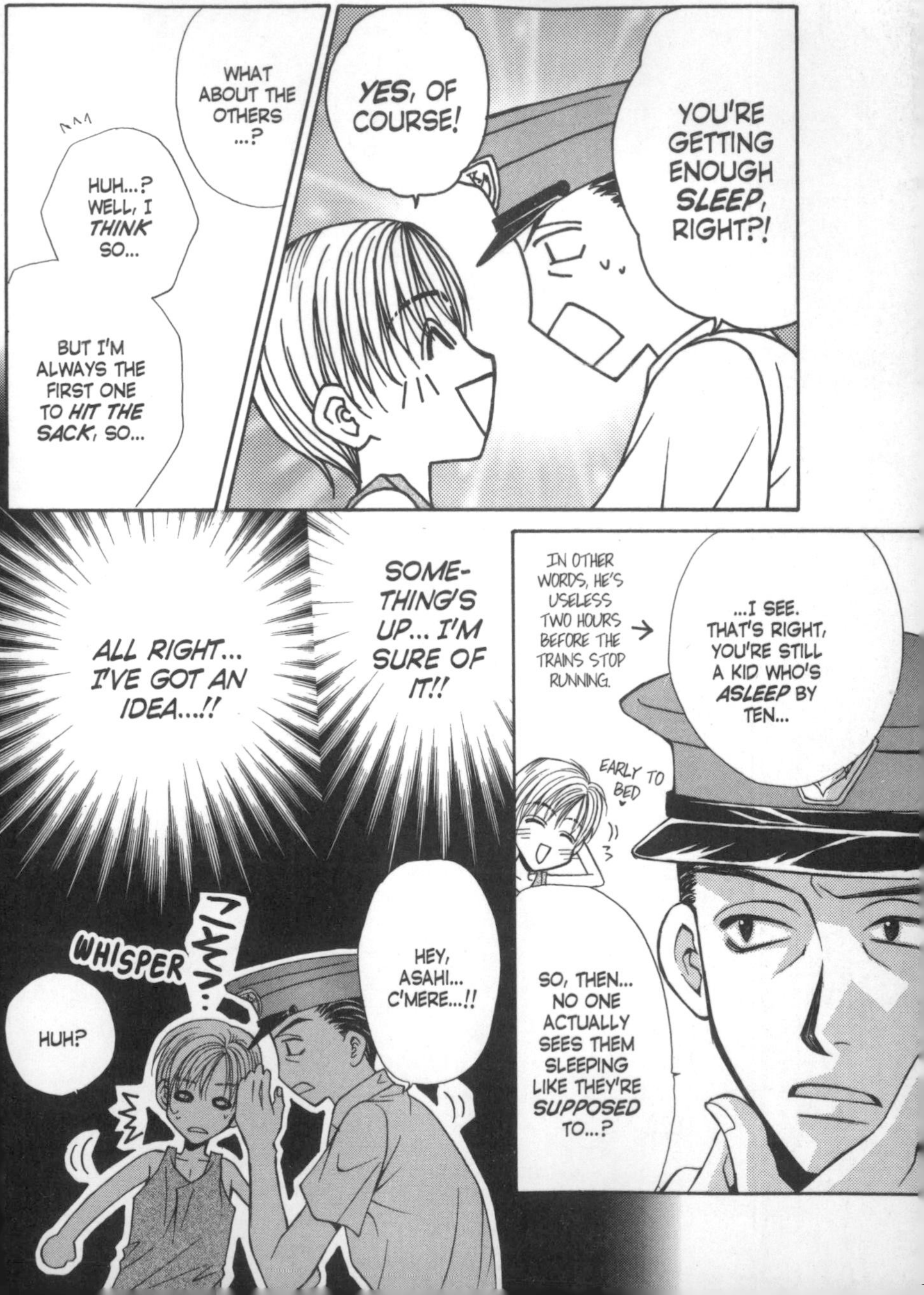
YOU'RE GETTING ENOUGH SLEEP, RIGHT?!
YES, OF COURSE!
WHAT ABOUT THE OTHERS ...?
HUH...? WELL, I THINK SO...
BUT I'M ALWAYS THE FIRST ONE TO HIT THE SACK, SO...
...I SEE. THAT'S RIGHT, YOU'RE STILL A KID WHO'S ASLEEP BY TEN...
IN OTHER WORDS, HE'S USELESS TWO HOURS BEFORE THE TRAINS STOP RUNNING. →
EARLY TO BED
SO, THEN... NO ONE ACTUALLY SEES THEM SLEEPING LIKE THEY'RE SUPPOSED TO...?
SOME-THING'S UP... I'M SURE OF IT!!
ALL RIGHT... I'VE GOT AN IDEA...!!
HEY, ASAHI... C'MERE...!!
WHISPER
HUH?

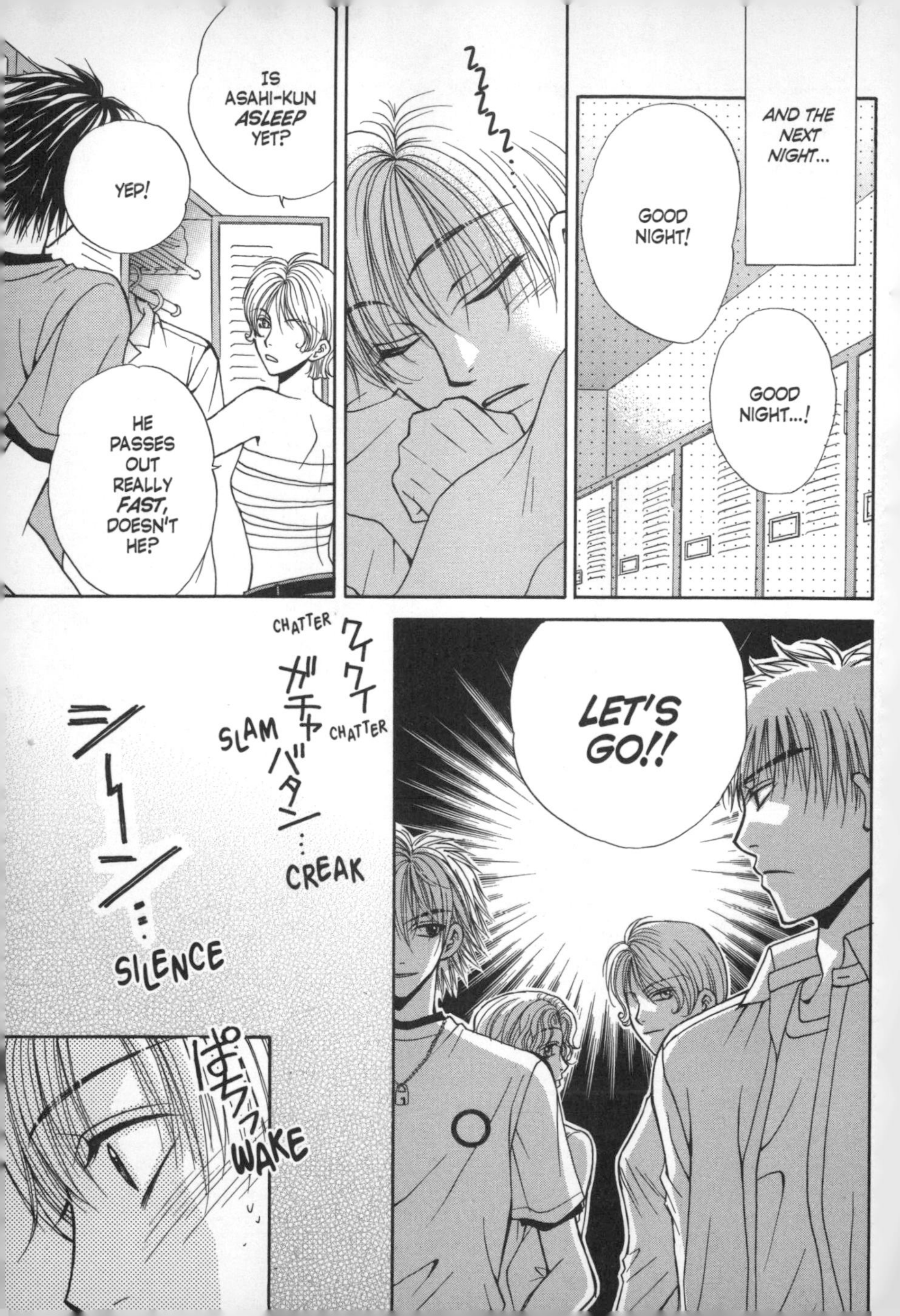
AND THE NEXT NIGHT...
GOOD NIGHT!
GOOD NIGHT...!
ZZZZZZ...
IS ASAHI-KUN ASLEEP YET?
YEP!
HE PASSES OUT REALLY FAST, DOESN'T HE?
LET'S GO!!
ワイワイ CHATTER CHATTER
ガチャバタン... SLAM CREAK
シーン... SILENCE
ぱちっ WAKE

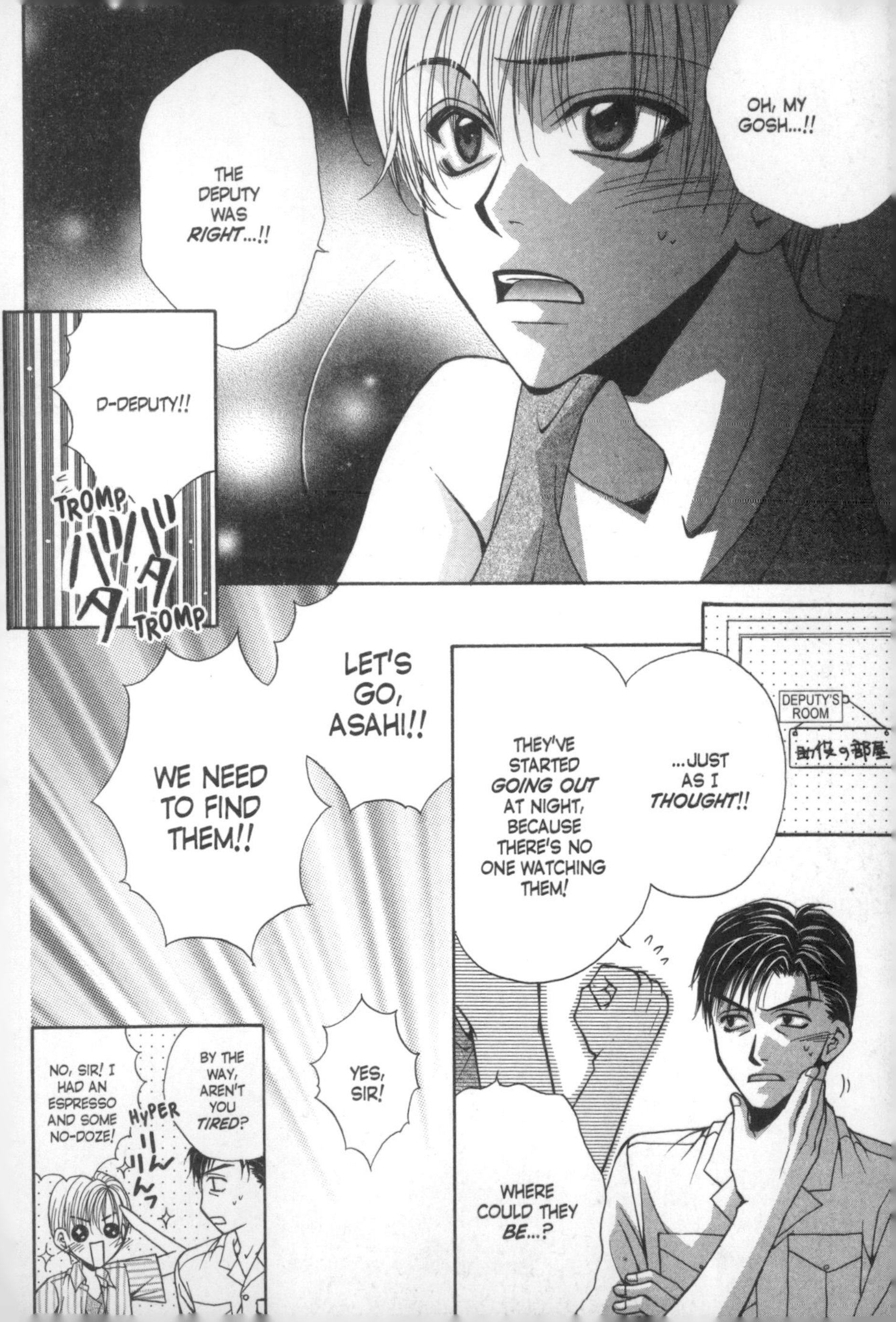
OH, MY GOSH...!!
THE DEPUTY WAS RIGHT...!!
D-DEPUTY!!
TROMP
バタ
バタ
TROMP
DEPUTY'S ROOM
助役の部屋
...JUST AS I THOUGHT!!
THEY'VE STARTED GOING OUT AT NIGHT, BECAUSE THERE'S NO ONE WATCHING THEM!
WHERE COULD THEY BE...?
LET'S GO, ASAHI!!
WE NEED TO FIND THEM!!
YES, SIR!
BY THE WAY, AREN'T YOU TIRED?
NO, SIR! I HAD AN ESPRESSO AND SOME NO-DOZE!
HYPER

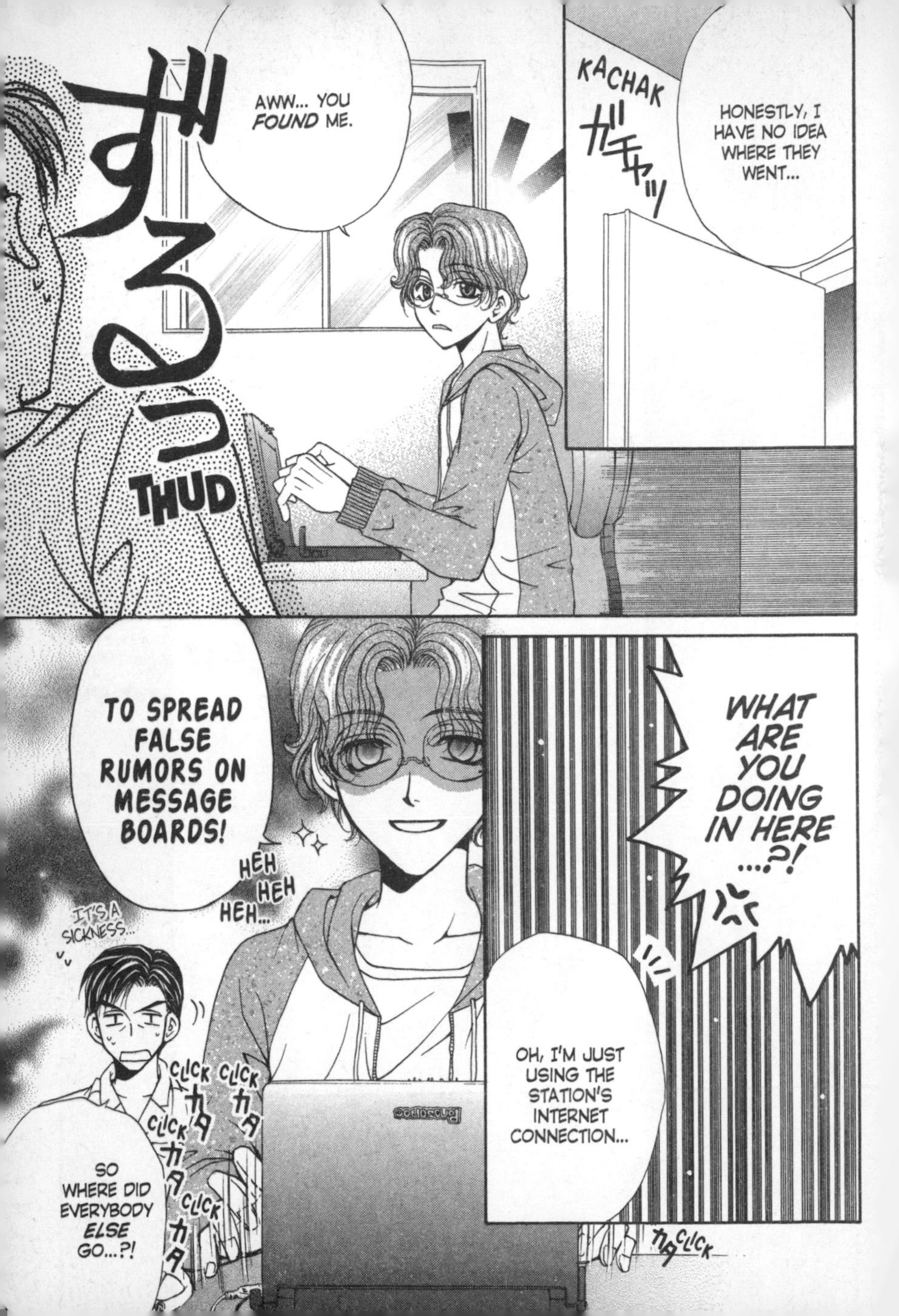
KACHAK
ガチャッ
HONESTLY, I HAVE NO IDEA WHERE THEY WENT...
AWW... YOU *FOUND* ME.
ずるっ
THUD
WHAT ARE YOU DOING IN HERE ...?!
OH, I'M JUST USING THE STATION'S INTERNET CONNECTION...
カタ CLICK
TO SPREAD FALSE RUMORS ON MESSAGE BOARDS!
HEH HEH HEH...
IT'S A SICKNESS...
CLICK カタ CLICK カタ CLICK カタ CLICK カタ
SO WHERE DID EVERYBODY *ELSE* GO...?!

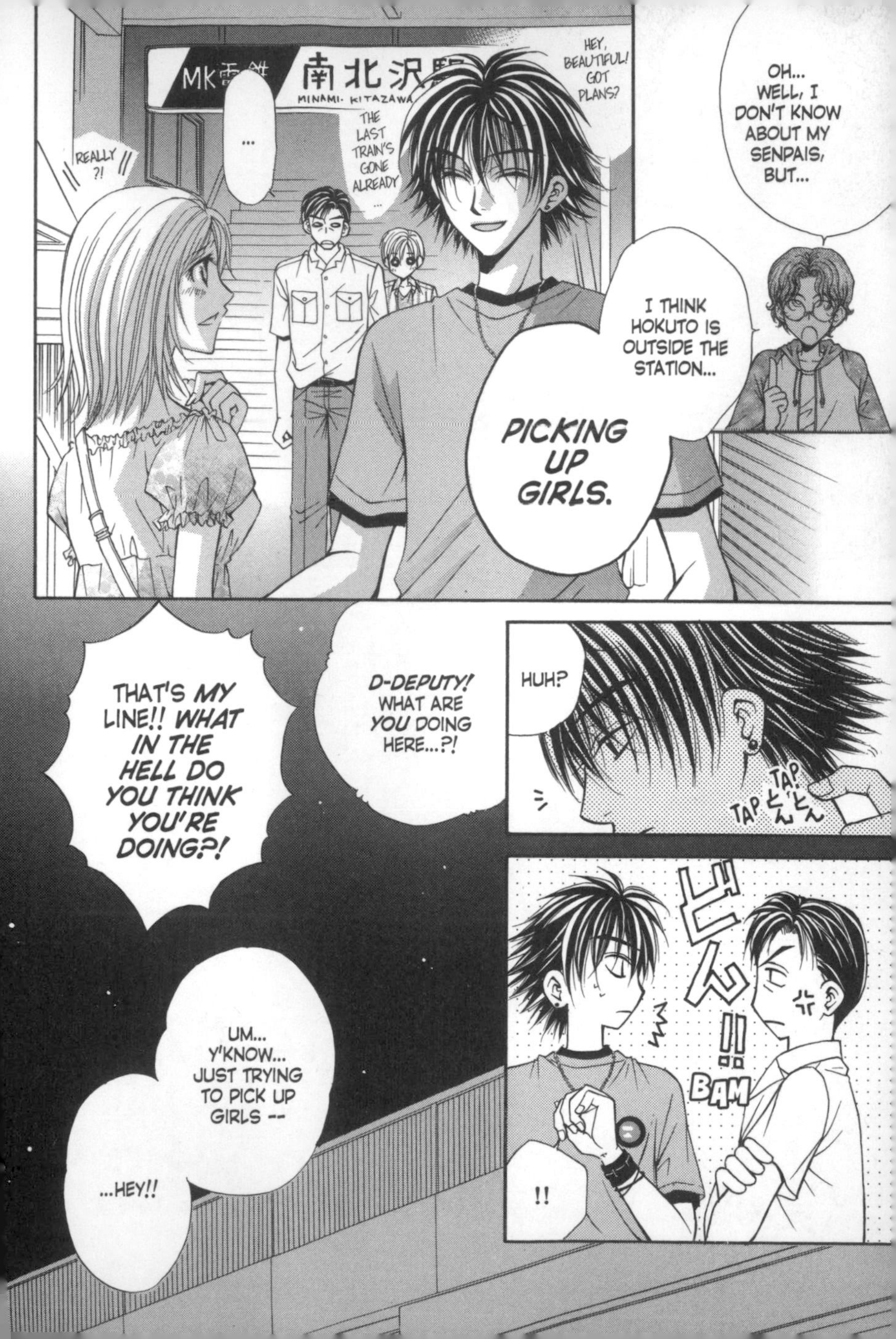
OH... WELL, I DON'T KNOW ABOUT MY SENPAIS, BUT...
I THINK HOKUTO IS OUTSIDE THE STATION...
PICKING UP GIRLS.
HEY, BEAUTIFUL! GOT PLANS?
南北沢
MINAMI-KITAZAWA
THE LAST TRAIN'S GONE ALREADY...
...
REALLY?!
HUH?
TAP TAP とんとん
どん!!
BAM
!!
D-DEPUTY! WHAT ARE YOU DOING HERE...?!
THAT'S MY LINE!! WHAT IN THE HELL DO YOU THINK YOU'RE DOING?!
UM... Y'KNOW... JUST TRYING TO PICK UP GIRLS --
...HEY!!

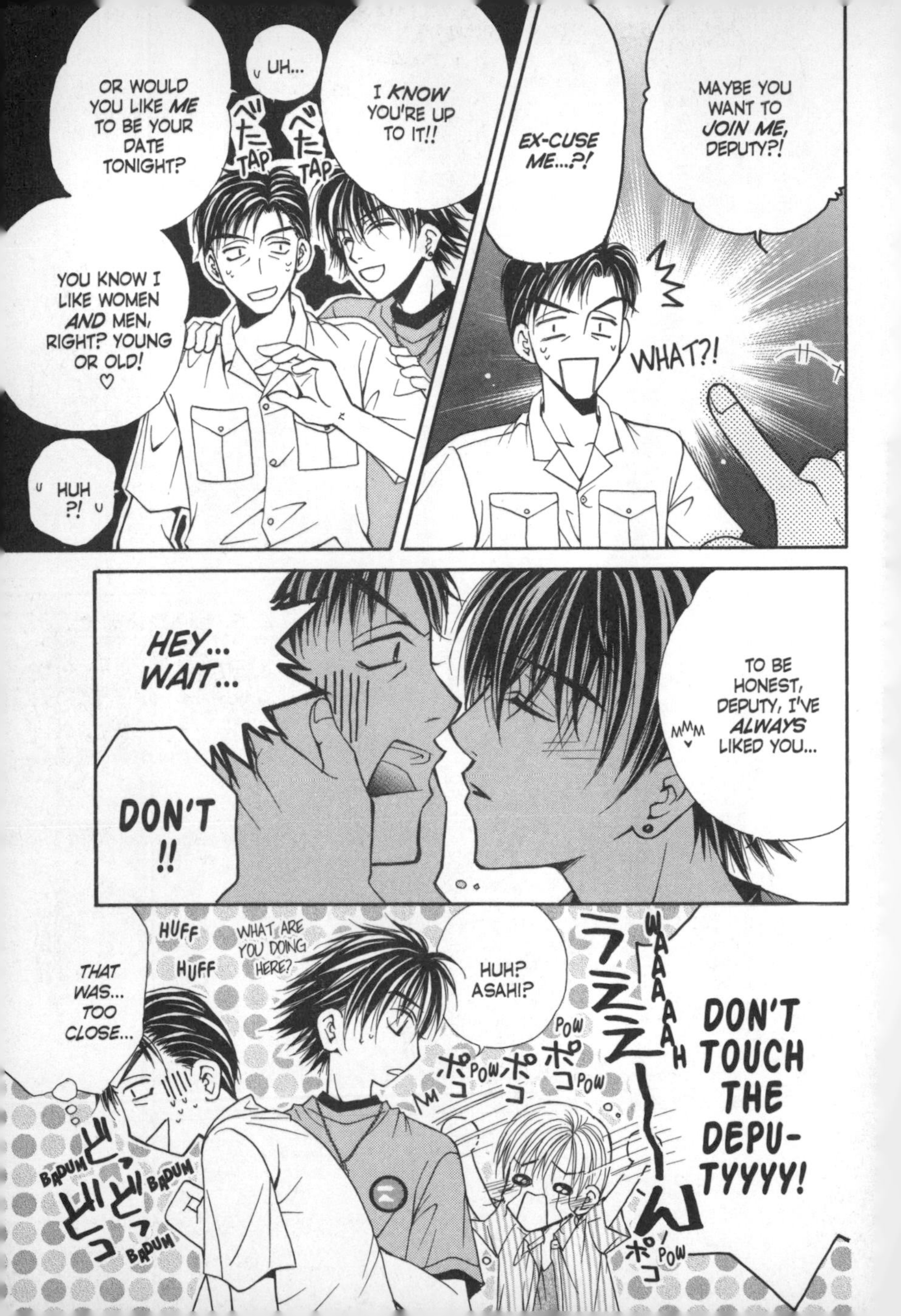
MAYBE YOU WANT TO JOIN ME, DEPUTY?!
EX-CUSE ME...?!
WHAT?!
I KNOW YOU'RE UP TO IT!!
UH...
べた TAP
べた TAP
OR WOULD YOU LIKE ME TO BE YOUR DATE TONIGHT?
YOU KNOW I LIKE WOMEN AND MEN, RIGHT? YOUNG OR OLD! ♡
HUH?!
TO BE HONEST, DEPUTY, I'VE ALWAYS LIKED YOU...
MMM
HEY... WAIT...
DON'T!!
DON'T TOUCH THE DEPU-TYYYY!
WAAAAAAH
ポコ POW
ポコ POW
ポコ POW
HUH? ASAHI?
WHAT ARE YOU DOING HERE?
HUFF
HUFF
THAT WAS... TOO CLOSE...
BADUM
BADUM
BADUM

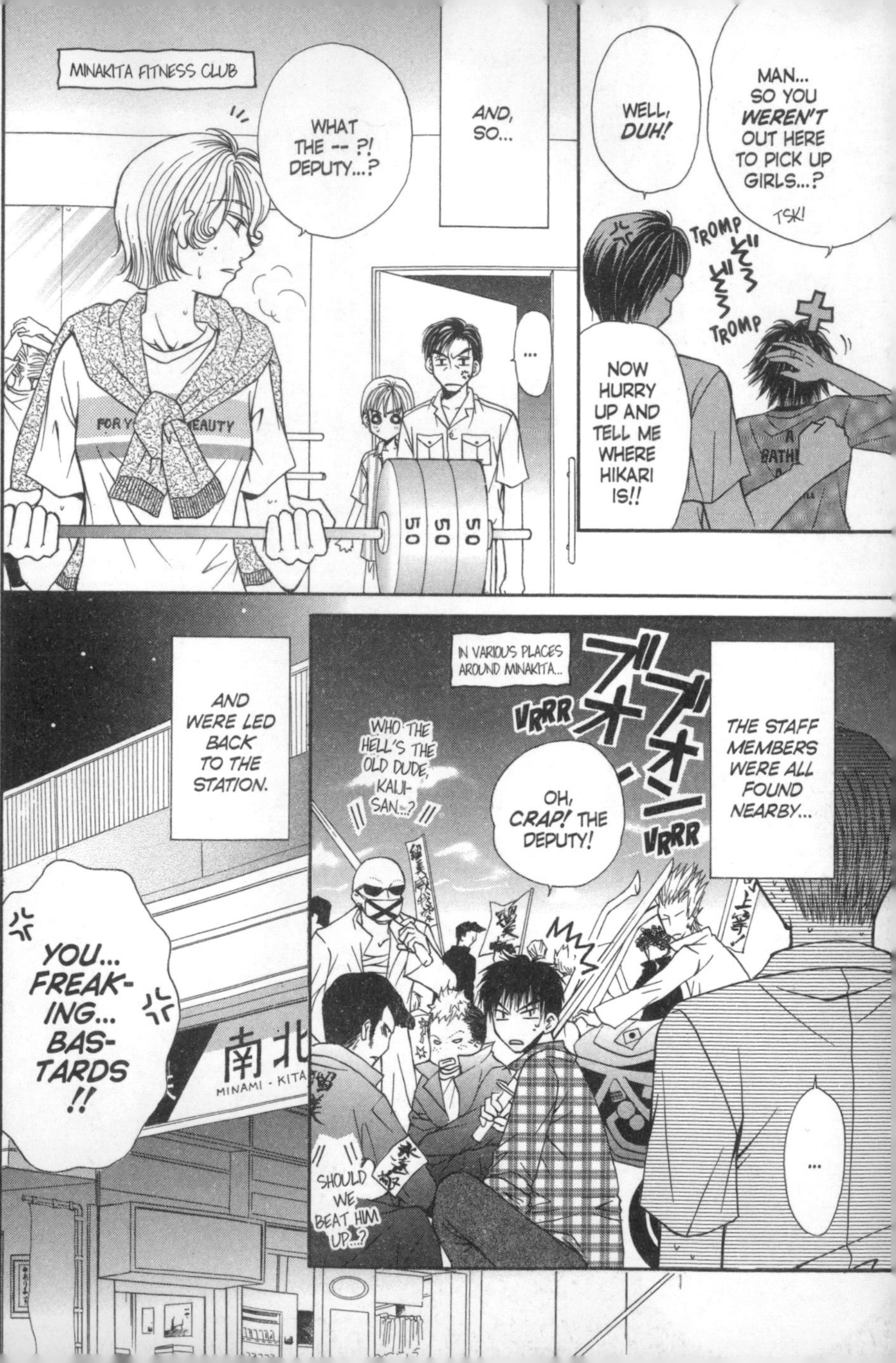
MAN... SO YOU WEREN'T OUT HERE TO PICK UP GIRLS...?
WELL, DUH!
TSK!
TROMP
TROMP
NOW HURRY UP AND TELL ME WHERE HIKARI IS!!
AND, SO...
MINAKITA FITNESS CLUB
WHAT THE -- ?! DEPUTY...?
...
50 50 50
THE STAFF MEMBERS WERE ALL FOUND NEARBY...
IN VARIOUS PLACES AROUND MINAKITA...
VRRR
VRRR
OH, CRAP! THE DEPUTY!
WHO THE HELL'S THE OLD DUDE, KAIJI-SAN...?
SHOULD WE BEAT HIM UP...?
...
AND WERE LED BACK TO THE STATION.
YOU... FREAKING... BASTARDS!!
南北
MINAMI - KITA

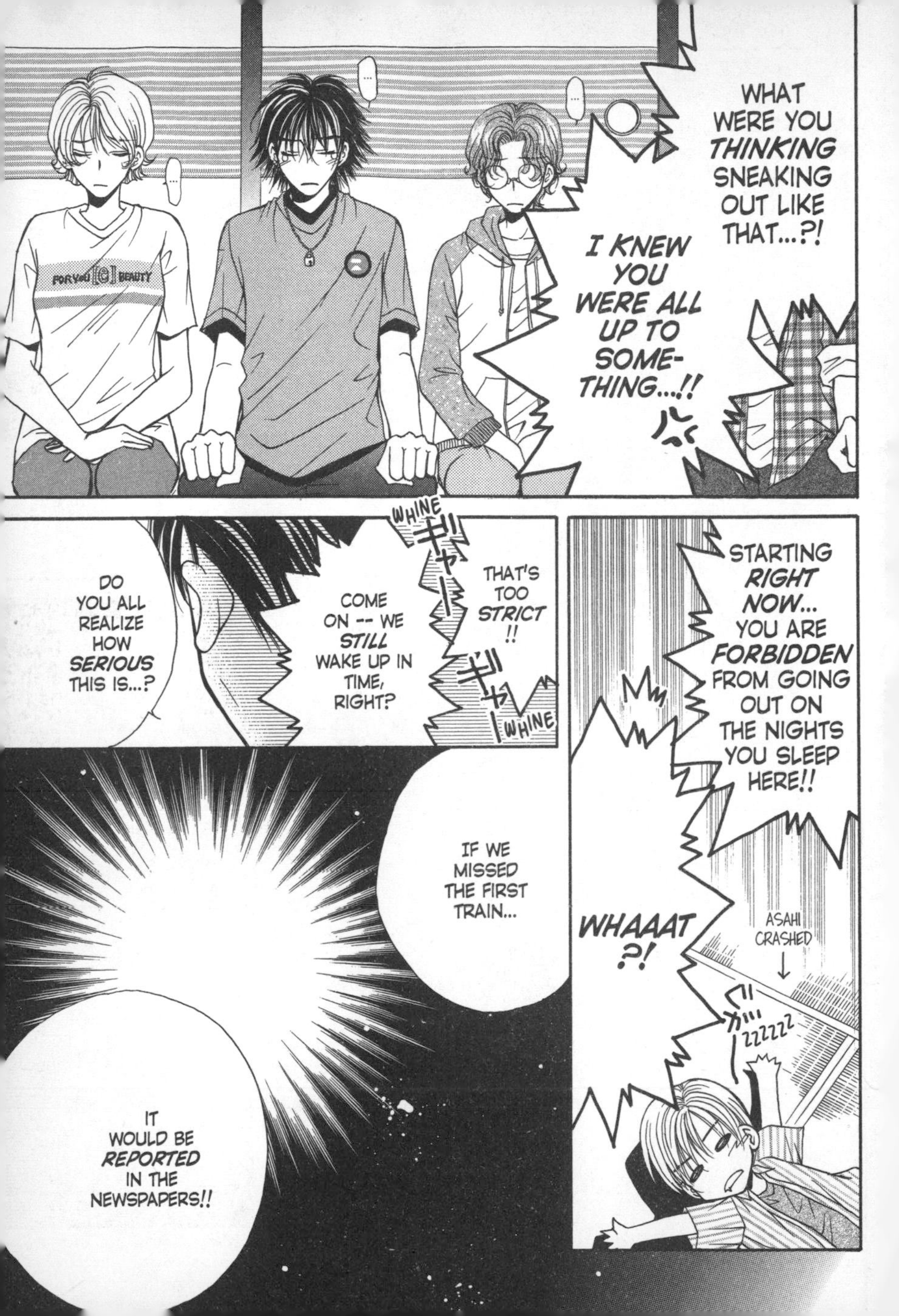
WHAT WERE YOU THINKING SNEAKING OUT LIKE THAT...?!
I KNEW YOU WERE ALL UP TO SOME-THING...!!
...
...
...
STARTING RIGHT NOW... YOU ARE FORBIDDEN FROM GOING OUT ON THE NIGHTS YOU SLEEP HERE!!
WHAAAT?!
ASAHI CRASHED
ZZZZZZ
WHINE
THAT'S TOO STRICT!!
WHINE
COME ON -- WE STILL WAKE UP IN TIME, RIGHT?
DO YOU ALL REALIZE HOW SERIOUS THIS IS...?
IF WE MISSED THE FIRST TRAIN...
IT WOULD BE REPORTED IN THE NEWSPAPERS!!

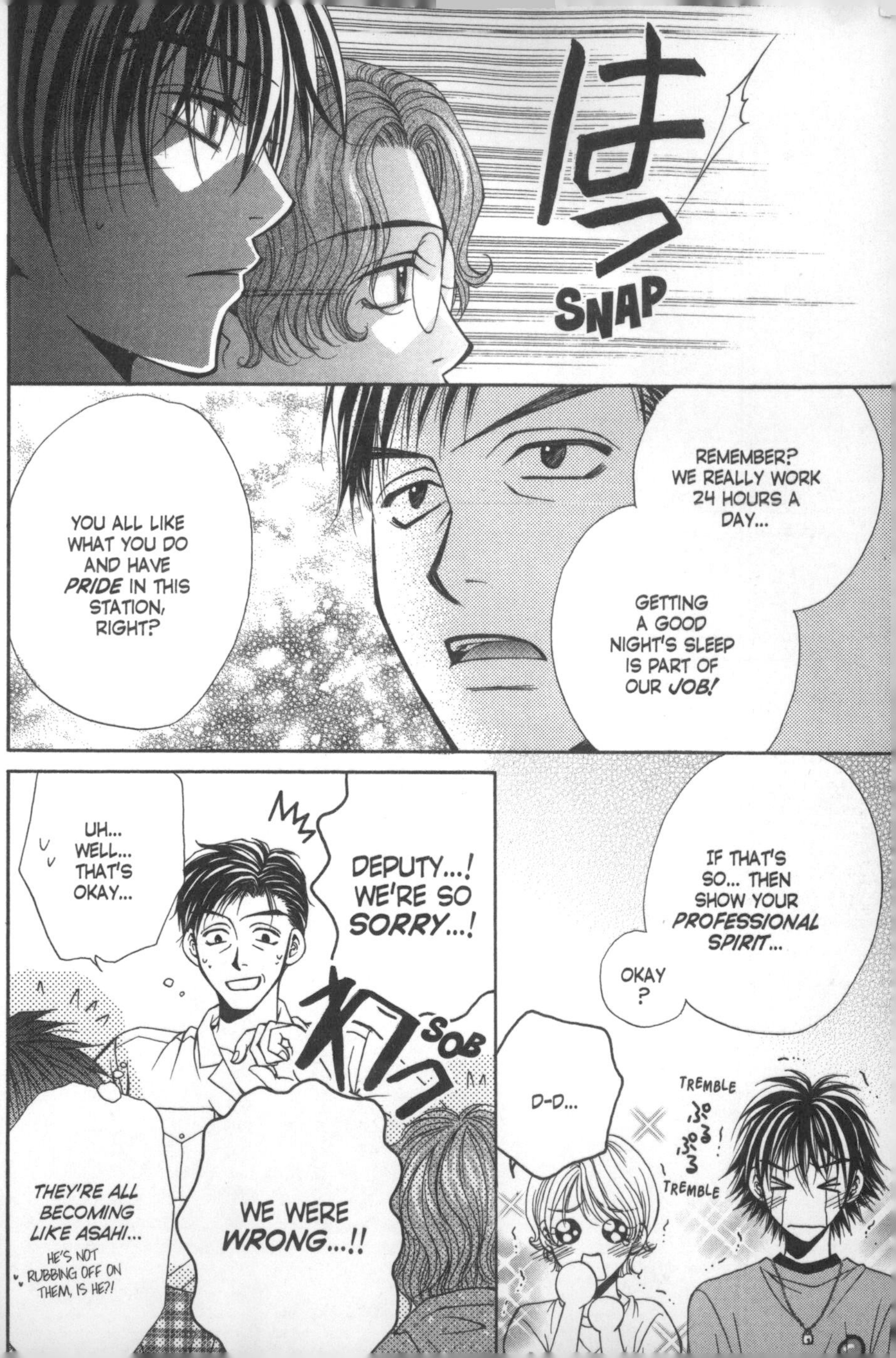
はっ
SNAP
REMEMBER? WE REALLY WORK 24 HOURS A DAY...
GETTING A GOOD NIGHT'S SLEEP IS PART OF OUR JOB!
YOU ALL LIKE WHAT YOU DO AND HAVE PRIDE IN THIS STATION, RIGHT?
IF THAT'S SO... THEN SHOW YOUR PROFESSIONAL SPIRIT...
OKAY ?
D-D...
TREMBLE
ぷるぷる
TREMBLE
DEPUTY...! WE'RE SO SORRY...!
UH... WELL... THAT'S OKAY...
SOB
WE WERE WRONG...!!
THEY'RE ALL BECOMING LIKE ASAHI...
HE'S NOT RUBBING OFF ON THEM, IS HE?!

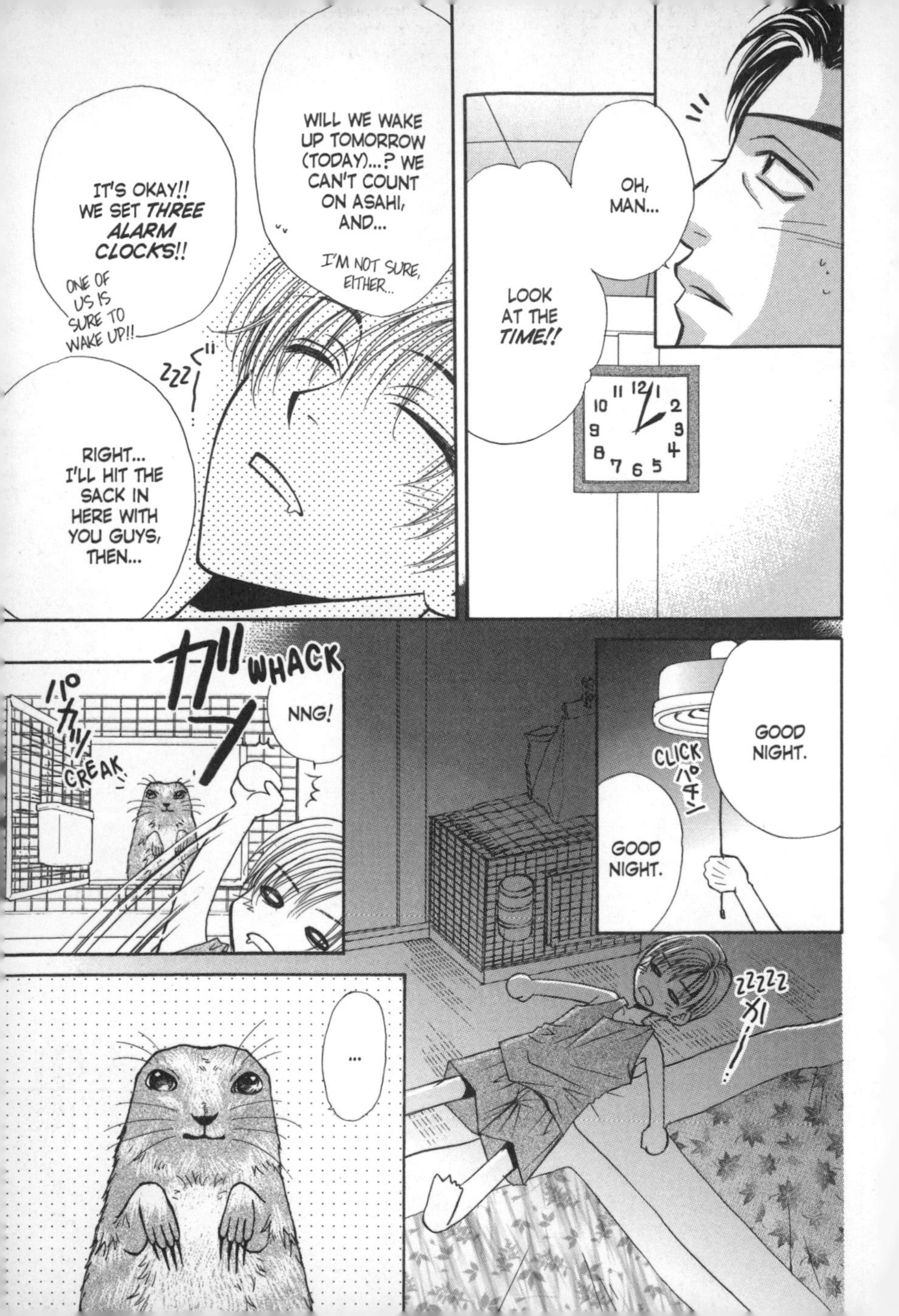
OH, MAN...
LOOK AT THE TIME!!
WILL WE WAKE UP TOMORROW (TODAY)...? WE CAN'T COUNT ON ASAHI, AND...
I'M NOT SURE, EITHER...
IT'S OKAY!! WE SET THREE ALARM CLOCKS!!
ONE OF US IS SURE TO WAKE UP!!
ZZZ
RIGHT... I'LL HIT THE SACK IN HERE WITH YOU GUYS, THEN...
GOOD NIGHT.
CLICK
GOOD NIGHT.
ZZZZZ
WHACK
NNG!
CREAK
...

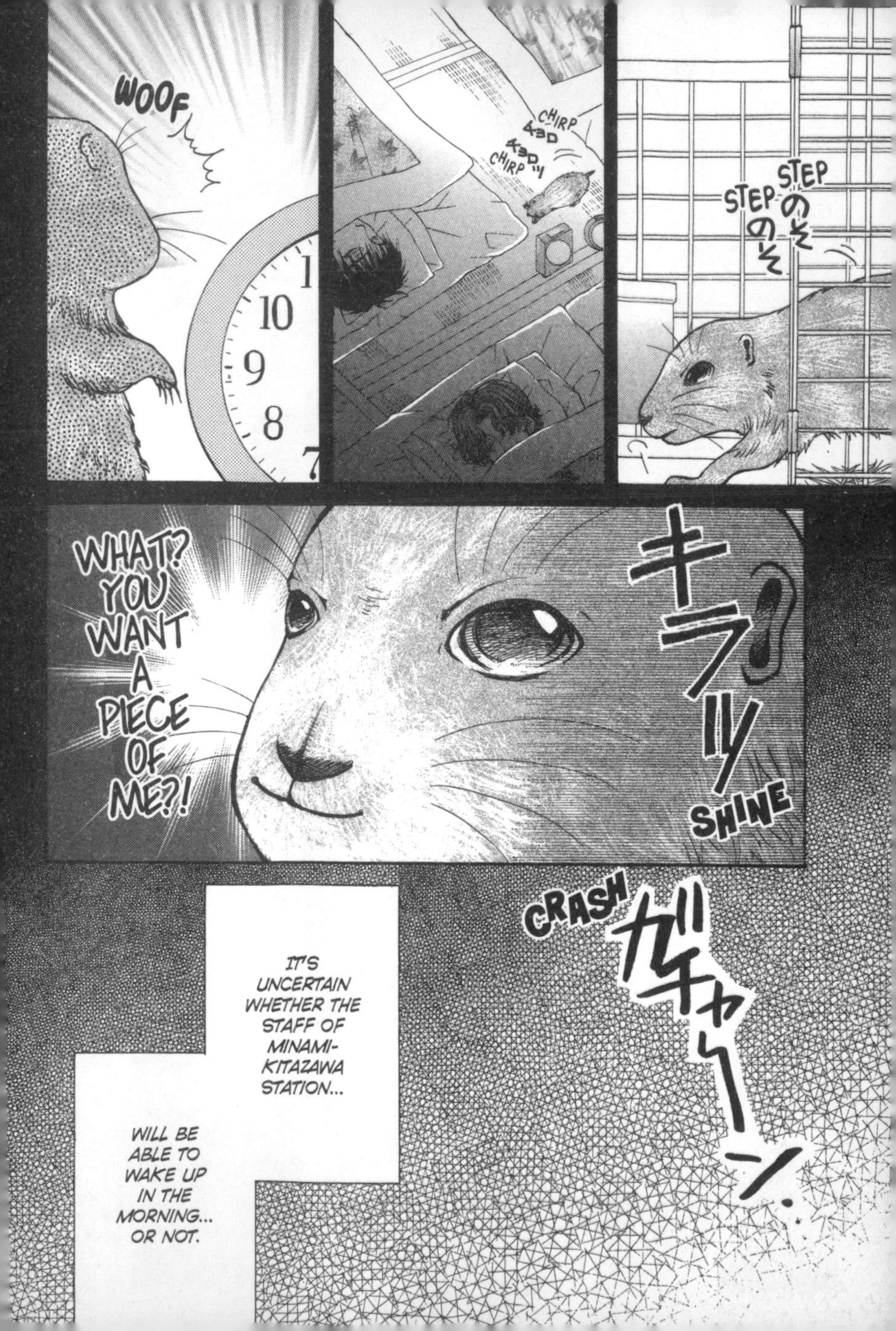
STEP STEP
のそのそ
CHIRP CHIRP
WOOF
キラッ
SHINE
WHAT? YOU WANT A PIECE OF ME?!
CRASH
ガチャーン!
IT'S UNCERTAIN WHETHER THE STAFF OF MINAMI-KITAZAWA STATION...
WILL BE ABLE TO WAKE UP IN THE MORNING... OR NOT.

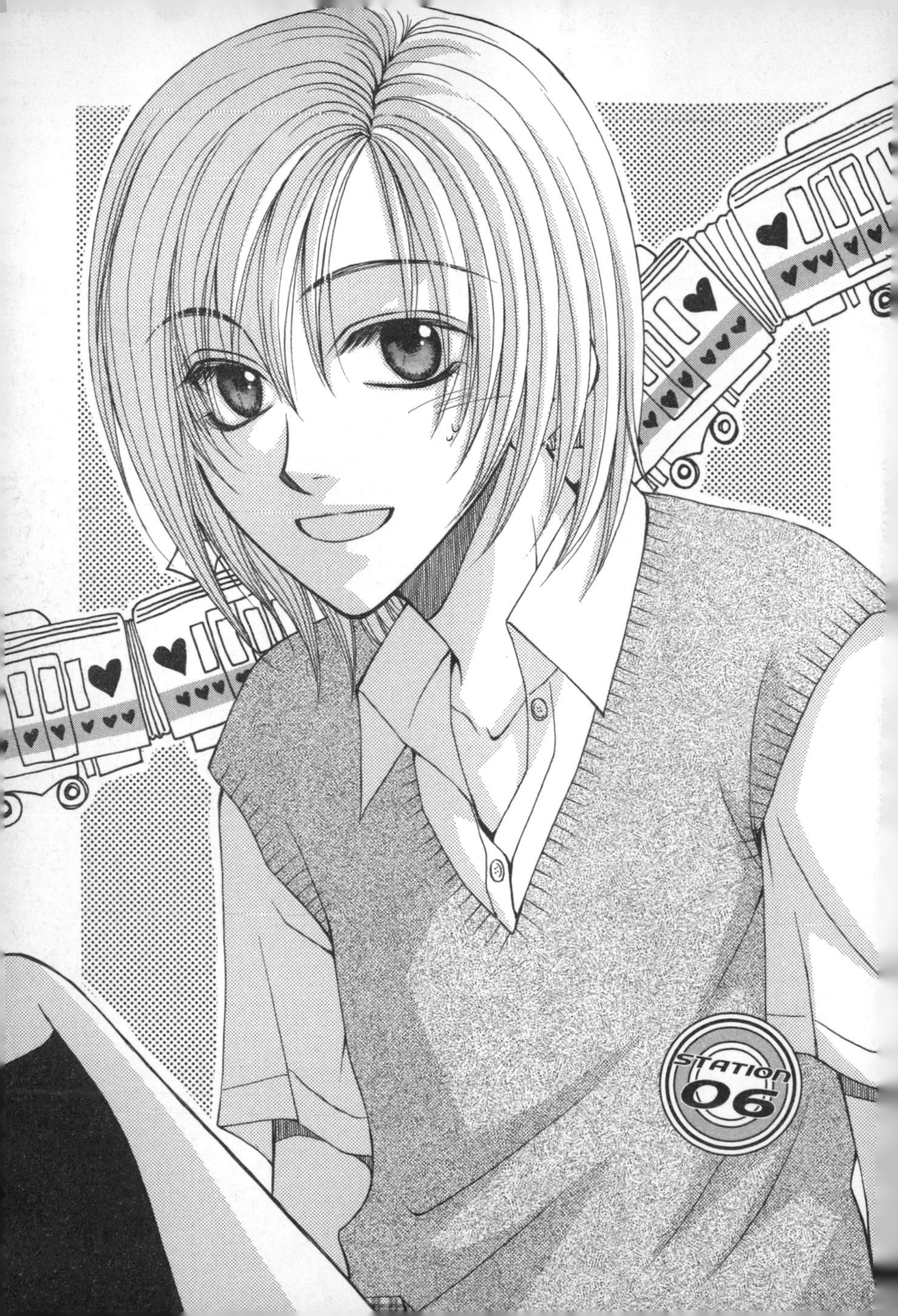
STATION
06

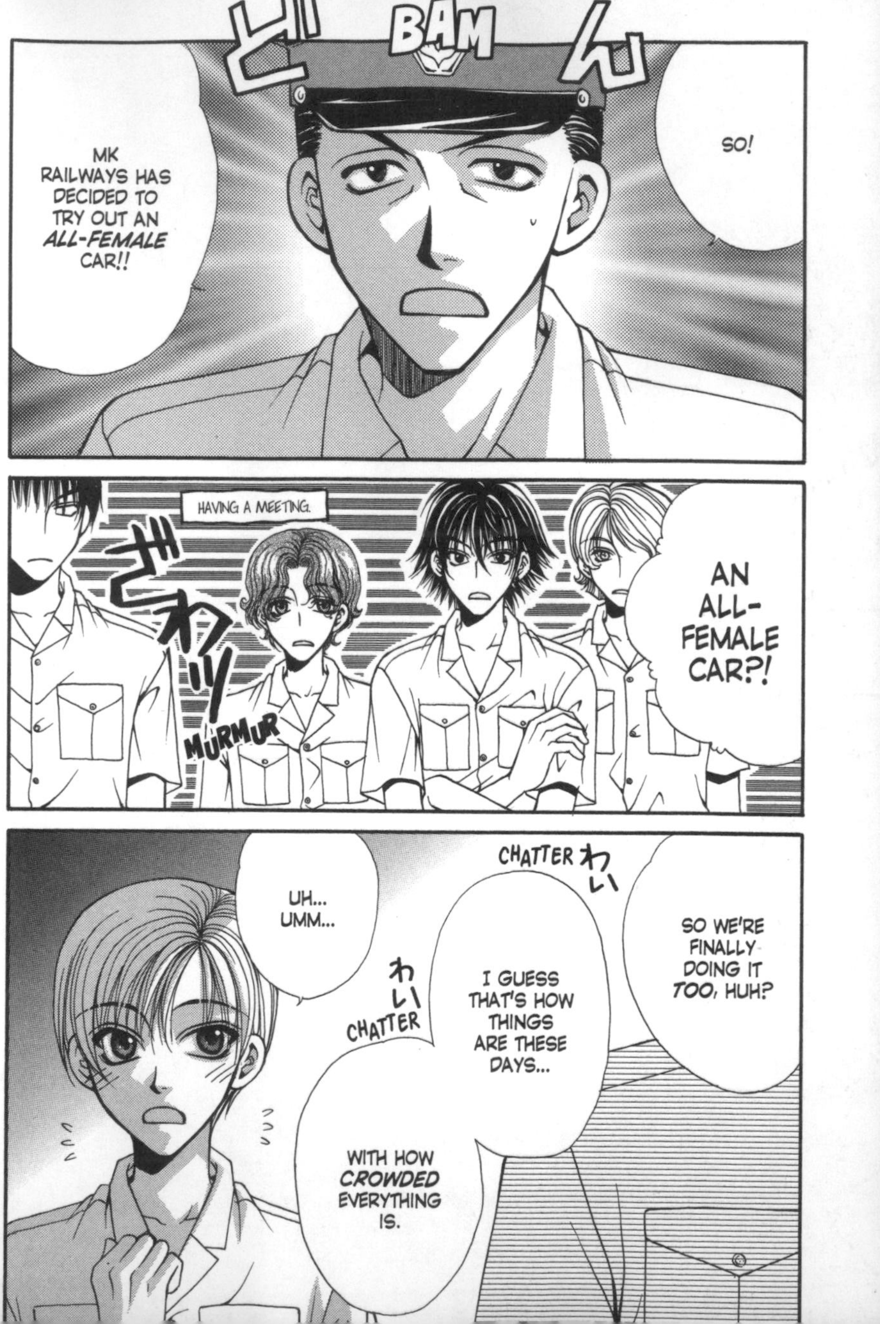

どん
BAM
SO!
MK RAILWAYS HAS DECIDED TO TRY OUT AN *ALL-FEMALE* CAR!!
HAVING A MEETING.
AN ALL-FEMALE CAR?!
ざわっ
MURMUR
SO WE'RE FINALLY DOING IT *TOO*, HUH?
CHATTER わい
I GUESS THAT'S HOW THINGS ARE THESE DAYS...
わい CHATTER
WITH HOW *CROWDED* EVERYTHING IS.
UH... UMM...

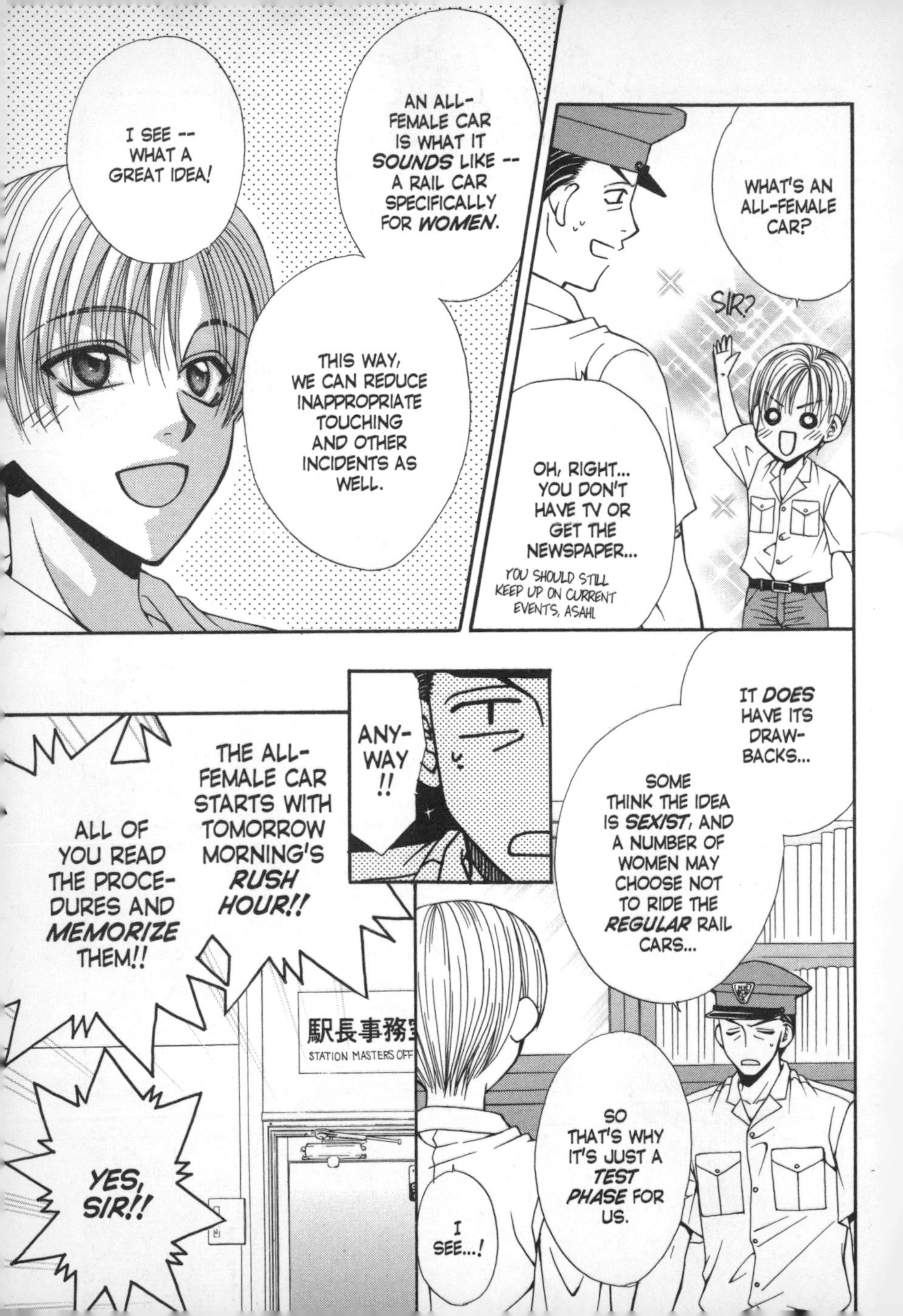
WHAT'S AN ALL-FEMALE CAR?
SIR?
OH, RIGHT... YOU DON'T HAVE TV OR GET THE NEWSPAPER...
YOU SHOULD STILL KEEP UP ON CURRENT EVENTS, ASAHI.
AN ALL-FEMALE CAR IS WHAT IT *SOUNDS* LIKE -- A RAIL CAR SPECIFICALLY FOR *WOMEN*.
THIS WAY, WE CAN REDUCE INAPPROPRIATE TOUCHING AND OTHER INCIDENTS AS WELL.
I SEE -- WHAT A GREAT IDEA!
IT *DOES* HAVE ITS DRAW-BACKS...
SOME THINK THE IDEA IS *SEXIST*, AND A NUMBER OF WOMEN MAY CHOOSE NOT TO RIDE THE *REGULAR* RAIL CARS...
SO THAT'S WHY IT'S JUST A *TEST PHASE* FOR US.
I SEE...!
ANY-WAY!!
THE ALL-FEMALE CAR STARTS WITH TOMORROW MORNING'S *RUSH HOUR!!*
ALL OF YOU READ THE PROCE-DURES AND *MEMORIZE* THEM!!
駅長事務室
STATION MASTERS OFF
*YES, SIR!!*

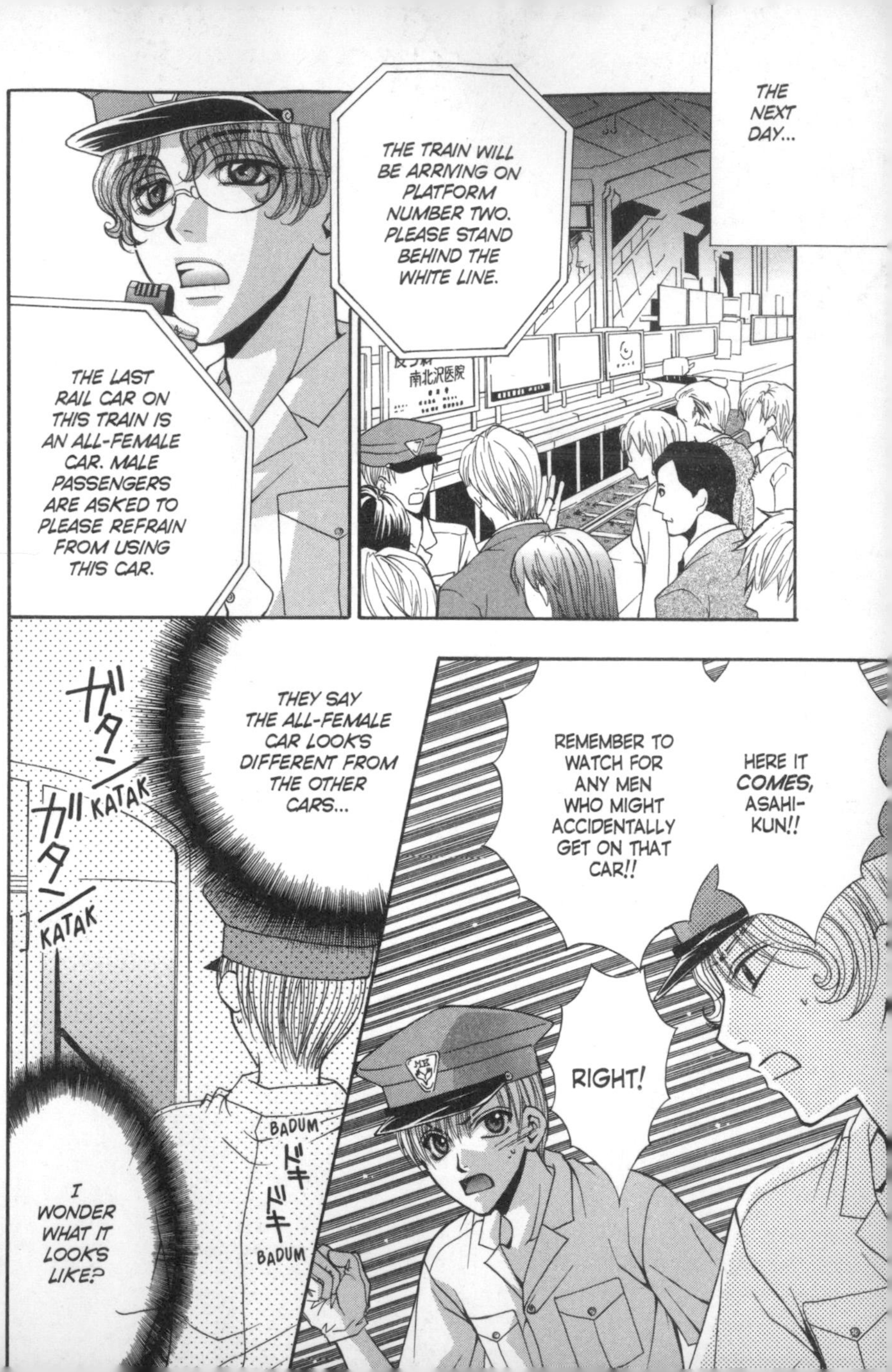
THE NEXT DAY...
THE TRAIN WILL BE ARRIVING ON PLATFORM NUMBER TWO. PLEASE STAND BEHIND THE WHITE LINE.
南北沢医院
THE LAST RAIL CAR ON THIS TRAIN IS AN ALL-FEMALE CAR. MALE PASSENGERS ARE ASKED TO PLEASE REFRAIN FROM USING THIS CAR.
HERE IT COMES, ASAHI-KUN!!
REMEMBER TO WATCH FOR ANY MEN WHO MIGHT ACCIDENTALLY GET ON THAT CAR!!
RIGHT!
THEY SAY THE ALL-FEMALE CAR LOOKS DIFFERENT FROM THE OTHER CARS...
ガタン
KATAK
ガタン
KATAK
BADUM
ドキ
ドキ
BADUM
I WONDER WHAT IT LOOKS LIKE?

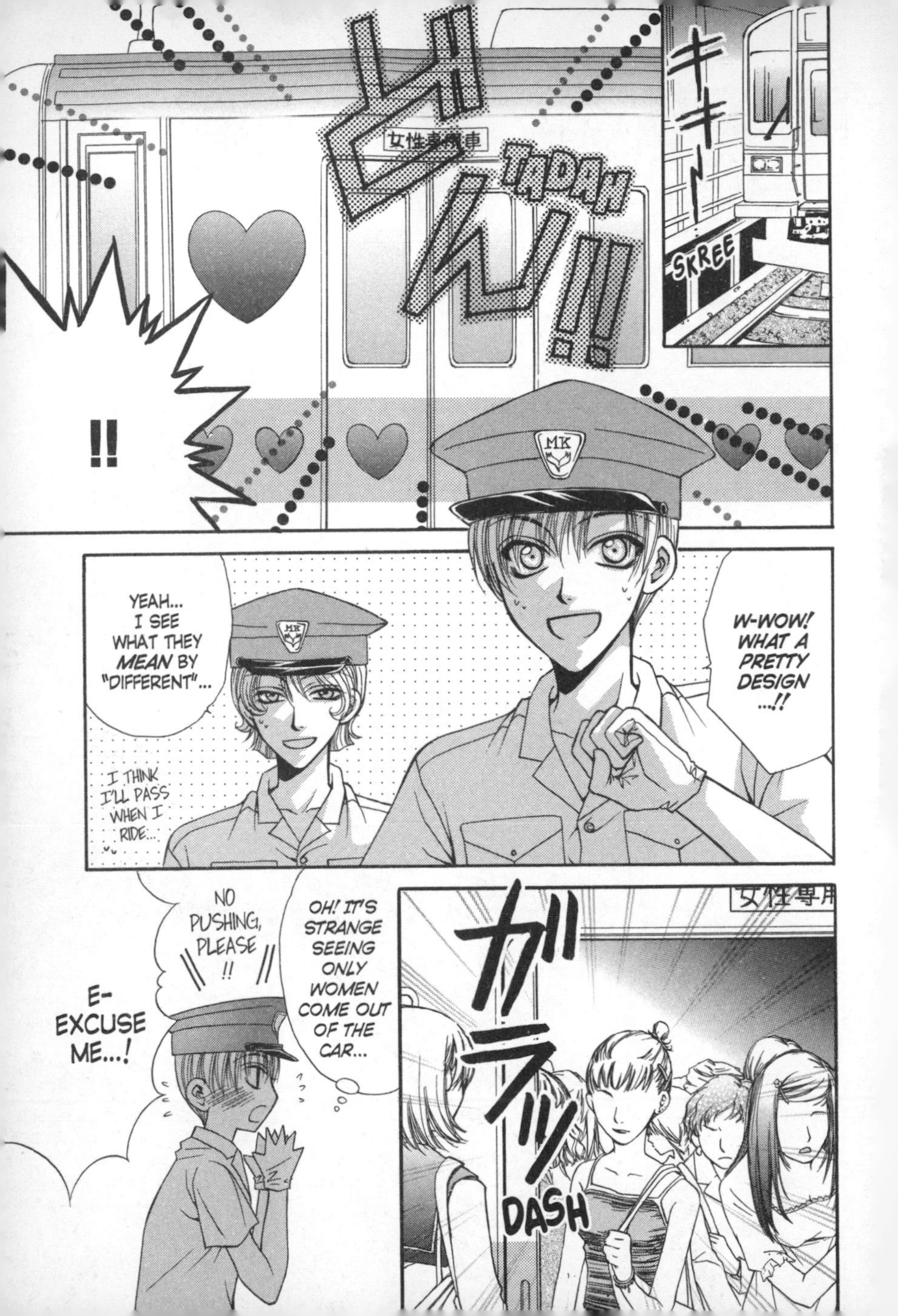
SKREE
TADAH
!!
W-WOW! WHAT A PRETTY DESIGN ...!!
YEAH... I SEE WHAT THEY *MEAN* BY "DIFFERENT"...
I THINK I'LL PASS WHEN I RIDE...
女性専用
DASH
OH! IT'S STRANGE SEEING ONLY WOMEN COME OUT OF THE CAR...
NO PUSHING, PLEASE !!
E-EXCUSE ME...!

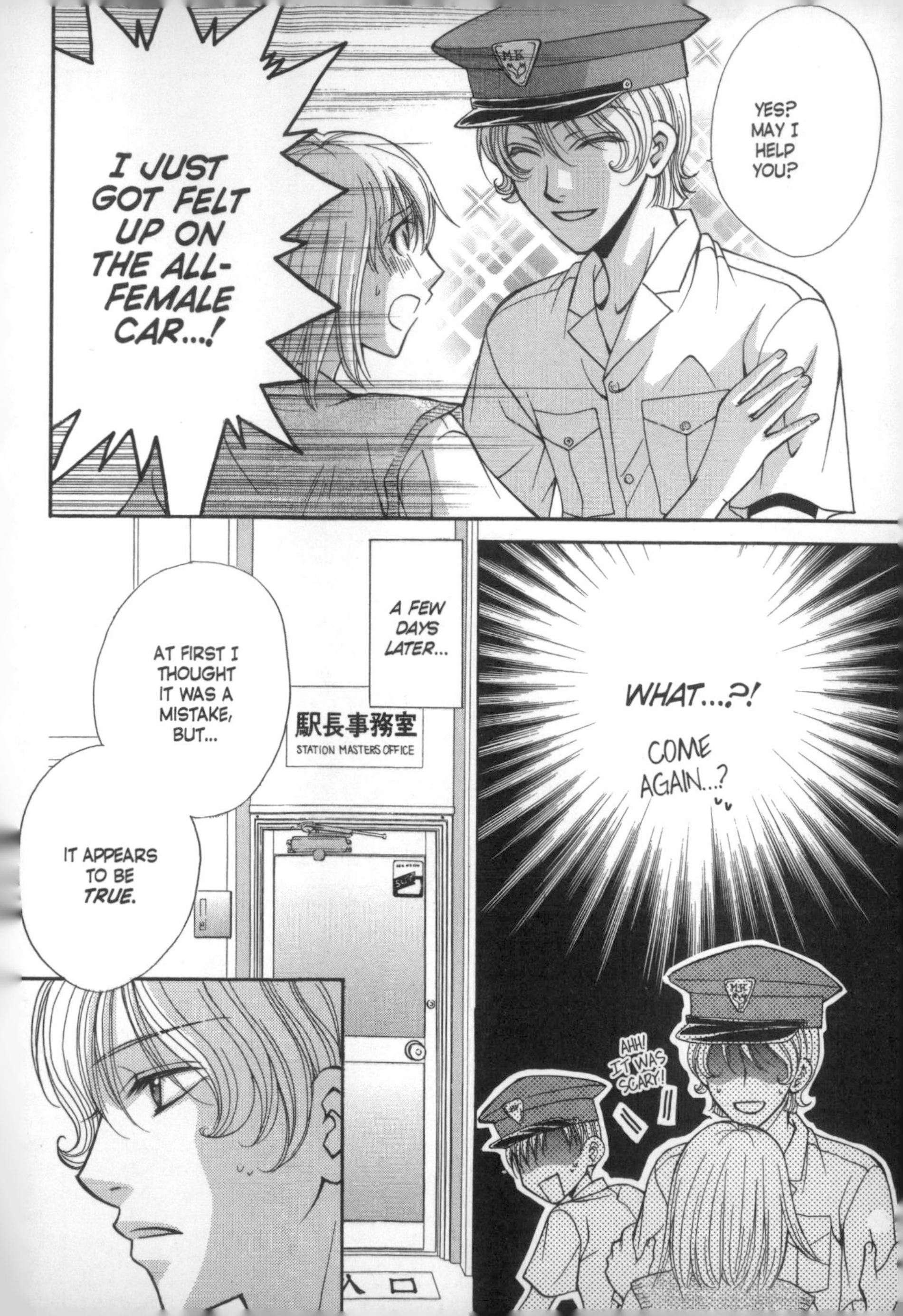
YES? MAY I HELP YOU?
I JUST GOT FELT UP ON THE ALL-FEMALE CAR...!
WHAT...?!
COME AGAIN...?
AHH! IT WAS SCARY!
A FEW DAYS LATER...
駅長事務室
STATION MASTERS OFFICE
AT FIRST I THOUGHT IT WAS A MISTAKE, BUT...
IT APPEARS TO BE TRUE.

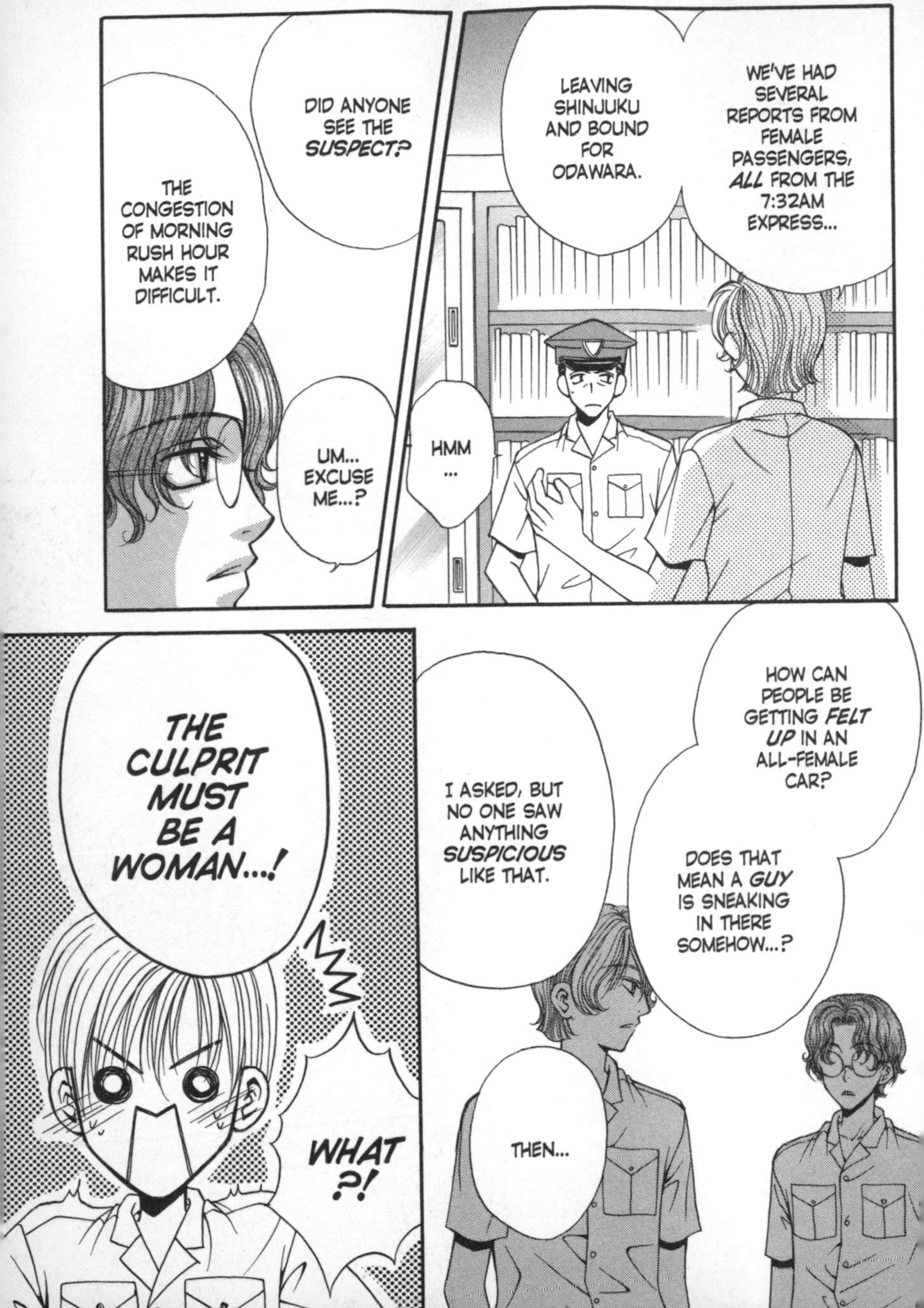
WE'VE HAD SEVERAL REPORTS FROM FEMALE PASSENGERS, ALL FROM THE 7:32AM EXPRESS...
LEAVING SHINJUKU AND BOUND FOR ODAWARA.
HMM ...
DID ANYONE SEE THE SUSPECT?
THE CONGESTION OF MORNING RUSH HOUR MAKES IT DIFFICULT.
UM... EXCUSE ME...?
HOW CAN PEOPLE BE GETTING FELT UP IN AN ALL-FEMALE CAR?
DOES THAT MEAN A GUY IS SNEAKING IN THERE SOMEHOW...?
I ASKED, BUT NO ONE SAW ANYTHING SUSPICIOUS LIKE THAT.
THEN...
THE CULPRIT MUST BE A WOMAN...!
MM
WHAT ?!

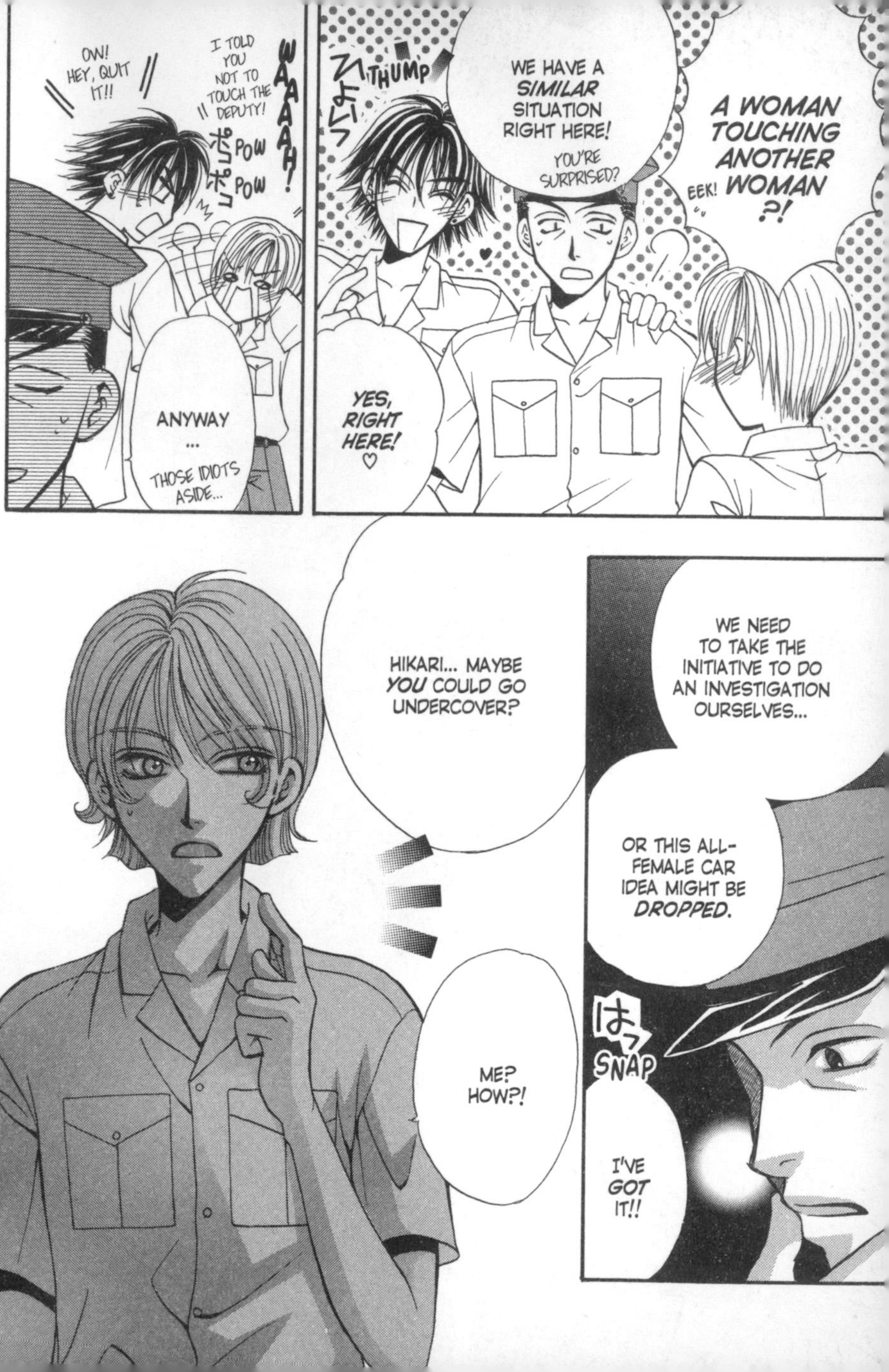
A WOMAN TOUCHING ANOTHER WOMAN ?!
WE HAVE A SIMILAR SITUATION RIGHT HERE!
THUMP
ひょいっ
YOU'RE SURPRISED?
EEK!
YES, RIGHT HERE! ♡
WAAAAH!
I TOLD YOU NOT TO TOUCH THE DEPUTY!
OW! HEY, QUIT IT!!
ポコ POW
ポコ POW
ANYWAY ... THOSE IDIOTS ASIDE...
WE NEED TO TAKE THE INITIATIVE TO DO AN INVESTIGATION OURSELVES...
OR THIS ALL-FEMALE CAR IDEA MIGHT BE DROPPED.
はっ SNAP
I'VE GOT IT!!
HIKARI... MAYBE YOU COULD GO UNDERCOVER?
ME? HOW?!

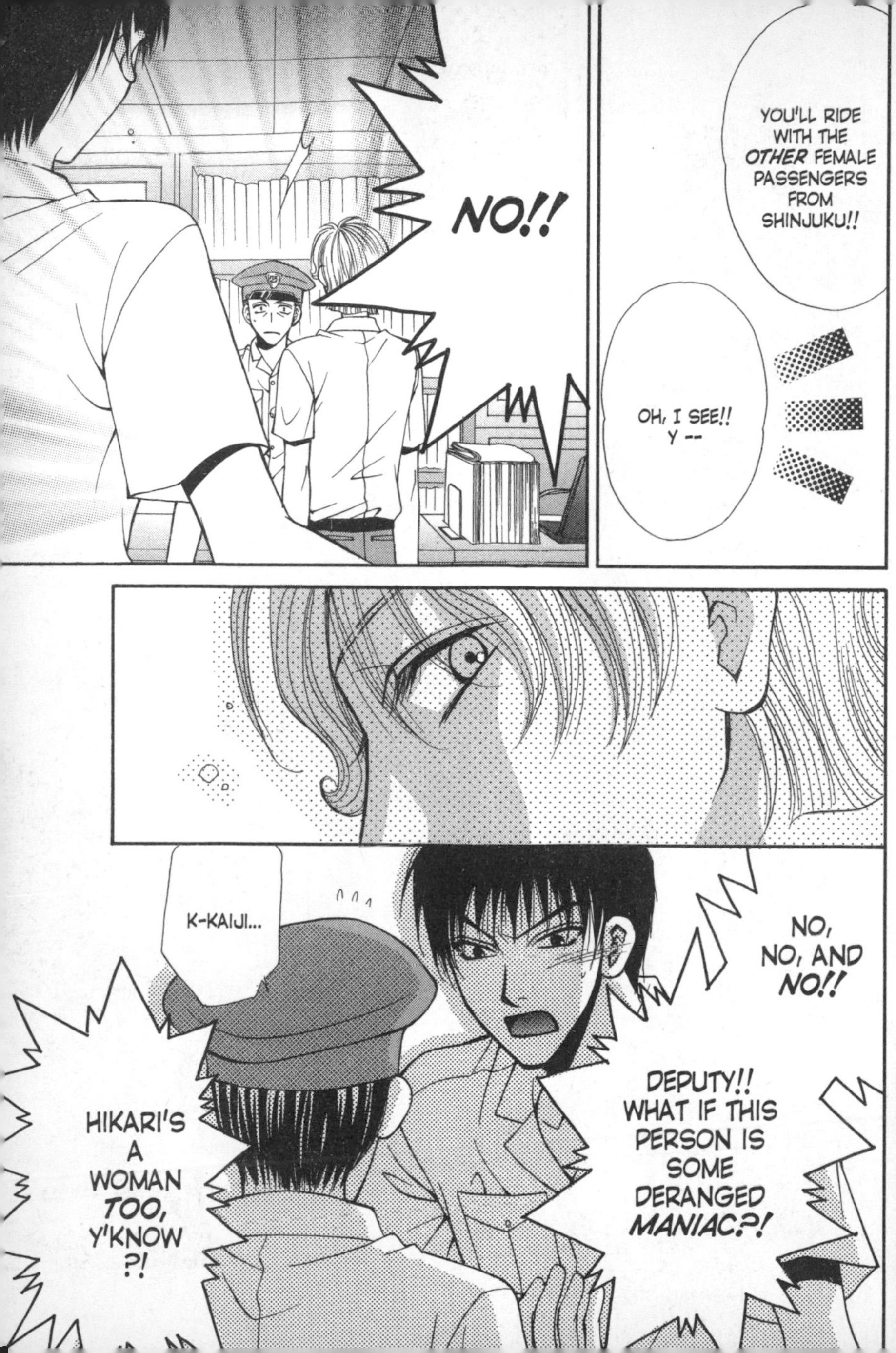
YOU'LL RIDE WITH THE *OTHER* FEMALE PASSENGERS FROM SHINJUKU!!
OH, I SEE!! Y --
NO!!
NO, NO, AND *NO!!*
K-KAIJI...
DEPUTY!! WHAT IF THIS PERSON IS SOME DERANGED *MANIAC?!*
HIKARI'S A WOMAN *TOO,* Y'KNOW ?!

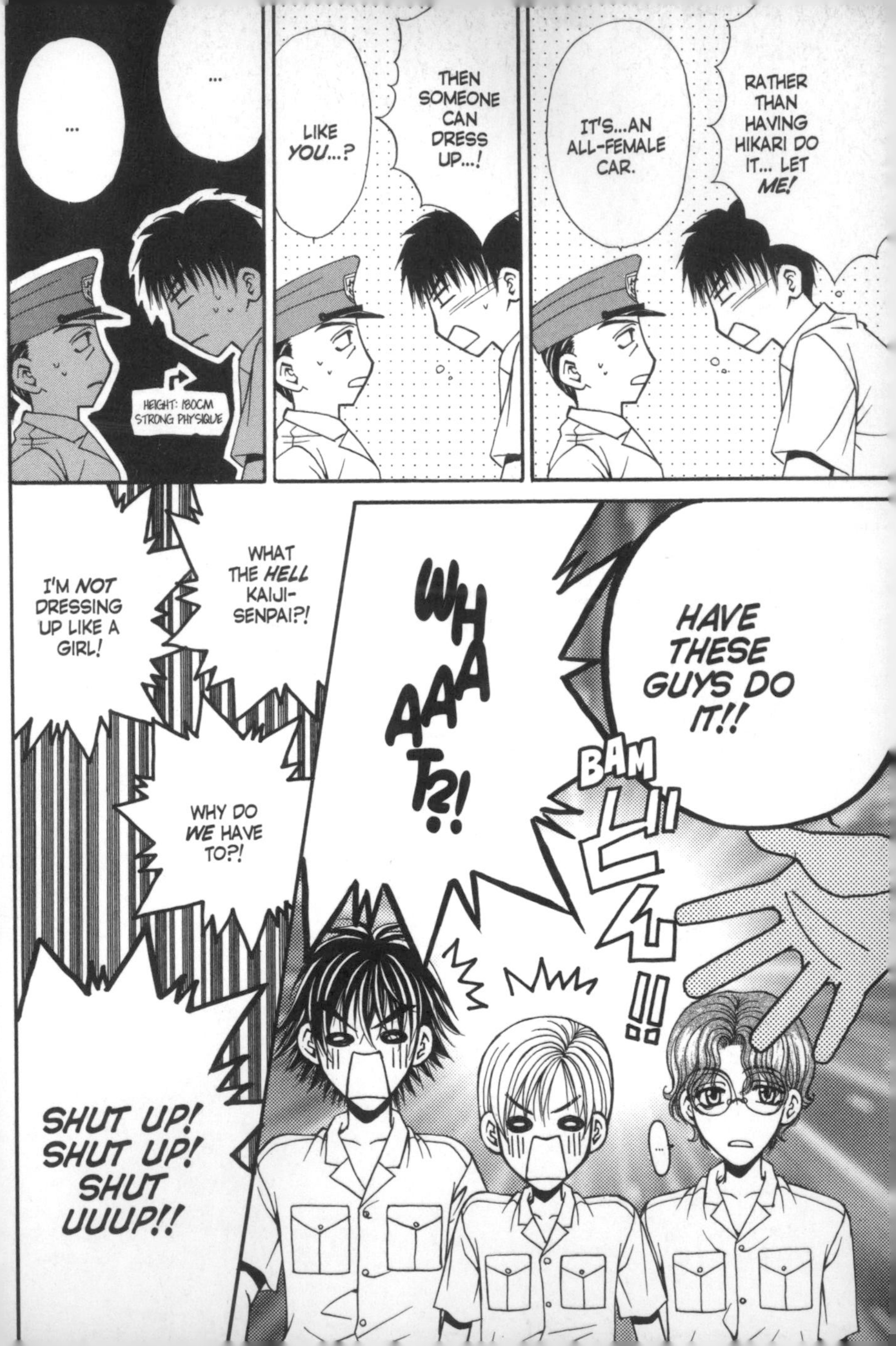
RATHER THAN HAVING HIKARI DO IT... LET ME!
IT'S...AN ALL-FEMALE CAR.
THEN SOMEONE CAN DRESS UP...!
LIKE YOU...?
...
...
HEIGHT: 180CM STRONG PHYSIQUE
HAVE THESE GUYS DO IT!!
BAM
WHAAAAT?!
WHAT THE HELL KAIJI-SENPAI?!
I'M NOT DRESSING UP LIKE A GIRL!
WHY DO WE HAVE TO?!
...
SHUT UP! SHUT UP! SHUT UUUP!!

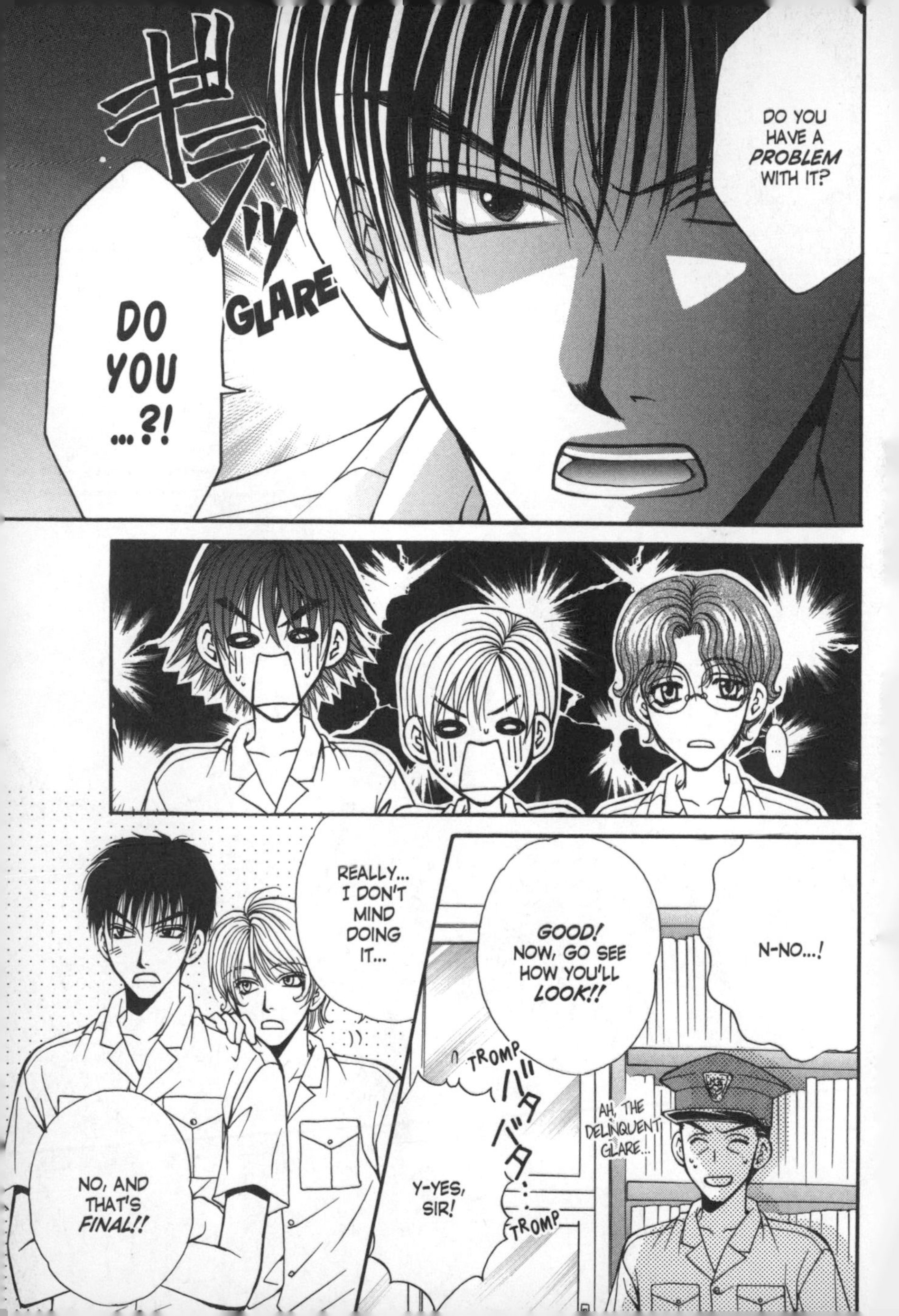
DO YOU HAVE A PROBLEM WITH IT?
ギラッ
GLARE
DO YOU ...?!
...
N-NO...!
GOOD! NOW, GO SEE HOW YOU'LL LOOK!!
AH, THE DELINQUENT GLARE...
TROMP
バタバタ
TROMP
Y-YES, SIR!
REALLY... I DON'T MIND DOING IT...
NO, AND THAT'S FINAL!!

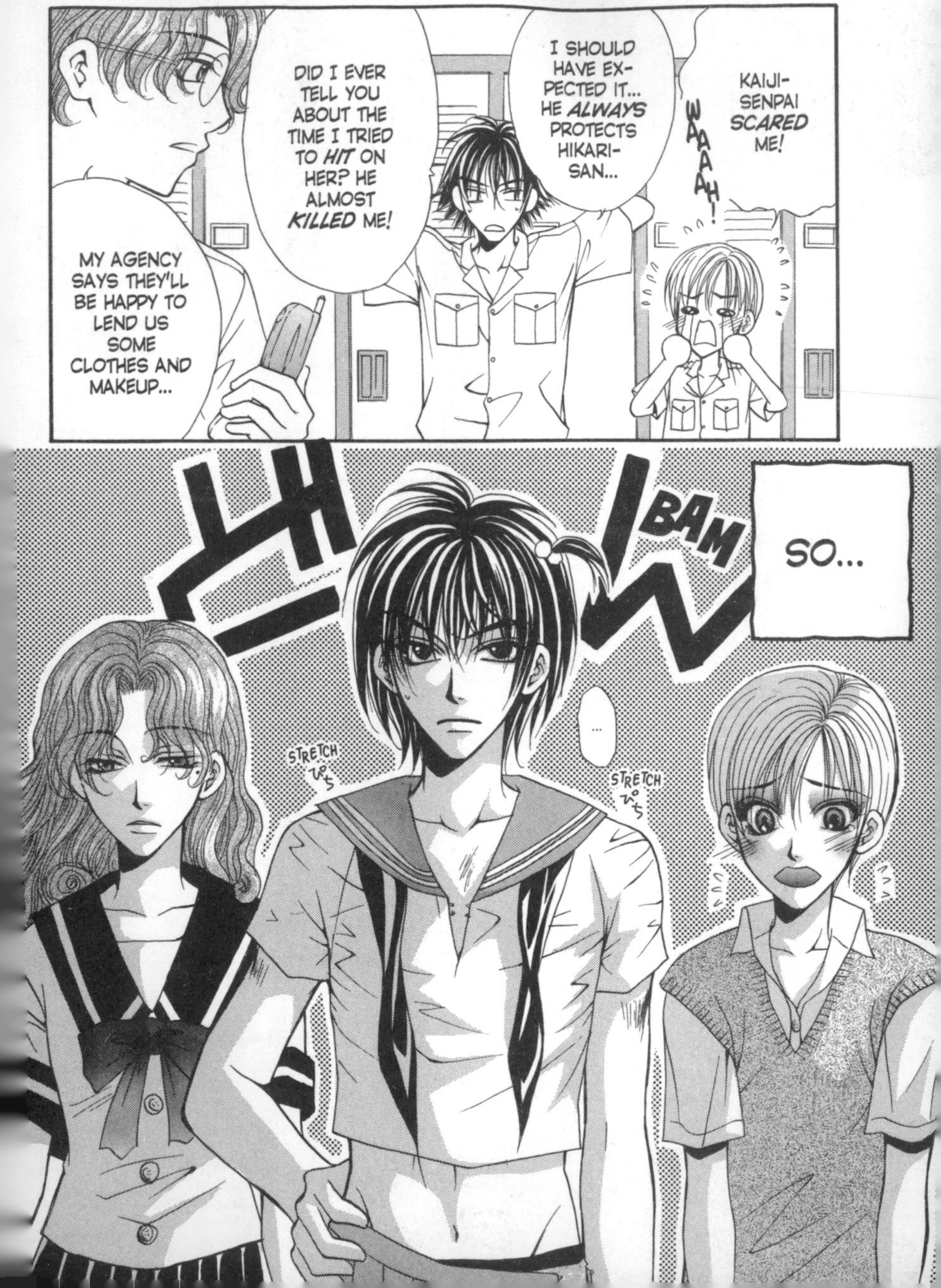
KAIJI-SENPAI SCARED ME!
WAAAAH!
I SHOULD HAVE EX-PECTED IT... HE ALWAYS PROTECTS HIKARI-SAN...
DID I EVER TELL YOU ABOUT THE TIME I TRIED TO HIT ON HER? HE ALMOST KILLED ME!
MY AGENCY SAYS THEY'LL BE HAPPY TO LEND US SOME CLOTHES AND MAKEUP...
SO...
BAM
...
STRETCH
STRETCH

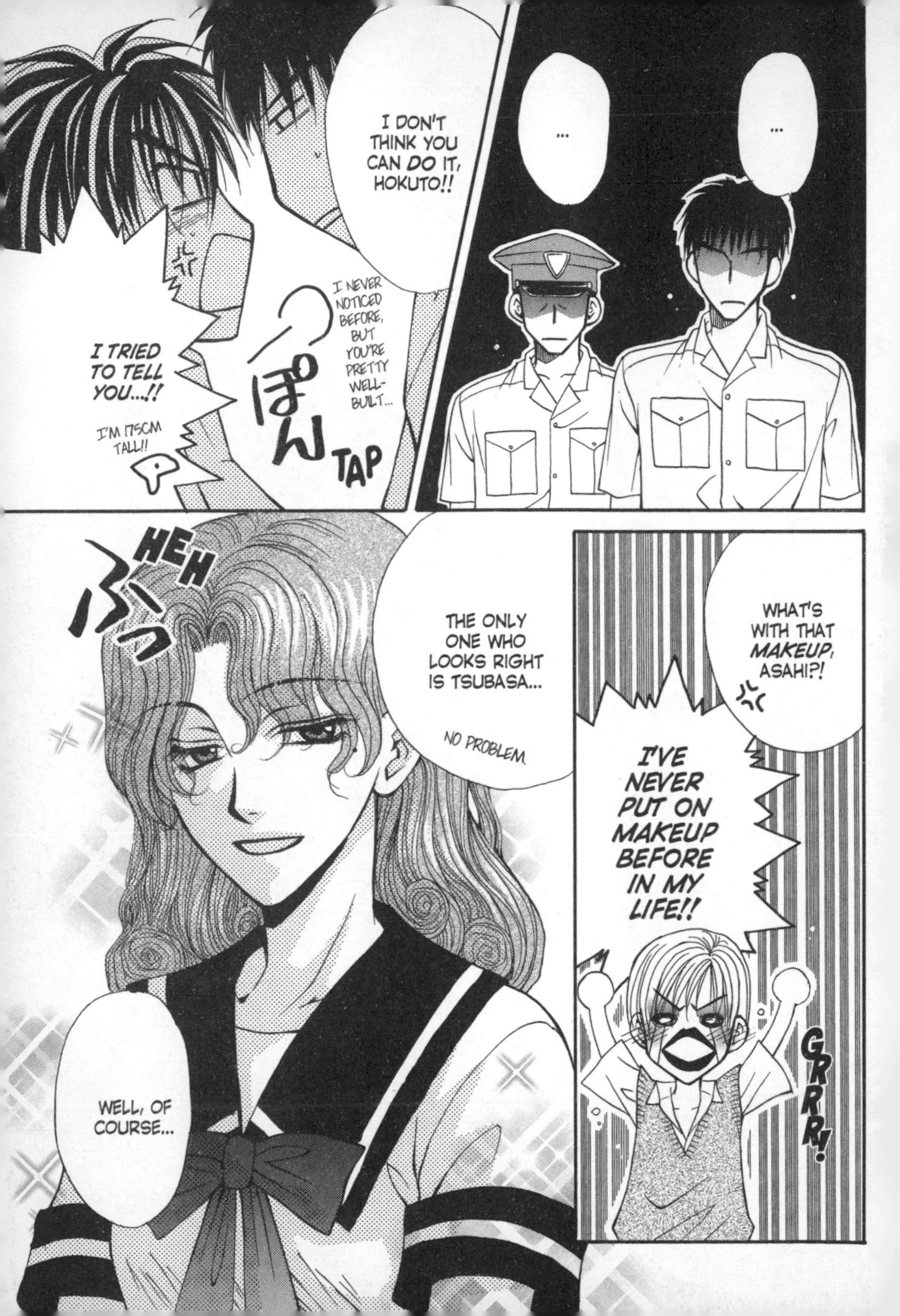
...
...
I DON'T THINK YOU CAN *DO* IT, HOKUTO!!
I NEVER NOTICED BEFORE, BUT YOU'RE PRETTY WELL-BUILT...
ぽん TAP
I TRIED TO TELL YOU...!!
I'M 175CM TALL!!
WHAT'S WITH THAT *MAKEUP*, ASAHI?!
I'VE NEVER PUT ON MAKEUP BEFORE IN MY LIFE!!
GRRR!
THE ONLY ONE WHO LOOKS RIGHT IS TSUBASA...
NO PROBLEM.
ふっ HEH
WELL, OF COURSE...

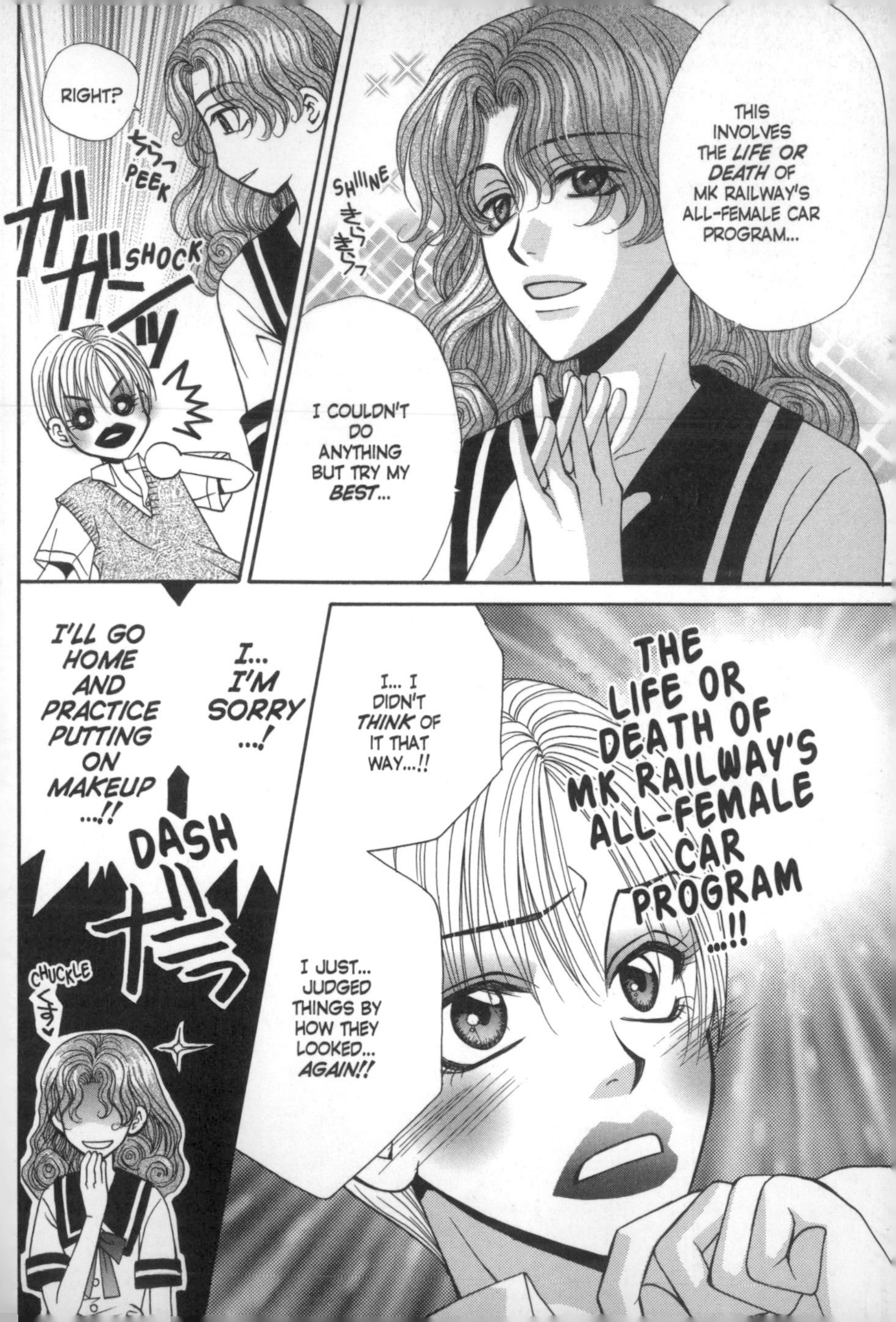
THIS INVOLVES THE *LIFE OR DEATH* OF MK RAILWAY'S ALL-FEMALE CAR PROGRAM...
SHIIINE
きらきらっ
I COULDN'T DO ANYTHING BUT TRY MY *BEST*...
RIGHT?
ちらっ
PEEK
SHOCK
THE LIFE OR DEATH OF MK RAILWAY'S ALL-FEMALE CAR PROGRAM ...!!
I... I DIDN'T *THINK* OF IT THAT WAY...!!
I JUST... JUDGED THINGS BY HOW THEY LOOKED... *AGAIN!!*
I... I'M SORRY ...!
I'LL GO HOME AND PRACTICE PUTTING ON MAKEUP ...!!
DASH
CHUCKLE
くすっ

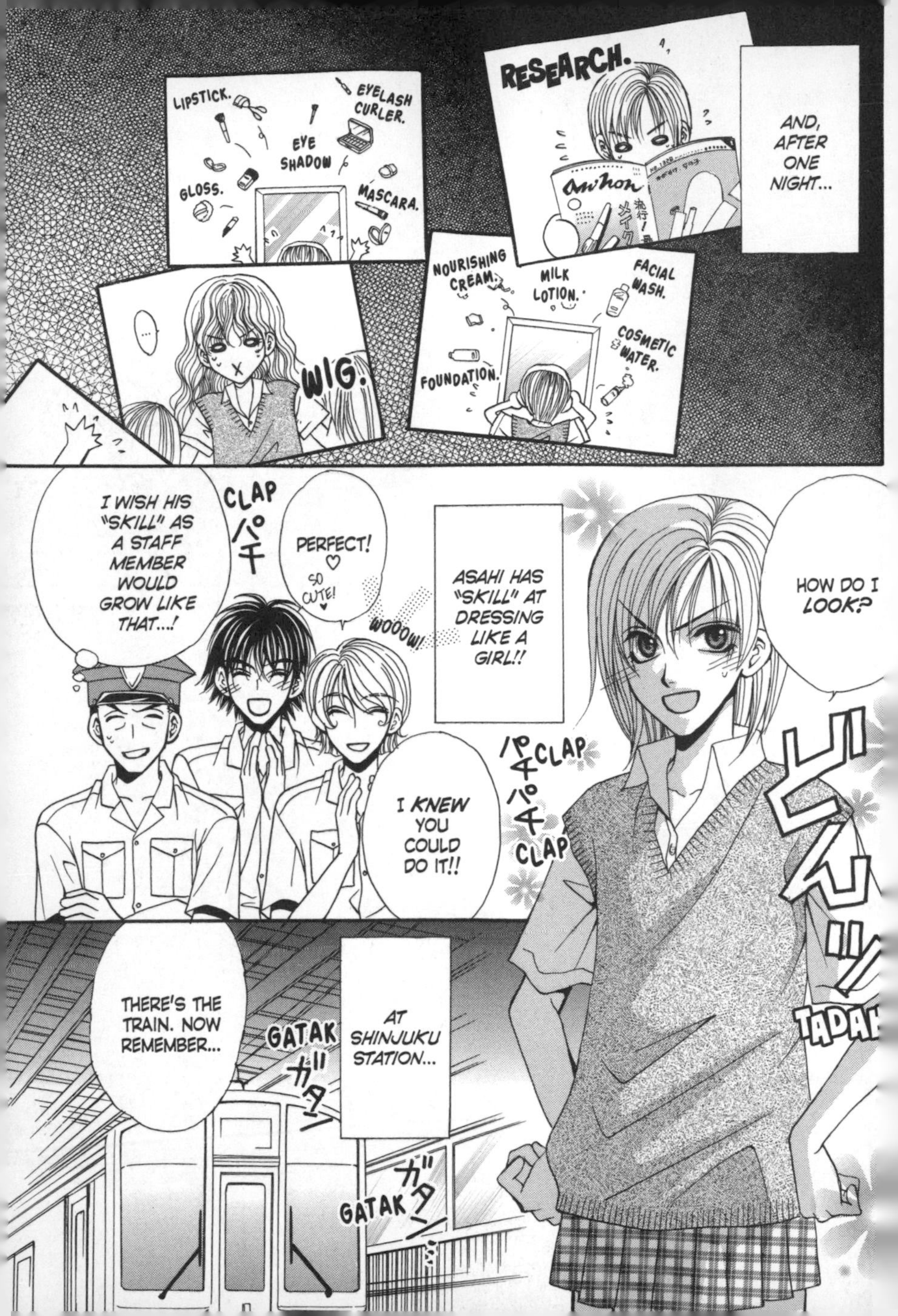
AND, AFTER ONE NIGHT...
RESEARCH.
LIPSTICK.
EYELASH CURLER.
EYE SHADOW
GLOSS.
MASCARA.
NOURISHING CREAM.
MILK LOTION.
FACIAL WASH.
COSMETIC WATER.
FOUNDATION.
...
WIG.
HOW DO I LOOK?
TADAH
ASAHI HAS "SKILL" AT DRESSING LIKE A GIRL!!
PERFECT! ♡
SO CUTE! ♥
WOOOW!
CLAP パチ
I WISH HIS "SKILL" AS A STAFF MEMBER WOULD GROW LIKE THAT...!
パチ CLAP
パチ CLAP
I KNEW YOU COULD DO IT!!
AT SHINJUKU STATION...
THERE'S THE TRAIN. NOW REMEMBER...
GATAK ガタ
GATAK ガタ

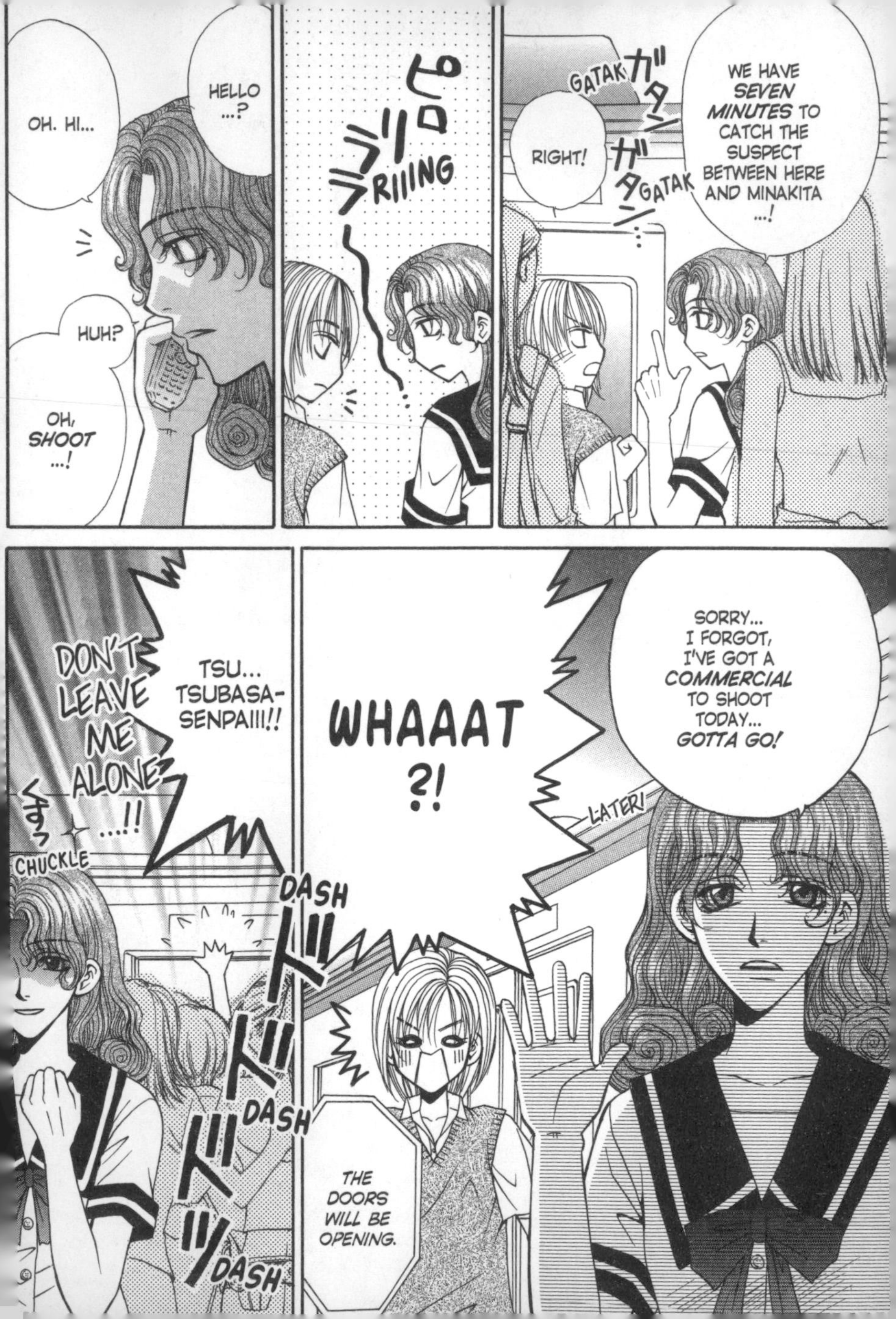

WE HAVE SEVEN MINUTES TO CATCH THE SUSPECT BETWEEN HERE AND MINAKITA ...!
GATAK ガタン
GATAK ガタン
RIGHT!
ピロリラ~
RIIIING
HELLO ...?
OH. HI...
HUH?
OH, SHOOT ...!
SORRY... I FORGOT, I'VE GOT A COMMERCIAL TO SHOOT TODAY... GOTTA GO!
LATER!
WHAAAT ?!
THE DOORS WILL BE OPENING.
TSU... TSUBASA-SENPAIIII!!
DON'T LEAVE ME ALONE ...!!
DASH
DASH
DASH
くすっ
CHUCKLE

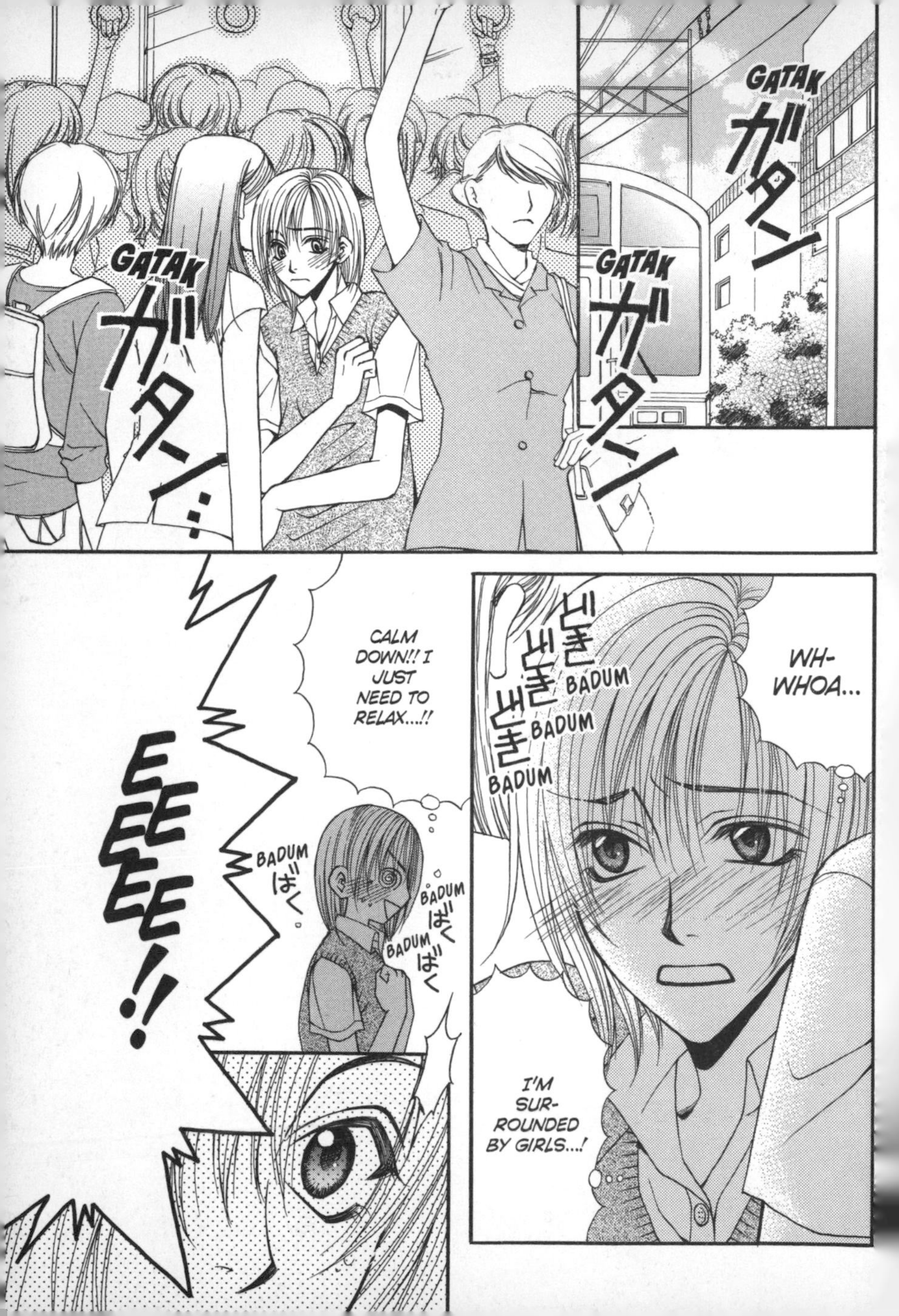
GATAK
ガタン
GATAK
ガタン
GATAK
ガタン…
どきどきどき
BADUM
BADUM
BADUM
WH-WHOA...
I'M SUR-ROUNDED BY GIRLS...!
CALM DOWN!! I JUST NEED TO RELAX...!!
BADUM
ばく
BADUM
ばく
BADUM
ばく
EEEEEE!!

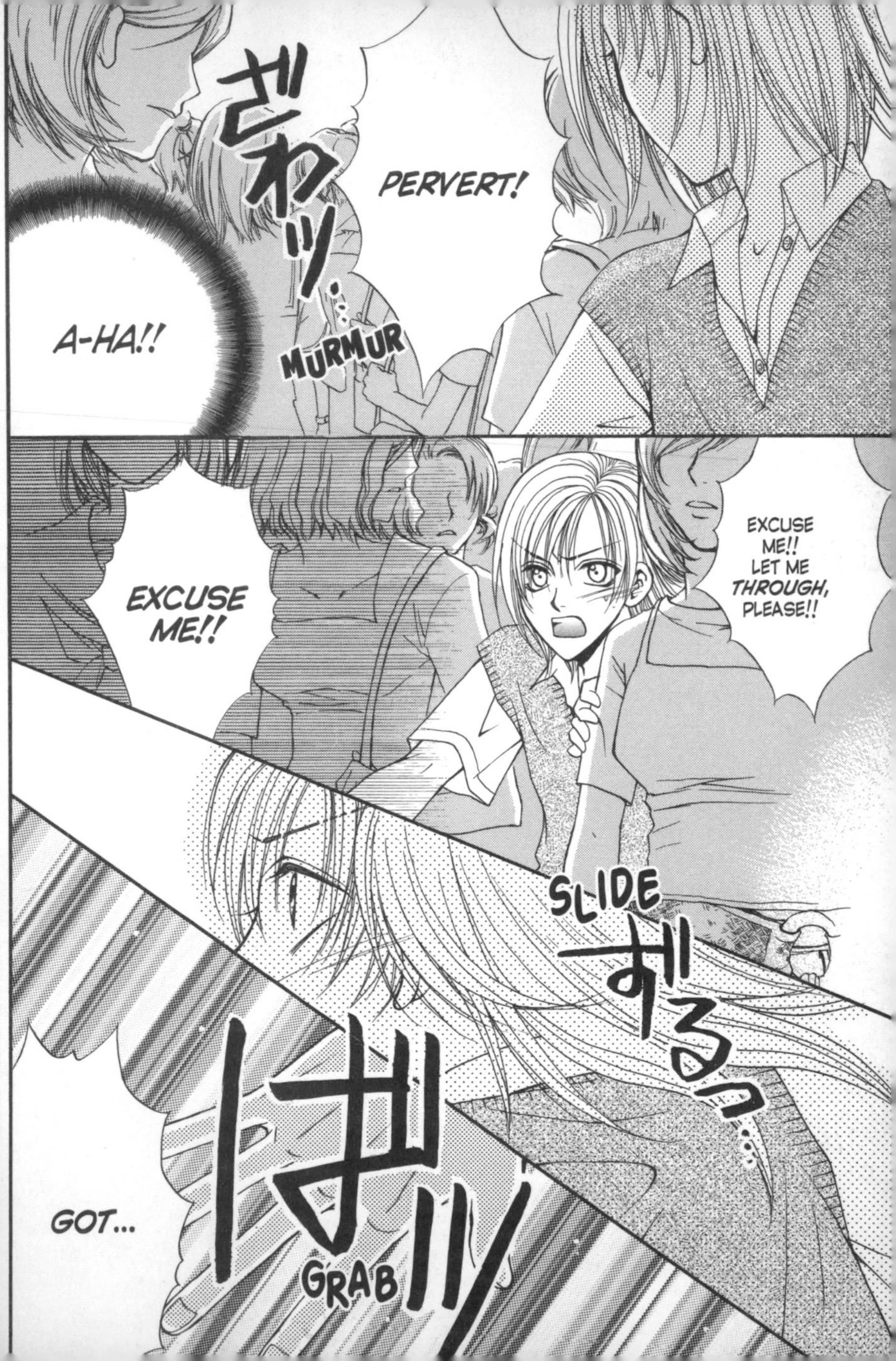
PERVERT!
ざわッ…
MURMUR
A-HA!!
EXCUSE ME!! LET ME THROUGH, PLEASE!!
EXCUSE ME!!
SLIDE
するっ…
GOT...
ばッ
GRAB

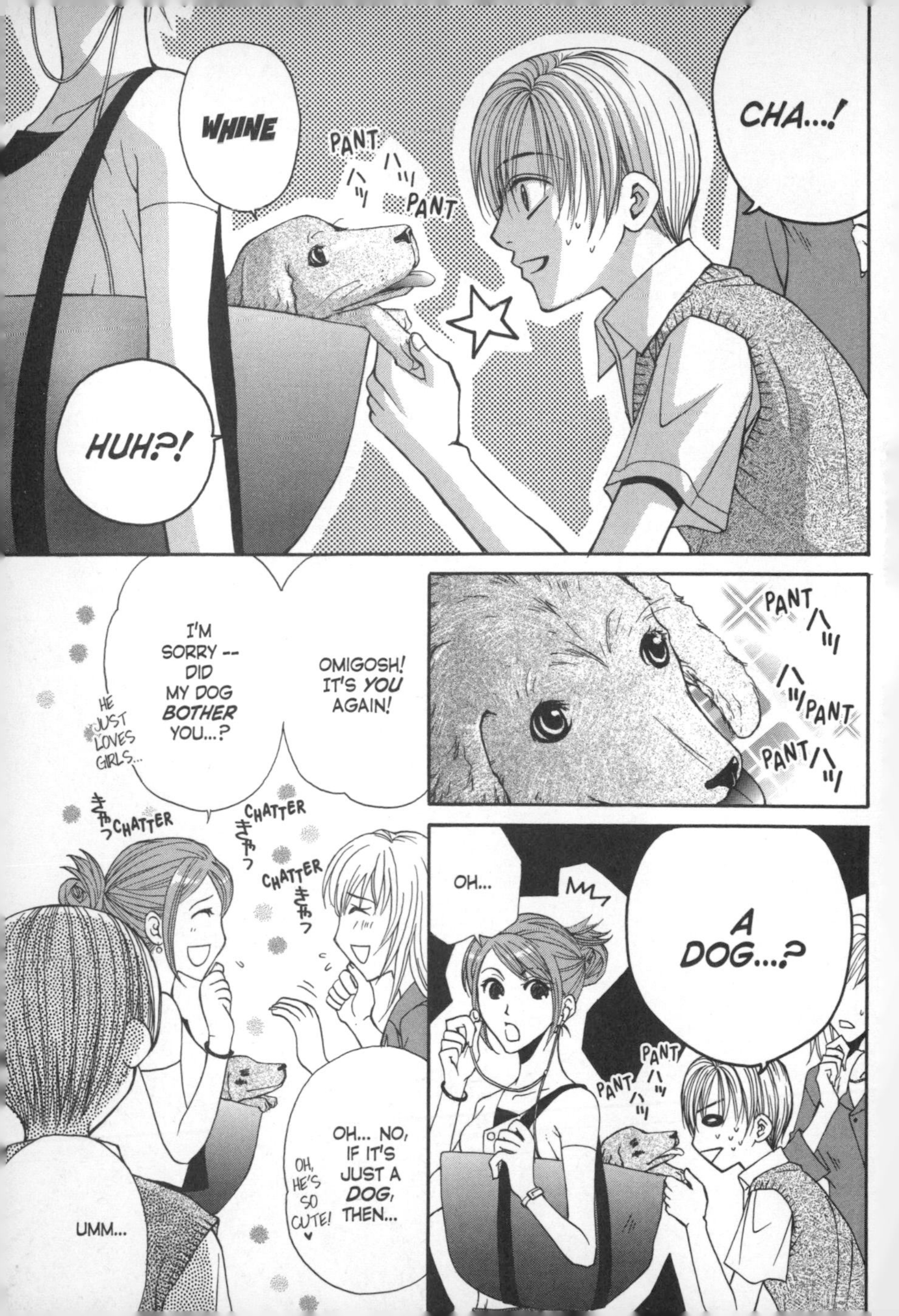
CHA...!
PANT ハッ
PANT ハッ
WHINE
HUH?!
PANT ハッ
ハッ PANT
PANT ハッ
A DOG...?
OH...
PANT ハッ
PANT ハッ
OMIGOSH! IT'S YOU AGAIN!
I'M SORRY -- DID MY DOG BOTHER YOU...?
HE JUST LOVES GIRLS...
CHATTER きゃっ
CHATTER きゃっ
きゃっ CHATTER
OH... NO, IF IT'S JUST A DOG, THEN...
OH, HE'S SO CUTE! ♥
UMM...

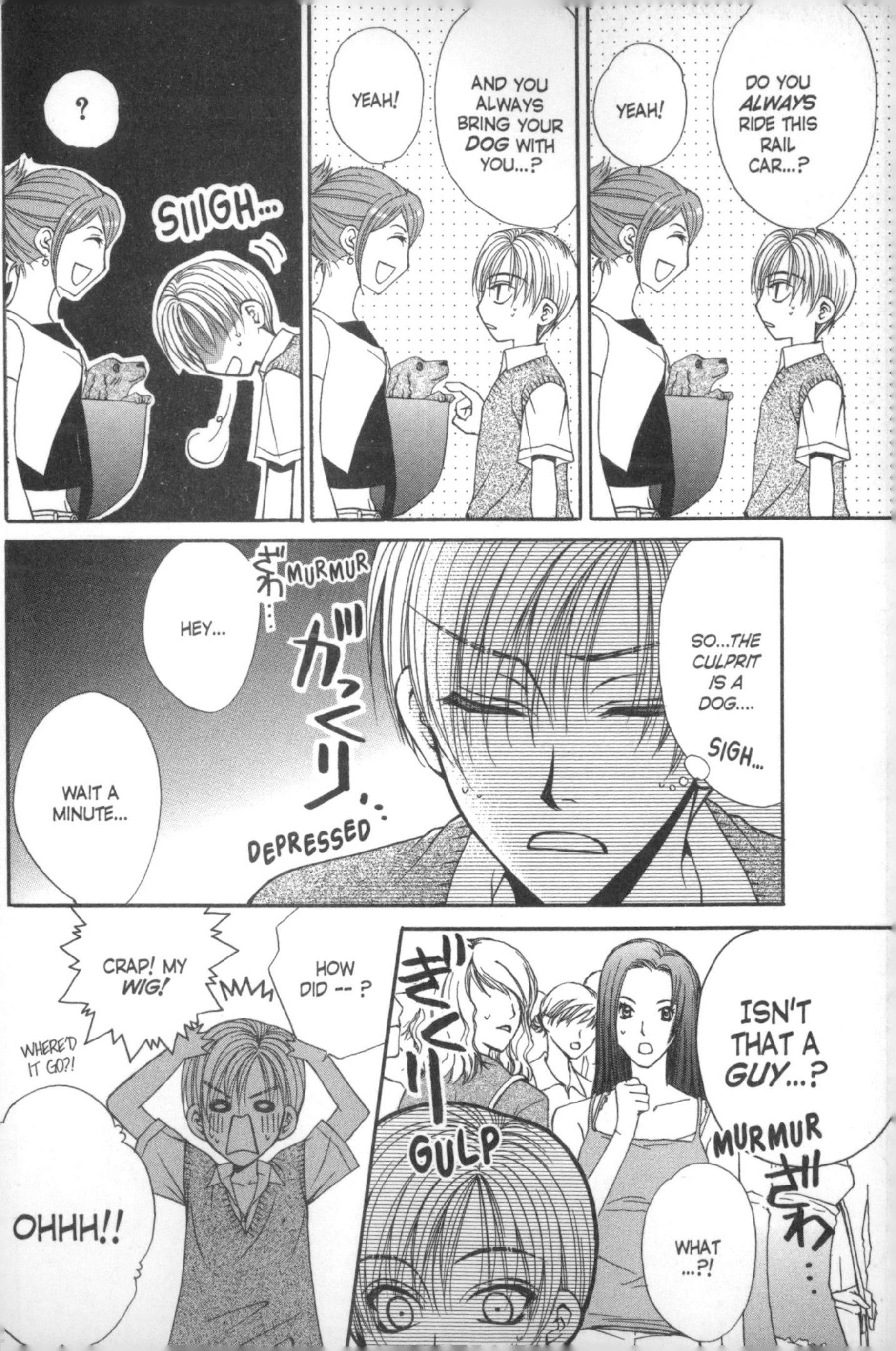
DO YOU ALWAYS RIDE THIS RAIL CAR...?
YEAH!
AND YOU ALWAYS BRING YOUR DOG WITH YOU...?
YEAH!
?
SIIIGH...
SO...THE CULPRIT IS A DOG....
SIGH...
がっくり
DEPRESSED
ざわ...
MURMUR
HEY...
WAIT A MINUTE...
ISN'T THAT A GUY...?
MURMUR
ざわ...
GULP
WHAT ...?!
HOW DID -- ?
CRAP! MY WIG!
WHERE'D IT GO?!
OHHH!!

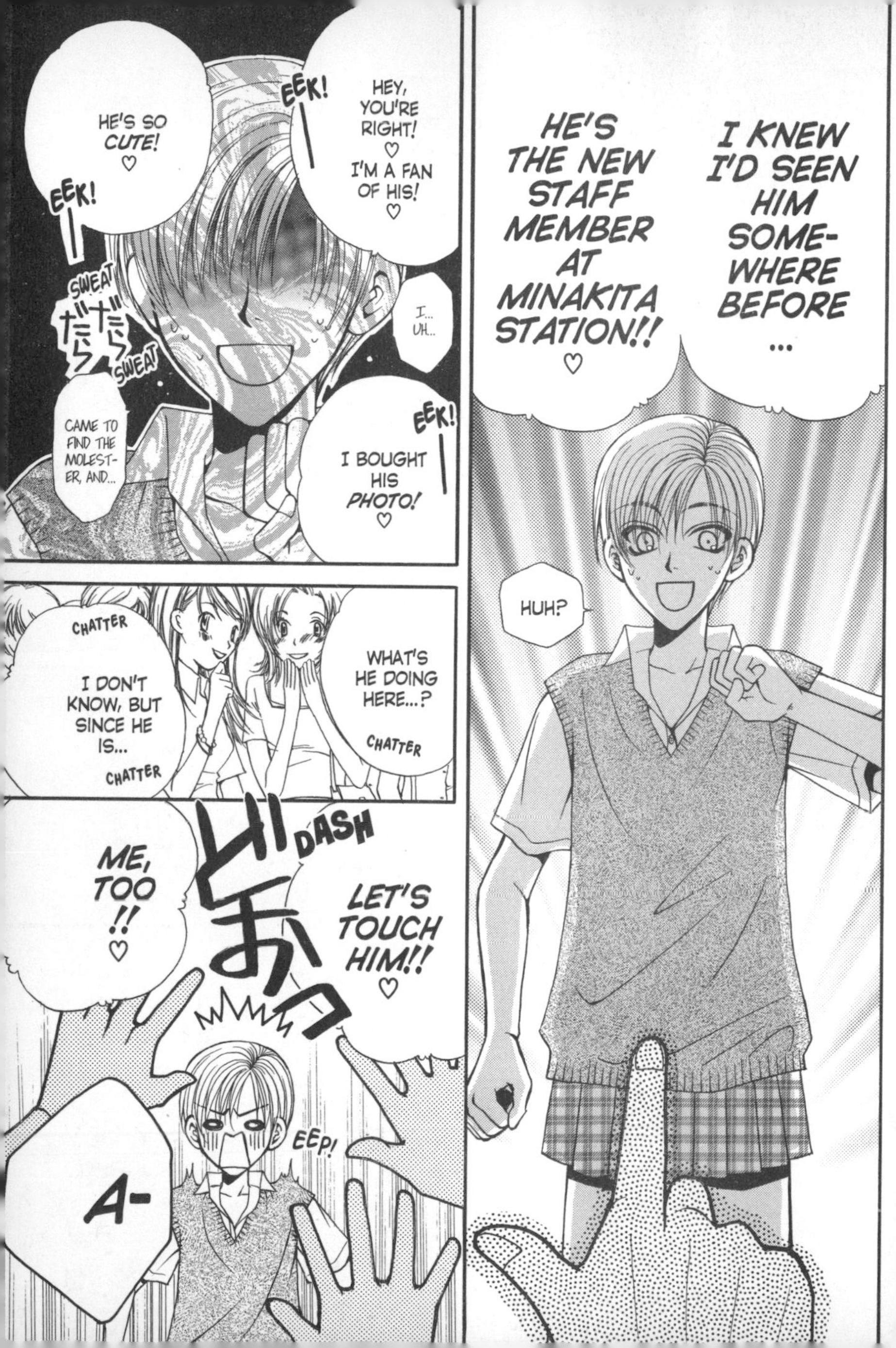
I KNEW I'D SEEN HIM SOMEWHERE BEFORE...
HE'S THE NEW STAFF MEMBER AT MINAKITA STATION!! ♡
HUH?
EEK!
HEY, YOU'RE RIGHT! ♡ I'M A FAN OF HIS! ♡
HE'S SO CUTE! ♡
EEK!
I... UH...
SWEAT SWEAT
EEK!
I BOUGHT HIS PHOTO! ♡
CAME TO FIND THE MOLEST-ER, AND...
WHAT'S HE DOING HERE...?
CHATTER
I DON'T KNOW, BUT SINCE HE IS...
CHATTER
CHATTER
DASH
LET'S TOUCH HIM!! ♡
ME, TOO!! ♡
EEP!
A-

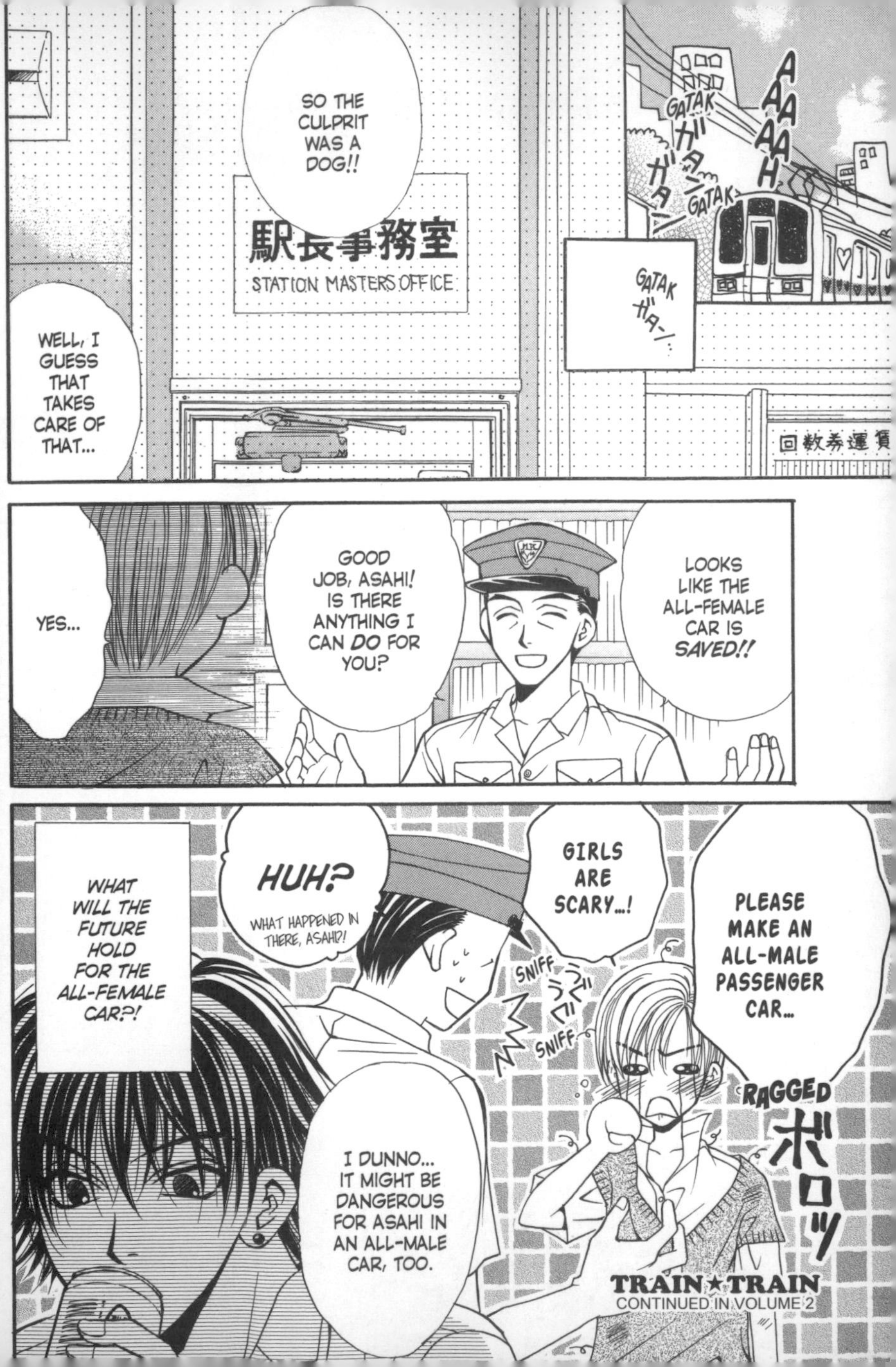

AAAAAH
GATAK
ガタン
GATAK
GATAK
ガタン
回数券運賃
SO THE CULPRIT WAS A DOG!!
駅長事務室
STATION MASTERS OFFICE
WELL, I GUESS THAT TAKES CARE OF THAT...
LOOKS LIKE THE ALL-FEMALE CAR IS SAVED!!
GOOD JOB, ASAHI! IS THERE ANYTHING I CAN DO FOR YOU?
YES...
PLEASE MAKE AN ALL-MALE PASSENGER CAR...
GIRLS ARE SCARY...!
SNIFF
SNIFF
HUH?
WHAT HAPPENED IN THERE, ASAHI?!
RAGGED
ボロッ
WHAT WILL THE FUTURE HOLD FOR THE ALL-FEMALE CAR?!
I DUNNO... IT MIGHT BE DANGEROUS FOR ASAHI IN AN ALL-MALE CAR, TOO.
TRAIN★TRAIN
CONTINUED IN VOLUME 2

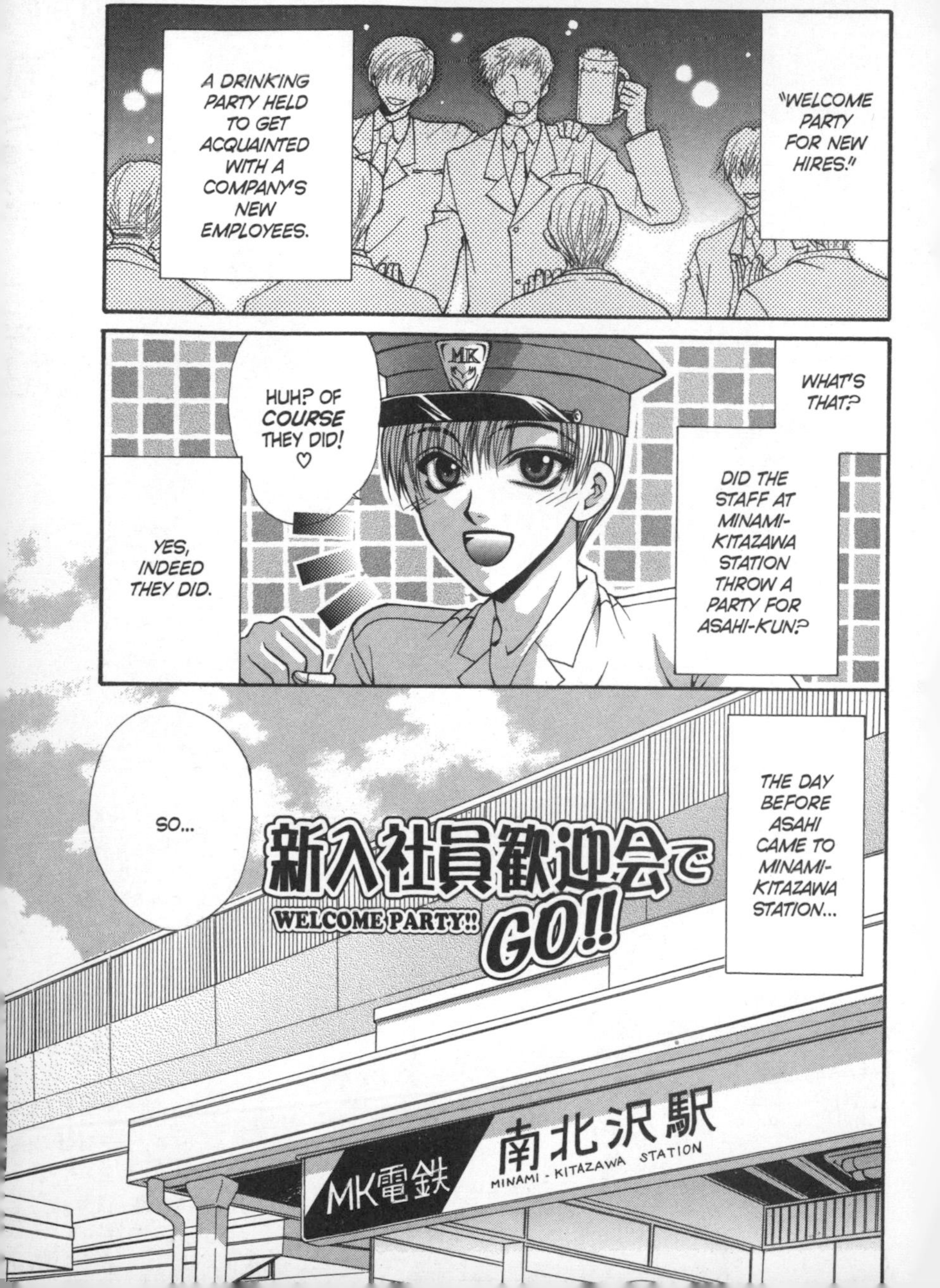
"WELCOME PARTY FOR NEW HIRES."
A DRINKING PARTY HELD TO GET ACQUAINTED WITH A COMPANY'S NEW EMPLOYEES.
WHAT'S THAT?
DID THE STAFF AT MINAMI-KITAZAWA STATION THROW A PARTY FOR ASAHI-KUN?
HUH? OF COURSE THEY DID! ♡
YES, INDEED THEY DID.
THE DAY BEFORE ASAHI CAME TO MINAMI-KITAZAWA STATION...
新入社員歓迎会でGO!!
WELCOME PARTY!! GO!!
SO...
MK電鉄
南北沢駅
MINAMI - KITAZAWA STATION

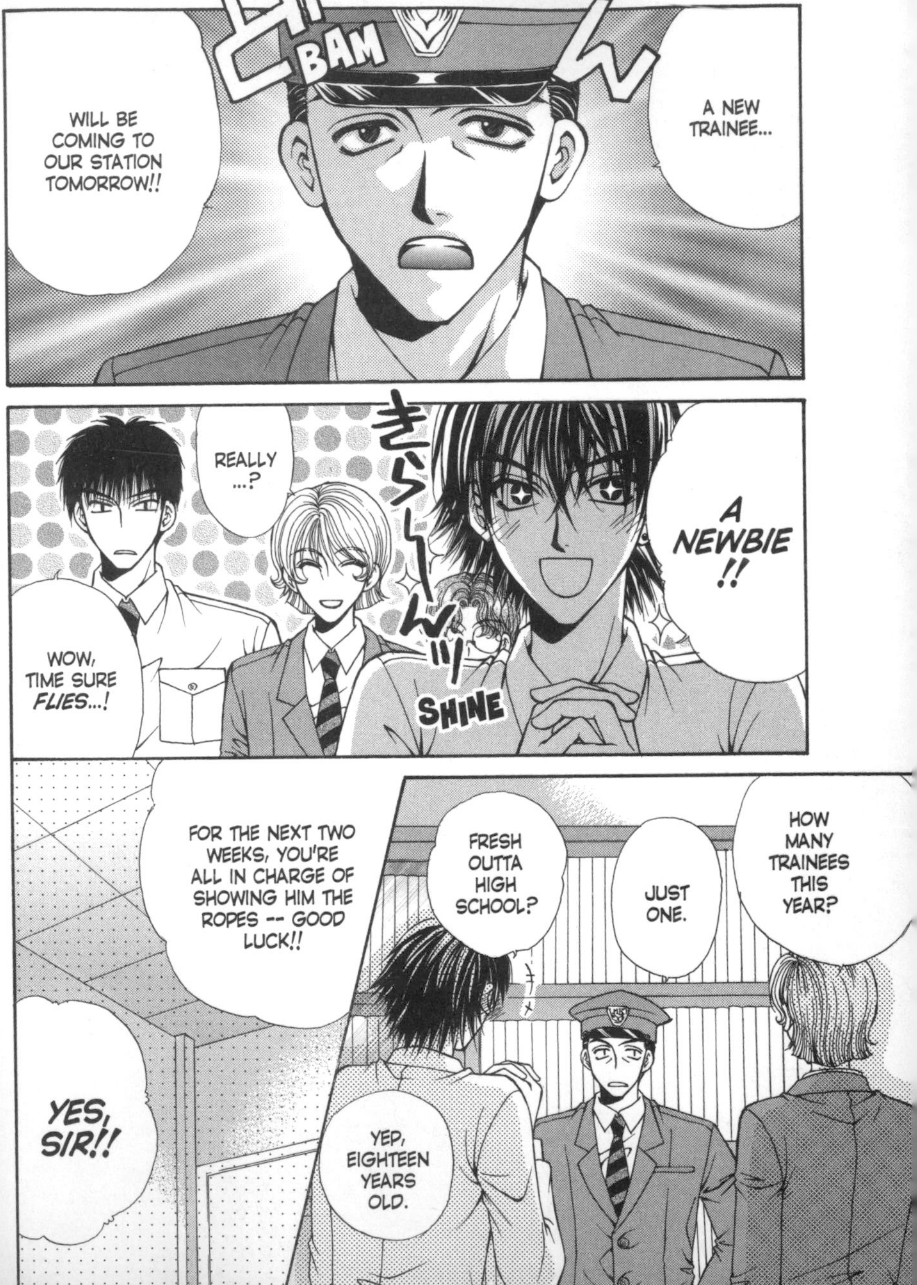
どん
BAM
A NEW TRAINEE...
WILL BE COMING TO OUR STATION TOMORROW!!
A NEWBIE!!
きらーん
SHINE
REALLY...?
WOW, TIME SURE FLIES...!
HOW MANY TRAINEES THIS YEAR?
JUST ONE.
FRESH OUTTA HIGH SCHOOL?
YEP, EIGHTEEN YEARS OLD.
FOR THE NEXT TWO WEEKS, YOU'RE ALL IN CHARGE OF SHOWING HIM THE ROPES -- GOOD LUCK!!
YES, SIR!!

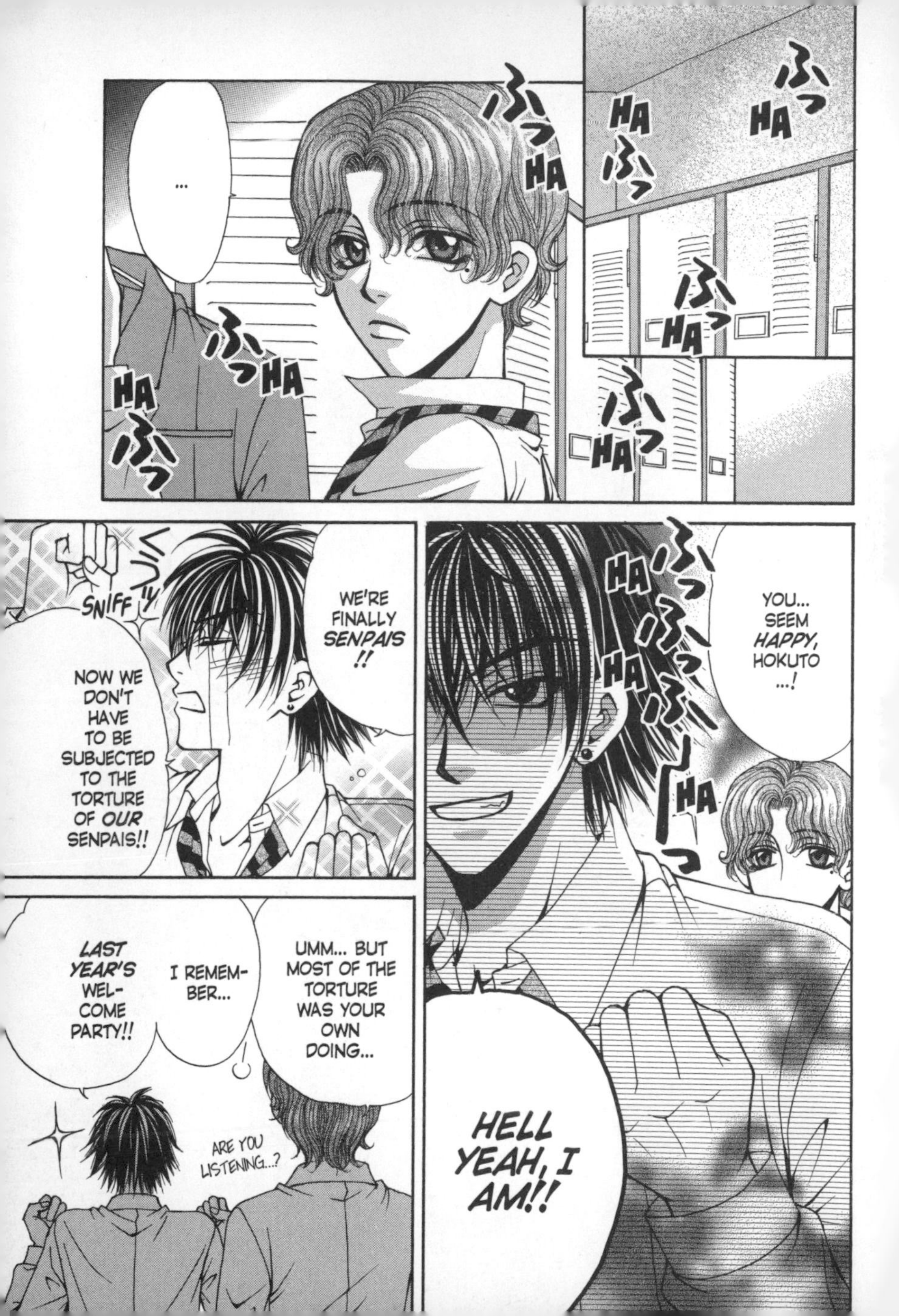

ふっ HA
HA ふっ
ふっ HA
ふっ HA
...
ふっ HA
HA ふっ
ふっ HA
HA ふっ ふっ HA ふっ HA
YOU... SEEM HAPPY, HOKUTO ...!
HELL YEAH, I AM!!
WE'RE FINALLY SENPAIS!!
SNIFF
NOW WE DON'T HAVE TO BE SUBJECTED TO THE TORTURE OF OUR SENPAIS!!
UMM... BUT MOST OF THE TORTURE WAS YOUR OWN DOING...
I REMEM-BER...
LAST YEAR'S WEL-COME PARTY!!
ARE YOU LISTENING...?

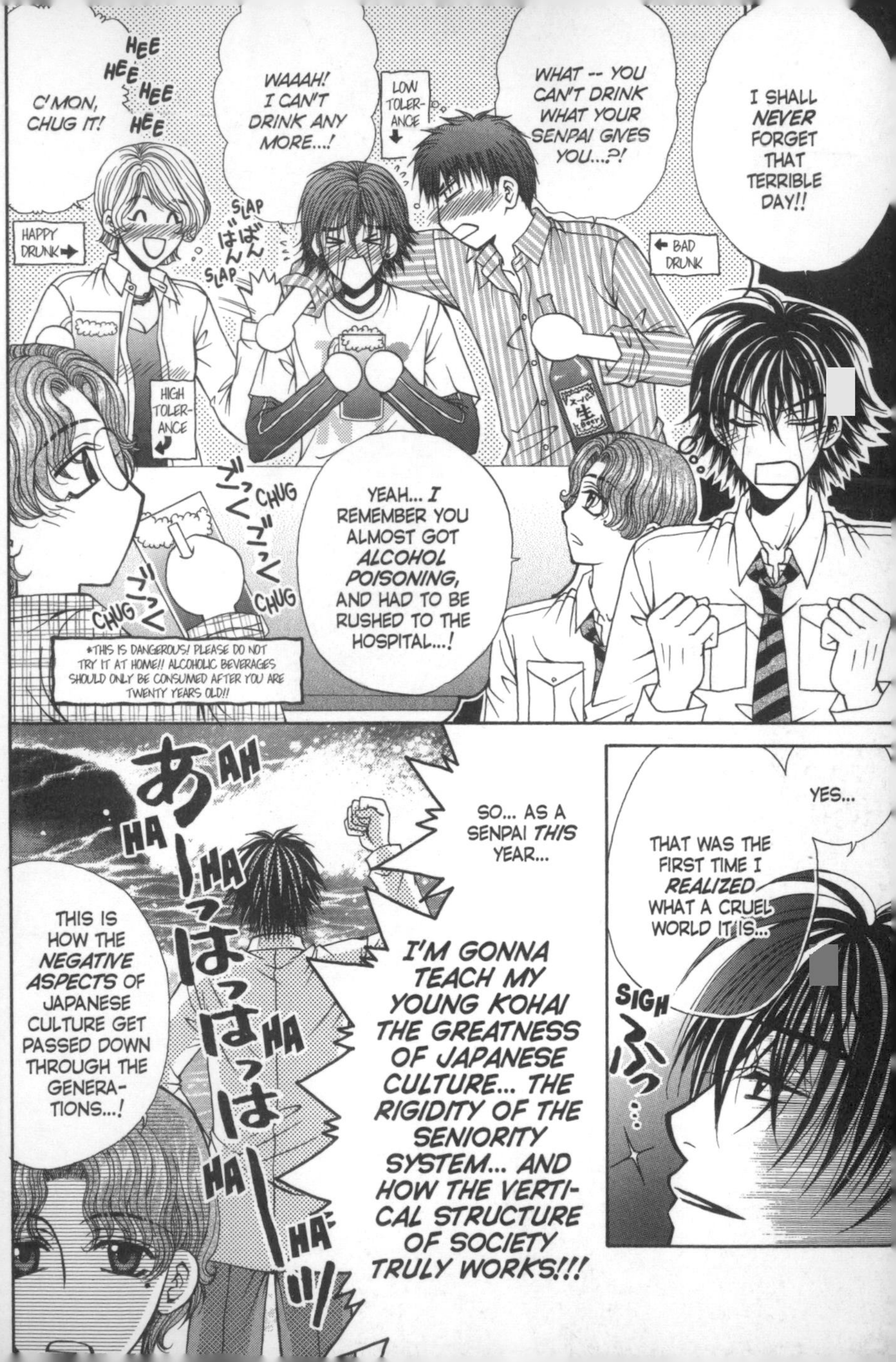

I SHALL NEVER FORGET THAT TERRIBLE DAY!!
WHAT -- YOU CAN'T DRINK WHAT YOUR SENPAI GIVES YOU...?!
LOW TOLERANCE
WAAAH! I CAN'T DRINK ANY MORE...!
HEE HEE HEE HEE
C'MON, CHUG IT!
BAD DRUNK
SLAP ばんばん SLAP
HAPPY DRUNK
HIGH TOLERANCE
YEAH... I REMEMBER YOU ALMOST GOT ALCOHOL POISONING, AND HAD TO BE RUSHED TO THE HOSPITAL...!
CHUG ごくごくごく CHUG CHUG
*THIS IS DANGEROUS! PLEASE DO NOT TRY IT AT HOME!! ALCOHOLIC BEVERAGES SHOULD ONLY BE CONSUMED AFTER YOU ARE TWENTY YEARS OLD!!
YES...
THAT WAS THE FIRST TIME I REALIZED WHAT A CRUEL WORLD IT IS...
SIGH ふっ...
SO... AS A SENPAI THIS YEAR...
I'M GONNA TEACH MY YOUNG KOHAI THE GREATNESS OF JAPANESE CULTURE... THE RIGIDITY OF THE SENIORITY SYSTEM... AND HOW THE VERTICAL STRUCTURE OF SOCIETY TRULY WORKS!!!
AH HA HA HA HA HA HA!! あーはっはっはっはー
THIS IS HOW THE NEGATIVE ASPECTS OF JAPANESE CULTURE GET PASSED DOWN THROUGH THE GENERATIONS...!

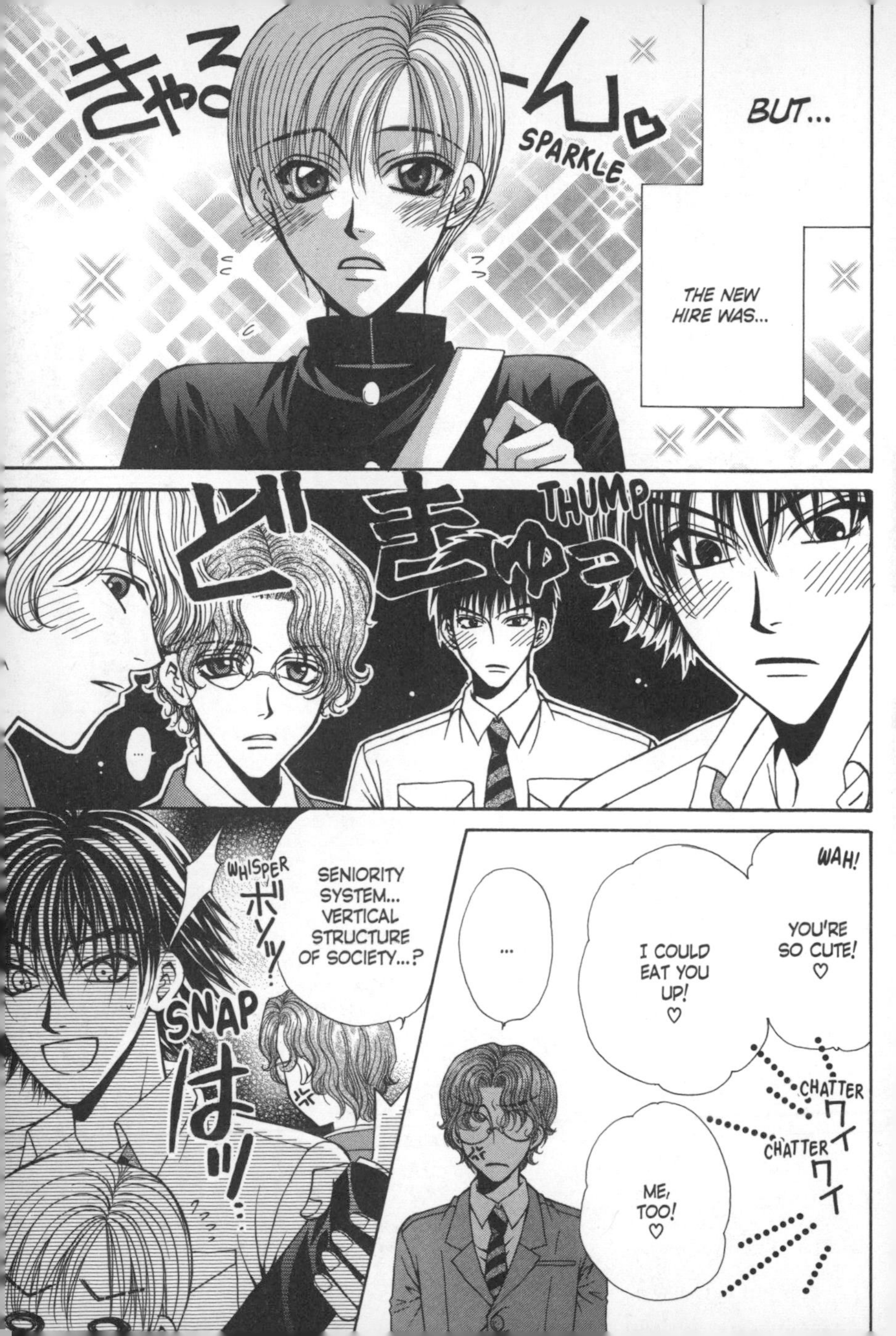
BUT...
THE NEW HIRE WAS...
SPARKLE
THUMP
...
WAH!
YOU'RE SO CUTE! ♡
I COULD EAT YOU UP! ♡
...
CHATTER ワイ
CHATTER ワイ
ME, TOO! ♡
SENIORITY SYSTEM... VERTICAL STRUCTURE OF SOCIETY...?
WHISPER ボソッ
SNAP はッ

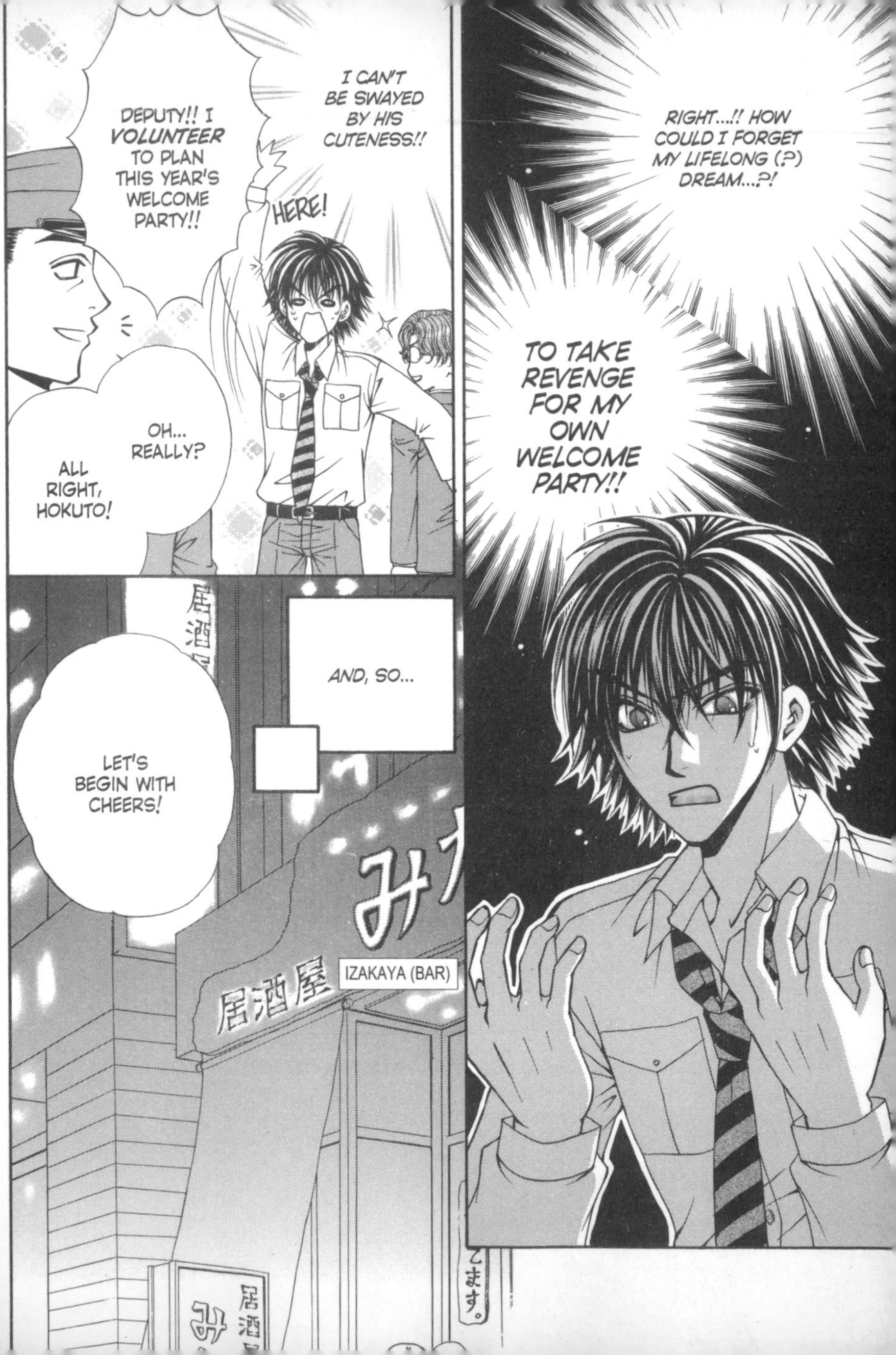
RIGHT...!! HOW COULD I FORGET MY LIFELONG (?) DREAM...?!
TO TAKE REVENGE FOR MY OWN WELCOME PARTY!!
I CAN'T BE SWAYED BY HIS CUTENESS!!
DEPUTY!! I VOLUNTEER TO PLAN THIS YEAR'S WELCOME PARTY!!
HERE!
OH... REALLY?
ALL RIGHT, HOKUTO!
AND, SO...
LET'S BEGIN WITH CHEERS!
居酒屋
IZAKAYA (BAR)

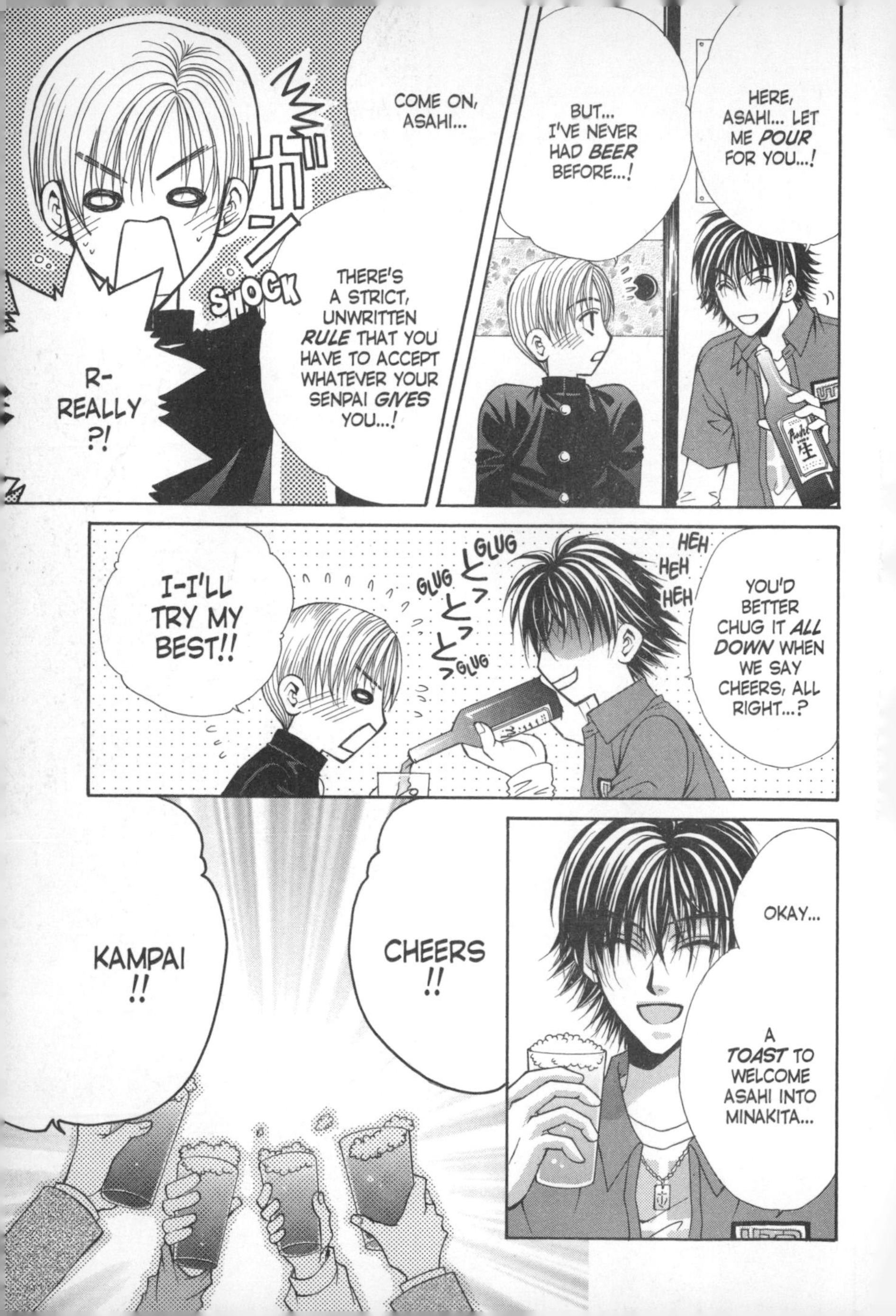
HERE, ASAHI... LET ME POUR FOR YOU...!
BUT... I'VE NEVER HAD BEER BEFORE...!
COME ON, ASAHI...
THERE'S A STRICT, UNWRITTEN RULE THAT YOU HAVE TO ACCEPT WHATEVER YOUR SENPAI GIVES YOU...!
ガーン
SHOCK
R-REALLY?!
YOU'D BETTER CHUG IT ALL DOWN WHEN WE SAY CHEERS, ALL RIGHT...?
HEH HEH HEH
GLUG とととGLUG GLUG
I-I'LL TRY MY BEST!!
OKAY...
A TOAST TO WELCOME ASAHI INTO MINAKITA...
CHEERS!!
KAMPAI!!

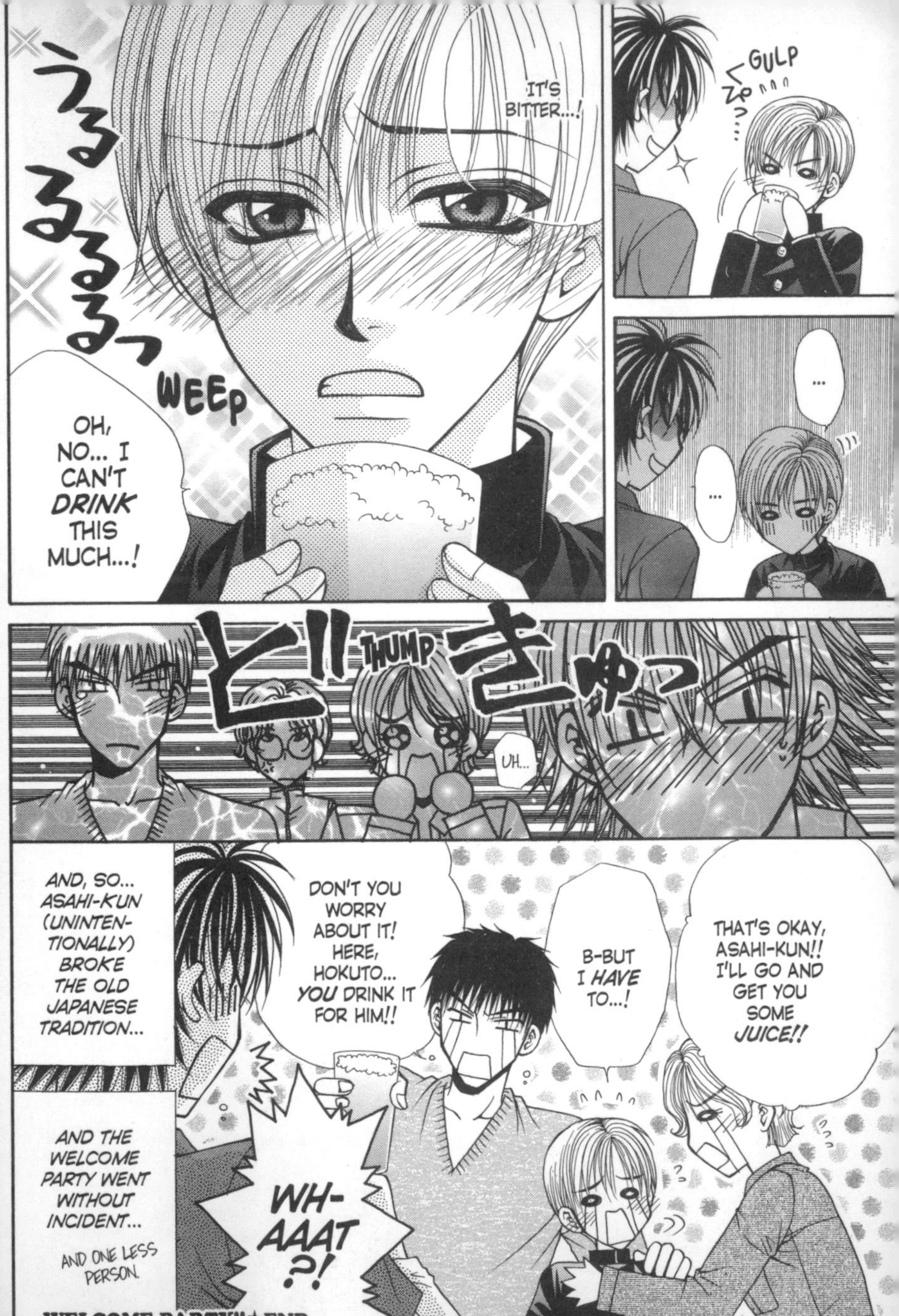
GULP
...
...
IT'S BITTER...!
うるるるるっ
WEEp
OH, NO... I CAN'T DRINK THIS MUCH...!
きゅっ
THUMP
と!!
UH...
THAT'S OKAY, ASAHI-KUN!! I'LL GO AND GET YOU SOME JUICE!!
B-BUT I HAVE TO...!
DON'T YOU WORRY ABOUT IT! HERE, HOKUTO... YOU DRINK IT FOR HIM!!
AND, SO... ASAHI-KUN (UNINTENTIONALLY) BROKE THE OLD JAPANESE TRADITION...
WH-AAAT?!
AND THE WELCOME PARTY WENT WITHOUT INCIDENT...
AND ONE LESS PERSON.

**WELCOME PARTY!!★END**

# トレ☆トレ 4コマシアター

# TRAIN★TRAIN 4-PANEL COMIC THEATRE

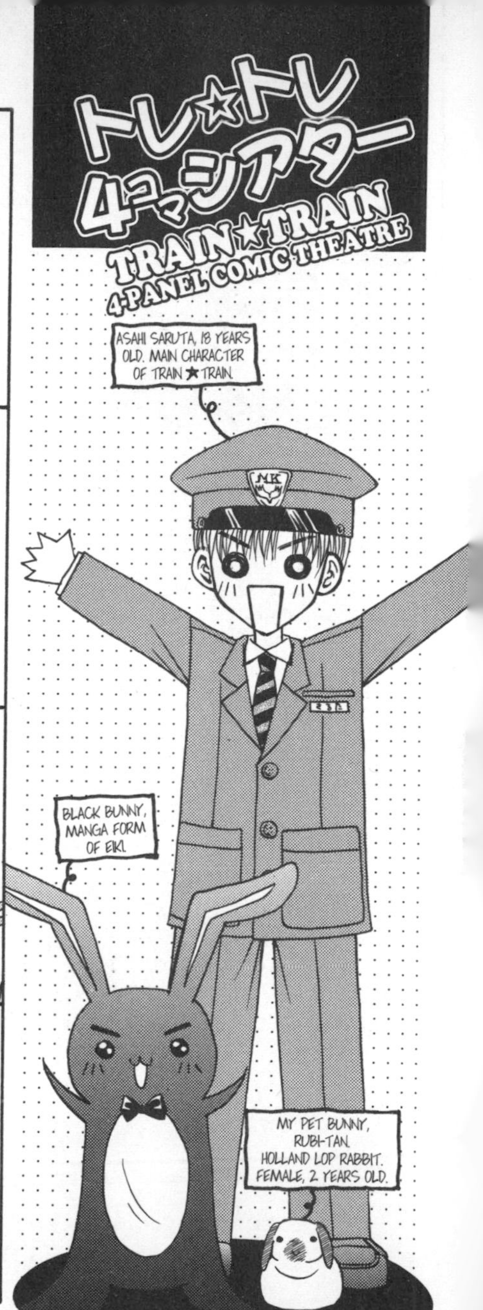
ASAHI SARUTA, 18 YEARS OLD. MAIN CHARACTER OF TRAIN★TRAIN.
BLACK BUNNY, MANGA FORM OF EIKI.
MY PET BUNNY, RUBI-TAN. HOLLAND LOP RABBIT. FEMALE, 2 YEARS OLD.

## RE-ADVERTISEMENT!!

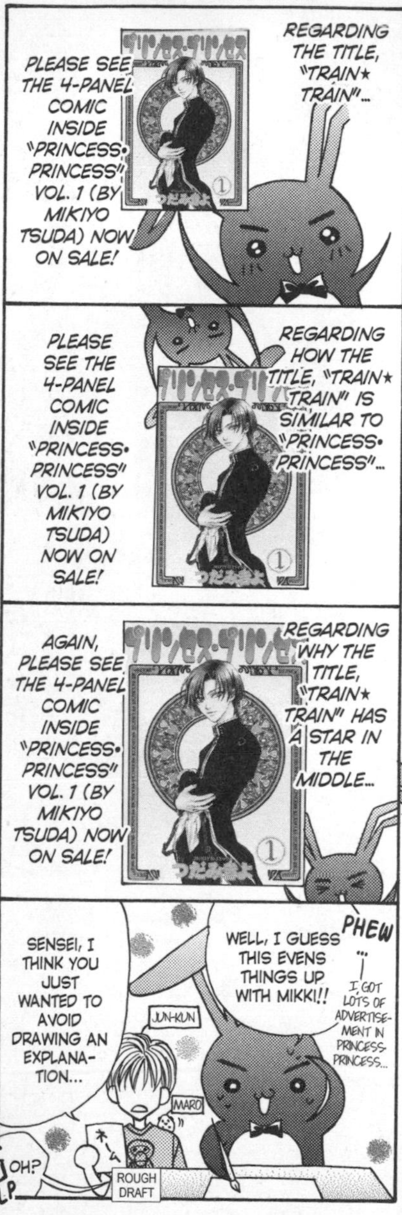
REGARDING THE TITLE, "TRAIN★ TRAIN"...
PLEASE SEE THE 4-PANEL COMIC INSIDE "PRINCESS• PRINCESS", VOL. 1 (BY MIKIYO TSUDA) NOW ON SALE!
REGARDING HOW THE TITLE, "TRAIN★ TRAIN" IS SIMILAR TO "PRINCESS• PRINCESS"...
PLEASE SEE THE 4-PANEL COMIC INSIDE "PRINCESS• PRINCESS" VOL. 1 (BY MIKIYO TSUDA) NOW ON SALE!
REGARDING WHY THE TITLE, "TRAIN★ TRAIN" HAS A STAR IN THE MIDDLE...
AGAIN, PLEASE SEE THE 4-PANEL COMIC INSIDE "PRINCESS• PRINCESS" VOL. 1 (BY MIKIYO TSUDA) NOW ON SALE!
PHEW
WELL, I GUESS THIS EVENS THINGS UP WITH MIKKI!!
...I GOT LOTS OF ADVERTISE-MENT IN PRINCESS PRINCESS...
SENSEI, I THINK YOU JUST WANTED TO AVOID DRAWING AN EXPLANA-TION...
JUN-KUN
MARO
ROUGH DRAFT
OH?
GULP

YOUR NAME IS...

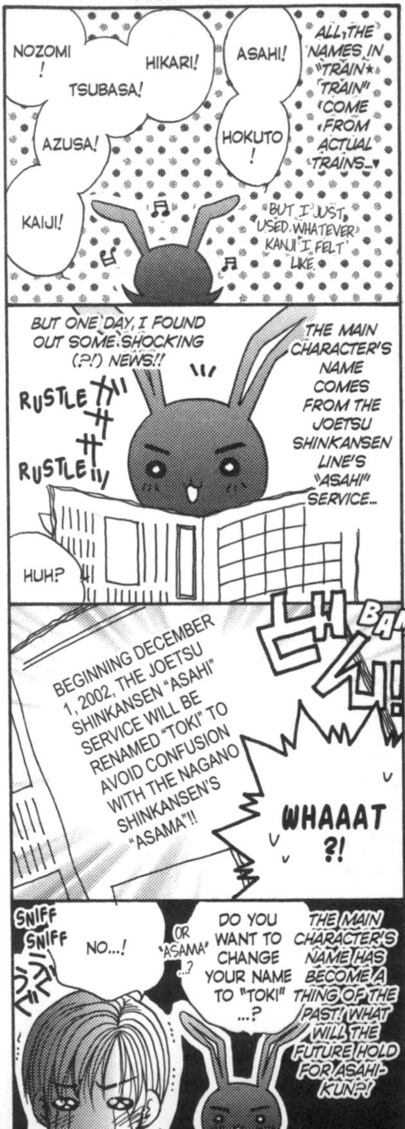
ALL THE NAMES IN "TRAIN★TRAIN" COME FROM ACTUAL TRAINS...♥
ASAHI!
HIKARI!
NOZOMI!
TSUBASA!
HOKUTO!
AZUSA!
KAIJI!
BUT I JUST USED WHATEVER KANJI I FELT LIKE.
THE MAIN CHARACTER'S NAME COMES FROM THE JOETSU SHINKANSEN LINE'S "ASAHI" SERVICE...
BUT ONE DAY, I FOUND OUT SOME SHOCKING (?!) NEWS!!
RUSTLE
RUSTLE
HUH?
BAM
BEGINNING DECEMBER 1, 2002, THE JOETSU SHINKANSEN "ASAHI" SERVICE WILL BE RENAMED "TOKI" TO AVOID CONFUSION WITH THE NAGANO SHINKANSEN'S "ASAMA"!!
WHAAAT?!
THE MAIN CHARACTER'S NAME HAS BECOME A THING OF THE PAST! WHAT WILL THE FUTURE HOLD FOR ASAHI-KUN?!
DO YOU WANT TO CHANGE YOUR NAME TO "TOKI"...?
OR "ASAMA"...?
NO...!
SNIFF SNIFF

GETTING PHOTOS.

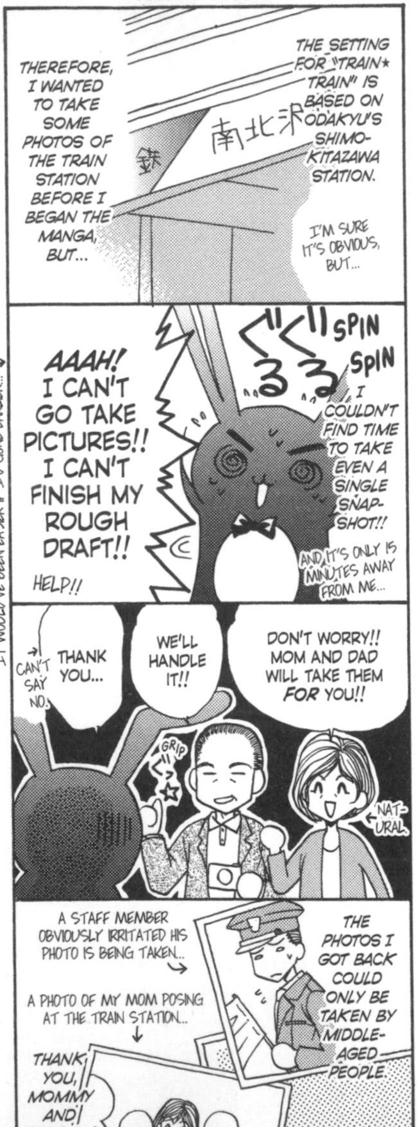
THE SETTING FOR "TRAIN★TRAIN" IS BASED ON ODAKYU'S SHIMO-KITAZAWA STATION.
南北沢
THEREFORE, I WANTED TO TAKE SOME PHOTOS OF THE TRAIN STATION BEFORE I BEGAN THE MANGA, BUT...
I'M SURE IT'S OBVIOUS, BUT...
SPIN SPIN
I COULDN'T FIND TIME TO TAKE EVEN A SINGLE SNAPSHOT!!
AAAH! I CAN'T GO TAKE PICTURES!! I CAN'T FINISH MY ROUGH DRAFT!!
AND IT'S ONLY 15 MINUTES AWAY FROM ME...
HELP!!
DON'T WORRY!! MOM AND DAD WILL TAKE THEM FOR YOU!!
WE'LL HANDLE IT!!
THANK YOU...
CAN'T SAY NO.
GRIP
NATURAL.
THE PHOTOS I GOT BACK COULD ONLY BE TAKEN BY MIDDLE-AGED PEOPLE.
A STAFF MEMBER OBVIOUSLY IRRITATED HIS PHOTO IS BEING TAKEN...
A PHOTO OF MY MOM POSING AT THE TRAIN STATION...
THANK YOU, MOMMY AND DADDY...!

IT WOULD'VE BEEN EASIER IF I'D GONE EARLIER...

SHINSHOKAN'S KUMA-SAN ALSO HELPED ME WITH SOME PHOTOS.
THANK YOU VERY MUCH!

## SARASHI.

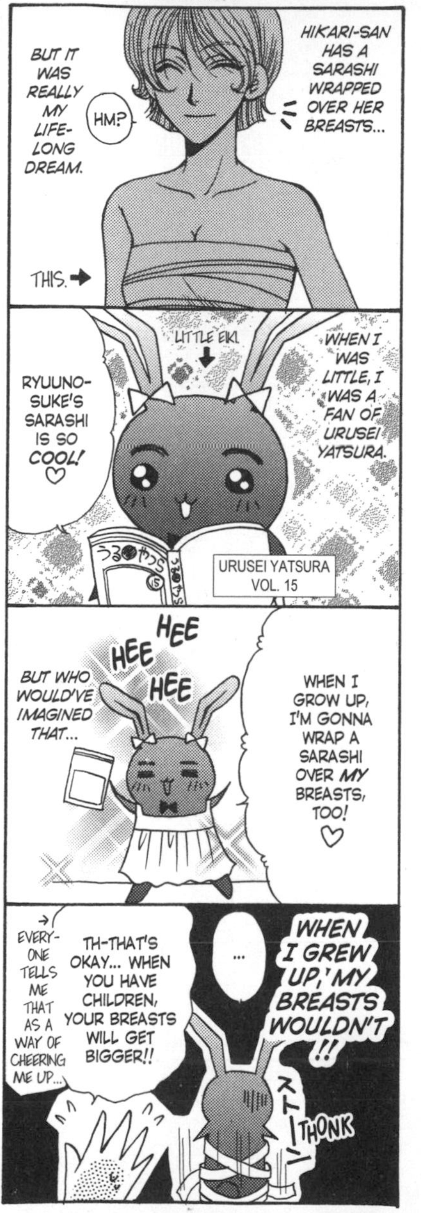
HIKARI-SAN HAS A SARASHI WRAPPED OVER HER BREASTS...
HM?
BUT IT WAS REALLY MY LIFE-LONG DREAM.
THIS. ➔
WHEN I WAS LITTLE, I WAS A FAN OF URUSEI YATSURA.
LITTLE EIKI
RYUUNO-SUKE'S SARASHI IS SO COOL! ♡
URUSEI YATSURA VOL. 15
WHEN I GROW UP, I'M GONNA WRAP A SARASHI OVER MY BREASTS, TOO! ♡
HEE HEE HEE
BUT WHO WOULD'VE IMAGINED THAT...
WHEN I GREW UP, MY BREASTS WOULDN'T!!
...
TH-THAT'S OKAY... WHEN YOU HAVE CHILDREN, YOUR BREASTS WILL GET BIGGER!!
EVERY-ONE TELLS ME THAT AS A WAY OF CHEERING ME UP...
ストーン
THONK

## PURE.

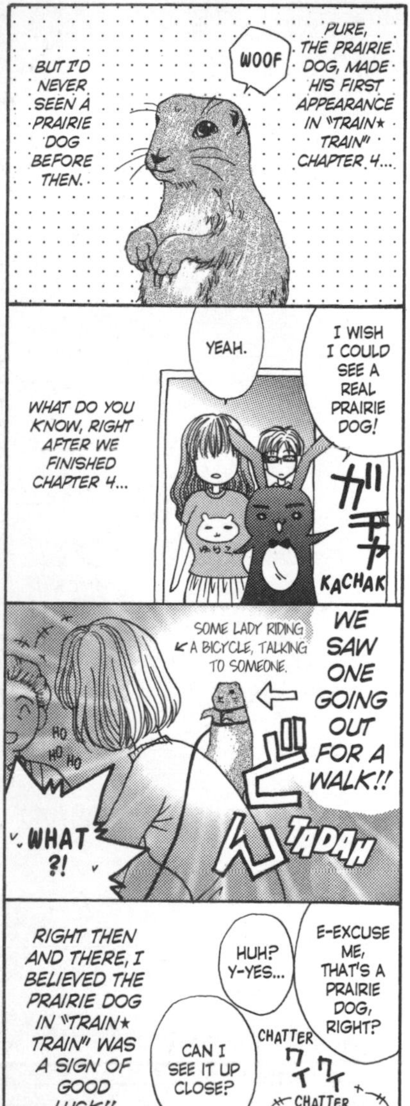
PURE, THE PRAIRIE DOG, MADE HIS FIRST APPEARANCE IN "TRAIN★TRAIN" CHAPTER 4...
WOOF
BUT I'D NEVER SEEN A PRAIRIE DOG BEFORE THEN.
I WISH I COULD SEE A REAL PRAIRIE DOG!
YEAH.
WHAT DO YOU KNOW, RIGHT AFTER WE FINISHED CHAPTER 4...
ガチャ
KACHAK
WE SAW ONE GOING OUT FOR A WALK!!
SOME LADY RIDING A BICYCLE, TALKING TO SOMEONE.
HO HO HO
どん
TADAH
WHAT ?!
E-EXCUSE ME, THAT'S A PRAIRIE DOG, RIGHT?
HUH? Y-YES...
RIGHT THEN AND THERE, I BELIEVED THE PRAIRIE DOG IN "TRAIN★TRAIN" WAS A SIGN OF GOOD LUCK!!
CAN I SEE IT UP CLOSE?
CHATTER
ワイワイ
CHATTER
OH, SURE...

**TRAIN★TRAIN 4-PANEL COMIC THEATRE★END**

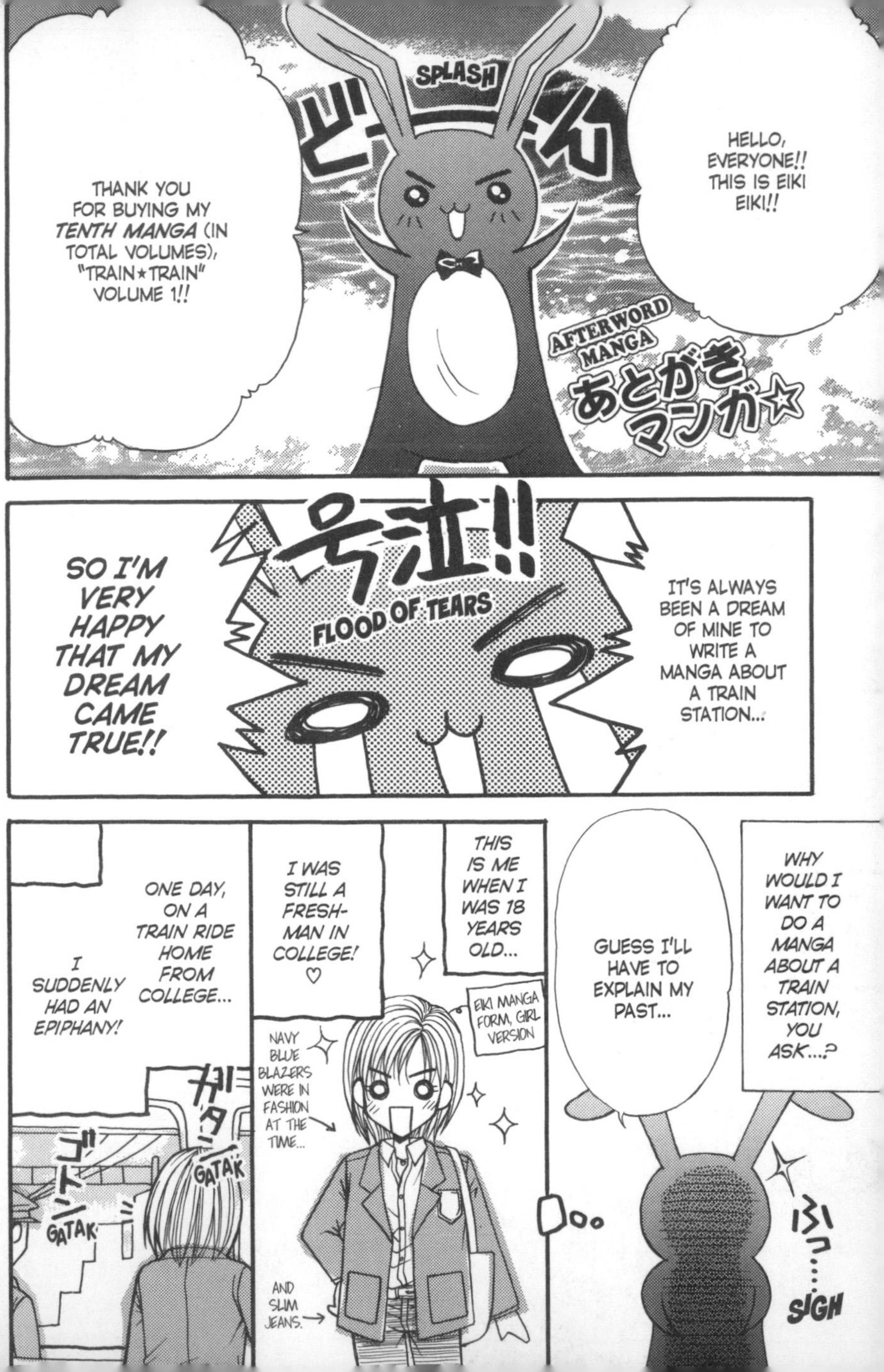
HELLO, EVERYONE!! THIS IS EIKI EIKI!!
どーん
SPLASH
AFTERWORD MANGA
あとがきマンガ☆
THANK YOU FOR BUYING MY *TENTH MANGA* (IN TOTAL VOLUMES), "TRAIN★TRAIN" VOLUME 1!!
IT'S ALWAYS BEEN A DREAM OF MINE TO WRITE A MANGA ABOUT A TRAIN STATION...
号泣!!
FLOOD OF TEARS
SO I'M VERY HAPPY THAT MY DREAM CAME TRUE!!
WHY WOULD I WANT TO DO A MANGA ABOUT A TRAIN STATION, YOU ASK...?
GUESS I'LL HAVE TO EXPLAIN MY PAST...
ふっ…
SIGH
THIS IS ME WHEN I WAS 18 YEARS OLD...
I WAS STILL A FRESHMAN IN COLLEGE! ♡
EIKI MANGA FORM, GIRL VERSION
NAVY BLUE BLAZERS WERE IN FASHION AT THE TIME...
AND SLIM JEANS.
ONE DAY, ON A TRAIN RIDE HOME FROM COLLEGE...
I SUDDENLY HAD AN EPIPHANY!
GATAK
GATAK

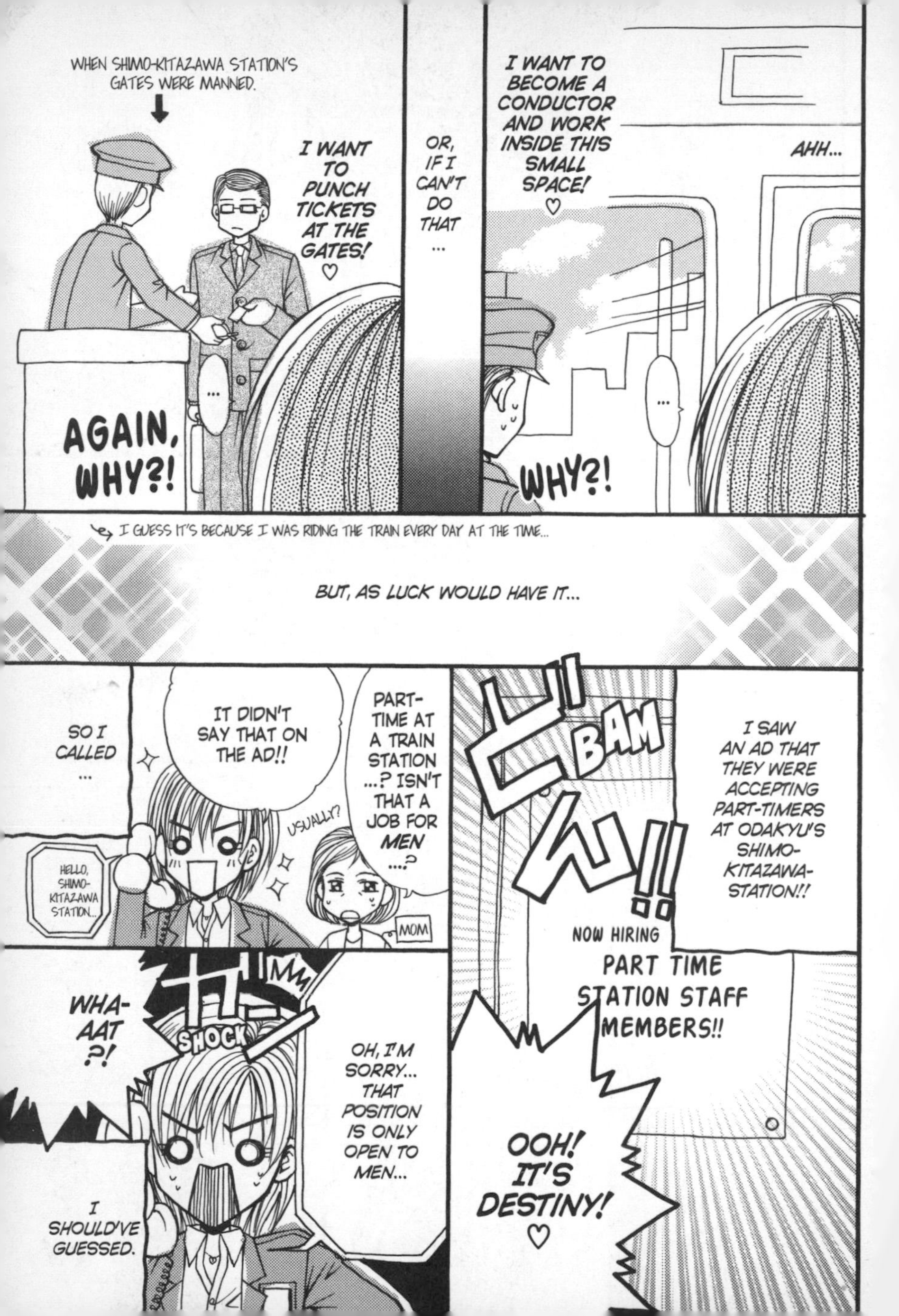
AHH...
I WANT TO BECOME A CONDUCTOR AND WORK INSIDE THIS SMALL SPACE! ♡
...
WHY?!
OR, IF I CAN'T DO THAT ...
I WANT TO PUNCH TICKETS AT THE GATES! ♡
WHEN SHIMO-KITAZAWA STATION'S GATES WERE MANNED.
...
AGAIN, WHY?!
I GUESS IT'S BECAUSE I WAS RIDING THE TRAIN EVERY DAY AT THE TIME...
BUT, AS LUCK WOULD HAVE IT...
I SAW AN AD THAT THEY WERE ACCEPTING PART-TIMERS AT ODAKYU'S SHIMO-KITAZAWA-STATION!!
どん
BAM
NOW HIRING
PART TIME STATION STAFF MEMBERS!!
OOH! IT'S DESTINY! ♡
PART-TIME AT A TRAIN STATION ...? ISN'T THAT A JOB FOR MEN ...?
USUALLY?
MOM
IT DIDN'T SAY THAT ON THE AD!!
SO I CALLED ...
HELLO, SHIMO-KITAZAWA STATION...
OH, I'M SORRY... THAT POSITION IS ONLY OPEN TO MEN...
SHOCK
WHA-AAT ?!
I SHOULD'VE GUESSED.

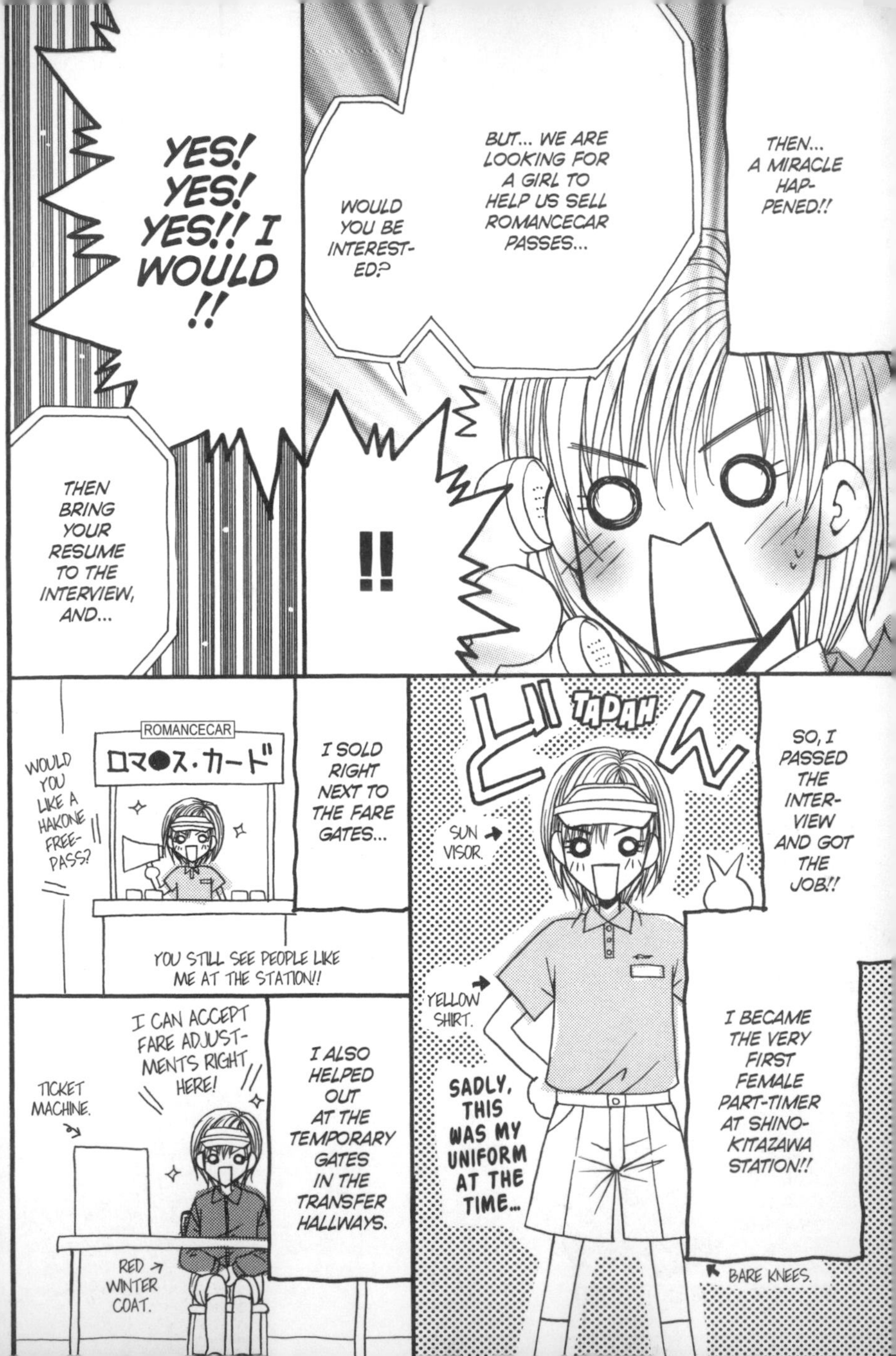
THEN... A MIRACLE HAP-PENED!!
BUT... WE ARE LOOKING FOR A GIRL TO HELP US SELL ROMANCECAR PASSES...
WOULD YOU BE INTEREST-ED?
!!
YES! YES! YES!! I WOULD!!
THEN BRING YOUR RESUME TO THE INTERVIEW, AND...
SO, I PASSED THE INTER-VIEW AND GOT THE JOB!!
どん
TADAH
SUN VISOR.
I BECAME THE VERY FIRST FEMALE PART-TIMER AT SHINO-KITAZAWA STATION!!
YELLOW SHIRT.
SADLY, THIS WAS MY UNIFORM AT THE TIME...
BARE KNEES.
I SOLD RIGHT NEXT TO THE FARE GATES...
ROMANCECAR
ロマ●ス・カード
WOULD YOU LIKE A HAKONE FREE-PASS?
YOU STILL SEE PEOPLE LIKE ME AT THE STATION!!
I ALSO HELPED OUT AT THE TEMPORARY GATES IN THE TRANSFER HALLWAYS.
I CAN ACCEPT FARE ADJUST-MENTS RIGHT HERE!
TICKET MACHINE.
RED WINTER COAT.

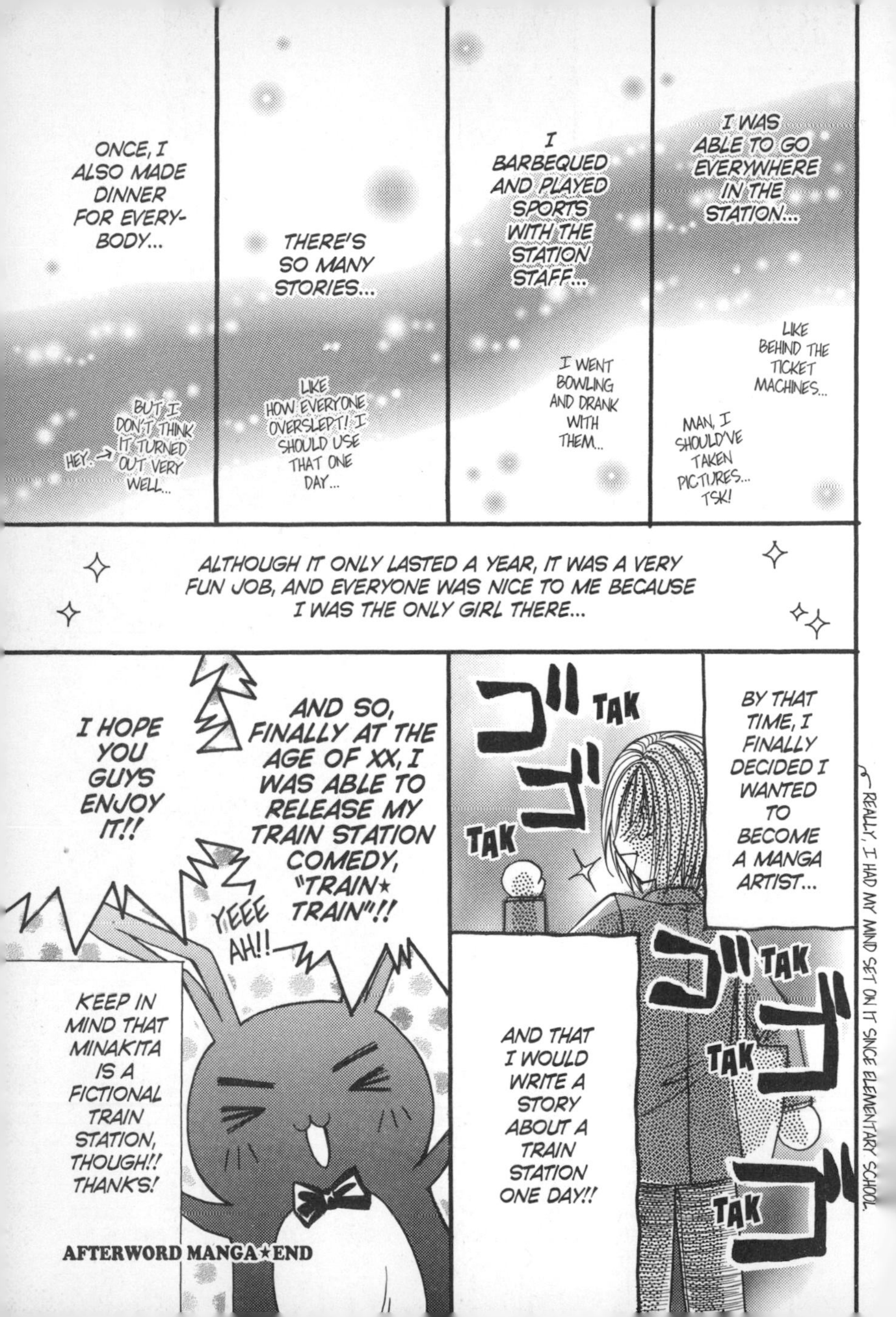
I WAS ABLE TO GO EVERYWHERE IN THE STATION...
LIKE BEHIND THE TICKET MACHINES...
MAN, I SHOULD'VE TAKEN PICTURES... TSK!
I BARBEQUED AND PLAYED SPORTS WITH THE STATION STAFF...
I WENT BOWLING AND DRANK WITH THEM...
THERE'S SO MANY STORIES...
LIKE HOW EVERYONE OVERSLEPT! I SHOULD USE THAT ONE DAY...
ONCE, I ALSO MADE DINNER FOR EVERY-BODY...
BUT I DON'T THINK IT TURNED OUT VERY WELL...
HEY. →
ALTHOUGH IT ONLY LASTED A YEAR, IT WAS A VERY FUN JOB, AND EVERYONE WAS NICE TO ME BECAUSE I WAS THE ONLY GIRL THERE...
REALLY, I HAD MY MIND SET ON IT SINCE ELEMENTARY SCHOOL.
BY THAT TIME, I FINALLY DECIDED I WANTED TO BECOME A MANGA ARTIST...
TAK
TAK
AND THAT I WOULD WRITE A STORY ABOUT A TRAIN STATION ONE DAY!!
TAK
TAK
TAK
AND SO, FINALLY AT THE AGE OF XX, I WAS ABLE TO RELEASE MY TRAIN STATION COMEDY, "TRAIN★TRAIN"!!
I HOPE YOU GUYS ENJOY IT!!
YEEE AH!!
KEEP IN MIND THAT MINAKITA IS A FICTIONAL TRAIN STATION, THOUGH!! THANKS!
AFTERWORD MANGA★END

# AFTERWORD.

- THANK YOU FOR BUYING MY TENTH MANGA! ♡ MY TENTH VOLUME... WOW, I'M SO HAPPY! IT'S ALL THANKS TO EVERYONE WHO HAS GIVEN ME SUPPORT THROUGH THE YEARS! ♡
- THIS WORK HAD MANY CHALLENGES, INCLUDING BEING THE FIRST TIME I WROTE YOMIKIRI-STYLE (CHAPTER-STYLE), BEING MY FIRST TRUE COMEDY, AND HAVING MY PROTAGONIST BE A NEW CHARACTER TYPE FOR ME. SO, IT IS TAKING ME LONGER TO REFINE THE STORY, BUT I'M ENJOYING THE FUN AND EXCITEMENT OF DOING SOMETHING I ALWAYS WANTED TO DO. I HOPE MY EXCITEMENT REACHES THE READERS... DID IT???
- I TRIED MY BEST TO ADD AMUSING EXTRA CHAPTERS AND AFTERWORDS. HOW WERE THEY? I LOOK FORWARD TO HEARING YOUR THOUGHTS AND IMPRESSIONS, AND ABOUT WHICH CHARACTERS YOU LIKE THE BEST!! ♡
- IF YOU SEND ME A NEW YEAR'S CARD, I USUALLY REPLY, BUT I ADMIT THAT IT MIGHT TAKE A WHILE. IF YOU DON'T MIND, THOUGH, FEEL FREE TO SEND ONE TO THE PUBLISHER AT MY ATTENTION. ♡ I LOOK FORWARD TO ALL THE DETAILED THOUGHTS AND COLORFUL ILLUSTRATIONS! ♡
- IN CLOSING, I'D LIKE TO SAY THANKS AGAIN FOR READING THIS MANGA. IF YOU FIND SOMETHING YOU LIKE IN IT, EVEN JUST A LITTLE BIT... I WILL BE VERY HAPPY! ♡ SINCE "TRAIN☆TRAIN" IS A YOMIKIRI-STYLE MANGA WITH A SHORT NUMBER OF PAGES IN EACH, IT MIGHT TAKE A WHILE FOR THE SECOND VOLUME TO COME OUT... BUT I HOPE TO SEE YOU THERE! ♡ (IF YOU CAN'T WAIT, IT'S SERIALIZED MONTHLY IN WINGS MAGAZINE). HOPEFULLY, WE'LL GET SOME BACKGROUND ON THE SENPAI CHARACTERS IN VOLUME TWO!! WELL, I HOPE TO SEE YOU SOON!! 'BYE FOR NOW!!

EIKI EIKI 9/2002 LOVEXXX


- SPECIAL THANKS (PREFIXES ABBREVIATED)

ASSISTANTS ▶ JUN UZUKI & YURIKO NAKAZATO (MY SUPER DUO!! THANKS, AS ALWAYS!!)
JUNKO (SUPER ASSISTANT!!)
NATSUO MORIHIRA & MOTOYA HINO (SUPER BG CHARACTERS!!)

SPECIAL GUEST ▶ MAO KUON (I'M SORRY TO MAKE YOU DRAW OLD MEN AND WOMEN...)

TRAIN STATION STAFF ▶ TAKAHIRO TAMURA (JR EAST RAILWAYS) YOUR STORIES PROVIDED A LOT OF INSIGHT!

EDITORS ▶ MIKI ISHIKAWA, IKUKO KURINO, YUKI ISEMURA, WINGS EDITING STAFF, SHINSHOKAN PUBLISHING, EVERYONE ELSE THAT HELPED PUT TOGETHER THIS MANGA.

LAST BUT NOT LEAST... TO YOU, THE READERS... I GIVE A VERY SPECIAL THANKS! I LOVE YOU ALL! ♡
THANK YOU ALL VERY MUCH!!

CM
MY NEXT MANGA WILL BE MY FIRST PROJECT WITH ANOTHER PUBLISHER, "D2 – THE RESIDENTS OF ZASSOUKAN" (FROM ZASSHOUSHA PUBLISHING). IT'LL BE ON SALE IN DECEMBER OF 2002, AND WILL BE MY FIRST 4-PANEL COMIC STRIP MANGA! IT MIGHT BE HARD TO FIND AT SMALLER STORES, BUT YOU CAN PRE-ORDER IT!!
THEY PUBLISH THE MANGA INFO MAGAZINE, "PAFU"
AFTER THAT WILL BE A COMPILATION FROM DEAR PLUS COMICS, INCLUDING "YUIGON" AND THE OTHER-SIDE VERSION OF "PRIME MINISTER." I'LL WORK HARD TO RELEASE THAT IN DECEMBER, TOO!!
WISH ME LUCK!

ASAHI-KUN AND PURE

UNDER-COVER MASTERPIECE THEATER.

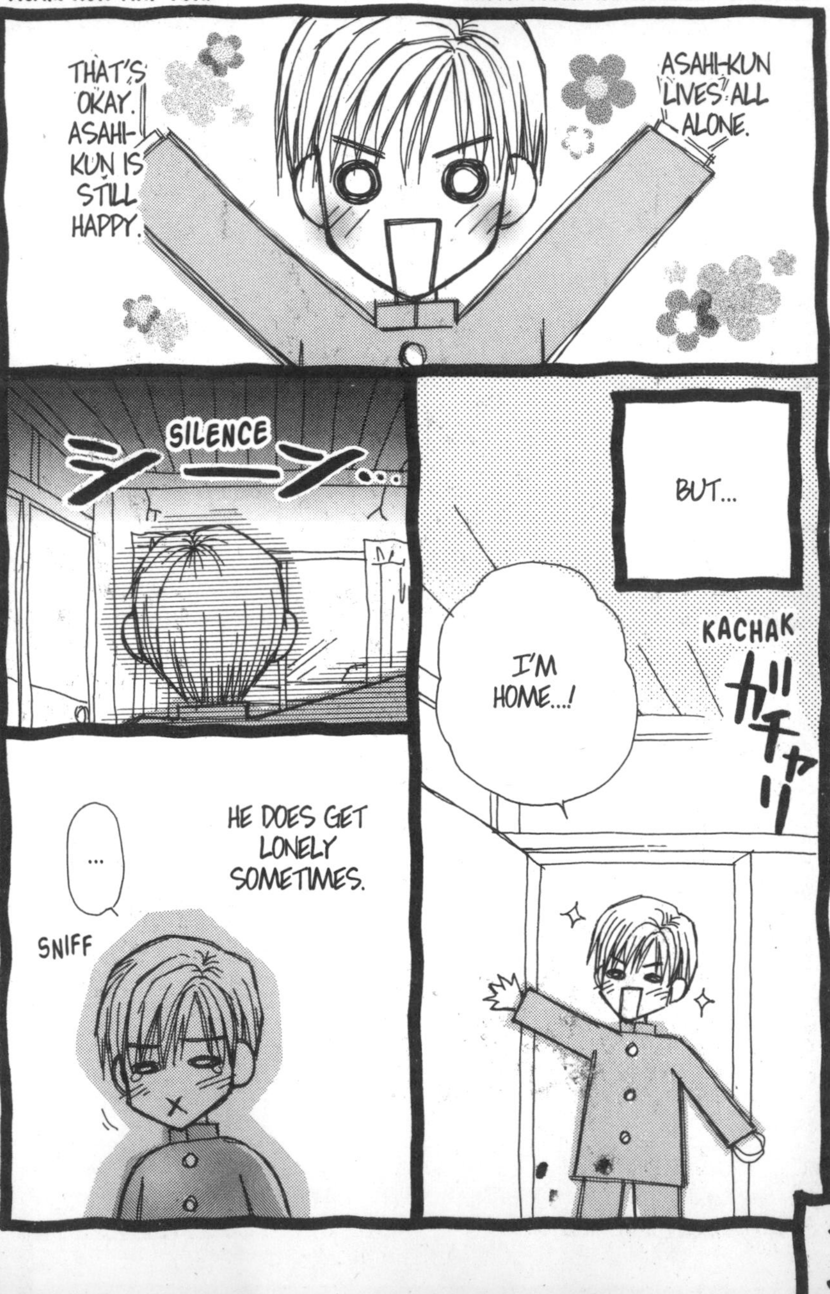
ASAHI-KUN LIVES ALL ALONE.
THAT'S OKAY. ASAHI-KUN IS STILL HAPPY.
BUT...
KACHAK
I'M HOME...!
SILENCE
HE DOES GET LONELY SOMETIMES.
...
SNIFF

1

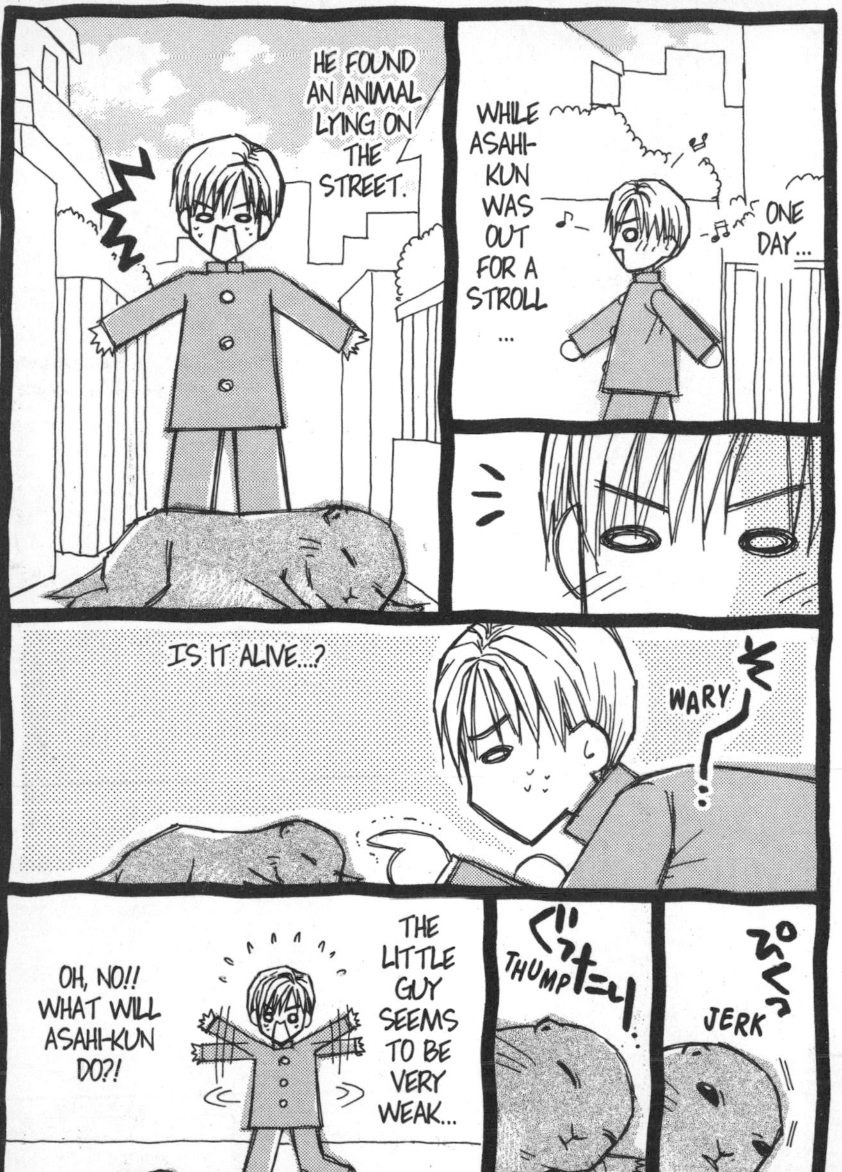

ONE DAY...
WHILE ASAHI-KUN WAS OUT FOR A STROLL ...
HE FOUND AN ANIMAL LYING ON THE STREET.
IS IT ALIVE...?
WARY
JERK
THUMP
THE LITTLE GUY SEEMS TO BE VERY WEAK...
OH, NO!! WHAT WILL ASAHI-KUN DO?!


CONTINUED IN VOLUME 2.

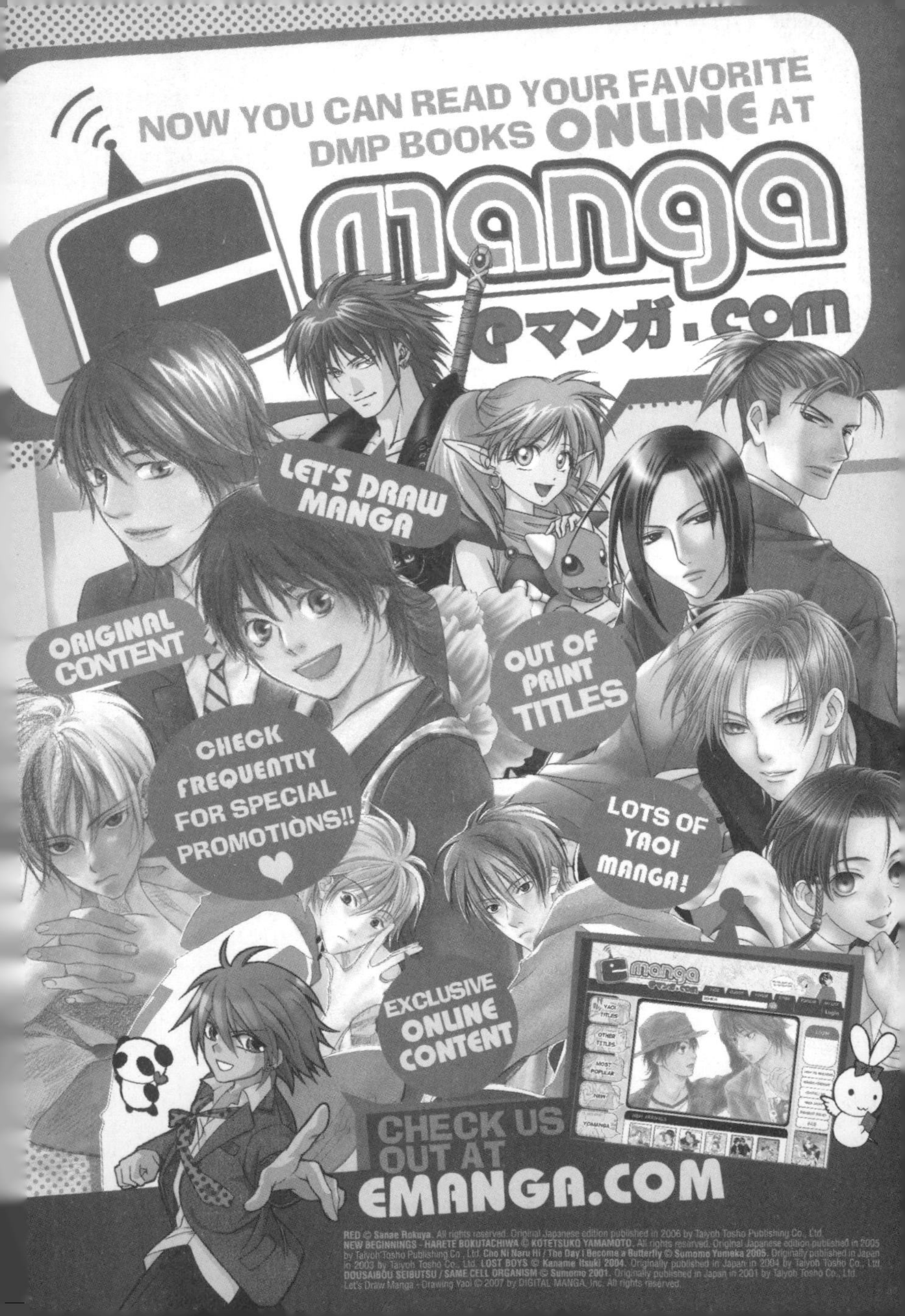
NOW YOU CAN READ YOUR FAVORITE
DMP BOOKS ONLINE AT
emanga
eマンガ.COM
LET'S DRAW MANGA
ORIGINAL CONTENT
OUT OF PRINT TITLES
CHECK FREQUENTLY FOR SPECIAL PROMOTIONS!!
LOTS OF YAOI MANGA!
EXCLUSIVE ONLINE CONTENT
CHECK US OUT AT
EMANGA.COM
RED © Sanae Rokuya. All rights reserved. Original Japanese edition published in 2006 by Taiyoh Tosho Publishing Co., Ltd.
NEW BEGINNINGS - HARETE BOKUTACHIWA © KOTETSUKO YAMAMOTO. All rights reserved. Original Japanese edition published in 2005 by Taiyoh Tosho Publishing Co., Ltd. Cho Ni Naru Hi / The Day I Become a Butterfly © Sumomo Yumeka 2005. Originally published in Japan in 2003 by Taiyoh Tosho Co., Ltd. LOST BOYS © Kaname Itsuki 2004. Originally published in Japan in 2004 by Taiyoh Tosho Co., Ltd. DOUSAIBOU SEIBUTSU / SAME CELL ORGANISM © Sumomo 2001. Originally published in Japan in 2001 by Taiyoh Tosho Co., Ltd.
Let's Draw Manga - Drawing Yaoi © 2007 by DIGITAL MANGA, Inc. All rights reserved.

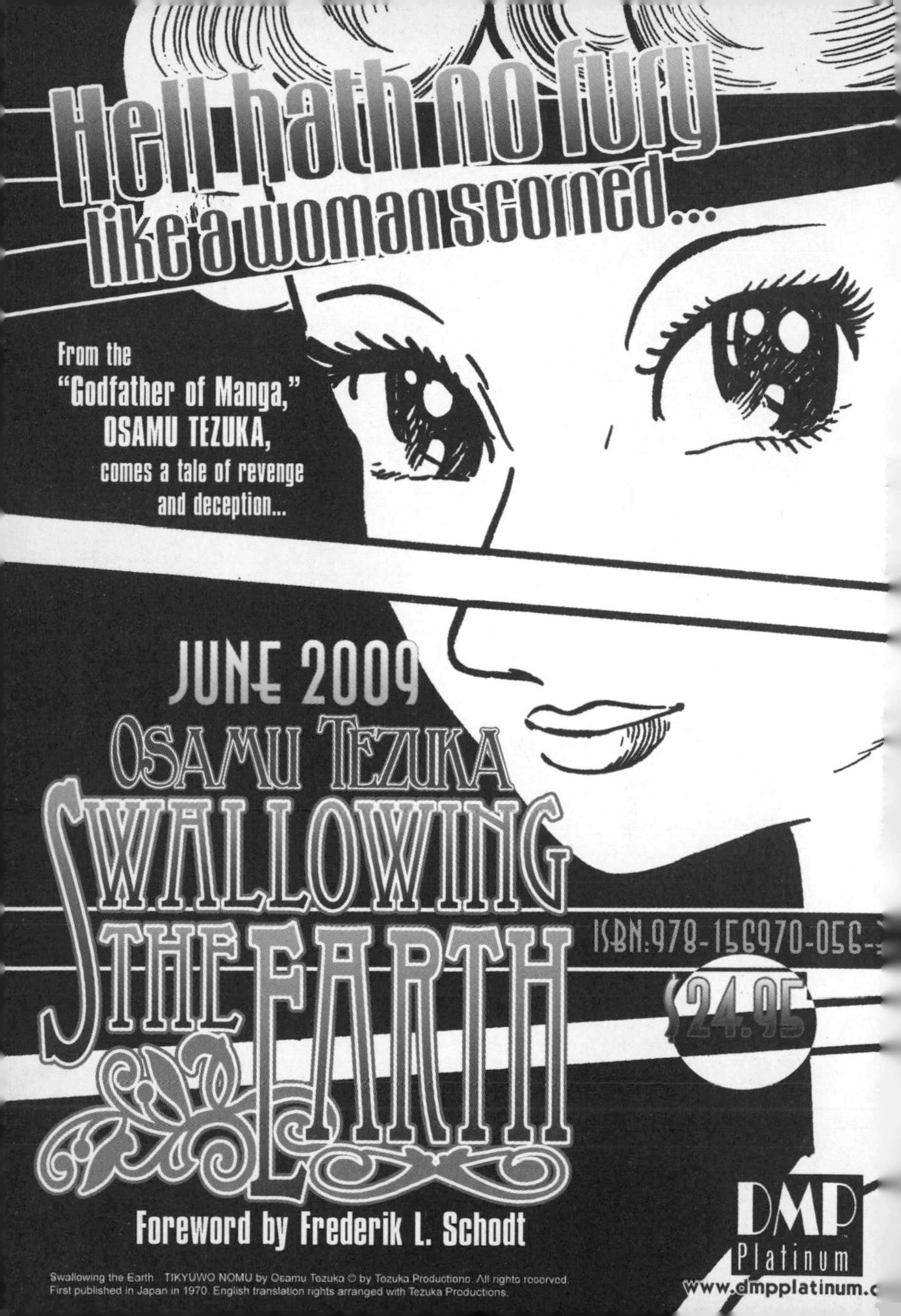
Hell hath no fury
like a woman scorned...
From the
"Godfather of Manga,"
OSAMU TEZUKA,
comes a tale of revenge
and deception...
JUNE 2009
OSAMU TEZUKA
SWALLOWING THE EARTH
ISBN:978-156970-056-
$24.95
Foreword by Frederik L. Schodt
DMP
Platinum
www.dmpplatinum.c
Swallowing the Earth TIKYUWO NOMU by Osamu Tezuka © by Tezuka Productions. All rights reserved.
First published in Japan in 1970. English translation rights arranged with Tezuka Productions.

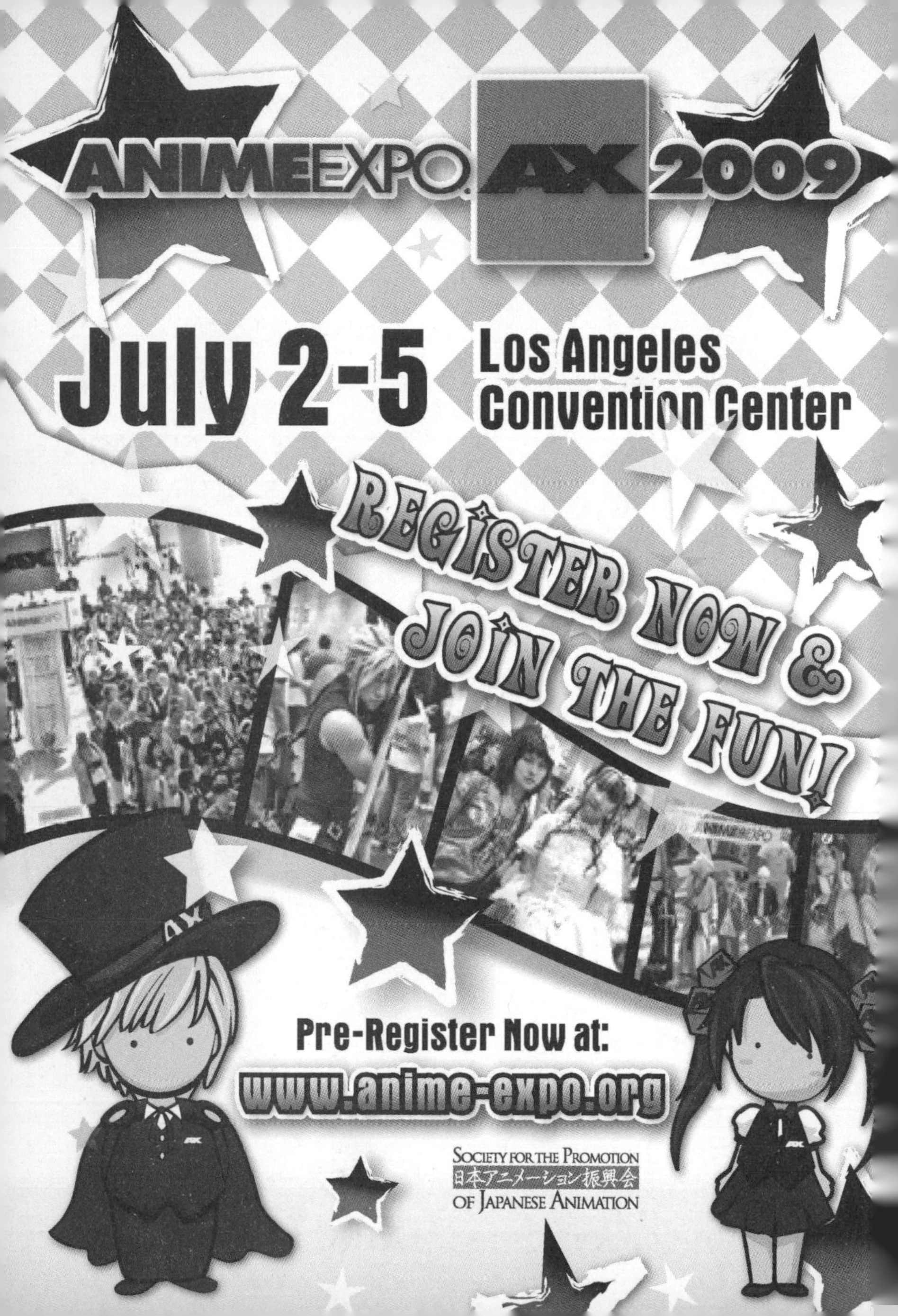
ANIME EXPO
AX
2009
July 2-5
Los Angeles
Convention Center
REGISTER NOW &
JOIN THE FUN!
Pre-Register Now at:
www.anime-expo.org
SOCIETY FOR THE PROMOTION
日本アニメーション振興会
OF JAPANESE ANIMATION

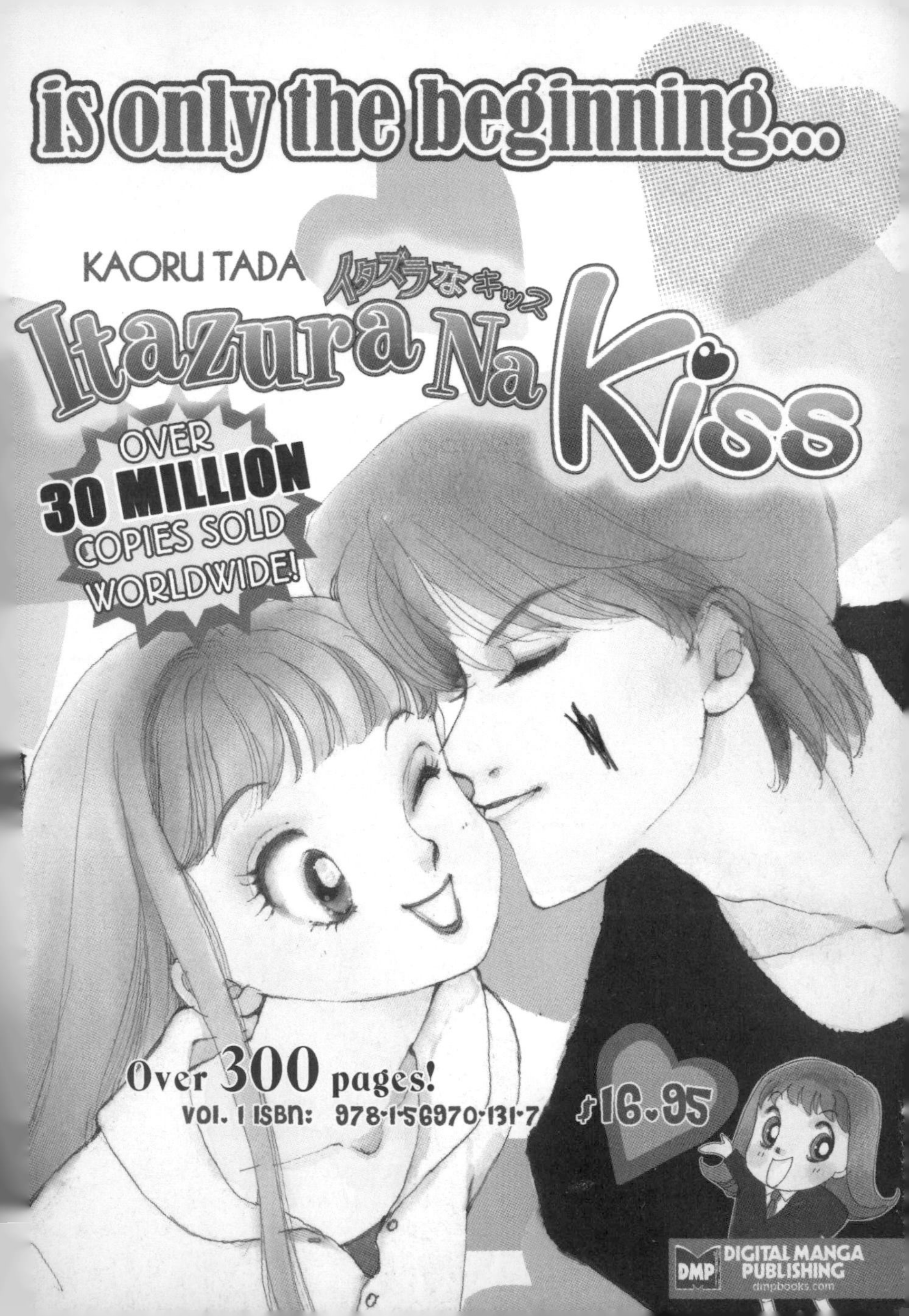
is only the beginning...
KAORU TADA
イタズラなキッス
Itazura Na Kiss
OVER 30 MILLION COPIES SOLD WORLDWIDE!
Over 300 pages!
VOL. 1 ISBN: 978-1-56970-131-7
$16.95
DMP
DIGITAL MANGA PUBLISHING
dmpbooks.com

# One mischievous kiss

## The classic and timeless manga that set the standard for ALL shojo manga is finally available for the first time EVER in English!

Kotoko (The non-genius)

Naoki (The genius)

| LONGON BOROUGH TOWER HAMLETS | |
|---|---|
| 910 000 00204348 | |
| HJ | 27-Nov-2009 |
| | £9.99 |
| THISCA | |

VOL.1

The road to true love is never easy!

# NOVEMBER 2009

# Other Way!

This book is printed right-to-left to preserve its original native format. So all speech bubbles, effects and panels are reversed! If you don't want to spoil the action-turn the book around to start at the beginning, and just go in the order as shown below!

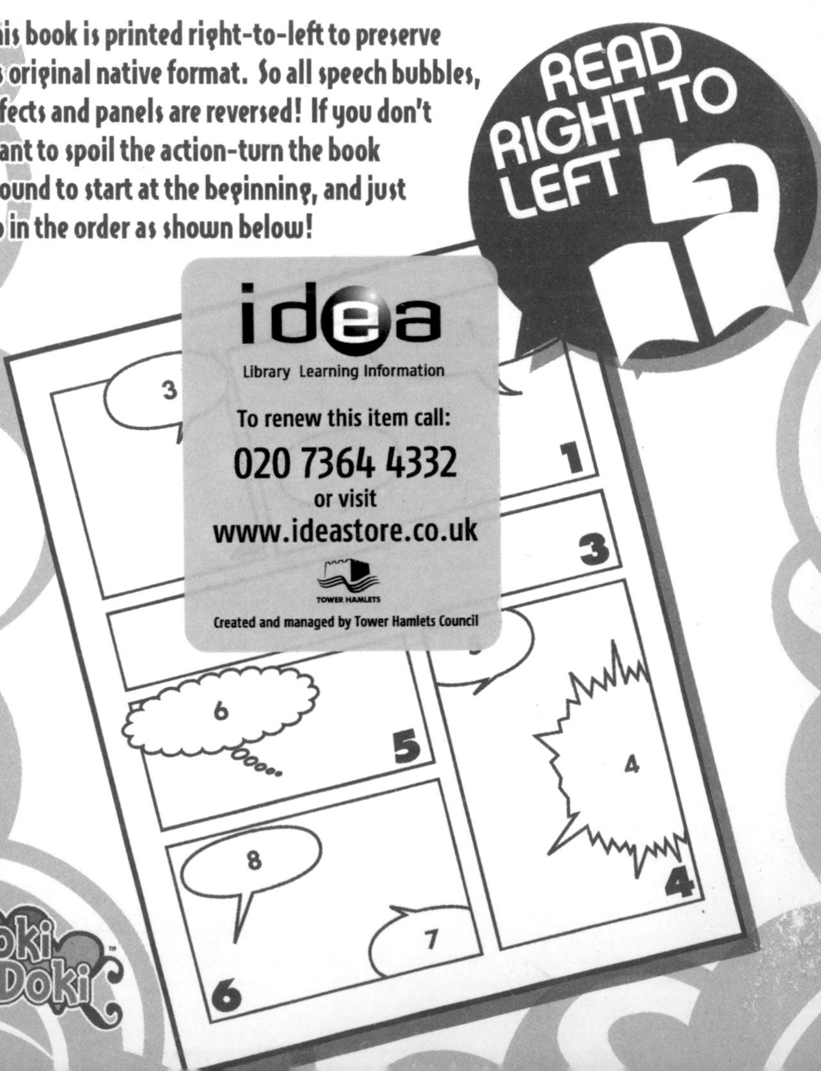
READ RIGHT TO LEFT
1
3
3
4
4
5
6
6
7
8

Doki Doki™